George Anthony Denison

Notes of my life

1805-1878. Second Edition

George Anthony Denison

Notes of my life
1805-1878. Second Edition

ISBN/EAN: 9783337053819

Printed in Europe, USA, Canada, Australia, Japan

Cover: Foto ©ninafisch / pixelio.de

More available books at **www.hansebooks.com**

NOTES OF MY LIFE,

1805—1878.

BY

GEORGE ANTHONY DENISON,

VICAR OF EAST BRENT, 1845;
ARCHDEACON OF TAUNTON, 1851.

Εἷς Κύριος, μία Πίστις, ἓν Βάπτισμα.
"One LORD, one Faith, one Baptism."—*Eph.* iv. 5.

SECOND EDITION.

Oxford and London:
JAMES PARKER AND CO.
1878.

PREFACE.

I MAKE no apology for publishing "Notes of my Life." Contemporary biography is allowable, and may be useful when it is Autobiography; but hardly, I think, otherwise.

If it is said that Autobiography betrays an overweening self-conceit, the answer to this is the facts of the case.

The conflict between the Church and the World is a perpetual conflict, admitting of no armistice.

In the end, the Church finally overcomes the World, under HIM WHO is her LORD and MASTER, her Example, her Hope, her Peace.

"These things I have spoken unto you, that in ME ye might have Peace. In the World ye shall have tribulation: but be of good cheer; I have overcome the World." (St. John xvi. 33.)

Meantime, in proportion to faithfulness or unfaithfulness, particular Churches overcome the World, or are overcome by the World.

Again, sometimes the conflict, as respects a particular Church, assumes a definite and comprehensive character, and arrives at a distinct and decided issue within the limits of a single life. My own life supplies an instance.

Lastly, it has happened that my life has been for the last forty years largely, intimately, actively concerned with the details of the conflict.

I make therefore no apology for publishing " Notes of my Life."

In respect of the " Education" question, I write in the position of a man irretrievably defeated. The adversary and the supporter have combined against me, and, after a fight of twenty-five years, it was waste of time to fight any more. I retired thereupon into passive resistance.

My apprehensions and my arguments remain, indeed, just where they were thirty-three years ago; save only that all the apprehensions have become facts, and all the arguments have been proved to be sound by succession and culmination of results.

I have letters lying before me in great numbers, from great names, congratulating me through many years upon what I had been enabled to do in this matter for the Church of England. I was at no time able to accept the congratulation as well-founded; I feared what was coming; and in 1853-5 was compelled to part with it altogether; in 1853, as respected the Church at large, and in 1855, as respected the Diocese of Bath and Wells. I felt it indeed to be my duty to the Church to persevere actively after 1855, and down to 1870; but it was as hoping against hope.

If I had retained any hope of the public issue as long ago as 1851, I should not have then made the Vicarage of East Brent the private training and middle schools which I made it to be.

These schools were largely promoted by kind friends, and worked excellently well till 1854. In 1854, in consequence of the pressure upon my time and energies caused by the prosecution against me in the matter of "THE REAL PRESENCE," I was compelled to close them.

G. A. D.

East Brent, 1878.

CONTENTS.

CHAPTER I. 1805—1819.
HOME AND SCHOOL.—Home.—Sunbury.—Southwell.—Eton . pp. 1—11

CHAPTER II.
DECAY OF GREEK AND LATIN.—Its causes and remedies.—Connected closely with decay of "Education" in our time.—Antiochus Epiphanes, second century before CHRIST.—Julian the Apostate, fourth century after CHRIST.—Government of England in "Church and State," nineteenth century after CHRIST . . pp. 12—43

CHAPTER III. 1819—1832.
HOME TUITION.—Oxford.—Ch. Ch.—Oriel.—Ordination . pp. 44—53

CHAPTER IV. 1832—1838.
CUDDESDON, Curacy of.—Outline of Catholic Revival.—General Position then and subsequently.—"Tory," "Whig," "Liberal," "Conservative."—Distinction between "Tory" and "Conservative."—Medical and other experiences . . . . pp. 54—77

CHAPTER V. 1828—1878.
THE OPPOSING FORCES . . . . . pp. 78—87

CHAPTER VI. 1838—1845.
BROADWINSOR.—First relations with Committee of Council on "Education" . . . . pp. 88—94

CHAPTER VII. 1845—1852.
EAST BRENT.—Bishop Bagot.—Examining Chaplaincy.—Ritual, germ of.—Bristol, and other Church Unions.—Development of Policy of Indifferentism.—Minutes of 1846.—Withdrawal of application for assistance under Minutes.—Letter to Mr. Gladstone, 1847.—Refusal to admit further Government Inspection.—Position of Mr. Gladstone in relation to the "Schools question."—Management Clauses.—National Society.—Letter to Bishop Bagot, 1849.—Summary of "Schools question," from beginning of century to 1840.—From 1840 to 1852.—John Keble.—Communication from the Derby Government, 1852.—Action thereupon.—Letter to Chris-

topher Wordsworth.—Final defeat upon the Management Clauses.
—Extent of the defeat.—Revival of Convocation.—Gorham Case.—
Protest.—Declaration.—Meeting.—Bishop Bagot.—Synod of Exeter.—"Why should the Bishops continue to sit in the House of Lords?"—Archdeacon of Taunton.—East Brent Middle and Training Schools.—Holy Communion at Visitation.

First indications of policy of Elementary "Education" Act of 1870, in Manchester and Salford "Education" scheme.—Papal aggression. — Sanford Correspondence. — Preparation for Holy Orders . . . . . . pp. 95—221

CHAPTER VIII. 1853—1858.

EAST BRENT.—Prosecution for teaching THE REAL PRESENCE.—Bishop Spencer.—Bishop Bagot.—Resignation of Examining Chaplaincy.—Sermons on THE REAL PRESENCE in Wells Cathedral.—Mr. Ditcher.—Lord Auckland, Bishop of Bath and Wells, refuses to have anything to do with Prosecution.—Commission at Clevedon, 1855.—Court at Bath, 1856.—Deprivation.—Appeal to Court of Arches.—Letter from Bishop of Exeter.—"Saravia on the Holy Eucharist."—C. S. Grueber and John Keble.—Protest of Pusey, Keble, Bennett, and others, against Judgment of Court at Bath.—First Harvest-home at East Brent, 1857.—Appeal sustained upon first point of law, 1857.—Counter appeal of Prosecutor rejected by Judicial Committee of Privy Council, 1858.—Welcome home, and Address of Parishioners.

Mr. Henley in the House of Commons, 1855, 6.—His majority against Lord John Russell and Sir J. Pakington.—Divorce Act.—Crimean War . . . . . . pp. 222—275

CHAPTER IX. 1858—1870.

EAST BRENT.—Convocation.—General review.—Education question—Burial question inseparably connected with revival of Discipline.— Spiritual Censures-Act of 57 Geo. III. c. 127.—"Essays and Reviews."—Dr. Colenso.—Bishop of St. David's.—Bishop of Capetown.—Professor Jowett.—Dr. Pusey.—Oxford Declaration.—Dr. Temple, Bishop of Exeter.—Protest, and action thereupon.—Court of Final Appeal.—Conscience Clause.—Letter to Mr. Hardy.—Bishop Wilberforce.—Earl of Carnarvon.—Defeat of Mr. Gladstone for Oxford.—Irish disestablishment . . . pp. 276—339

CHAPTER X. 1870—1878.

EAST BRENT.—Defeat in Lower House *in re* "Conscience Clause."—Reversal of action of Lower House, since revival in 1852, upon the Education question.—Illness.

"Ritual."—Gradual change of mind thereupon.—Norwich Congress.—Letter of Archbishop of Canterbury, 1865.—Discussion in, and Committee of, the Lower House, 1866.—What "Ritual" is.—Necessary connection of it with Doctrine.—My own partial adoption of "Ritual."—How I should act if prosecuted under the Public Worship Regulation Act.—How, if the Synod were to declare against "Ritual."—Fallacy of claiming Authority for Diocesan in matter of "Ritual," under paragraph in Preface to Prayer-Book.—Fallacy of picking and choosing among points of "Ritual."—Reference to meeting in St. James's Hall, 1867.—Difference with the Bishop of Bath and Wells.—Recovery of Curate's Licence.—Money-cost thereof.—Judgments of the Judicial Committee.—Synod of Lambeth, 1867, 1878.—Committee on Canons.—Causes of withdrawal from active work of Convocation, 1878.—" Ritual."—Committee of Revision.—Desecration of the Blessed Sacrament by Judgment upon Appeal of the Judicial Committee in Jenkins *v.* Cook.—Confession to, and Absolution by, the Priest.

Church League.—Confraternity of the Blessed Sacrament.—Society of the Holy Cross.—Letter to Bishop of Ely.—Reprint of portion of it.—My Curates.—Memorial on the Holy Eucharist, 1867.

pp. 340—374

CHAPTER XI.

SUMMARY OF ARGUMENT AND POSITION.—Secession to Rome.—Difficulties of Scripture . . . . pp. 375—398

APPENDIX A.—Epistle of Julian the Apostate . . p. 399
  „   B.—East Brent Waterworks . . . p. 405
  „   C.—Dilapidations, Report of Committee, Diocese of Bath and Wells, 1876 . . . p. 408
  „   D.—Extract from Phillimore's Ecclesiastical Law

p. 416

NOTES OF MY LIFE.

CHAPTER I.

HOME AND SCHOOL. 1805—1819.

I WAS born, Dec. 11, 1805, at Ossington, in Nottinghamshire: one of a family of fourteen children, nine sons, five daughters, living to man's and woman's estate; the nine sons, and three of the daughters, my mother's children. My dear father died in 1820, aged 62; he sat in Parliament, I think, for Colchester; afterwards for Minehead: my dear mother died in 1859, aged 82. Two sons, one daughter, are still living; I am the eldest survivor.

We were brought up lovingly, tenderly, gently, wisely; never coddled, always cared for; in true subjection, but free from fear. We had also the advantage, at Eton and at home, 1809—1823, of the preparing for, the supplementing and improving of our school education, by a man of a very rare combination of great qualities. The absolute authority over us of Charles Drury, always tempering itself, never broken or impaired; his high principle, his cogent discipline; his exact and refined scholarship; his great teaching power; his wit and humour, in my experience unequalled; his genial companionship, so full of all manner of amusement and pleasant memories; our affection, respect, and love, with the abiding sense of great benefits received, the natural fruits of all the relations between us; all these are principal parts of a great inheritance.

Six of us were at Eton; one at Harrow; one was brought up for the navy: he died at the age of thirty-one, loved and valued by all who knew him. Six were at Oxford, as Undergraduates; four at Ch. Ch., one at Oriel, one at Balliol.

My eldest brother, John Evelyn, Viscount Ossington 1872; married, 1827, Lady Charlotte Bentinck, third daughter of the Duke of Portland; and after some thirty years of Parliamentary life, became Speaker of the House of Commons, 1857; resigned, 1872. Died, 1873.

Edward, First Class in Classics, Fellow of Merton, became Bishop of Salisbury in 1837; married, 1839, Louisa Mary Ker Seymer, 2nd. Hon. Clementina Hamilton, 1845. Died, 1854.

William, went from Eton to Woolwich, then into the Engineers; married, 1838, Caroline Hornby. After employments at home and abroad, he became in 1846 Governor of Van Dieman's Land; Governor-General of Australia, K.C.B., 1855; Governor of Madras, 1861. After Lord Elgin's death, he acted for some months as Governor-General of India. Died, 1871.

Henry, Double-first Class, Fellow of All Souls. Was paralysed by an injury received in Australia; returned to England, 1841, and, after many years of great suffering, died, 1858.

Stephen, First Class in Classics, Stowell Fellow of University; married Susan Fellowes, 1845; was for many years Deputy Judge Advocate. Died, 1871.

Frank was the Sailor. Died, 1841.

Alfred, after some twenty years of laborious, honourable, and successful life in Australia, returned finally to England, 1859, and became Private Secretary to the Speaker.

Charles was in the 52nd Regiment, and became Colonel in it. He had sundry Staff employments in India; and afterwards, till he was compelled by failing health, caused by sun-stroke, to retire from active life, was Chief Commissioner of Civil Service at Madras. Died, 1877.

I was First Class in Classics, Fellow of Oriel, and gained the Chancellor's Prizes for Latin, and English Essay, 1828, 1829. Married, 1838, Georgiana, eldest daughter of the Rt. Hon. J. W. Henley.

My sister Charlotte, daughter of my father's first marriage, married Charles Manners Sutton, then Judge Advocate General; afterwards, for seventeen years Speaker of the House of Commons, and Viscount Canterbury.

Matilda, the second sister of the first marriage, married Thomas Smith, Esq.

Julia married the Rev. Henry des Vœux; Henrietta, John Henry Jacob, Esq. My surviving sister, Charlotte, is the wife of the Right Hon. Sir Robert Phillimore.

In life and in death the love between us all has been unbroken. It is not that upon many points there has not been much difference of thought and judgment; but it has never touched the love. For myself, I cannot say, having lived all my life upon a diet of very strong and definite conclusions, religious and political, that I have had from brothers and sisters absolute sympathy with me in respect of such conclusions, and of my action upon them. Such family sympathy is a very rare thing. It was one of my dear brothers who said I was "St. George without the dragon;" another who said that one day I might not improbably "upset the coach." But, with much difference, there has been no alienation, or loss of love. My eldest brother, afterwards Viscount Ossington, who succeeded to the family property in 1820, did all, and more than all, to help our dear mother in her wise and loving care for us. His own fatherly care for us, and his loving and generous kindness, never failed.

The first thing I can recall is looking out of a window in the house at Ossington at my dear father's troop of volunteers, in or about 1808. When I was six years old I went with my dear brother William to school at Sunbury. Those were not days of petting and coddling children, and stuffing them upon the hamper system; nor of making children virtually their own masters. If they had been such days, I think our case would have been an exception; I am certain we should not have been petted, coddled, "hampered," nor made our own masters. I remember well my school outfit, when I was six, the fourth son of a country gentleman of considerable estate.

I had a small hair-trunk, containing a spare jacket, and

a pair of stiffest corduroys, so stiff that, in their new and uncreased condition, with a little adjustment they might be made to stand upright of themselves; six shirts, two night-shirts; eight pairs of blue cotton stockings; eight small chequed pocket-handkerchiefs of a stern material; a black ribbon for my neck; a hat, and two pairs of shoes; a plum-cake; and some small money in an old-fashioned purse. The cake, having left its fragrance throughout the garments, was transferred to the cupboard of the Master's wife, and disappeared speedily under the combined efforts of the master, mistress, and their children, myself and school-fellows. In a few days, my application for a slice for two or three, and "a bit for the Doctor, my dear, and a bit for me, my dear, and a bit for Tommy and Betsy," finished up my cake.

There were two curious bits of discipline at that school: one, that whenever a boy committed a grave offence, every boy of the school was made a party to it; and a penitential letter was written home by every boy precisely in the same terms. Here is an instance. One night, as we followed the ushers two and two down a passage from the school-room to our bedrooms, William said to me, "George, I hate that usher fellow."

"So do I," I said.

"I shall spit on his back," said he.

"Please don't," said I, "we shall both be strapped."

Strapping was administered with a piece of carriage-trace with the buckle-holes in it, through which the air rushed as the strap descended on the hand. "I shall spit on his back," said he; and, as I expected, the usher having, I suppose, heard whispering, turned round, and William was caught in the act. The next morning, after the due personal treatment of the leading culprit by a process more painful than strapping, we were all drawn up in single file in the school-room, and every boy, older and younger, had to write from dictation, and then to copy from his slate on a sheet of letter-paper, the letter following. Letters then cost eightpence each.

"My dear Parents,

"We have committed a great sin. For William Denison spat on the usher's back as we went to bed.
"I remain,
"Your affectionate Son,
"Arthur Shirt."

There were four Shirt brothers in the school, Arthur, Lionel, Frederick and Augustus Shirt. I draw a veil over the feelings and expressions of the Shirt parents upon opening the four letters, price 2s. 8d. The like thing happened again while I was there, upon the occasion of buying apple-tarts from an old woman over the play-ground wall. In this case the sin was of a more general character, but as in the other case, was made universal.

"My dear Parents,

"We have committed a great sin. For we have bought apple-tarts without the leave of the Master, when we have plenty to eat, and that of the best quality.
"I remain, &c."

The other point of discipline was, that every boy who had not conducted himself well during the week had no mutton-pie on Saturday. Now this gave the mutton-pie a moral elevation which, in its own nature, it did not deserve, being composed of what was left on the plates in the preceding days of the week.

William had been at school at Esher, with our elder brothers, Evelyn and Edward, before Sunbury. There, one Sunday morning, having lost his hat, he was made to go to church in a straw coal-scuttle bonnet of one of the daughters of the house. The ways of discipline are various. At present, there being no such thing as discipline, it is interesting to recall instances.

At home, as at school, we had our mischievous recreations.

We had one day a narrow escape. We were about eleven and ten years old.

We had a room to ourselves in the north wing of the house. William said to me, "Let's make some gunpowder."

I said, "I don't know how, and am afraid."

"Oh," he said, "I know how very well, and I ain't a bit afraid."

I said, "How long have you known?"

"Always," said he.

So we got the materials and mixed them, a good big heap, in one of the window-seats of the room. "Now then," said I, "let's try it;" and I took a broad-bladed kitchen-knife, and taking some of the mixture up, put it into a candle close by. Happily for ourselves, the house, and family, it was not very well made, and did not explode; but out of the candle there came a number of little blue balls of fire hopping all about; one or more hopped into the heap. In a moment the room was full of little blue balls of fire hopping over the carpet, over the beds, under the beds, over us, over everything. We rushed to the water-jugs, and then, making no head against the blue balls, screamed for help. Under a heavy drenching the blue balls vanished as quickly as they had come, leaving their mark in hundreds of black spots.

When we came to be "examined" and "taught," I remember the same question was put to William that I had asked him: How long he had known how to make gunpowder? His answer was the same as to me, "always." He protected me, as on another occasion, insisting that the blame was all his.

Another day we did a curious piece of mischief, and very properly suffered for it.

A clergyman of a neighbouring parish, an old friend of my father's, was very often at Ossington, and had a room in the south wing which went by his name, where we often played tricks with his clothes and shoes, left there from time to time. One day he said to us, "Boys, come and see me, and we will catch eels in my brook." Next day we went. He was not at home. "Very odd," we said, "bringing us all this way for nothing; no worms ready, and no message where we are to try for eels;' looked into the dining-room, found nothing to eat. "We' won't stay, of course; but we must let him know we have been here."

In the dining-room was a good mahogany table, second-hand, just bought a bargain, as good as new: we took our knives and cut upon it, "William and George Denison." I often think that, though we did not escape a flogging, we came off very much too lightly.

When William went to Eton, I was transferred to a Grammar-School of much repute at Southwell. Having been driven there in much state, four-in-hand, and deposited with my small hair-trunk and my cake, I made acquaintance with my schoolmaster and schoolfellows.

The schoolmaster was a good, kindly man, and a good scholar; the classes of schoolfellows much mixed. I was taught to sing, so far as such an accomplishment was possible to me, "Jessie of Dumblane," "The Woodpecker tapping," and "Mr. Boney, if you please, let alone the Portuguese," by a son of the butcher at Newark who supplied our family with meat. In our equestrian combats among the gravestones, in the Minster-yard, which was our playground, my best horse was the hatter's son. There was another school in the town, which looked down upon us with much contempt. The boys had to pass through the churchyard on their way to the fields beyond. Then we avenged our honour. Lying in wait behind the gravestones, we sallied out upon them, and punched their heads; occasionally bringing them in gentle contact with a gravestone. Our church was the beautiful old Minster; its choir at that time, as at this, in great repute.

While I was at Southwell, I made two attempts to improve the fashion of my outer wardrobe, which had always issued, and continued so to do when I was at Eton, from the primitive shop of the Ossington tailor; as, to the great punishment of our feet, the family boots and shoes issued from the shop of the village shoemaker. When I came to wear top-boots for hunting, I was obliged to rise very early; it took so much time to get them on, and more time in the evening to get them off. I represented that I needed repair and reinforcement; and, having obtained leave from home, proceeded to order a suit from the Southwell artist. The material throughout, as selected by me, was a bright green pepper-and-salt; the decoration of it, smooth white metal buttons, about the size of a half-crown. I was much mortified, having asked and received permission to go out into the town, to find that my appearance did not excite the general admiration I expected.

My other attempt was more ambitious. The "Brummel," the original type of the frock-coat, was captivating all hearts. It was my first ambition to possess a "Brummel." So I represented again at home that, as the cold weather was coming on, I should be glad of a great-coat; and, upon permission given, did my best to combine a great-coat with a "Brummel," with velvet collar—the correct thing. Going home for the Christmas holidays, I issued from a side-door in my "Brummel," ready for church, before the eyes of the astonished family; and it was with much difficulty that decency of conduct was re-established at the church-door.

I never had but one serious conflict with the Southwell authorities. I forget other particulars, but recall two: one, that I threw a brass candlestick at the usher's head; the other, that, having been upon this sent to bed, I was hauled out of it in my night-shirt, and taken to by the usher with an ash-plant, in the presence of the boys who had witnessed the assault, and who were not displeased to see the little gentleman taken down.

It was not till some time after leaving Southwell that I recovered the more polished pronunciation of the English tongue.

"What is it, George," my brothers asked, "that you call your school-feast?"

"We call it, 'Potation.'"

"What is Potation?"

"Ploom boon and nagus," said I.

However, I learnt a good deal of Latin and some Greek at the school, and was sorry to leave it, though it was for Eton, in 1817, when I was eleven and a-half.

I was not an idle boy, and had been fairly taught; so I found myself in the upper remove, fourth form, to start with; and when I left Eton at Christmas, 1819, was in the upper division of fifth form, being just fourteen.

At Eton I witnessed the Marriott rebellion; the scene in the upper school at "Prose;" the eggs thrown at Keate by many hands, but not before his back was turned. Not one of them hit him, though they spattered him plentifully from the wall and the door-frame. His return, with several masters, in a few minutes; his order to seize the first boy that said a word; the expulsion then and there of a good many boys, and the end of the rebellion; as tidy a bit of sound and wholesome discipline as one would desire to see.

I witnessed also the stand made by the upper boys with Chapman, Captain of the school, now Bishop, at their head, on Barnespool bridge, against the bargees. It made a great impression upon me, and more than fifty years after I told Bishop Chapman that I had greatly respected him all that time. "What for?" he said; and I told him.

The bargees were furious against a particular boy, and came roaring down the street from the river, saying they would have him, and throw him over the bridge. I got near enough to hear what passed; but, being a small boy, was disposed towards the rear, if it came to a fight. Chapman stood in the middle of the bridge, at the head of the boys; a short, stout boy, with his fists ready, at his side. When the bargees came close, and demanded the boy, swearing they would have him, come what might, the only words that Chapman spoke were, "You'd better not try."

The bargees looked at the boys, and the boys looked

at the bargees; the bargees began to waver, the boys stood fast. No rush was made, no blow struck. The enemy fell back slowly by twos and threes, and the boys remained masters of the bridge.

It is reported of the Duke of Wellington that he said, "Waterloo was won in the Eton playing-fields." I never hear this repeated without thinking of Bishop Chapman, and the army of his boyhood.

I suffered at Keate's hands three times; twice for playing tricks in my Dame's house, once for bathing at a forbidden hour, or rather, I ought to say, and with shame I say it, for fibbing to Keate when he caught us, just as we turned into his lane on our return. We ran and hid, but were ferreted out. Approaching Keate, with my hat off, and my wet towel hanging out of it, I stated to him that it was a mistake to suppose I had been bathing. He looked at me, and said nothing; but next morning, as I richly deserved, I suffered heavily.

I was very happy at Eton, in spite of my clothes. There was one boy only, I remember, whose clothes were made by Stultz, and the boys used to follow him up and down with admiring eyes. He had a swallow-tailed bright blue coat, with gilt buttons, and other things conformable. By his side, the contrast with the artistic developments of the Ossington tailor was very humbling. But I was very happy, clothes, boots, and shoes, and made fast friends there, as I had done at Southwell. I have now, at the age of seventy-two, survived them all; as, indeed, I have nearly all my intimate friends made at Oxford.

Upper School boys, when "taking leave" in my time, used to slip a £10 note into Keate's hand. Being in some fright when I found myself alone with him in chambers, just as I was putting out my hand I dropped the note on the floor. My tact, if I had any, deserted me, and I stooped to pick it up and present it. So doing, my hand came in collision with Keate's foot, which had followed the note, and covered and secured it. Since that time, a great deal of what is called "Reform" has taken place in this and other things at Eton. I don't observe that the "Reform" has done Eton any good. There was a good deal of a sort of prudery and false delicacy, I remember, talked about the note-giving practice. It was nine years after, that, going from Oxford to Eton, I came upon Keate at the corner of his "lane." Off went my hat. "Ah, Denison," he said, "very glad to see you." He had a wonderful faculty of recalling faces.

CHAPTER II.

Decay of Greek and Latin.

THIS seems to be a convenient place for some enquiry into the causes of the decay of "Greek and Latin," as a primary and principal element of the higher education.

This matter lies very deep. It is, no doubt, a detail; but it is one of those details which are hardly distinguishable from principles.

It lies as deep as the entire revolution of our time, which has degraded everywhere, in England, the Schools and Universities of the Church into places either of no religion at all, or, what is even worse, into places of quasi-religion. For good, plausible but unreal, pretentious but untrue, is always a more powerful instrument in the hand of the Tempter, than openly-proclaimed and undisguised evil.

The shallowness of prevailing democracy; the race of the material life; the yielding up the soul to the mastery of "the pride of life;" with the natural and necessary issue of these things, the preference for material above moral and religious considerations; these instruments of power for evil have combined to bring about the revolution. English people, aye, even Church-people, are congratulating themselves upon it. Schools and Universities of the modern type; the science and the art, the scholarship and the criticism of Century XIX., are to do what the Church of CHRIST has failed to do. They are to "regenerate" England. The Church of the past and the present; the Church of "the one Faith," has failed. The Church of the future, the Church of all faiths and no faith, man's Church, not GOD'S, is coming to the rescue.

Alas, for the awful punishment and retribution that has come upon this Church and People! Alas, for the vengeance upon neglect, misuse, abuse, of most precious Gifts of GOD! Alas, for the blindness of Bishops, Priests People! They could not, they cannot, see that, as respects the Parish School, the nursery of the Parish Church, what they had to do was, as in the case of other Schools and of the Universities, to bring their own care and use of GOD'S Gift something nearer to the level of the Gift itself; not to aid in its disparagement and ultimate rejection, upon ground of social or political expediency, or miscalled peace; least of all upon ground of money-grants by the Civil Power, given only upon conditions destroying the Church character of the school, and the Trust and the Commission of the Parish Priest in the school.

And for all other Schools, and for Universities in England which can, under whatever pretext, be forced under the cognisance of the Legislature and its instruments indifferent to religion; sound and excellent as the Schools and Universities may have been in conception, institution, and foundation,—sound and excellent as human things may be; guarded by the founders jealously, with all safeguards judged to be necessary and sufficient for preserving for all time their Church character, devised to the glory of GOD, the good of His Church, the saving of souls; all these having come into contact with the worldliness, and the selfishness, and the rapacity of many generations, and having been poisoned at their source, have finally fallen an easy prey to that indifferentism in religion—the parent of unbelief—which is in every country the natural outcome of the growth and prevalence of the temptation of "the pride of life," and of the democratic principle, the most powerful springs of all public action in England in Century XIX.

Alas, I say, once more for ourselves, and for our children, and for our children's children! The evil is wider, and deeper, and more enduring than words can tell.

It is curious to note here, that there have been in the last 2,000 years three principal instances of the formal repudiation by the Civil Power of the Trust and of the Commission of the Church in the matter of Education.

JEWISH CHURCH.—I. The instance of the reign of Antiochus Epiphanes, A.C. 174, 1 Maccabees i. 11—15.

CHURCH OF CHRIST.—II. The instance of Julian the Apostate, A.D. 362.

Tillemont, vol. vii., in Article IX. of his Life of Julian, in the *Mémoires Hist. Eccles.*, tells us the whole story. Julian issued an Edict in 362, giving Christian teachers the option of either confining themselves *exclusively* to *religious* instruction in churches, and catechetical classes,= sermons and Sunday-schools; or, if they chose to teach secular literature in public schools with state support, then they must refrain from any words or actions which would imply the falsity of the pagan systems and deities referred to in such literature. And to make this scheme work better, he set up *School Boards* in every town, consisting of the Town Council and certain other notables, who were to elect all the masters, subject to confirmation by the Crown. For edict, see Baronius; see also Appendix.

CHURCH OF CHRIST.—III. The instance of the Imperial Government of England in Church and State, A.D. 1840—1870.

I return to the decay of Greek and Latin, as a primary and principal instrument of the higher education.

Up to a late period of English life, definite teaching of Religious Truth as delivered by the Church was the avowed basis, and "Greek and Latin" the primary instrument, of our higher "Education." Both are disappearing.

It will appear in the course of the enquiry, that the causes of the joint disappearance are curiously interwoven and linked together: combining to produce that substitution of English "Instruction" for English "Education," which is a leading, perhaps *the* leading when all its issues are taken into account, and the most unhappy characteristic of our time.

"Religious liberty," degenerating, as all experience shews inevitably, into "licence," just as "Civil liberty" degenerates inevitably into Democracy, is fast filling the place of the implicit acceptance of Religious Truth as sealed and delivered by Authority of the Church.

The race of life, in a country where the supply of candidates for all callings, professions, and employments, largely exceeds the demand [a], has evolved the habit of assigning the early years of life to the acquiring the knowledge wanted for particular employments, so that bread-winning may begin the sooner; instead of assigning them to studies which in themselves are not, as a rule, productive of income, but are best fitted to exercise and sharpen the mental power; and to enable it to engraft upon itself, so exercised and sharpened, as occasion may afterwards arise, the particular knowledge wanted for a particular calling.

Add to this the truly miserable way in which it has been attempted to teach Greek and Latin, and you have the account, amply sufficient but not satisfactory, of the decay of Greek and Latin.

That it is a great national misfortune it is impossible to doubt; whether we look to the injury done to the mental powers, or to the loss of the principal ingredients of scholarship and taste. A "scholarly" man, even with all our fast-multiplying population, is a much rarer individual in England than he was fifty years ago.

First, then, let me say, that in proportion as there is in any country less care for the "one Faith,"—that is, for Truth exact, and definite, and always the same, as being matter of Divine Revelation and not of human discovery, —there will be always less care, becoming less and less continually, for exact and thorough scholarship. The original records of Revealed Truth are Hebrew and Greek. The earliest and best commentaries upon them are Greek and Latin. What is to become of Theology when the knowledge of Greek and Latin is gone, or, at

---

[a] The only exception that I know of is that of Holy Orders in the Church of England. A very adequate cause for the deficiency is to be found in the "policy," Ecclesiastical and Civil, of our time.

most, confined within a narrow circle, is easy to say, but it is not comforting to say.

Secondly, there is the truly miserable way in which Greek and Latin have been taught.

No man has any reason to be surprised, when, as matter of fact, some twelve to fifteen years of a boy's life have been spent almost exclusively about Greek and Latin, and at the end he can hardly produce anything in either, except what would properly result in a flogging if justice were done. No one, I say, can be surprised that people in general, and especially parents who have to pay very heavily for no result in this particular, should make up their minds that boys had better be taught something else.

Now this conclusion, however reasonable it may appear to be on the surface, where most of us now arrive at our conclusions, is hard upon Greek and Latin. It is not Greek and Latin at all; it is the truly miserable way of attempting to teach them which is in fault. They would have done great things for the boy, greater far than any other branch of human study, not excepting even the exact sciences, if they had been properly handled. As it is, they are made to bear a burden of obloquy, and alleged uselessness and waste of time, for which they are in no respect answerable.

I will say later what my indictment against the way of attempting to teach Greek and Latin is, and how I would have it mended. Here, I propose to go into some examination of the new system of "Instruction," which, possessing neither of the elements of the old system of "Education,"—neither, that is, definite Religious teaching as by Authority for its basis, nor knowledge of Greek and Latin for its instrument,—has, to the great and lasting unhappiness of this people, taken the place of the old system of "Education." It is no more than might have been looked for in a country where respect for authoritative religious teaching has fallen so low as it has in England; and "private judgment" of every man has been, not by Civil only, but by Ecclesiastical authority, encouraged to usurp its place; where also the vast resources applicable to the best teaching of Greek and Latin literature have been so miserably abused, as to waste altogether, in the great majority of cases, the time and the money expended upon it. It is no more than might have been expected, but it is not the less for that a most unhappy issue: one which, in my judgment, has laid the foundation of a perverted and corrupted system of culture of heart and mind, of decaying scholarship and degenerated taste.

I shall have to return later to details of the conflict between the system of "Education" and the system of "Instruction." Here I confine myself to some general account of both systems. I am writing to "Church-people."

The system of "Education" is that of training childhood and youth to do their duty in that station of life to which GOD has called them.

It lays, first, a sound and substantial basis of religious principle, and of the moral principles derived and issuing therefrom; a basis which is, not of man, but of GOD only. These are ingrained into, and engrafted upon, the soul, regenerated in Holy Baptism, by authority derived from GOD; and to be exercised, first by the parents, then by the school-teacher. This is done, not by appeal to the reasoning power, but to the duty of implicit obedience; and the means employed are perpetual repetition and inculcation; as the old maxim has it, *inculcanda repetenda*. The obedience claimed is obedience to the Book of GOD; the Holy Scriptures of the Old and the New Testament, as first sealed by the Church Catholic under the guidance of the HOLY SPIRIT; as committed to the Church to keep, and to deliver, and to interpret; a Book to which nothing may be added, nor anything diminished therefrom; and which is not to be dealt with upon the same rules which are applicable to books of man.

Thus, so far, "Education" provides, by early and steady and faithful anticipation, at least some security against the greatest temptation of man, sure to beset the soul in later years, the temptation of "the pride of life [b]."

The foundation being laid, what follows? To enshrine and convey all in the words of the Church's formularies, and, with perpetual reference to these, to exercise and sharpen the mental power, without putting undue and excessive strain upon the mind, or the body, of the young. The parents' and the school-teachers' business being to guide and encourage, but not to supersede the pupil's own intelligence; and, before assisting in any difficulty, to call for steady, honest, and repeated application on the part of the pupil. Wheresoever this rule is transgressed, teaching degenerates into "cramming."

The mind of the child and the youth thus dealt with, comes to apprehend what is its own proper work; to begin with the assumption, and to abide and rest in it, that the highest use of reason is to submit reason to Revelation, as delivered and interpreted by the Church. Feeling its ground sure under its feet, it applies itself to gather for itself greater weight and more incisive power, to be applied specially to the particular requirements of its calling; and so founded, prepared, and encouraged, proceeds to educate itself throughout this life for heaven.

This is some brief account of what is meant by "Education" in the Church of CHRIST. Let me repeat, that the education of early home, and school, and University life is the training mind and body to educate themselves in after life. The setting and the whetting of the machine, so that it may cut sharply and truly. "Instruction" duly given, is, of course, a part of "Education," but can never be substituted for it without the deepest injury, private and public.

The system of "Instruction" is not only a different, but an opposite thing. It is a thing of a lower and, almost exclusively, an earthly type. It is opposed in respect of its basis, its manner, and its end. It does not lay its basis in authority, parental or other, as derived from

[b] ἀλαζονεία τοῦ βίου. 1 St. John ii. 16.

Holy Scripture[e]. It does not therefore, by natural consequence, demand obedience of heart and mind to Divine authority, as committed and entrusted to man. It knows of no hearty obedience, except such as the child or youth may give of himself. For every system must have some basis; and Divine authority being, by the nature of the case, discarded from the system of "Instruction," which is, to say the least, indifferent in the matter of Creeds and Church, there remains only the authority of the individual will to fill the vacant throne. Now the authority of the individual will cannot consist together with, but excludes, humble, reverent, implicit, and unquestioning reverence for the Book of God, as committed to, and delivered, and interpreted by the Church. To such extent does the difference and the opposition between the two systems run. When it is traced to its source, it is found that the opposition lies at the root. A child and youth is "educated" for the heavenly life, through the earthly life: a child and youth is "instructed" for the earthly life only. Religion is the essence of "Education:" it is the accident of "Instruction." Religion is the beginning, the middle, and the end of "Education." It is the chance, and not very welcome, companion of "Instruction." "Education" bases itself upon the Creeds and the Catechism of the Church; "Instruction" not only neglects, but puts aside Creeds and Catechism.

In sum, "Instruction" deals with the child and the youth as bound by no authority but his own, and as not meant for obedience, except in so far as comes either of fear, or of sense of interest. And it does not concern itself with Holy Scripture any more than with the Church of CHRIST, except as one among many subjects for "free enquiry."

The democratic principle has received a new and para-

[e] My dear brother William used to say that, as the duty and the blessing of obedience of children to parents rests, in the highest sense of both, on the authority of the Bible; and as the authority of the Bible had come to be so commonly called in question amongst us, it was nothing surprising that the obedience should be so fast disappearing as a matter of every-day experience.

mount development here in England in Century XIX., in the persons of young children. A development happily expressed by somebody as follows: "There have been priest-ridden ages, and king-ridden ages; ours is a child-ridden age."

Loving and tender, thoughtful and considerate care for children, is a beautiful and GODlike thing. Deference, subordination, submission to children, is, under all its aspects, a hideous thing.

Nevertheless, it is dominant now in England, thanks to the domestic "policy" of the last forty years, which has formally subjected all considerations of religious truth and religious obedience to considerations of "social requirement," "economical adjustment," and "political necessity;" has devolved the responsibility of parents upon the schoolmaster or mistress, by whom it is feebly, if at all, discharged; has taken for its watchword "free enquiry" alike into all things; and has set up for its idol indifferentism in religion.

There is a subordinate difference between the two systems, in respect of the manner and the matter of teaching. I shall have occasion to speak of it presently. But as it belongs principally to higher-class education, it may be passed by here.

The system of "Education" is that upon which, I thank GOD always, I was brought up. I shudder to think of what might probably have become of me, if I had been brought up under the system of "Instruction," as the vast majority of English children are now. I was brought up in the habit of implicit reverence for the integrity of Holy Scripture, in humble, and dutiful, and unquestioning acceptance of Creeds and Catechism. I was taught to hold—what I have held always with tenacity of grasp, closer as life draws to its close—that implicit belief in the Ever-blessed Trinity, in the Incarnation, in the Atonement, in the holy Sacraments, and the Priesthood, as the means whereby the Atonement is applied throughout the life here to the individual soul; I was taught to hold, and have held always, that all these are "necessary to salvation," where within man's reach, i.e. where they "may be had;" I was taught to live, as I trust to die, clinging with heart and soul to "One LORD, one Faith, one Baptism."

And yet, I shall be replied upon here,—Your comparative estimate of the two systems, and of their issues, can hardly be a sound and correct estimate. Look at the position which religion occupies in the mind and in the life now, and contrast it with that which it occupied some forty years since, before the new system of "Instruction" was born. Look at the little speaking about things religious then; at the comparatively rare knowledge of such things; at the scanty observances in church and out of church; and look at all these things now. Look, again, at the self-denying life of young men and women, of which our time shews so many bright examples. In a word, look at the general position before the revival, and at the position since; under the old system of "Education," and under the new system of "Instruction."

The reply is plausible, and deludes people who, as is most common in our day, judge and decide upon great questions without pausing to think a little. It is plausible, but it is in fact compounded only of two fallacies, the fallacy of time, and the fallacy of cause.

For the first of these, the men who, under GOD, originated and shaped, and have hitherto conducted the revival, were brought up under the old system, not under the new. This is true, without an exception. Nor, again, has there been time yet to place beyond dispute, however cogent the "*à priori*" argument, the true character; to develope the inherent and irredeemable vice, and the practical vital mischief of the new system; pervading, as it does, Universities, Public Schools, Private Schools, Schools still *called* Schools of "the National Society for the Education of the Poor in the principles of the Established Church," but *being really* State schools for the "Instruction" of children in no principles at all. The

argument is necessarily as yet, for the most part, an
"*à priori*" argument. The "*à posteriori*" argument is on
its way, is coming inevitably, is not yet fully come. It
has not yet had time.

Then for the "fallacy of cause." My rejoinder is this.
The revival is not *of* the new system. It is, on the contrary, the recoil and the reaction *from* it throughout.
Men were raised up by GOD to see in certain facts of
the position in Church and State, certain assumptions
on the part of the Civil Power; certain developments
and consequences not less sure than evil. They were
called to revive religion in the face of a Civil Power
proclaiming Indifferentism; of an Episcopate and Priesthood and People offering nothing to be called resistance,
in the face of the new system of bringing up childhood
and youth; a system born of Indifferentism, as against
Religion. They obeyed the call, and have prospered in
the good work unto which they have been sent.

In sum, any one, really considering the matter, will
see that it is absurd to claim for a system, which is in its
essence irreligious, to claim for this, as its genuine fruit,
revival of religion. The contradiction is manifest in terms
and in things. It may be plausible enough in a time
which is always in such a hurry, that it never stops to
go half-an-inch beneath the surface; and which, in spite of
all its intellectual pretension, is a very shallow time; but
the most absurd things are often the most plausible.

When therefore, I say, as I have said many times, that
I bless GOD for the days which I have been spared to
see, even with all their incipient and multiplying evil;—
for days in which, as was not the case in the time of
my childhood, and youth, and earlier manhood, they that
fear THE LORD speak often one to another[d],— days
in which the knowledge of religious books and things
has been wonderfully widened and deepened amongst us,
—days in which religious observances, and specially the

---

[d] Malachi iii. 16.

Celebration of the Blessed Sacrament, have become a part of the daily life,—and last, not least, days in which we see all around us the self-denying life of so many among the young, men and women. In one word, days of a great revival of the true Religion of CHRIST; of His Faith, and of His Worship, among all orders and conditions of men;—when I say that I bless GOD for His mercy in permitting me to see all this, I am not attributing it, as to its native source and cause,—how is it possible I should do so?—to the system of Indifferentism in Religion, now publickly and formally endorsed by Power Civil and Ecclesiastical, and made an integral part of the administration in "Church and State;" but to its real motive cause, as in a case in which the good Providence of GOD has brought, and is bringing good out of evil; to the recoil and reaction from that system, from the "public policy" of Indifferentism in Religion as evidenced indisputably by many things, and especially by the system of "Instruction" in place of "Education," however such Indifferentism be advocated and enforced by the voice and by the example of those set in high places. The movement comes, as true movements always do, from below. It is not the Bishops at all: it is only partially the Priests and Deacons. It is not the Synods: it is not the Parliament: it is not the Crown, that has helped to the Revival. Nay, rather, all these have opposed it, in principle and in detail. It is principally the faithful Laity of all orders and conditions, the "working man" as the "gentleman," who are, under GOD, the Revivers of the true Primitive and Catholic Faith and Worship of the Church of England.

I have always thought the people of the Church of England the worst used of all people, under the halting and stammering voice and shifting order of "the Establishment^e." They are beginning to make a noble return for the ill-usage now.

[e] Every parish is liable to diametrically opposed teaching by successive Incumbents: to have two or more religions delivered to them instead of one and the same always. It is very hard measure for a Church to deal to her children.

Education, then, having degenerated into Instruction, Instruction, in its turn, has been depraved into "cramming," the necessary complement of the modern test of professional competency, competitive examination.

Competitive examination is a monstrous abortion, filled with poison, intellectual and physical: cramming is its proper child. I do not believe that the mind and body of any people can stand, for long, competitive examination, and its necessary complement, cramming: and the English, who, with all their faults, have a good deal of rough common sense, are already beginning to find this out. I forget who it was who said of the English that, taking them man by man, they were almost idiots, but that, somehow or other, in the mass and in the end, they commonly came right. The experience of my life does not incline me to assent to this statement in either part of it, certainly not to the latter portion of it. The corporate mind of England has, in many principal things, gone deplorably wrong. Nevertheless, it must be allowed that, sooner or later, after making the worst mistakes, and suffering largely in consequence, the rough common sense returns to the surface.

The Education, then, properly so called, of early life at home and at school and at college, is the training mind and body to educate themselves in after life: the setting and the whetting of the machine, so that it may cut sharply and truly. In the case of a people believing in CHRIST, and especially of a people having, as a nation, a branch of the Church Catholic for their National Church, all such Education is to be based upon certain exact rules and principles; rules and principles of Divine Authority, and as such always the same. The carrying out of these principles in the several stations to which GOD calls men, is the beginning and the middle and the end of the Christian life. Every man, no doubt, has to be instructed specially for his particular calling; but this instruction is not Education. It is only one, a necessary but subordinate and subsidiary, part of it. It can therefore never be substituted for it, as is now, most unhappily, the rule prescribed by public authority, and even not demurred to on the part of the Church, without the deepest and most lasting injury.

Then, of all ways of Instruction, the modern way, devised to meet the demands of the race of life, is the worst, and the most filled with harm to mind and body. The modern way is "cramming," forced upon us, as a necessity, by the rule of "competitive examination." Now a crammed boy is a pitiable thing. He is like a receiver, sometimes full to bursting, at other times quite empty. But at no time does he pump into himself at all; somebody else pumps into him. In other words, he does not use his own mind at all, except in taking in formulæ and facts conveyed to it by another mind. As soon as the pumping stops, the receiver empties itself rapidly. First there is a vacuum, then a sense of utter feebleness, then a collapse.

I may not be worth much as it is, and many people call me an educated idiot; but of this I am sure, that if I had been "crammed" I should be beneath all men's contempt.

With regard to "competitive examination," the silliness of supposing that, at its best, it can ever be a reliable test of, and a sufficient guide to, a wise and judicious selection of public servants, or of any other servants, is a wonderful thing. What it amounts to, and issues in, is that a boy or girl being crammed by somebody whose trade it is to collect and provide answers to questions, knows and can produce the answers. Now such knowledge is, at the most, a part only, and a subordinate part, of the competency required. And yet it is all that the examination can touch: on the other hand, "success" or "failure" is regulated by the issue. It is really nothing but a popular fallacy, and an imposition upon the public; it is true that it serves the public quite right; it is only throwing their own folly back in their own face. Competitive examination, with its half-witted officer, "cramming," is the child of democratic shallowness. The mass of men never go deep into things; and if we are to be governed, as we are now, by the masses, we must be content to be a shallow people. Now Democracy likes the way to public employments to be open to it; and Democracy is quite right here. But when the way of getting public employments is measured by the advantage accruing to the public service thereby, it may very likely be true, and, as matter-of-fact, commonly is true, that the way which the Democracy favours is the wrong way, and leads only to a general incompetency and incapacity, as soon as real difficulties arise to test it.

For my part, I believe that the old way of nomination to public offices, watched and guarded by an ever-vigilant public opinion, was a very much better thing in all respects than competitive examination,—even if this could be had, which it cannot, apart from "cramming."

Take a well "educated" boy, and he will soon master the particular knowledge required. Take a well "crammed" boy, and as soon as his mind, looking as if it were full, but really empty, is turned down upon anything not within the circle of his formulæ and facts and borrowed premisses and conclusions, it is impossible to conceive a creature more inane, jejune, blundering, ignorant, and helpless.

My dear friend, the present Warden of All Souls College, gave me, some time ago, a powerful illustration of the difference between Education and Instruction. He said:—

"Certain of our fellowships having been applied, under the Oxford 'Reform' Bill, to the promotion of the study of History and Law, we have been scrupulously careful in respecting such application, and in our capacity of examiners, of duly and faithfully discharging our trust. Now it has happened, very remarkably, that in no single instance has it been the candidate who had got his honours in History or Law, that has passed the best examination for the fellowship. It has, without exception, been the candidate who has got his honours in the Classical School, and has afterwards, with a view to a fellowship in History or Law, turned his mental power, so trained, whetted, sharpened, and working upon its own sound basis, down upon the particular subject-matter with which he was preparing himself to deal."

I have also an illustration, worth recording, of the "cramming" fallacy.

In the earlier years of this fallacy, a well-known Civil Service Examiner told me the story following. He began by saying, "Archdeacon, I know you hate us and our doings."

"Well," I said, "I don't like you certainly, or your work. Civil Service Examiners, with their 'competitive' trash,— School Inspectors, with their negation or disparagement of the One Faith,— and Commissioners generally with their blue-books, are people officially very odious in my view of men and things."

"Well, then," he said, "I will tell you something that will please you. Last week we had an examination for a Clerkship in the ——— Office. Three candidates."

"Oh," I said, "a 'dummy' case. Two Whig dummies, and one other, who is to have the Clerkship." I should observe here, for the information of a simple and confiding and much-suffering people, that a 'Whig dummy' is a poor creature who has failed once or twice, but is allowed to 'try' again; that is, to 'fail' again. It was an invention of the Whigs, to give the examination the appearance of equitable and tender consideration, while securing the success of the third man; and is truly Whiggy.

"Well," he said, "I know nothing about dummies; but here is the story."

"Prodigious!" I "mentally ejaculated," as the pure English of novels of our time has it, "Here's a Civil Service Examiner who knows nothing about dummies." But, wanting to hear his story, I restrained my natural feelings, and he went on.

"The examination ended, and election took place yesterday. I should tell you at this point that candidates are examined, 1. in the ordinary routine knowledge of office work; 2. in special and higher knowledge. Our man knew absolutely nothing of No. 1; but in No. 2 he shewed so remarkable and unusual proficiency, that we gave him the preference over the other candidates, who did extremely well in No. 1, but more or less feebly in No. 2. We made a special case, as in a special instance of original and acquired power. This morning the successful candidate went to the ——— Office, and was received by the Secretary."

Having duly congratulated him upon his appointment, the Secretary said:

"Mr. ———, there are circumstances attending your appointment of a marked and unusual character; and, if you have no objection, I should be glad to ask you a question or two for my better information.

"You are a very young man, and are reported to me as having succeeded in this competition entirely upon one ground, that of your answers to that higher class of questions which Examiners always put, but do not often get answers to. Upon this, though you are also reported to me as knowing nothing of the routine which it will be necessary for you to know as soon as possible, you have had the preference given you. Will you let me ask you how long ago it is since your attention was first turned to the subject, and what have been your means of acquiring the knowledge you possess. It may be of advantage to the public service that I should know this."

The Clerk looked at the Secretary and said, "I think, my Lord, you said that the appointment was mine. I trust to shew that I can well discharge its duties. But, I think your Lordship said that I am appointed."

"O yes," the Secretary said, "you're all safe; now, then, tell me, as fast as you can,—I have only a few minutes."

"Well," said the Clerk; "your Lordship shall know all about it. I think your Lordship said that I had—"

"Oh," said the Secretary, "don't be frightened, you're not going to lose anything."

"Well, then, my Lord, you ask me how long ago it is that I first thought of standing for this Clerkship. My Lord, it is just three weeks to-day since I first thought of it. I enquired who was the best crammer for the ——— Office in London, and I went to him. He said, after a little talk, 'It's absurd; waste of time, and robbing you of your money. You have got about a fortnight, more or less; you know absolutely nothing, and have not the ghost of a chance.' 'Very well, Sir,' I said, 'good morning, I'll go somewhere else.' I had got as far as the door, when he said, 'Stay a minute, you have made up your mind?' 'To be sure, I have,' I said, or 'I should not have come to you.' 'Well, then,' he said, 'I may as well have the handling of you.' Perhaps, my Lord, he saw I was not quite a fool. 'Now,' he went on, 'I have been at this work several years, and I know all about it. Mind, there are questions in the examination ordinary and extraordinary. We haven't a minute to give to the first: for the second, I know pretty well what will be asked. Now, if you will give yourself up to me, body and soul, for this fortnight, to do what I tell you, and nothing else; to eat, drink, sleep, wake, work, just as I bid you, and nothing else,—I see you are sharp enough, and I may be able to give you the ghost of a chance.' 'I agree,' I said. The result is, my Lord, that I am here to-day the successful candidate, and, as for my knowledge of the matters in which I have been examined and succeeded, I have not got any. I have been well crammed, and have been able to take it in, and that's the whole account of the matter."

What sort of public servant the man made I never heard. But any start in life more calculated to do a man harm, it is difficult to conceive. It must be a very strong mind indeed, which could bear up against the impetus given to conceit and presumption, and generally to a plausible and superficial life. No doubt he was a sharp, clever man, but, I suppose, few would say that his sharpness and cleverness would not have been better things without his "cramming;" and that for the true purposes of life, he would have done much better to have waited, and taken time to educate himself.

If competitive examination be a sound thing, then ecclesiastically it should be applied to Bishop-making; judicially, to Judge-making; legislatively, to M.P. making; administratively, to Prime Minister and Cabinet making.

But it is not a sound thing, and the argument for it, like many other arguments much relied upon for the management and conduct of public affairs, *proves too much.*

I repeat, then, that the silliness of supposing that competitive examination can, at its best, be any sufficient and reliable test of competency is a wonderful silliness. What it amounts to, and issues in is, that a boy or girl being able to produce answers to certain questions, in whatever way this ability has been acquired, is competent to fill this or that public post. Now such ability is only a part, and a very subordinate part, of any such competency. There are things which no competitive examination can touch; but which enter largely into all thoughtful consideration of what is the turn of a boy's mind, and his aptitude, ascertained to those who know him well, for a particular occupation. I hold, therefore, that competitive examination is a gigantic popular fallacy, and believe that it will prove as gigantic a failure.

In like manner, as the loss of care and love for the "one Faith," as delivered by authority of the Church, has been the loss of the basis of Christian Education, and the cause of its decay and well-nigh ruin; so, what I have called the truly miserable way of teaching Greek and Latin, has been the decay, and bids fair to be the loss, of the chief instrument of the higher Education.

It is, I know, a heavy indictment, and demands substantial proof. I do not think it is far to seek.

Bad teaching of a language, and consequent ignorance of its literature, with loss of all the time given to the supposed learning of it, comes either of incompetency of the teacher, the system of teaching being in itself good; or of such incompetency, coupled with a system in itself bad.

I make my indictment on both counts. To teach Greek and Latin well, you want men who know it well. Now, if the teacher has been badly taught himself, how is he—as the rule—to know well what he teaches others? Here and there, the *nativa vis* comes in and makes an exception. But the instances are very few, and I am writing about a national defect and want.

You want then, everywhere, in private schools, public schools, Universities, men imbued thoroughly with the letter and the spirit of Greek and Latin; men who have the languages, as it is said, at their fingers' ends. You want these men everywhere; but you have not got them; you have not had them, you are not going to have them, under the present system of teaching. After making due allowance for exceptions, the general fact past, present, prospective, remains.

And it is aggravated by this consideration, that the funds and other appliances for the due remuneration of first-class teaching-power are immense here in England; but are wasted upon the remuneration of second or third-rate teaching-power.

When I was Editor of the "Church and State Review," a paper which, though written by many first-rate hands, was so sound and able, and so little exciting and scurrilous that it did not live long, I had some articles written by such hands upon this matter, discussing the way of teaching Greek and Latin well, and going into detailed calculations founded upon unexceptionable data, and shewing that the remuneration of teachers was so high, that it was only reasonable to expect to find first-rate teaching-power, and that you did not find it. The articles are to be found in Appendix to Blue Book of Public School Commissioners.

My dear kind friend, the late Lord Lyttelton, whom I could never agree with, but always loved much, said to me: "Well, you see we have printed your articles."

"Yes," I said, "I see that: but you have not done anything to enforce them by your authority."

"Well," he replied, "there are difficulties."

"No doubt there are," was my rejoinder; "but what is the use of a commission, which leaves a chief blot just where it found it?"

When I had the articles written, I had an eye principally to Eton. Eton ought upon all accounts to be first in scholarship, as she is in a good many things. But certainly, she has no pre-eminence here. Rather, especially of late years, the reverse.

She teaches Greek and Latin; how shall I say that she teaches it? Well, I will say infamously, like other schools. But then, there being a larger proportion of rich idle boys at Eton than anywhere else, and less stimulus in consequence to mental exertion, Eton comes off badly in the race.

I prove my indictment positively, negatively,—the two intermixed, for it is not easy to separate them,—what is done, what is not done?

Now take an Eton boy's day, so far as his "learning" is concerned. I am speaking of nearly sixty years ago. But the system of that time has left its mark upon this generation; and I don't believe, from all I can make out, that the matter is much mended now.

Before 'school' you went to your tutors to be "construed," that is, to have done for you what you ought to have done for yourself as well as you could, according to your knowledge and your powers. But you were not asked to exercise your powers at all. Here, let me remark by the way, was the first development of that monster vice "cramming." You went into school: most days you came out just as you went in, not having been "called up," called, that is, to produce anything out of your "construing." How could it be otherwise in a class of some forty boys?

But, supposing real and frequent "construing." Now, such "construing" is, no doubt, an integral part of language-teaching, but is very far from being the most essential part. Translation is the most essential part. I don't remember translation at Eton.

But, again, supposing you had frequent translation into English, and out of English, translation upon paper — exercises of written translation, to be carefully examined, and corrected one by one; very good, so far well. But you have not come yet to the chief instrument of teaching a language well; I mean oral translation—*viva voce*, translation from English into Greek and Latin.

All this was lacking at Eton; and it is therefore nothing surprising that my recollections tell me of very little learnt in school, and of not much learnt out of school, at Eton, after the first half-year, when I was there in the hands of my dear old tutor, Mr. Drury[f].

Now suppose, once a day at least, a "school" of the kind following.

The boys, not more than twenty-five in a class,—the number is quite as many as a teacher ought to have in hand at once,—to come into school. To bring with them—though writing down anything would not be *the* business of that school-hour—a ruled note-book and pencil for entering anything they might wish to make a note of.

The teacher to be ready with a passage of sufficient length from one of our best Prose English writers. The boys to know nothing beforehand of the passage chosen.

Then as to the placing the passage before the boys.

This might be done in one of three ways:—

1. By the class having a small library of cheap editions of—to begin with—one or two of our best prose writers. Thirty copies, say, of each, to be left in the class-room: a small sum charged to each boy in the class would soon raise a sufficient fund to start with, and additions of like works might be made as time went on.

2. The passage might be written legibly on a blackboard just before the boys were admitted, to be placed well in sight of the whole class.

3. By the use of some one of the many inventions of

---

[f] I left Eton, Christmas, 1819, after having been there two years and a-half; I was just fourteen, and had got that time into Upper Division, Fifth Form. I went home to be in Mr. Drury's hands, with younger brothers, till I went to Christ Church, January, 1824.

our time for cheap and rapid printing, a sufficient number of copies of the passage might be struck off just before school each day.

I think plan 1. greatly to be preferred.

Then the teacher to tell the head boy of the class to read a sentence from the passage aloud; and, having done this, to proceed to read it into Latin, or into Greek if it was a Greek day.

In the oral rendering of the passage five things would have to be cared for:—

1. The knowledge of the equivalent word, or form of expression.
2. The grammar.
3. The idiom.
4. The taste and elegance of expression.
5. The form and turn of sentence.

A boy at fault in 1. or 2. to be stopped at once, and the next boy put on till the defect was supplied, or the fault rectified. The boy succeeding in this to go up to, or towards, head of class.

Interposition of, and enquiry by, the teacher in respect of 3, 4, 5, to be regulated by his own judgment; and to be made a ground of promotion in the class.

In this way, instead of the possible unamended ignorance of a "construing" class, or, at least, of most of the boys in it; and of the depressing dulness of only one boy at a time occupied with "construing" what had been "construed" to him by somebody else, every boy would be searched into more or less, stimulated and interested: most boys would be kept on the alert. A great advantage would be gained by grammar being taught in the process of learning language, and not by rote; and when school was over boys would go away, feeling that they had learnt something; and had some thoughts of the correct use and the force and power of language; of its taste and elegance, as derived from closer inspection of its best models put into their minds and hearts; and so be led to think of their school-hours as times of gain and improvement, instead of shiftless loss of time and deadening of energies.

I was not taught by way of oral translation; I believe, if I had been, I should have been a much better scholar than I am. I was taught by constant written translation of both kinds, which is the next best instrument, and in no case to be neglected or superseded, as well as by careful and exact construing.

So much, then, for construing and translation, oral and written. It hardly requires to be pointed out, that for each and all, but especially for oral translation, you must have as a really efficient teacher a first-rate scholar; a man thoroughly imbued with the letter and the spirit of Greek and Latin. And I say again, that the remuneration of teachers accessible in England, especially in our public schools, ought to ensure and command the services of such men.

Next to construing and translation, there is the learning Greek and Latin Prose by heart. A thing quite as useful and improving, if not more so, as learning Verse by heart; but in my recollection not part of the system.

Now, if it be said, all this about oral translation is very good for a more advanced class, but very difficult of application to younger boys, my reply is, that I think the objection not founded; and that a little thought and care would point out how it might be most profitably adjusted to the case of younger boys.

It was when I was seventeen that my attention was first called to the power of oral translation. I think I have read since that Montaigne and Milton, two of the best scholars of the world, strongly advocate it, as taught by their own experience of it.

I was saying to a friend in London, what a poor miserable thing my knowledge of French was, as I had picked it up at school, and at home by help of my sisters' governesses in the holidays. He said, "Why don't you try the

Hamiltonian system?" and he directed me to a house in the Strand. I went and said I wished to attend the class. When I got into the room I found about a dozen people, younger and elder, sitting round a table, each with a copy of the "Vicar of Wakefield" in his hands; a copy was given to me.

"Read into French," said the teacher. It was a stern and painful necessity, but the thing had to be done by unassisted effort. As I blundered on, I was corrected by the teacher himself, or through the other pupils, in points of words equivalent,—grammar, idiom, taste and elegance of expression, form and turn of sentence; and, lastly, what I have said nothing about, in speaking of Greek and Latin, because I know nothing, and don't believe anybody does, in point of pronunciation.

All the French I ever had, and I had in early life a decent quantity for reading and writing, — talking I never much attained to [g],—I got in eighteen lessons in the Strand; and from that time I have never ceased to believe that the primary way of learning a language is oral translation, and that you cannot begin with it too young.

I pass on to that most remarkable engine for stultifying the powers of thought and imagination and taste, the promiscuous requirement of "Latin theme" and "Latin verse." Of all things absurd, I know of no one more absurd; of all incomprehensible delusions, no one more incomprehensible; of all wastes of time, no greater waste; of all cruel requirements, no one more cruel; of all conspiracies against taste and elegance, no one more successful; of all contrivances to make Greek and Latin hateful and contemptible, no one so ingenious or so powerful; of all abortion making, no one more prolific

---

[g] Nevertheless, I record here what I have always thought a very remarkable instance of the power of French politeness. I was talking with a French gentleman at a *table d'hôte*, at Rouen, and apologising to him for my deficiencies of expression. "Mais non," he said, "Monsieur apparemment a vecu long temps à Paris." "Oh dear," I said to myself, "what a polite people it is."

than this same promiscuous Latin theme and verse making.

Take any fifty schoolboys, and see what is proposed, and what comes of it.

Every boy is to produce a "theme," a thing upon a thesis, some thesis of life and morals. You ask all the fifty boys indiscriminately to set to work "thinking," and to give you their thoughts in a language which they are learning only, and have not mastered at all.

Now, by far the greater part of any fifty boys havn't got any "thoughts" upon life and morals, beyond the simplest truisms, and can't get any "thoughts." They won't come for the asking. There is then a good deal of cruelty, as well as of absurdity, in asking them for what they cannot get, however they may try to get it.

But it is said,—after the manner of the Committee of Council on "Education,"—this is to do boys great dishonour. Without going so far as the Committee, who contend that at seven years of age a boy may be considered as able to form his own intellectual and intelligent estimate of religious dogma, we protest against its being taken for granted that schoolboys in general do not think much and deeply upon life and morals. Let me grant then, for argument's sake, that they all have thoughts waiting only to be evoked into expression. Just look at the absurdity and the cruelty of telling a boy to do two things at once, which are not only incompatible, but which fight with one another for the mastery during the whole process; you tell him to "think," and to express his thoughts in a language, at the best, as yet very imperfectly known and understood by the thinker. It is simply silly—a bad kind of silliness. It is worse; it is very cruel to the boy—stultifying and discouraging. It is to delude "the little victims" into the belief that they are employing themselves, when it is a sheer waste of their time.

There is always a good deal of risk in forcing the young thinking power. But, if you must have a boy set "thinking," in the name of common sense, ask him to give you his thoughts expressed in a language with which he is most familiar, and which comes more or less naturally to his call,—his own language. Don't be asking him to do two things at once, which cannot be done well at once, if done at all.

And just look at what comes of all this.

A "theme," in my time—perhaps it is so still—was a thing of fourteen lines, not less; Latin by courtesy, seldom exceeding fourteen lines, except in the case of an ambitious thinker. Fourteen lines,—how many words to a line? Five words will be very handsome. Five fourteens, seventy words,—an Essay on life and morals in seventy words,—seventy words, not of Latin, but of Latin-English, and of more than doubtful equivalence, and correctness in point of grammar; expressing one, perhaps two, thoughts arrived at either by an excruciating internal process, or by external suggestion,—commonly the last.

I suppose the number of "themes," beginning *omnes homines*, and ending *faciunt*, to have been very large every week.

So much for the normal prose Latin exercise—the development of assumed original thinking-power, expressed in a language not the thinker's own, and, at the best, very imperfectly grasped by the thinker.

O insulsum et crudele pædagogorum genus!

Then for promiscuous verse-making — original Latin verse, Odes upon Spring, and the like. Why this is, if possible, more absurd still, and of a wider and more comprehensive cruelty. For, granting that there may possibly be out of fifty boys five who can "think" a little, and it is a large allowance, the chances against finding one imaginative boy among the fifty are infinitely great.

And yet all the boys, every one of them, is bound here to "imagine" something by the conditions of their school-life. And, as in the "theme" case, to express their little "imaginations" in Latin verse.

Everybody who knows anything of Eton knows very well what came of this requirement. It lies in two words, "Old Copies."

Sometimes it issued in bold plagiarism. I remember an instance of a very near and dear relative.

He was, in common with all the other boys of his part of the school, told to write some original Latin Alcaic stanzas on "The Eagle."

His imaginative power was unequal to the call. He produced one stanza. Here it is :—

> *"Jovis Volucris vivit in arduo*
> *Saxo, polum quod sustinet arduum;*
> *Dilexit et princeps Deorum*
> *Jupiter hunc avium ferocem*
> *Regem, ministrum fulminis alitem*
> *Perfecit illum mortalibus citum."*

The vital mistake is, in supposing that what you want to do is, to *get from* boys, who have no natural powers that way, imagination and invention. Whereas, what you want to do is, to *put into* boys correctness, taste, elegance of expression.

I conclude absolutely, as I began, against promiscuous Latin "theme" and "verse" making. I conclude it upon every ground.

I say "promiscuous," for I need hardly add, that I would not only not debar, but would encourage, a boy shewing signs of thinking power. I would encourage him to use and develope it humbly, soberly, temperately; to think and to express his thoughts as occasion served. But, unless he was also a promising scholar, I would not encourage him to express his thoughts in Latin or Greek. It would not be real Latin or Greek; it would be Latin or Greek English. To write well in a given language, you must be able, more or less, to think in that language. It must come as natural and familiar to you as your own language is.

Neither, again, would I debar a boy, shewing signs of imaginative power, from original verse-making at school, even as an ordinary habit of the school life. But if it is to be Greek or Latin verse, he should first know a good deal of Greek and Latin. His imagination should not be weighted with a continual and harassing search after words and phrases. These should come readily, gracefully, naturally to his hand.

I have found great fault; I am bound to suggest a remedy. It seems to me easy and complete, as in the construing and translation case.

For Latin Prose, in the place of promiscuous Latin theme-making, I would have either 1. translation from English, or 2. some original account of historical facts, 3. some biographical notice of eminent men, or 4. some letter-writing or conversation. In two and three, the boys to be directed to authentic sources for the facts, or having them supplied by the teacher.

For Greek and Latin verse, I would have, in the place of promiscuous verse-making, calling upon boys for imaginings, which either they have not got, and cannot get, and which have been many times better expressed by poets, I would have close and faithful, but free rendering into verse, Greek or Latin, of passages in English or other poetry, if a boy has sufficient knowledge of other poetry.

In both cases, the boys would not be asked to do two incompatible things at once. 1. To think, or to imagine; 2. to express thought and imagination in languages they are learning, and are not yet familiar with. The facts, and the imagination, and the taste being supplied *ab extra*, they would be able to give all their energies pleasantly and productively, to correctness and elegance of expression.

I have for many years pondered upon these suggestions; have, as I have had opportunity, tested them in practice; and have thought that, if I were to begin work over again, I should keep a school, being first in Holy Orders, for "Education" in all its parts, strictly such as I have endeavoured to describe in outline.

If Greek and Latin is ever to re-assert its place as the true primary instrument of the higher "Education," as the best, because at once the hardest and the most polished, whetstone for sharpening and reducing into graceful form and shape the mental powers; if it is to be rescued from the undeserved and calamitous oblivion into which it is fast falling; I am persuaded that this is to be done only by such a reform of the teaching process as I have sketched above.

It may be that it is too late. That what has been betrayed is beyond our recall; that we may not look, as a people, to recover what has been so idly and shamefully lost,—I fear greatly that it is so. The opposing influences of this world's life are so active, pressing, seductive, powerful.

But of one thing I see no room to doubt, and that is, that a school, based upon the One Faith, as committed to the Church to deliver as of authority; and using Greek and Latin as its primary instrument of teaching, after the manner I have suggested, would very soon appropriate to itself all prizes and distinctions, and be in all highest honour.

I contend that I have sustained my indictment in all its counts.

1. That the system of teaching Greek and Latin in England is radically bad.

2. So bad that, if it were by common consent amended, it must be some little time before the supply of teaching-power could equal the demand.

3. That parents and children have right to complain heavily. Parents, that they were so badly taught themselves; and that they have to pay so extravagant a price for an inferior article in the case of their children.

If it is replied,—Do you, then, mean to say that scholarship in England is a very rare thing? Relatively a very rare thing: absolutely not. I have not said or suggested that it is a rare thing absolutely. It would be to state what is no less silly than untrue.

What I do say is,—

(*a.*) That the supply of it falls very far short of the demand.

(*b.*) That so much of it as is ready to hand is there in spite of the system, and not as the fruit of it.

(*c.*) That an exorbitant price is paid for an inferior article.

(*d.*) That the general issue is just what might be expected.

>Wasted years.
>Grumbling parents.
>Disgusted children.

There has never been a time when the class, either absolutely or relatively rich, has more urgent need for the best and soundest culture of heart and mind.

Democracy, in all its phases, from the claim of equal right to govern, down to Communism of possessions, is coming fast to the surface; and opening wide the maw, which does not close till society is swallowed up, and has to be reconstructed by the force of the stronger hand.

I say, then, to put the matter on the lowest ground, that of "British interests,"—as the ascendancy of the love of the material now describes our national duty,—that money, with the leisure for mental cultivation which money commands; the position and the influence which are the natural adjuncts of money, whether employed well or ill; that all these have at this time a special call to provide and care for such culture of heart and mind as commands the affection and the respect of men; disposing them to feel and to understand that, however full of surface plausibility the argument for democracy may be, the fact remains,— regard being had always to the rule of equity by which it is open, as it is in England, to every man to win his way from the lowest to the highest position in the social scale, —the fact remains, that distinction of classes, and right of the higher classes to govern, are integral parts of human society, by the laws which govern its being; and that what the great mass of a people have a right to, and will prefer greatly if they are wise, is not to govern but, to be governed well.

Where this is not found, this good government, there, sooner or later, the evil culminates ; law and order give way to force and rapine ; society, after terrible convulsion, has to be re-constructed upon the basis of military despotism, and the history of a people to begin again.

CHAPTER III.

Home Tuition.—Oxford.—Ordination.
1819—1832.

LEAVING Eton, Christmas, 1819, I was placed under Mr. Drury, with younger brothers, at home. I came into Edward's place, who was just gone to Oxford.

In 1820, my dear father died. My dear mother was left at forty-three with thirteen of us. Two besides myself are living still, my sister Charlotte, my brother Alfred. Evelyn came into my father's place.

I was four years under Mr. Drury; it is to these years that I owe such success in after life as I have been able to attain.

I recall, as if it were yesterday, the foundation of my four years' training.

Very soon after Christmas holidays, 1819-20, Mr. Drury said to me, "George, you are a very ignorant and a very careless boy."

"Dear me," I said; "I was high in the school for my age when I left. I was in Upper Division at fourteen; I used to do a good many boys' exercises besides my own; I was never flogged for my lessons. It is true I was never 'sent up for good;' but I always considered that it must have been a mistake on Hawtrey's part and Young's part."

"Maybe," he said; "but I think you'll be flogged for your lessons, whatever your merits, requited or unrequited, may have been at Eton, if you don't mind what you are about."

"Flogged," I said; "I thought that was all over."

"Not a bit of it," he said. "This morning you made two gross grammatical blunders in your Greek; if you make another I shall flog you."

I saw he was in earnest and held my peace, and thought I had fallen out of the Eton frying-pan into the Ossington fire.

A few days after I made another blunder, and, sure enough, I was flogged; I never made any more,—I had learnt to mind what I was about.

All honour to judicious flogging. Schools, with all their pretentiousness and fine talk, are not worth half so much as they used to be even in this one respect, let alone many others. But my discipline was of a yet higher character; it was home discipline. We lived very much to ourselves in a wing of the house, and it was no use making a noise about it; to say nothing of the childishness of making a noise about being flogged. If we had, besides, nobody would have paid the smallest attention to our noise. We lived under a real good despotism. My brothers, Henry and Stephen, were under Mr. Drury with me all the time, and my brother Frank part of it. They are all, as my three elder brothers, and my youngest, gone before me. Mr. Drury also.

It was a happy time. Plenty of work; plenty of play. Every morning at eight exactly, winter and summer, I had to be at his bedside with fifty lines of Milton, till I had learnt all "Paradise Lost" by heart. This has been a great help to me. Then work till 1 P.M., before and after breakfast. Play till four. Work till six; again, eight to ten.

Plenty of fishing, shooting, hunting. We were in the Rufford country, not many miles from the kennels; and there were some meets in five other countries, within fifteen miles: we youngsters, of course, confining our attention strictly to the Rufford hounds. Evelyn very kindly mounted me once a fortnight; I had a horse to myself. I never could sleep the night before hunting-day; my brothers had ponies. It was also law that, any other day, as soon as the hounds were heard in our woods, we put down books and were off, out of the door or the window, whichever was the quickest way, to the stables, where all was ready beforehand. One of the gardeners was our special ally, quite as fond of hounds as we were. Directly we saw his face at the window, away we went.

It was a strict and close, a kindly and easy rule. Sharp discipline, loving intimacy: no fear; great obedience. It was boyhood well and tenderly cared for.

In the autumn of 1823 I went to Oxford for matriculation at Christ Church; wrote my name in a book at the Deanery; saw the Dean a minute or two; went to the Vice-Chancellor, and came away next day. That night I saw something of the Christ Church life, and it astonished me a good deal.

Boys are examined for matriculation now. I don't believe any good comes of it. I am sick of even hearing of examinations. There are so many of them now, that there is no time left for anything else but cramming. I remember years after, when I wanted a horse, going to Charles Simmonds about one. I said, "Well, Simmonds, much riding now?"

"Bless you, Sir," he said, "the gentlemen han't any time. They're being examined morning to night."

"Aye," I said, "after they are in bed, and before they get up. Truly a miserable delusion."

January, 1824, I went up to reside. My Tutor was C. T. Longley, afterwards Head Master of Harrow; Bishop of Ripon, Durham; Archbishop of York, Canterbury. I believe he was all but ruined by his preferments. A kinder and pleasanter man did not live; a good scholar and historian.

I was a member of "Loder's," and had a great many dear friends in and out of the Club; others outside "The House." At that time Christ Church used to get a very large proportion of Classes and Prizes. The "Debating Club" began in my time in private rooms; there used to be a great deal of ridicule and childish tricks played. I spoke once, and Digby Wrangham called me "Cerberus," because I arranged my speech under three heads. I collapsed. Smoking came in in 1826; also slang: we are indebted for the growth of slang principally to Dickens.

Long Vacation, 1826, I went with my dear friend, P. M. Smythe, to "read" in Guernsey. We entered at

Elizabeth College, and used to go and "read" every day in one of the class-rooms with Dr. Stocker, of St. John's College, then Principal. He was a good scholar, and there was no "cramming," but a good deal of kicking us by the boys, as we passed through the school-room. They resented the intrusion, and the loss of their teacher for the time. Years afterwards I was invited to attend the Jubilee dinner at the College, but, as nobody offered me a bed, I thought it a little too far to go from East Brent. There were two other Oxford men, and three Cambridge, at Guernsey at the same time, and it was very pleasant. I remember T. V. Short, late Bishop of St. Asaph, then Senior Censor, telling me that he heard we had played so many freaks in the island, that the organization of a police was for the first time judged to be necessary. It was jocose of him, but imaginative. I believe, indeed, that there was no police when we went, and that there was after we came away; but *post hoc* is not *propter hoc*. Our freaks were of a very innocent description. The only thing I remember, was our carrying off a little black man from over a tobacconist's door. It was entered next day among my luggage as "Guernsey lilies," and found its way to Christ Church.

I came back to Oxford about the middle of the time to stand for a demyship at Magdalen, which I did not get; Roundell Palmer was elected. I mention it, because I am indebted to it for something I value very much.

It was the only time I ever saw Dr. Routh. Twenty-eight years afterwards, in 1854, the year before he died at the age of ninety-nine, he sent me his last publication, with an autograph letter asking my acceptance, and saying he wished to "see and" converse with me when I was next "in Oxford, upon a subject which interested us both." Something prevented me from going at the time, and I never saw him again. I have always much regretted it.

When I got my First Class, Michaelmas, 1826, Longley mentioned me, as the custom was, in his Censor's speech at Christmas in Christ Church hall. He said of me, *Sim-*

plex iste et modestus juvenis. It was very kind of him; some, perhaps, thought him jocose.

Many years after I said to him at York, "Dear Archbishop, when any one abuses me, as some ill-informed people do occasionally, I always quote you."

"Me," he said, "what did I ever say for you?"

"Oh," I said, "you don't remember, of course; but I remember very well your Censor's speech in 1826. I was your first pupil, you know, that got a First Class. You said of me, *Simplex iste et modestus juvenis.*"

"It's quite impossible," he said; "I never could have said that of you."

A coach used to run then three days a-week from Oxford to Cambridge. It saved me the round by London, and I went by it sometimes as far as the old great north road.

It was called "the pluck coach," because so many of its passengers were misfortunates at Oxford, going to try their luck where it was thought easier to command, at the sister Academe.

I got on the box one November morning, just after I had done in the Schools. We toiled up Headington-hill in a fog: I think I was the only passenger. Whereupon the coachman not being cheerful, and I being very cold, conversation languished. No doubt I looked yellow and pinched; and if I had not been ashamed, should have got down and gone inside. But young men in those days never went inside if they could help it.

Presently, after a heavy silence, he said: "Don't seem very well, sir; down like. You 'aven't been and got plucked, 'av've?"

I think I knew then that I had my First Class in my pocket; but I didn't tell him. I said, "Oh no, not exactly."

Then we were very pleasant.

The Ireland Scholarship began 1825. Herman Merivale, Mr. Drury's nephew, was the first Scholar. I tried in 1826, and was beat by H. H. Dodgson. Dr. Lloyd, afterwards Bishop of Oxford, then Reg. Div. Prof., a great friend of Evelyn's, was an examiner. He said to me afterwards, "Why, George, we all thought the two first days you were going to get it; but you dropped in your Greek verse." I worked at Greek verse, and tried again, 1827, but could not make up lee way, and was beat again by the present Dean of Wells.

1828, I got an Oriel Fellowship. Charles Neate, afterwards my very dear friend, and the late Bishop Trower were elected the same time.

Questions in "science" were part of the examination. Luckily for me, the answers didn't go for much. I never had any turn that way. But I read up Bonnycastle and Mrs. Marcet, &c.; arming myself, as I vainly imagined, with the necessary "knowledge," i.e. I set about "cramming" myself. I had never been "crammed" by anybody, and I made a nice mess of it, as the "crammed" always do, whether they "succeed" or not.

There came a paper of twelve questions. I proposed to myself to answer them all, out of the stores of my "knowledge." I richly deserved to suffer for this folly. Having had a good deal to do with "examining" myself, I always have warred against the specific thing of which I was guilty here, answering by guess. In matters of science, it is of all things specially ludicrous, and meriting punishment. When I had done, I thought the answers had a suspicious appearance; and so I did another set. Then I said to Trower, who was sitting next me, "Now, Trower, look here, I have got two sets of answers to this paper. Will you just run your eye over them? Whatever you may tell me will make no difference. I have made up my mind to send in No. 2; but knowing nothing about it myself, I have a fancy for hearing a little from you who do know a good deal what both are like."

He read both. I saw him laughing, not loud but deep.

"Well," he said, in set 1 there is one answer out of twelve tolerably correct; in set 2 no answer anything like correct."

I sent in No. 2; but I got my Fellowship, *minus* "Science."

1828, I got the Chancellor's Prize for Latin Essay; 1829, for English Essay.

The Oriel Common-room was a curious place at that time,— Whately, Arnold, Blanco White, Senior, Keble, Newman, R. Wilberforce, R. H. Froude, Hampden, Dornford; Hawkins had just succeeded Copleston, Bishop of Llandaff, as Provost; Pusey had gone that year to Ch. Ch., as Hebrew Professor.

It was as dull a place socially as I can remember anywhere: men were stiff, and starched, and afraid of one another; there was no freedom of intercourse. Whether the restraint of the old Common-room in Oxford, or the free thinking and licence of the new, is to be preferred, I am not going to discuss here. I have, of course, my settled opinion about it.

The summer of 1829 I went abroad for a year; the first part of the time with Mr. Drury.

At Cologne he said to me, "George, we shall be at S. Bernard in six weeks."

"Well," I said.

"Well, you stupid boy, we shall want an impromptu. We had better begin at once."

So we invented and polished away for six weeks, up the Rhine, Switzerland, St. Gothard, Milan.

It used often to make me laugh, though at times it was severe, that, many years after his recognised despotism had ceased, I was still to him his boy, subject to freest criticism and absolute dominion. He weighed a good many stone then: some years after, when I got him to let himself be weighed in S. James'-street, he was very angry with me because he came out of the scale over twenty stone; he held me responsible for the enormity. I used always when we travelled together to pack his portmanteau, tie his shoes, and pick up his stick. The day we got to Milan, we were dining at the *table d' hôte*, a large, mixed society of many nations besides our own. I suffered severely that day; it was well-merited punishment. There was some general talk about cameo: in worse than childish ignorance I rushed upon my fate, remarking complacently that the best cameos were mosaiques.

Mr. Drury was on the other side of the table, some little way up. Down he came upon me: "Why, you great fool, they are all shells."

I shrunk into *my* shell.

It had been the same sort of thing all along, in my brothers' case, and in my own; a curious mixture of the freest familiarity and the most absolute and unresisting subjection. Instance after instance crowds upon my memory, full of wonderful amusement, never interfering with respect and love. He died in 1868, at the age of eighty, bound up with all our interests and affections for nearly sixty years.

The rebuke at Milan did for me what the flogging at Ossington had done ten years before; it made me mind what I was about. It was to be sure publicly administered, and to the young of our time may seem somewhat harsh; just like the flogging appears unbearable to silly people, of perverted understanding and diseased feelings. A young man of twenty-four who talks like an idiot, is a greater offender than a boy of fourteen who makes grammatical mistakes; and requires even sharper correction; differently administered, indeed, but in proportion to the offence. Boys are not commonly conceited; young men commonly. If you disliked your tutor at school, you called him a beast; at College, you called him a fool. Young men especially want "taking down;" and it is to be noted that this was, and may be is, the phrase applied at Eton to the denuding of the boy preparatory to flogging. So beautiful is the harmony of just correction, physical and moral.

We came to S. Bernard towards the close of our six weeks. Going away the next morning, I waited to see what he would do. It was almost too much for me. Nothing came up to the moment of actual departure, when, as if suddenly awakened to a sense of duty, he said aloud, "But we have forgotten to record our best thanks to our good, kind hosts." (All this in his own particular French; a kind I have never heard the like of before or since[a]; the most daring outrage upon language and pronunciation I have ever come across :) "Have the goodness to bring me the book."

A monk brought the book: he took the pen, looked to the sky, and the mountains, and the snow, with pauses here and there for renewed inspiration, and dashed off our impromptu, *currente calamo*, as well he might. I contained myself with extreme difficulty, and much bodily pain.

The late Sir R. Wilmot Horton, who was there at the time, told us afterwards that when we were gone there was much talk over us and the verses. Their great beauty was on all hands admitted: some envious body suggested previous preparation; he was soon put down. Upon one point all agreed, viz. That I could not have produced so fine a thing; I was much too young.

Years after, I asked a friend who was going to S. Bernard to look into the book of 1829 for our impromptu. The leaf had been cut out. Evidently our six weeks labour had not been for nothing; the impromptu was a gem.

We parted at Geneva : Mr. Drury to return to England; I for Italy, by the Rhone, the Corniche, to Genoa, Florence, Rome, Naples, — returning to England in May, 1830. Evelyn had, with his constant considerate kindness, supplied me with the means of going further; but I wanted to get home, and did not use them. I was silly enough to leave Italy without seeing Venice; and have not been able to go there since.

---

[a] The night before, he was talking freely with a Frenchman at dinner. "Monsieur, quelle grande quantité d'ecrevisses vous avez ici partout sur les montagnes." "Pardon, monsieur, vous avez dit d'ecrevisses?" "Oui, monsieur, d'ecrevisses partout enormes, d'une grande profondeur, pleines de glace et de neige." "Mais oui, les crevasses comme vous dites, monsieur, sont terribles, vastes, et profondes." Truly a Frenchman is a polite man.

January, 1830, I became Tutor at Oriel. 1832, retaining my Tutorship, I succeeded my dear friend the present Dean of Peterborough, who had been made Head Master of Charter-house, as Curate of Cuddesdon, under Richard Bagot, Bishop of Oxford, 1829; Bishop of Bath and Wells, 1845. I was ordained Deacon, Trinity Sunday, 1832; Priest, Christmas, 1832.

CHAPTER IV.

CUDDESDON. 1832—1838.

ORDAINED Deacon and Priest in 1832, at the age of twenty-seven, I found myself entering upon my office contemporaneously with the first public beginnings of the Catholic Revival in England.

The Revival had two principal sources: one in Spirituals; one in Temporals.

The source in "Spirituals" was the defects, and consequent ultimate failure, of the "Evangelical" movement. But all this notwithstanding, let it be said humbly and thankfully, that to that movement England owes very much. It recalled men from a dry, cold and powerless morality, to the prime source of all that is most excellent in the regenerated nature, the love of CHRIST; but it failed in respect of care for the means ordained of CHRIST for the perpetual administration of His Kingdom upon earth, and for the regeneration and renewal of the individual soul. It appealed rather to inward feeling than to evidence of life: it thought much of CHRIST, little of the Church of CHRIST: much of THE SPIRIT of CHRIST, little of the order of His grace: much of preaching, little of the Sacraments: least of all did it think of the Real Presence of CHRIST in the Holy Eucharist under the form of Bread and Wine: nothing consequently of the Adoration of HIM there Really Present upon Consecration of the elements; and of the re-presentation of His one Sacrifice therein, and the pleading of It, ἀνάμνησις, before THE FATHER by THE SPIRIT.

This is the more remarkable, because the Wesleys had grasped it all, and had taught it expressly and powerfully; as any one may see by the Collection of Hymns published in their joint names at Bristol, 1760, Fifth Edition.

It is true that twenty years later, when the schism had been sealed by Wesley's act in ordaining, another Hymn-book, omitting the above Primitive and Catholic teaching, obtained chief currency among Wesleyans. But this fact is only one evidence among many of the rapid downward tendency of schism; a very remarkable evidence no doubt, but still only one among many.

But, whatever may be the account of the fact, it remains that the "Evangelical" system failed from the first, as the Wesleyan system had finally failed.

The enthusiasm evoked by teaching of this mutilated character carried in itself the seeds of its own decay. "Evangelicalism" was once a great power in England; it is not so now. After a while, it came to be felt that a system of religious teaching which, so to speak, left out integral parts of Religion, could not be sound and true, could not therefore satisfy the need of the soul. What was wanted, was the system which combines all the inheritance of the Servant of CHRIST, as bequeathed to him by CHRIST through THE SPIRIT. The system combining all that is objective, all that is subjective in Religion; all that is external to man and independent of man; all that is internal to man, and dependent upon the act of his free-will: the system caring for both parts of man's nature, in body and in soul; first caring for Doctrine, then for Ritual, its natural, and sooner or later, its necessary exponent. The system resting neither in faith without works, nor in works without faith: the system beginning and ending with CHRIST and His Sacraments, not with preaching CHRIST apart from HIS Sacraments.

In a word, what was wanted was the system of the Church Primitive and Catholic. The recalling into active life this system was, as it is still, England's need. The Church was failing within, and sorely pressed without. GOD in His mercy put it into the hearts of chosen men of His faithful servants, to lead the way in supplying the one thing which could satisfy the need; and the publication of "Tracts for the Times" began.

If it be said, in answer to my words just above about "Ritual," that this portion of the Revival does not find, except by necessary implication, a place in "Tracts for the Times," the obvious rejoinder is, that what had *first* to be expounded and enforced was, the positive teaching of the Church as of Divine Authority and Commission in matters of Faith. This had to be made, under GOD, to take the place of that negative religion which is the plague-spot of the English mind. I believe that, fifty years ago, if you had taken a hundred (so-called) "educated" English Church-people, and asked them what their Faith was not, they would have told you, and have thought it a good and sufficient answer, that it was not Roman Catholic, without knowing much, if anything, of what the Roman Catholic Faith is. If you went on to ask them what their Faith was, they would have had no answer to give; no answer with any substance in it; something about the Prayer-Book and the Articles; of which, as is said curiously enough in the Royal Declaration prefixed to the Articles, "Men of all sorts take the Articles of the Church of England to be for them;" and so in like manner of the Prayer-Book. The answer, therefore, does not amount to much in the way of definiteness touching Faith.

The Doctrinal Position cleared and established, especially the position of the Doctrine of the Sacraments, which has been for the last three hundred years, and is still, the great stumbling-block of the English mind; and the authority of the Church as against that of "private interpretation" of Holy Scripture vindicated, it is only to obey a law of our nature to place next in order, as concurrent throughout more or less, and developing itself as the circle of true belief becomes wider and more comprehensive, care for reverence of worship, and, where practicable, for magnificence of ceremonial. This is what the vulgar English mind calls "Ritualism," looking upon it, in its inveterate ignorance and prejudice, only as a rag of Roman Catholicism. What that great theologian, the present Prime Minister, called "the Mass in masquerade," "understanding neither what he says, nor whereof he affirms." The English mind, even in the highest places, is not deep either theologically or ecclesiastically, and prides itself upon what it is pleased to call "common sense belief;" i.e. natural religion, as opposed to belief in Revealed Religion, in the Mysteries of GOD, and especially in His Holy Sacraments.

The Prime Minister does not think—he knows too much for that, but to suit his political occasions he allows himself to appear to think—that "Ritualism" is going to be "put down" by Act of Parliament. So he leads his Conservatives, with a good many Liberals—always ready for any tyranny except when it concerns themselves—in the "putting down" folly; and then asks Churchmen to support his Government.

Now I happen to know something of the inner history of the passing of the "Public Worship Regulation Act." It came to me one afternoon at Plymouth, October, 1876, from the lips of the man to whom the Archbishop of Canterbury told it.

"The morning of the day of second reading," said the Archbishop, "I got a note from the Prime Minister to say that Government could not let the Bill go on."

"What did you do?" I said.

"I got into a Hansom cab, and went to Sir William Harcourt. I knew that a great many Conservatives would not lose the Bill if they could help it; and that, if Sir William and his men knew what the position was, they and these Conservatives together were strong enough to make the Minister alter his hand. So I got into a cab, and went to Sir William Harcourt. At 4 P.M. the Minister went to the House, having left his Cabinet with the understanding that he was going to do as stated in his letter to me, and, we must suppose, thinking so himself. But when he got into the House, he saw at once that the coalition was there in strength; changed his hand, made his speech, and the second reading was carried."

"Well," I said, "Archbishop, rather strong for the Archbishop of Canterbury, that *coup* of yours, about Hansom cab and Sir William Harcourt."

"Oh," he said, "if I hadn't done it the Bill was lost."

The Cabinet, no doubt, felt very like men dragged through not pleasant dirt. But, the thing that had to be done was to keep the party together.

So much for "Church and State;" for the Archbishop, who asks Churchmen to confide in him; for the Prime Minister, who calls upon Churchmen to support his Government.

I have heard "High Churchmen," men from whom I should least have expected such a thing, affirm two or three years ago, that there is no necessary connection between Doctrine and "Ritual," i.e. no necessary connection between Faith and Worship. It used to make me smile, and wonder what they would say next. I observe, however, that for the last year, or thereabouts, it has been found out that the affirmation is not worth much,—will not "hold water."

But it is manifestly absurd, and needs no detailed exposure, to say that because the writers in "Tracts for the Times" do not say much about "Ritual," it is to be inferred from their silence that they shared in the fallacy; and that the necessary connection of "Ritual" with the acceptance of the Doctrine of "THE REAL PRESENCE," and its ultimate adoption as the rule of Worship, was not present to their mind. It would be a curious piece of inconsequence and shallowness to saddle the fallacy on them. Let it be left for the use of those who are divided between "Church" and "State."

The source in Temporals was the changed relations of "State" to "Church,"—not the growing tendency only, but the development in act, of the policy which subordinates considerations of religion to social and political exigencies, and claiming still to have a "National Church," enters upon a course which, sooner or later, makes a "National Church" an impossible thing.

The seeds of the policy were sown in 1688. They bore

fruit first in the closing the doors of Convocation, "the Church of England by representation." The account of this commonly received in England, and thought sufficient is, that the Houses could not agree; that the Lower or Priests' House was to blame, and that Government shut the doors of both Houses. This is a sample of what is called "historical fact:" I know nothing more misleading than historical fact.

The conflict between the Houses lay very deep; and the account of it, and of its issue is quite simple. The conflict was the old conflict between Temporal and Spiritual. The Bishops' House represented the first; the Priests' House represented the second: the Government sided with its natural allies the Bishops, and specially with Bishop Hoadley[a]; and as it was politically convenient and palatable to the Crown to put down the Priests' House with a high hand, and as it left the Bishops more free to go their own way, Convocation was closed in 1717, and continued closed till 1852,—one hundred and thirty-five years. The difficulty about its being thus disabled from granting subsidies to the Crown had been got rid of forty years before, by the Act 16 and 17 Caroli II., in the time of Archbishop Sheldon[b].

Secondly, the seeds bore fruit in the religious torpor of Century XVIII., when, to use the words of Mosheim, "ecclesiastical literature sank to a low ebb, and spiritual religion to a lower."

When, Wesleyanism and Evangelicalism having been tried and found wanting, Churchmen began to awake again some fifty years ago, the Parliamentary condition was fast passing into active assault and half-paralysed defence, that is to say, into the condition in which it has remained

---

[a] Hoadley born, 1676; Priest, 1700; Bishop of Bangor, (which Diocese he never visited in the six years of his Episcopate) 1715; of Hereford, 1721; of Salisbury, 1723; of Winchester, 1734; died, 1761. Dean Hook says,— "He seems at first to have speculated in orthodoxy, and there is a work of his on Episcopacy which may even now be read with advantage. But the Whigs were in power, and their hatred of Church principles being strong, Hoadley soon perceived that the way to preferment was to assail the Church, and undermine the principles of Christianity."—*Hook's Life of Hoadley*.

[b] See Appendix D, p. 416.

ever since; and which will doubtless end in its natural issue, a condition of triumphant assault and complete paralysis of defence. In 1832, the numbers and the power of those who, either as Roman Catholics or Nonconformists, were not of the National Church, had become formidable; and the mind of the English Statesman, having lost its stay and its balance, took refuge in the rule that considerations of the position and the claim of the National Church must be made to give way before the claim of social, or political, or economical expediency; and the policy of Indifferentism succeeded to the policy of "Church and State."

I do not go here into the broad question of "Church and State:" I have in other publications stated my conclusions upon it, and should only be repeating myself.

All that I say here is this, that there was in "Church and State" fifty years ago, something of the nature of a principle; something which a Statesman could appeal to without stultifying himself.

Whatever may have been its value, it is gone now; though it be often appealed to still, as though it remained unchanged and unimpaired. But it is to be observed that, of late years, men are beginning to use language compounded of fear and worldliness: "It will last my time." This is in many ways significant.

The repeal of the Test and Corporation Act in 1828: the Roman Catholic Emancipation Act in 1829, with all its weak and futile devices and contrivances for preventing the vote of a Roman Catholic member upon questions affecting the "National Church:" the Reform Act of 1832, giving an impulse to democracy, which has never ceased since to gain strength year by year, with the election of many Nonconformist members: the doing away of ten of the Irish Bishoprics: the admission of Jews into Parliament,—all these things, natural in their order and sequence, and having one common origin in the march of democracy and consequent policy of Indifferentism, combined to stir the minds of faithful men touching the great and urgent need of Catholic Revival.

The National Church had leaned far too much upon the reed of State connection, as it leans upon it still even after the costly experience of the last forty-five years, though the reed has gone into the hand and pierced it. Henceforth, the Church, if to be found faithful, must be wearing other armour, and be fighting with other weapons.

And so, in the mercy of GOD, the Catholic Revival set forth, and moved slowly, but steadily upon its way.

Looking back upon the forty-five years, it is a wonderful sight. Full of sorrow, full of rejoicing; full of hope, full of fear; full of darkness, full of light.

Looking nearer and more intently, the sight has two parts; the one distinct from the other: one is that of the corporate condition of the Church as the "National Church;" the other, that of the individual condition of members of the Church, and of congregations.

On the latter side are men and women, soldiers of CHRIST, resting patiently, yea, and thankfully, under all trials in the Church of their Baptism; contending earnestly for the Faith once delivered to the Saints; committed to the Church to keep and to deliver throughout all time: ready to suffer for the Faith, and, if called thereto, suffering cheerfully; knowing that it is by suffering at the hands of the world, and not by the world's "successes," that they can best serve and follow CHRIST. Faithful men and women; individuals and congregations; Priests and People; here and there, but at large intervals of time and space, a Bishop.

On the other side is the Church Corporate, bound up with, and bound by the State—subjected, and subjecting itself more and more year by year, to the will of a Civil Power of all religions and of no religion; and listening, not unwillingly, to proposals for constructing the Church anew, after man's device, and, as it is said, for "adapting it to national requirements."

On the side of the faithful there is an unearthly and fast-gathering light, filled with struggling shapes, fighting, beaten, conquering, suffering, rejoicing, smitten, crowned [h]. On the other side there is the darkness that may be felt.

Let us turn from figure to fact. What have the forty-five years seen in respect of the Church Corporate here in England?

They have seen her robbed of her Church-rate upon pretext of conscience: on the same pretext, robbed of her Schools and her Universities: robbed of her Endowments and "Charities," devised exclusively for Church purposes, and trusted to the keeping of "Church and State" by pious donors, as devised "for ever:" robbed of her Jurisdiction in things Spiritual^c, as guaranteed to her in Century XVI.: on the eve of being robbed of her Churchyards, on the way to her Churches: outwardly retaining power and place, privilege and possession; but no longer with any influence as a "Church" upon public policy.

They have seen the Doctrine of THE REAL PRESENCE condemned by the six Doctors of Oxford University, in the person of Dr. Pusey. They have seen the Hampden case. They have seen the Gorham Judgment. They have seen the four years' prosecution of myself for the Doctrine of THE REAL PRESENCE. They have seen *in eadem materia* the "Bennett" Judgment, in which the Court of Final Appeal, transgressing its own rules and limits, prescribed what is, and what is not, the Doctrine of the Church of England, and disparaged to the utmost of its powers, what it did not dare to condemn by Sentence. They have seen "Essays and Reviews." They have seen Dr. Colenso. They have seen "Inspiration of Holy Scripture" and "Eternal Punishment" made "open questions." They have seen a huge wave of Scepticism and Infidelity, and of "oppositions of Science,

---

^b "As deceivers, and yet true; as unknown, and yet well known; as dying, and, behold, we live; as chastened, and not killed; as sorrowful, yet alway rejoicing; as poor, yet making many rich; as having nothing, and yet possessing all things."—2 Cor. vi. 8—10.

^c Constitution of Judicial Committee of Privy Council; 2 and 3 William IV. c. 92. August 7, 1832; entitled "an Act for transferring the Powers of he High Court of Delegates both in Ecclesiastical and Maritime Causes to His Majesty's Council." 3 and 4 William IV. c. 41. August 14, 1833; entitled "an Act for the better administration of Justice in His Majesty's Privy Council." Public Worship Regulation Act, 1874.

falsely so-called [d]," rising in the Universities and Schools, and sweeping over the whole country. They have seen the present Master of Balliol endowed in Oxford as Regius Professor of Greek. They have seen the Divorce Act and the Divorce Court. They have seen divers prosecutions for "Ritual," that is, for restoring more or less the Law of this Church and Realm, as set out in "the Book of Common Prayer and Administration of the Sacraments," in respect of the Catholic Ceremonial and Worship of the Church of England. They have seen every possible attempt made by Authorities Ecclesiastical and Civil against the revival of the Catholic element of the Church of England; no attempt made by the same authorities against the ultra-Protestant element; and this, though the first have on its side ninety parts in a hundred of all the devotion, self-denial, learning, knowledge, reverence, Worship, care for souls, to be found in the Church of England. They have seen no efforts worthy of the name against neglect of the Church's plainest and most undisputed laws on the part of Bishops, Priests, Deacons; no crusade against the secular life of perfunctory discharge of the *minimum* of the Priest's duty. They have seen in these divers prosecutions for "Ritual," Judgment after Judgment of the same Court of Final Appeal, contradictory and stultifying one of them the other of them, by a process of perpetual interchange. They have seen the "miscarriage of justice" in the "Essays and Reviews" case; in the "Colenso" case; in the "Liddell" case; in the "Mackonochie" case; in the "Purchas" case; in the "Ridsdale" case; in the "Tooth" case; in the "Edwards" case. They have seen an ex-Judge of the Divorce Court selected to decide in the first instance in Spiritual causes, under an Act passed for the express purpose, as avowed by the Minister in his place in the House of Commons, of "putting down Ritual," and sitting at Lambeth Palace in the house of the chief promoter of the Act under which he sits. They have seen the desecration of the Blessed Sacrament by the Judgment of the Court of Final Appeal

[d] 1 Tim. vi. 20.

in the "Jenkins and Flavel Cook" case. They have seen a "new Lectionary," which, among blots upon it other and sundry, pulls out the corner-stone of the whole series of first Morning and Evening Lessons from "Trinity" to "Advent." They have seen a Committee for "revision of the Authorized Version," and one of its members a man who denies the GODHEAD of CHRIST; and who, as such member, is invited to receive the BODY and the BLOOD in Westminster Abbey. They have seen the Convocation of Canterbury either openly approving or acquiescing. They have seen an attempt, mainly promoted by the present Archbishop of Canterbury, to get rid of the Athanasian Creed. They have seen the same high authority, with others of his brethren the Bishops, proposing that Priests of the Church of England be required to bury the bodies of unbaptized parishioners with a "Service of the Church." They have seen an assault upon "Confession to a Priest," of which it is hard to say whether the blank ignorance, the unscrupulous calumny, or the passionate frenzy be most conspicuous; though Confession to a Priest be explicitly taught, encouraged, and provided for by the Church of England. They have seen the assault, in its substance, approved of by the Convocations.

These are some of the public acts of Bishops, Clergy, and People of the Church of England aided by allies other and sundry, in and out of Parliament; and of the Imperial Government, administering by its Judges, in all causes, Spiritual and Temporal, justice "truly and indifferently," in the course of the last fifty years.

One would think that it were more than enough to ruin "seven Churches;" and so it would be, were it not for the mercy and long-suffering of GOD. "Yet have I left me seven thousand in Israel, all the knees which have not bowed unto Baal, and every mouth which hath not kissed him [e]."

It is the worst aspect of the case that they have seen all

---

[e] 1 Kings xix. 18.

this aided, abetted, encouraged, welcomed by Bishops, Synods, Priests, People. They have seen labour for peace which is no peace; for unity which is no unity; building of walls with untempered mortar, decaying as soon as built, and sure to fall. They have seen her Synods admitted, as by indulgence of the Civil Power, not restored as of right and duty, to something looking like active life; but which was never meant to be active life by the power admitting, and never will be. The admitting was to be able to say that the grievance of Synods denied had no longer any place. The doors were opened, having been shut for 135 years because the Priests' House refused to concur in the Erastianism of the Bishops' House; and Churchmen might "meet and talk" once more in the Constitutional Synod: but as for "doing," it was never meant that they should "do" anything for the "Church," and never will be.

Many good friends of mine keep deluding themselves and others with the hope of what is called "Reform of Convocation"—meaning, as I am able to understand it, some better adjustment of the lower House. Well, supposing this was got, the real grievance would remain just where it was before; viz., that with a reformed Synod you would be just as unreal, and just as powerless as you are now. The House of Commons is not going to allow Convocation to "do" anything to make *Imperium in Imperio*.

Instances will come after. Here, I gather up the details into one issue.

On the other hand, under the good Providence of GOD caring for His Church as man cannot care, the forty-five years have seen a marvellous growth of the knowledge of things spiritual, and of the applying that knowledge to the daily life: of thousand-fold worship: of self-denial of the young, men and women: of concentration of purpose upon, and devotion to the work of CHRIST: of decency, order, reverence for things holy: of care to give the best of such things as we have to GOD: of labour of love for CHRIST'S sake. These things are seen more

F

or less everywhere, among all orders and conditions of men.

In a word, as the Church is being pulled down from within and from without, to suit the democratic, or the "scientific" man, or the "Broad Church" man, or the "Low Church" man, or the "no Church" man, or all of them together; and if defended at all in Parliament, defended as "the Establishment," not as "the Church," faithful hands within, faithful hands of all orders and conditions of men, are building it up upon the basis of Primitive and Catholic Truth and Order.

This is some brief summary of fact.

Every day forces it upon men's minds more and more. But there are many of us, aye, of those of us within the Church, who either as yet do not see it, or prefer, seeing it more or less, not to look at it.

It shews the process of dis-establishment, the natural and necessary consequence of those conditions of a people which present, on the one hand, a "Church" established by law; on the other, a legislative power of all religions and of no religion. Under such conditions, dis-establishment and dis-endowment (two things, but inseparably connected) are only questions of time and circumstance. The process is necessarily slow before reaching its final consummation; but it is sure.

Irish dis-establishment began forty-five years ago with the sweeping away of ten bishoprics: dis-endowment came 1868. English dis-establishment began 1828, with repeal of Test and Corporation Act: dis-endowment, first insidiously,—"unostentatiously," as the late Sir James K. Shuttleworth phrased it,—with inroad upon, and plunder of, Schools and Universities; formally, with Abolition of Church-rate, 1868.

For my belief at the time of my Ordination, it was in its substance what it is now. It has, indeed, in the forty-five years which intervene, been largely developed and consolidated; but in all its substance it is one and the same. I was then, as I am now, what has come to be called an "extreme High Churchman." It is a curious epithet to apply to belief, as if belief could be "extreme;" but it expresses well enough the opposite to the negative and compromising, and almost exclusively subjective character of English religion[1].

But I was, I regret to have to say it, no student of theology: I was as I had been educated: I thank GOD for the Education. I had not done, I was not doing much for myself. Certain broad outlines had been traced for me, and inside them I walked. My life of almost daily transit during half the year between Oxford and Cuddesdon was not favourable to study; and active occupation of time, health not very strong, and the comforts and enjoyments of my position, concurred to produce what I must needs describe as a negative result.

I cannot charge myself with not having taken thought for, and care of, my people: but measured by the standard of the Parish Priest's life which the Revival has established, my thought and care were only poor things. I found a parish of some five hundred souls, "church-going" people, with Holy Communion from time to time, and a number of Communicants relatively very large; with Sunday-school held in the church, with hardly anything to be called a daily school, and with no school-buildings; with a pretty old church, closed pews and open sittings; and I left all these things much as I found them. I was, indeed, only the Curate, but practically very like the Incumbent, so far as the management of the parish went; and I might have done a good deal for Cuddesdon which I left to be done by those who came after me.

In Oxford, I was very good friends with the writers

[1] It is noteworthy, that in politics, the world is indulgent to "extremes,"— thinks them silly, because it thinks all definiteness silly, except in thing material; but treats them with a half-pitying, half-contemptuous, indulgences In religion it regards them as a crime; an offence against society. No doubt the world finds them very inconvenient things in the path of its dominion.

of "Tracts for the Times," but was not intimate with them. I did not possess the necessary qualifications. I feel this keenly now,—I wish I had felt it keenly then.

Many years after, J. H. Newman wrote to me, asking me to use any influence I might have with Lord Derby's Government in favour of a (Roman) Catholic University in Dublin. He said that their choice lay between this and a College in Oxford, with a strong preference for the first. He went on to say that, knowing how decided my English Churchmanship was, he thought I would readily do what might be in my power against the College in Oxford.

My reply was, that I was against the College, but not for the University. I told him that their case, as between them and the Civil Power, was the strongest possible case. That a Civil Power, which looked favourably upon a creation such as the University of London, had no excuse for looking unfavourably upon a (Roman) Catholic University in Dublin; but that, so far as I was concerned, I did not see my way to having any hand in it.

In rejoinder came one of his kindly letters, saying, that he was as glad of the way in which I had received and replied to his request, as he would have been of my compliance with it.

He added, what moved me deeply,—I tell the story for two reasons, one, because it indicates how I stood as Fellow of Oriel, with Newman and his coadjutors; the other, because it testifies to his deep kindliness and true humbleness of heart :—he added, that he wished to say to me that he was sorry for instances of harshness towards me during our time together at Oriel.

I answered as I felt, and feel still, that I had no recollection of any such instances; and that, if there had been any such, the account of them I believed to be this, that he was at the time referred to much more in earnest than I was.

Many men's political "proclivities" underwent curious transmutations in and about 1832.

Among them I became, to my own great astonishment, a Liberal for six months, chiefly under the influence of my dear friend Harington, late Principal of Brasenose College. How exactly it began, and how it ended I cannot recall, but I know that the delusion did not survive six months. I was before, and have been since an "old Tory." I am quite of the man's mind, who when his friend said to him, "Why, you've changed sides;" said, "Well, yes, I was a Tory, and now I am a Radical; I thank Heaven I never was a Whig." So I say, I was and am a Tory. Forty-five years ago, I was fool enough for six months to be a Liberal: I thank Heaven I never was a Conservative. A Conservative is a Catholico-phobist; he is more, he is a Panto-phobist; he keeps what is trusted to him to keep till he is asked to give it up: then he gives it up as suits the political and party position.

Some years ago, my dear friend Upton Richards brought two nephews of his to me, saying, "Here are two boys you will like to know; good Conservative boys." Note here that boys begin having politics now, and quarrelling with those who have other politics, from four to five.

I said, "Oh no, something better than that." Off went the boys.

"Better! what's better than a Conservative? Papa's a Radical,—Mama's a good Conservative."

"Dear boys," I said, "you're going back to school to-morrow, and I daresay your kind uncle here will give you each a nice book to take with you. Now when you get to school there will come a big boy, and when he sees your nice book, will say, 'I say, you fellow, give me that book.' Then you'll say, in a whining, piping voice, 'No, I won't.' 'If you don't I'll thrash you.' 'There take it,' (blubbering).—That's a Conservative. Then to the other of you, another big boy for the other book. 'Give it me.' 'No I won't,' *not* in a piping voice. 'You'd better.' 'If you come an inch nearer, I'll knock you down.'—That's a Tory."

"Oh, we're Tories, Tories all over. Mama shall be

a Tory." Ever after they always asked where old Uncle Tory was.

In 1836 I gave up my Tutorship at Oriel, and became Treasurer. Treasurers of Oriel had a common fate, they kept the College accounts in some dozen books of bad Latin, accounts much intermixed and confused. At the end of three years, when they were just beginning to know something of their trade, they made room for the next Treasurer, and had to produce their balance-sheet. In the outset, it commonly appeared to the outgoing man that the College owed him a good deal; it ended as commonly in his owing the College a good deal. I came off easily, having been careful always to pay in and out of bankers.

I had two cottages at Cuddesdon, and used to have pupils there in Long Vacations, and sometimes to prepare for Oxford. Many happy friendships came of this. In 1837-8, I came into my brother Edward's place, as examiner for the Ireland; Lingen, and Fraser Bishop of Manchester, were the Scholars of the two years. I told Lingen some time afterwards, wishing to say something pleasant to him after fighting with him for many years as Secretary of Committee of Council, that he owed his scholarship to me. The two other examiners wanted to elect Fraser. I said, "No. Lingen has not made one mistake: Fraser is better in some things, but not so sound; besides, he will get it next year if he lives;" as he did. So we sat up all night reading over the papers, and about 4 A.M. they gave in.

Lingen wrote me in return a very kindly letter, telling me that there was hardly anything he could so ill bear to part with as his Greek and Latin; adding, that he reckoned he walked about 1200 miles in the year, between his office and his home; and that, as he walked, he was always turning things into Greek and Latin. He sent me two bits of the day before, and very good bits they were.

1838-9, I went to Eton to examine for the Newcastle; the late Bishop of Lichfield and the present Bishop of Chichester were my colleagues. Hawtrey received me with all his genial hospitality. It was pleasant times; one of the scholars elected was Balston, the late Head Master.

Hawtrey told me then, how that two successive nights his garden door had been painted red; the third night he lay in wait: about twelve he heard the brush, opened the door suddenly, and there was the Provost, Goodall, in full dress, with paint-pot and brush: closed the door hastily, and retired.

Next day he asked a common friend if he had seen the Provost lately, and how he was. "Oh quite well, I was with him rather late last night."

Eton men, and perhaps other men, will know very well who the painting Provost was.

When I was furnishing my house at Cuddesdon, my mother said to me, "George, you must have a medicine-chest; I will give you one."

"Please don't," I said, "I shall be killing men, women, and children."

"I will give you a little book with it, and you will be quite safe."

"Very well," said I; "thank you, dear mother."

I unpacked my little chest, and put it with the book in a corner of my bedroom, and for a year or more thought no more about it.

I had a gardener then, an old soldier, William Finlay; he had picked up somehow a great deal of very graphic language, which he used freely upon the ordinary occasions of life.

He came to me, and said: "I'm bad all over, inside and out, wants you to give me some physic. They tells me you've got a medicine-chest, and a book as belongs to it."

"Well," said I, "I have; what will you take?"

"Some rhubarb," said he.

"I'll look in the book," I said, "and see how much."

Now the book has—I have it still with the chest—at least my wife has, for I carefully made her a wedding present of both,—the book has at the beginning a table of doses; quite an inexcusable snare, I think, to simple people. It is constructed on a hypothetical principle: "*If* to an adult a dram, so much to other ages."

The hypothetical part escaped me; an adult, 1 dram—a dram, that's 60 grains,—magnesia to be added upon experience; how much? I suppose half—30 grains—90 grains in all.

I got a half-sheet of the "Times,"—I remember telling Mr. Delane, when they made me tell the story at a dinner at Bishop Wilberforce's, that it was the only use I could find for the "Times,"—put it on the dining-table and mixed up. It looked a good deal; but I said to myself, "Must be all right, here's the book; Finlay's an adult." He was over 70.

So I rang the bell. "Here's your physic; I hope it will put you all right."

"I be to take all that."

"Yes, that's just what the book says; small doses foolish things."

"All right," says he.

Then I began to encourage him. "Now, Finlay, you're not very well, don't try and do any work to-day; go home, keep yourself warm, and tell your wife to mix it up in some warm water,—not too much water; you'll be much better in the morning. I should, if I were you, take it at once."

"All right," he said.

Poor man, his confidence in me had no limits. I thought no more about it till next morning, my conscience was quite easy; I had done a wise and kind thing; I had made a good use of my dear mother's gift.

When I was dressing in the morning, I looked out of the window, and there was Finlay standing between me and the garden wall. He looked, so to speak, shadowy, almost ghostly; the wall, as it were, was visible through him; but, as it was daylight, I wasn't afraid. "Hope you're better this morning; glad to think you must be, or you would not have come up."

"Well," he said, "I be a trifle better."

"Ah," I said, "I thought so; you took your physic of course."

"Why, didn't you tell me to take it? I'll tell you all about it. I goes home to my wife, and says, 'There, you mix that up; mind, not much water.'

"'Lord's sake,' she said, 'you be not going to take all that; why it would kill a horse and a cow.'

"'You foolish woman, hold your tongue, go and do as I bids you. Master's got a book, and knows a sight more than you.' So she goes and mixes up in a slop-basin, and brings it back with a spoon standing up in the middle."

At this part of his report I began to have misgivings. He went on:

"I got him down; but it was a tough job,—and goes to bed."

I draw a veil over what followed. I reeled about with laughing, struggling to look sympathetic, but my misgivings increased.

His exact account of what had befallen him during the night I took down just as it came out of his mouth. I shall be happy to communicate it *ipsissimis verbis*, to anybody who may like to complete the tale.

"Well," I said, as soon as I could steady my voice, "go into the kitchen, and have some nice warm breakfast, and then we'll see what is to be done next."

Half-an-hour after I was on my way to Oxford as fast as I could go, and went to my dear friend Dr. Wootton. In the course of conversation, I asked him in a kind of careless way about rhubarb, as a guide for my parochial practice.

"Well," he said, "it's a fine medicine, and I give good doses of it."

"Yes, what is a good dose?"

"Eighteen grains is quite enough for anybody."

"Eighteen grains," I said, "why I gave a man sixty yesterday, and thirty magnesia."

He opened his great eyes and said, "Is he very old?"

"Yes, over seventy."

"Then perhaps "he" won't die. Go home as fast as you can, and pour in porter and port wine."

So far I had, with the best intentions, only made a mistake. It might have been wiser, no doubt, to have previously satisfied myself about the dose; but my intentions were very pure. For what I did afterwards I do not pretend to offer any excuse; but I tell the whole story as some warning to my younger brethren, who may be tempted to dabble in physic; and as shewing that "a little knowledge"—that is to say, about the worst kind of ignorance—"is a dangerous thing."

About ten days after my first escape and his, he came to me again,—what a precious thing unbounded confidence is to be sure; and how careful we should be not to abuse it.

But I confess that I did abuse it in this case. He went on:

"I should like some more of that there physic."

"Ah," said I, "I was sure it would do you so much good that, if you felt poorly again, you would come and tell me."

"Well," he said, "to be sure, who should I go to but you? I think, perhaps, I might have not quite so much as time before."

"Oh, no," I said, assuming an attitude of pensive consideration of the case, "of course not; this time I should not give you more than half of what I gave the first time."

"That will do very nicely," said he.

Half, was thirty grains rhubarb, fifteen magnesia; having regard to the antecedents of the case, and specially to Wootton's allowance of eighteen grains *ad max.:* I think many people have been hanged for a less offence than mine, in giving 45 + 15 on the second occasion.

However, Finlay survived it, and was alive ten years after; and upon the modern principle of English capital punishment that, whatever your intentions to kill may have been proved to be, you are not to be hanged if you don't succeed in killing,—a principle which has always been an extreme puzzle to me,—I am so far entitled to an acquittal.

After these two escapes, and a third, where I was really not to blame, in giving an aged woman ninety-three drops of laudanum in half-an-hour, dose after dose; being greatly exercised upon hearing of the use made of my liberal supply, but finding the old thing sitting on the end of her bed in a happy state, I locked up my little chest, put it away with book and key, and have kept aloof from it ever since.

At Cuddesdon all things were pretty much in my hands; and being of a despotic turn of mind, I ruled with a high hand. The outward discipline of the place was consequently somewhat exact, as the following instance serves to shew.

The church has a central tower, and north and south transept. I warmed the church by putting a stove in the centre of the space under the tower. The stove had a descending flue as far as north-east corner of north transept, where it mounted up the angle, and by a shameful blunder of construction, passed out close over the wall-plate.

Christmas morning it was very cold, and we had a roaring fire. The people were generally very quiet and orderly in church; but that morning I noticed that before I got to the end of the First Lesson everybody was fidgeting and looking about.

This increased so much, that I turned to the clerk, who by a peculiar arrangement sat just behind me, and said, "Mortimer, what is all this disturbance about?"

"Please, sir," he said, "if you don't stop reading we shall all be burnt alive."

"Burnt alive! what do you mean?"

"Please, sir, the church be on fire."

I looked over my right shoulder, and saw sure enough that in the corner, where the flue-pipe crossed the wall-plate, about 3 ft. square of the ceiling was red-hot.

Upon this I said to the people, "I see there is a little

accident, you had better go and get ladders and plenty of water."

Then, upon permission given, but not till then, out they went, and the church was cleared, so to speak, all in a moment.

When we came to pull off the roofing out burst the flames. We soon got the fire under; but if it had been after service, and I verily believe if, being in service, I had not told them to go, the church would have been burnt, and it may be some "burnt alive."

My cottage narrowly escaped destruction twice in the six years of my occupation. Once by the big fires I used to keep laying hold of a principal beam of the house cunningly laid across the chimney; the other time was upon a fête-giving occasion. There was to be a cricket-match in my field, and great preparations made for a banquet in a tent.

Getting up next morning, I smelt a fiery smell; opened the door, it was all over the house. Rang my bell for my servant Henry Gunn, lately promoted from the plough. "Henry, what's the meaning of all this smell?"

"Please, sir, it's the tarts."

"Go and tell the tarts they mustn't smell so much."

"Yes, sir."

I went down, and the servants came in to prayers, just as if nothing was the matter. The smell increased. After prayers I went into the kitchen to ask a question or two about the smell and the banquet generally. My cook said, "Please, sir, there's carrot-soup, and gravy soup; but if you please, sir, there's a bad accident happened upstairs."

"What's the matter?"

"Please, sir, the house is on fire."

Then she and the other maidens dissolved into tears. I rushed upstairs, and sure enough there were three men tearing up the floor in the maids' room, and pouring down water by buckets. I found that the flue of the oven had been ingeniously brought with its covering close to the floor-boards, and that the exigencies of the tarts being beyond Henry Gunn's control, had turned smouldering into flame.

Poor Henry Gunn; I often think I was unkind to him. In his first year, I think, a neighbour came to me to complain that he was very often at his house courting one of the maidens. I told him I would stop it. So I sent for Henry, and having asked his age, and being told nineteen, desired I might hear no more of it. He said I should not.

Mr. Drury came that day, and I told him.

"Foolish boy: waits at dinner I suppose?"

"Oh, yes."

"Then I'll tell you what we'll do. You shall begin with a story about James Pistol, and the dreadful consequences of his early and imprudent marriage; I will cap it with a story more dreadful about Philip Cannon. You again with even greater horrors about Frederic Musket; and I will come in finally with a climax about John Firearms. Mind you don't blunder, or send him out of the room for anything; let all be done easily and naturally, and it will be very wholesome to the boy."

It was all carried out. It seems to me now, as often since, that it was a great despotic cruelty.

Early in 1838, my brother Edward, Bishop of Salisbury, gave me the living of Broadwinsor, Dorset. Sept. 4, the same year, I married Georgiana, eldest daughter of Mr. Henley.

My Cuddesdon recollections are endeared to me by relations near and loving with the Bishop, Lady Harriet, and all their children. They are bound up with the prime blessing of all my life, my most beloved wife, with the ties uniting me to her dear father and mother, and all theirs.

I have had a long life, and many great privileges and blessings: next to my wife, no one greater than the intimate knowledge of, the deep love and reverence for Mr. Henley of more than forty years.

CHAPTER V.

The Opposing Forces. 1828—1878.

I SET down here as concisely as I can, what are the constituent parts of the opposing forces on the side of the assault, and of the defence, for the last fifty years. I began very early in the struggle to take a keen interest in it; my active personal share in it is a thing of about thirty-five years old.

On the side of the assault—
    1. The Nonconformist Power;
    2. The Roman Catholic Power;
    3. The Jewish Power;
    4. The Erastian Power;
    5. The Indifferent Power;
    6. The Critical and Scientific Power.

Most of these do not love one another more than they love the Church: but as against the Church they combine readily. The grounds of their hostility are of a mixed character. Note, that the Indifferent Power is always in its nature active as against Catholic Truth and order, if it be neutral as respects other things.

On the side of the defence—
    1. The Church Power;
    2. The Establishment Power.

At the time when the assault began to take its present form, the Church Power cannot be said to have been more than latent. Even now it has very little organised action, and no Corporate action. It is indeed gathering strength every year, by word and act of individual Churchmen and congregations; but there is as yet no concentrated and abiding strength about it. The lee-way it has to make up is very great, the adverse influences insidious and powerful, the surrenders under pressure many. It seems to me that modern Churchmen have yet to learn the lesson, that if they are to work for CHRIST, they must be content, aye and thankful, to suffer for CHRIST.

The Church Corporate cannot be said to be in substance other than Establishmentarian.

The Establishment Power is compounded of three things principally :—

(*a.*) The negative religion, which is the inheritance of Century XVI.

(*b.*) Ecclesiastical position, power, place and privilege, with corporate possessions, value a hundred millions, guaranteed by Common and Statute Law of "Church and State," as being what is left, after the wholesale plunder of Century XVI. The plunder has begun again, and will before long be consummated.

(*c.*) The *vis inertiæ* of Bishops, nominees of the Civil Power, passing commonly in action into the *Compromittendi vis:* sometimes, let us say unconsciously, into the *Tradendi vis*.

The Establishment Power is very far the largest of the two. The conditions of it are unfavourable to the growth of that true and abiding enthusiasm, without which no defence is worth much. We have just had a striking instance.

The assault has in its steady onward course reached the Churchyards.

Fifteen thousand Clergy sign a Declaration in this matter: no more than thirty thousand lay people. This is about as remarkable an evidence of lack of enthusiasm in the cause of the Establishment as could be adduced; so soon does the Temporal begin with failing the Spiritual, and ends in failing itself.

I could not sign the Declaration, because I have no sympathy with a movement which is content that the worst characters in a place, calling themselves Churchpeople, should have a legal right to burial with the full service of the Church, but will not hear of the body of the Nonconformist of the best character being buried in the Churchyard with Nonconformist service.

I am not for allowing the last at all; but the ground upon which I resist it is the "Church" ground, and not the "Establishment" ground. If I have to fight, I prefer to fight with clean hands.

All the fifty years of "defence" tell the same story: it is everywhere "Establishment," very little "Church." Negative religion, mixed, shifting, indefinite, contradictory teaching, can never bear fruit in the true and sound enthusiasm which is, under GOD, the life of the Church.

The assault marches on: the defence is not worthy of the name; it is one unbroken series of crushing defeats; it all points one and the same way. A national Church by law established, and a Legislature of all religions and no religion, cannot ultimately co-exist. When the Church of England loses "Establishment" and "Endowment," it will be because she has been defended as an "Establishment," and not as a "Church."

With regard to the Critical and Scientific Power, it is curious to observe how the poison of free enquiry has crept into the defence, almost as much as into the assault.

Some fifteen years ago, there were several volumes of answers to "Essays and Reviews:" I edited one myself. It struck me forcibly at the time, that the writers were commonly more occupied in giving "quasi-orthodox" explanations of what are called "difficulties in Scripture," than in rebuking the presumptuous folly of attempting to explain at all "the secret things" of GOD[a], lowering themselves thus down to the level of the assailant. If one has his "explanation," why not the other?

The Authority of the Church, which enjoins us to accept by faith what no amount of criticism or science can possibly explain, appeared to me not to be much taken into account in the matter, as the one all-sufficient and conclusive answer. Scepticism is very rife in England,— I believe that we are indebted for it almost as much to

[a] Deut. xxix. 29.

the answers to "Essays and Reviews," as to "Essays and Reviews" itself. ᵃ

People in England, well-informed people, talk very glibly about German Rationalism, German Neology, and the like; and, no doubt, Germany has had a large share in the unholy work of the un-Belief of the last three hundred years, and specially of our own day.

But people who live in a glass-house should not throw stones. In point both of time and substance, England is the parent of the un-Belief of the last three hundred years. Herbert and Hobbes were, next to Socinus, its first fathers [b].

Through France the poison passed into Germany. Germany has given it back with interest.

But why Germany more than France? For France has in like manner returned the gift with interest.

The answer has to be spoken out in the face of the " Protestantism " of Century XIX. It is because Germany is more generally " Protestant " than France.

Where "Protestantism" has most prevailed, denying the Authority, setting aside the Order; perverting, or disparaging, or both, the Sacraments of the Church Catholic; there, as matter not of *à priori* anticipation only, but as matter of historical fact and present experience, Infidelity has most prevailed. As a rule, continental " Protestantism " is un-Believing.

The Church of England is not "Protestant:" has been very careful never to call itself "Protestant." Indeed, what "Protestant Church" may mean, I do not know. The noun adjective and the noun substantive do not belong to the same category: cannot be fused into one descriptive appellation.

The Church of England is Catholic.

The term "Protestant" has passed, as it is in the nature of things it must pass, into a negative term only. There

---

[b] Lelius Socinus, born at Sienna 1525, died 1562. Lord Herbert of Cherbury, born 1581, died 1648. Thomas Hobbes of Malmesbury, born 1588, died 1679. Benoît de Spinoza, born 1632, at Amsterdam, died 1677.

is nothing really affirmative about it, save only so much as belongs to every man's affirming upon the ground of his own private judgment and interpretation his own particular religion to be exclusively Truth: and it is now commonly taken as intending all people of all beliefs and of no belief, save only The Catholic Belief.

Beginning with 1832, the assailant had not been idle. On the other side, the "Church" Power evoked in defence "Tracts for the Times." The "Establishment" stood upon two things: first, upon possession; second, upon "political wisdom," as shewn in the surrender of Sacred Trusts bit by bit.

The assaults upon "Church-rate," and upon "Church-schools," occupy the foreground of the battle of fifty years: if that be a battle, in which one side is advancing steadily, step by step, and the other side, either laying down its arms, or running away. I will touch here, and conclude upon "Church-rate,"— Church-schools I shall have to return to.

For the history of Church-rate, and the process of its destruction, I should be only repeating myself if I were to do more than refer to my book, "Church-rate, a National Trust," published 1861. I endeavoured to the best of my power to deal with the whole subject exhaustively throughout; and upon looking at it again very carefully, I believe myself to have done it.

In 1866, Church-rate was abolished: the manner of the defence had made any other issue impossible. It was a betrayal, not a fight.

To injury was added insult. A voluntary Rate, that is, a sham Rate, a thing as absurd, if not as dishonest, in conception, as futile in operation, was proposed in place of Church-rate. There is no such thing in the order of human contrivance as a Voluntary Rate: there is such a thing as a voluntary contribution upon the proportion of assessment. But why, except for the purpose of taking in that most gullible of Societies, the British Public, this should have been called a Voluntary Rate, I do not comprehend.

For the character of the general assault, that the non-Conformist and the Roman Catholic should combine against the Church of England, is no ground of reproach to either; they are only consistent with all their history. As for some of the allies they are content to be associated with in the work, that is another, and not a pleasant matter. It has a resemblance to something which is going on now in respect of the "Eastern Question." The Roman Church cannot abide the Greek Church, and so sides with the Turk against the Russian. When, four hundred and twenty-five years ago, the Turk walked into Constantinople, there was no element of his success so powerful as the quarrel between the Churches.

The ground of reproach is, that plea of religious conscience should be mixed up with picking your neighbour's pocket,—a plea insisted upon by the assailant in his own case, pooh-poohed by the same man in his neighbour's case; but in both cases alike ending with picking your neighbour's pocket.

For Church-rate, assailant said—"You have got something which it hurts our conscience to help to pay for. It is true we have always had the right to the use of it, when we like, and this we propose to retain; but you shall pay for repair and maintenance of it by yourselves."

For Schools, assailant said—" You have got something we are shut out from ; this hurts our conscience, we want to share in it; but it can only be upon our own terms. It is true that those terms cannot be reconciled with your principles and practice: that they are quite as much against your conscience as Church-rate was against ours; but never mind all that, we must share in what you have got of your own, when we have had it altered to suit us, and you shall help to pay for it, though it will then have become a thing from which your religious conscience revolts, *or at least ought to revolt.*"

Now, if the assault had been honest in respect of Church-rate, it would have said, — "Relieve us from Church-rate, and we will give up our share of Church and Churchyard."

And for Schools, it would have said in like manner,—
"Let our Schools be built and maintained by help of the
Civil Power, in all respects equally with your schools,
in due proportion to the wants of the populations severally, and we will give up all attempt to intrude ourselves into your schools."

But as neither of these arrangements would have answered the purposes either of the assailants themselves,
or of those "Churchmen" who promoted and aided in
the assault, neither of them was adopted.

On the side of the defence, there has not been, and
never will be so long as Parliament lasts, any real defence. The key to this, over and above its unfaithfulness,
is about as great a piece of silliness as may be. You
will not look at a disputed question from the adversary's
stand-point; you will only look at it from what is,
not so much your own stand-point, for then you would
stand fast, but, something which, under pressure, you
have made your stand-point. I think I had in my hands
in some ten years about thirty drafts of Bills for settlement of the "Church-rate" question; all of them, as
I pointed out at the time, open to this fatal objection.

The issue is, that you keep telling your adversary that
he asks for what he neither asks for nor cares to have;
and you offer this for his acceptance in lieu of what he
does ask for, and does care to have. This folly has just
been repeated in the "Burial" matter.

It tends naturally enough to irritate: has no tendency
to satisfy. It is very like telling a man he is a fool: a
thing which men resent much more than the being told
they are knaves. And the end of it is that you lose
everything, and he gains everything: as happens always
when one side stands fast, and the other shifts and dodges
about.

England is a great country, but it is a puzzling place
too. There is nothing too monstrous for the Whig oligarch to advocate as a sop to the democracy which, for

the present, is content to have him for leader: nothing too precious for the Conservative to surrender upon demand: nothing too gross or too cloying for the democrat to eat, provided always it is found him at other people's expense.

And all this always on plea of conscience. Why, this conscience doth make knaves.

Is it said, these are hard words? I know they are hard words; but I know nothing in the law of nature, or of Grace, or of both, to tell me not only that I may not use hard words in denouncing false principles, but to acquit me if, knowing the principles to be false, I do not denounce them. In this case, hard words become a duty. Let me distinguish a little.

Man is bound by the law of natural love, and by the law of heavenly charity to his fellow-man: man is not the judge of his fellow-man. Even when he is bound by duty to deliver him over to the death of this world, the judgment does not go beyond this world; it remembers itself and says, "The LORD have mercy on your soul." Innocent men have perished by public law, innocent, that is, of the crimes for which they have been condemned to die; and no man knows, or can know certainly, possibly not always the justly-condemned criminal himself, how it is that he stands, every particular of his case being taken into the account of Infinite knowledge, love, mercy, before the Judge of all men.

Let therefore charity, as between man and man, be the absolute bar to our "judging one another." Hard words as against this or that man, and much more as against classes of men, are only one form of "judging."

Our Blessed LORD, indeed, denounced classes of men; but it was Infinite knowledge, and wisdom, and power which did this: it is not for us. And be it borne in mind, that in doing it, He assigned the reason that the principles and practices of the class injured and ruined souls; but man may not denounce classes of his fellow-men, however much he may denounce the principles, which to the best of his judgment appear to him to guide them.

Now no doubt there is a difficulty in distinguishing between a man, and the principles which he represents; but the distinction has to be made and observed. It is contrary to Christian duty to use hard words about a man, however bad he may be, or appear to be: it is Christian duty to use hard words about an evil principle.

Our nature were indeed in worse case than it is, if the eternal principles of good were not absolutely and definitely fixed for us, delivered to us, and by Grace as definitely and absolutely ascertainable by each one of us, according to the measure of GOD'S gifts. Everything contrary to the eternal principles of good, is a principle of evil; and it is part of the charity which cares for souls to denounce evil principles unsparingly.

The lines of good and evil are very commonly much confused among men: it is so in large measure amongst ourselves at this time. What is the account of it? It is that men are much more given to build up every one his religious system for himself, than to receive it as delivered to him by the Church. But, it is said, the Church Catholic is much divided, where then is the guidance? The answer is, that in respect of the Incarnation, and the Atonement, and the Resurrection; in respect of Apostolical order and succession, the Creeds and the Sacraments, the trust, commission and authority of the Church, all branches of the Church Catholic are at one.

I say then again, our nature were indeed in evil case if all these things were not definitely and absolutely fixed for us, delivered to us, and by Grace as definitely and absolutely ascertainable by each one of us, according to the measure of GOD'S gifts. I say again, that it is part of the charity which cares for souls to denounce unsparingly, and in hard words—no words can be too hard—the principles of evil which reject them, either by way of direct denial, or by way of betrayal, or by way of compromise. Judge not men; but, as much as you can, judge and denounce unsparingly the principles of evil.

If, therefore, any man says to me, as many have said, "You speak of these things as if they were known to you as eternally true, and therefore condemn all who do not hold them as you do." I reply, "They are known to me as eternally true, and therefore I do so speak of them; but I condemn no man. If he is representing a principle of evil, I condemn the representation; the man I do not judge, much less condemn. I believe the things you refer to as I believe in my own life: I believe them as I believe in GOD. GOD'S Word tells me there is 'one LORD, one Faith, one Baptism;' I believe what I am told in GOD'S Word. GOD'S Word tells me to 'hear the Church;' I do hear it. GOD'S Word does not tell me to hear man as against the Church; I do not hear man as against the Church. I am bound by my duty to CHRIST, to denounce as unsparingly as I can everything that would persuade me to do it."

Do men tell me that the Church is only one sect among many, having great possessions and privileges, derived from the superstition of unenlightened times. I have only one answer. I say that it is a delusion of the Devil which makes men so to speak.

So much, then, for the use of hard words. For my countrymen, the people of England, and for myself, let me say this,—

Whatever my language in condemnation of principles of evil may have been and is, I have tried always— I know with what miserable imperfectness—not to judge my fellow-man. And however deeply and bitterly I see cause to lament the religious condition of this people, I am bound to believe, and I do believe, that it is the Bishops and Clergy who have here, as in all else, most to answer for. It would be well for us if those words of the Apostle were never absent from our minds and hearts, "Lest when I have preached to others, I myself should be a castaway."

CHAPTER VI.

BROADWINSOR. 1838—1845.

AFTER our marriage we went abroad for a little time, and then established ourselves, till I could build a house at Broadwinsor, at Waytown, in the parish of Netherbury, the house nearest to Broadwinsor that I could find. The Vicarage at Broadwinsor was a ruined cottage, with some three habitable rooms: there I housed my first Curate, Edward Wyndham Tufnell, afterwards Bishop of Brisbane; and for two years lived a life of almost daily transit, as I had done at Cuddesdon. The site of the old Vicarage became, some three or four years after, the site of the parish schools.

There was a strip of kitchen-garden, and a glebe field of some six acres: not a tree or a shrub in the glebe field, where I began with digging the well, and making the road for the new Vicarage.

Having borrowed two thousand pounds from the Bounty Board, I had to find the rest of my seven years' outlay as I could. I had no means of my own outside the marriage settlements; so I took pupils, insured my life largely, borrowed what I wanted, and have been half-ruined ever since. House, grounds, and stables, about £3,000; small church for west end of parish, £1,000; schools, £1,000. When we came to East Brent in 1845, I computed that I had left behind me at least £3,000 in seven years.

Broadwinsor is a parish of some five miles by three, lying in a very fine country, above the beautiful valley of Beaminster and Netherbury, under Lewsda nond Pillesdon hills, six miles north of the English Channel: population in 1838, about 1500. The parish church, substantially, I believe, sound, but of no beauty, and quite too small for the parishioners; locally also inconvenient to large numbers of them. It has, I hear, been beautifully restored of late years by the family of the present Vicar, Rev. S. C. Malan. No schools. The parish had been held for some years *in commendam* before my predecessor's Incumbency, who was Vicar ten years only; and altogether wanted a great deal of ecclesiastical repair. My Curate helped me admirably, and the people were not slow to answer to the call. I look back on the many instances of respect, and confidence, and attachment, throughout the seven years, with deep love and thankfulness.

Wages in Dorset in those times had an unpleasant notoriety; but Dorset was not the exception which it was commonly represented to be in and out of Parliament. Wilts, Somerset, Devon, might have been cited with about equal justice; and I was always told that what gave Dorset the advantage of being exceptionally abused, was certain personal Parliamentary antipathies. Be this as it may, wages were certainly many shillings lower at Broadwinsor than my north-country antecedents, lower than even my Oxfordshire antecedents, had prepared me to expect.

The parish was agricultural; but there was in it a sail-cloth manufactory, hand-loom weaving, employing a large number of hands, men and boys, women and girls.

When I had built the schools, we used to have a large attendance there week-days and Sundays,—Sundays especially; for many of the young men and women employed at the factory came to us to try to learn something,—reading, writing,—summing was a far-away accomplishment.

Now these young men and women worked at the factory ten hours a-day for five days, and eight hours on Saturday, and the wages were about 2s. 6d. a-week for young women, 3s. 6d., or thereabouts, for young men. The lowness of wages enabled the proprietor of the factory to compete with other factories worked by steam-power.

There was a good deal of rioting about 1841-2, rick-burning, and the like; we had some very rough hands amongst us, and things looked alarming enough. The farmers were too frightened to move, lest the move should bring them to be singled out for vengeance, and so they turned to me.

I went to the magistrates, and represented that I apprehended very serious consequences, unless immediate steps were taken to keep the rioters in check. My deposition and application were forwarded to the Home Office, and presently there arrived a splendid specimen out of the A division of police, and reported himself to me,—belt, bludgeon, dark-lantern, and small dog; I forget whether he had a pistol, but I think he had. It was about Christmas, I think, 1842.

I requested him to report to me from time to time as he saw occasion. In a week he came, and said that he did not think after all there was much the matter.

"Oh," I said, "take another week."

The Saturday following he came again, and said that it was not so quiet and respectable a place as he had supposed.

I asked the grounds of his change of mind.

He said that he was coming along the village street, and five or six rough fellows laughed at him.

"Ah," I said; "what did you do?"

"I went up to them and said, 'Now, my men, I'll take good care before I've been here many days, that a decent man can walk about here without being insulted by a pack of blackguards like you.'"

"Now, then, we're going to begin," said I.

Very soon after they assaulted him in force; and one of them, the ringleader, who used to boast that he had had fifteen warrants out against him, but that they could never find him, drew a knife upon him. "Go down to the magistrates at Beaminster," I said, "and get a warrant." Upon this the ringleader absconded, and never came back all the time I was Vicar; when I had been a little time at East Brent, his family, thinking that it all rested with me, wrote to me, to ask me to allow him to return.

Matters went on more or less quietly till Good Friday, 1843. When I came out of morning church, I was told that the village had narrowly escaped being burnt. I asked for the policeman; he told me that some dry stuff on the skirts of the village had been set on fire by some men in seven places, and that if the wind had been that way, the fire would have spread widely. I asked him where the men were.

"Five of them," he said, "in the lock-up."

"How did you get them in?"

"Well," he said, "I knew the cottage they commonly met in, and I went to them and said that I believed they could tell me about how the fire began, and that I wished they would come and shew me the exact place. I took them by the street in which the lock-up was, and when we got opposite it, said, 'Now, my men, this is Good Friday, and there will be no magistrates sitting, so I'll put you in here for the night.'

"'In there,' they said; 'but we won't go in there.'

"'The first man that says that again I'll knock him down.' In they all went."

The next morning the village was full of people; I got upon my horse, and rode into the middle of them with the policeman. Not a soul then, or at any other time, shewed me any disrespect; they knew well that the whole matter of the policeman was my doing; but they never gave any sign of a disposition to insult or thwart me. When we came to the lock-up, the policeman opened the door, brought out the five men, and we went with them to the magistrates. We let them off as easy as we could: one man was transported not long after for arson in another case, and the rioting subsided.

The people were very glad, especially the old women in the village. "Lor', Sir," they said to me, "afore this big gentleman come, we couldn't go out of our houses up and down street without pitch-polling over strings tied across the road; now it be all quiet like."

It was a great instance of what a single strong and resolute man can do with a mob. When I had left Broadwinsor about a year, he wrote to me to say that the parishioners thought they had no longer need of his services, and that he hoped I had some occupation for him at East Brent. I thanked him, and wished him well; but said that we were quiet people up here. It reminds me of the request of the first policeman stationed in the village of East Brent, that I would get him removed.

"Why," I said, "I thought you were very comfortable here, the people are so quiet."

"That's just it, sir, there are no outrages; a man's got no opportunities."

My sister Julia was talking with an old woman at Broadwinsor, and telling her how glad she was things were quieter. "It's Mr. Denison, ma'am; you see, they be bigly afeard on he."

"Dear," she said, "that isn't right, what they should be afraid of is doing wrong and offending GOD."

"Mabbe, ma'am, that's what it is as you says, but you see they beant come to that yet."

There was a large, most kindly and pleasant society all about us, simple and old-fashioned. Mr. and Mrs. Brookland and their daughter Emma were our closest friends. He was Vicar of the beautiful village of Netherbury; I remember well coming upon it for the first time in May, when I walked over from Broadwinsor, after my induction. It lay in the valley, and burst suddenly upon me as I reached the crest of the hill above it, with its broken ground, meadows and stream, full of timber and orchards in bloom; and its comfortable-looking houses, with its fine old Church and Vicarage. I thought I had never looked upon such a picture of an English village, and I do not think I ever have since.

The Brooklands are all long since dead. The father first; then the daughter, who died in this house the first winter we came to East Brent, of fever, caught in tending the sick; last, soon after, the mother. I never knew people with greater vigour, enjoyment, heartiness, and kindliness of life.

In 1843, having built my schools, I had my first fight with the Committee of Council on Education. They wanted a loose Constitution; I told them I would have nothing but a tight one, and they gave way.

I have had to do with many official people; with none for whom I have had throughout so deep a dislike, amounting to a shrinking from all contact, as "the Committee of Council on Education." All the evil of the time is, as it were, summed up and condensed in it: it is to me, always has been, as "the abomination of desolation, sitting where it ought not."

In 1843, my brother Edward, then Bishop of Salisbury, in the incapacity of the then Bishop of Bath and Wells, took charge, at the request of Sir R. Peel's Government, of the diocese of Bath and Wells; and East Brent falling vacant in 1845, he offered it to me.

I became Vicar of East Brent August, 1845; and with much regret said good-bye to all our good, kind friends in and about Broadwinsor.

The house at East Brent had been much enlarged, and the grounds beautifully laid out some seven years before, the same time that I was building at Broadwinsor. But there was not a sixpence of dilapidations at Broadwinsor: I got £50 at East Brent; but it cost me close upon £200 before I could get into the house. Possibly my successor at Broadwinsor has found out that there ought to have been some dilapidations there. I only record the fact.

Two years ago, finding very general discontent with the present Dilapidations Bill, and, as it seems to me, with the soundest reason, I moved at Wells for a Committee to report thereupon; I drew the Report which was adopted by the Committee, and is printed in Appendix. When we came to discuss the Report at Wells opinions were conflicting; and upon a further attempt, sanctioned by the Bishop, being made to ascertain if possible what the Clergy in their several Deaneries thought about the matter, the answers were not, either in point of general concurrence or of sufficient clearness, such as to supply ground for further proceeding.

I have never doubted, and great authorities have told me the same, that if the Report had been adopted in its substance, it would have supplied a very good basis for further legislation.

I suppose that Government, finding no concurrence of Clergy in the matter generally throughout the country, did not see its way to further legislation. And "dilapidations" law remains in all its most objectionable condition.

CHAPTER VII.

East Brent. 1845—1852.

A FEW weeks after my induction into the Vicarage of East Brent Bishop Law died, and Sir Robert Peel offered Bath and Wells to my dear friend Richard Bagot, Bishop of Oxford.

The Bishop sent for me, and asked me what I thought. I told him that I was an interested adviser in the matter, because I was just gone into the diocese myself.

"Oh," he said, "that's all nonsense; what do you think?"

I told him I thought he had better accept.

"Then you must be Examining Chaplain."

I agreed to be Examining Chaplain.

I found at East Brent a schoolroom built by my predecessor, Hon. W. T. Law; he had also rebuilt the chancel. The Trust-deed of the school places the management in the Vicar only.

I found also the germ of "Ritual," in preaching in the surplice; this may seem a small thing; but as it was quite enough then to almost convulse the country, it seems reasonable to conclude that parts of Ritual, however trifling they may appear to the untaught and ignorant, are not the small things which anti-Church policy, Episcopal policy, aye, and a great deal of "High Church" policy too, are busy in representing them to be. If it were not painful, it would be ludicrous; and, indeed, all the pain notwithstanding, it is ludicrous; to see and hear the same man, Bishop, Priest, Layman, saying that things are so trifling as to be unworthy of a moment's thought; and at the same moment struggling and striving unceasingly, fiercely, furiously, *per fas et nefas*, to "put those things down."

It shews how incorrect it is to consider the *differentia*

of the human animal as sufficiently expressed by the word "reasoning." For ignorance so clouds the reasoning-power, and passion and worldliness so pervert it, as to make it perpetually contradict and nullify itself after the very ridiculous example just instanced.

I came into the inheritance of a good deal of conflict between my predecessor and some of the parishioners. It soon settled down; and for twenty-six years, 1845 to 1871, there was, inside the parish, no perceptible disagreement. It is difficult to use words about the religious condition of a parish, without appearing to say more than is just, or less than is just, and so I say nothing. I have had daily Matins and Evensong for thirty-three years; increasingly frequent Celebration; for the last four years, Daily Celebration. And when I was younger and less occupied than I have been since, a large part of my time was given to looking after my people; but my engagements with the Bishop, and, in a year or two, the ever-increasing troubles as between "Church" and "State," engrossed a very large portion of that time, and my place in the work of the parish had, to a considerable extent, to be supplied by my Curate.

I think it was in the autumn of 1845 that I became member of the Bristol Church Union, then occupying the principal place among the Church Unions. Shortly afterwards I was elected, with three others, Secretary for the Union, and had a large share in all its action for several years. In the five years of Sir Robert Peel's Government, August 31, 1841, to that of Lord John Russell, July 6, 1846, the assault upon the Church made little open progress; but doubtless much was being done to consolidate the assailing forces, and prepare them for renewed attempts upon the first favourable opportunity. During those five years, even the assault as respects "Church-rate" made no public advance.

Lord John Russell's Government came into power July 6, 1846, and the Minutes of the Committee of Council on "Education," 1846, were issued from the Council Office.

The two component parts of the assault in England,

so far as taken publicly in hand, but not open and avowing its real character, from 1832 to 1846, are,—1. the demand of abolition of Church-rate, 2. the plot for "utilising" Church-schools for the purposes of the authors of the Committee of Council on "Education." I have said above, Chapter V., all that need be said by me now about abolition of Church-rate.

I pass on to review the successive steps by which the "Church-school" has been destroyed in England, and the "State-school" brought into its place.

There are many other elements of the general assault, aiming steadily throughout at one object,—the ultimate triumph of "Indifferentism." These will fall into their proper place in these "Notes," side by side with so much of resistance on the part of Churchmen as has been offered from time to time, and is being offered still. This is not much in quantity, nor again, with here and there an exception, very high in quality. It is hitherto desultory, unconnected, always halting on its way.

The data from which I write are :—

1. Personal recollection where clear and distinct.
2. A great mass of letters preserved in monthly packets for many years ; few of them speaking in any language but that of the warmest concurrence and encouragement.
3. Other documentary evidence in my possession.
4. Assistance of kind friends in supplying facts and dates about which I was uncertain.

If I do not publish letters to myself in evidence, it is, first, because this is in itself better avoided ; and next, because of the extreme difficulty of selecting from the great number in my possession. I could not, besides, do it without the writer's permission, or that of his nearest representative and· I had rather not put either of these in the position of having been asked.

Again, if in these "Notes" I give only a summary of the principal items of assault and defence under their several heads, linking them together in their natural connection, it is because I have myself published so much upon every one of them, and others have published so much, that my "Notes" would present a great amount of cumbrous and unnecessary repetition. All I aim at is, to represent the precise substance of the whole case under each one of its several heads, and to shew how all combine in one great assault. Alas, that I should have to add, in one more victory of the "World" of England over the "Church" of England.

What I have to do is, to trace for some fifty years, under all its phases, the progress and ultimate establishment of "Indifferentism" in England, as the rule governing all State policy in relation to the Church. The able, vigorous, steady efforts of its advocates, laying hold very adroitly of every advantage supplied to them by the connection of the Church with, and its consequent subordination to, a Civil Power of all religions and of none, with the short-sighted, feeble and desultory efforts of the "Establishment" to stem the tide. The paring down Religious duty to the level of social and political exigency, is the plague-spot of our Ecclesiastical position.

The public action of my life falls within the year 1847, and the time at which I write: thirty-one years.

It arose as follows:—

In 1846, my friend Rev. H. W. Bellairs, then Inspector of Schools under the Concordat of 1840, which *at that time* I supposed to be faithfully observed by the Committee of Council, advised me to apply for assistance to my parish school under the Minutes about to be issued.

In the "simplicity" and "modesty" of my nature[a], I listened to his alluring voice. I might have remembered that, some three years before, I had had strong grounds for suspicion about the purposes of the Committee of Council on Education, in the matter of the Trust-deed of the schools I had built at Broadwinsor; and, indeed, there was the fact staring all men in the face, that, in 1840, it had only been *by* a majority of two, 275 to 273 in the House of Commons, and *against* a majority of 111 in the House of Lords, that the Committee of

[a] Speech of Censor of Christ Church, Christmas, 1826.

Council had entered upon its ill-omened life. But I was in a generous and hopeful mood; and, like many other people before and since, I wanted help; and so I listened to the alluring voice, and made my application late in 1846, or early in 1847.

But before anything came of the application, I woke up to the truth of the position; being warned by a speech of Lord John Russell in the House of Commons, April 19, 1847; and wrote to put a question thereupon to the Secretary, April 23. I got no answer for nearly three weeks: my letter had been "mislaid." I have no doubt it had been "mislaid." The explanation, when it came May 12, 1847, was so wholly unsatisfactory, while pretending to be full of justice and equity, that I at once withdrew my application [b], and from that moment to this have remained in the attitude of antagonism to the Committee of Council. In 1849, I was further obliged by my duty to the Church to shut the doors of my school to the Government Inspector [c], and the antagonism already pronounced became absolute and final. It was not even affected by what passed between Lord Derby's Government and myself in 1852; for the condition, upon faith of which I withdrew my Resolutions at the annual meeting of the National Society for that year, was not fulfilled on the part of the Government.

Prior to 1847, though I had, on the one hand, watched anxiously the progress of the assault upon the position of the Church of England as by law established, during the nineteen years between 1828 and 1847; the gradual formation of the rule of "Indifferentism" on the part of the Civil Power, and all that positive and active antagonism to Catholic Truth and Apostolical Order, which, by a curious but necessary contradiction inherent in the nature of the case, is inseparable from "Indifferentism;" and had on the other hand noted the apathy, or the

---

[b] Correspondence with Secretary of Committee of Council, April and May, 1847.

[c] Correspondence with Secretary of Committee of Council, and other documentary evidence published therewith, March, 1849.

self-delusion of the "Establishment," and the awakening of the "Church" at the voice of "Tracts for the Times,"—though I had watched and noted all these things year by year, I had as yet taken no public part, and had published nothing.

My first public action, and the first things published by me, came, as I have just said above, out of the Minutes of the Committee of Council on "Education" 1846, and took the forms first, of a Correspondence between the Secretary of the Committee, then Mr. Kay Shuttleworth, and myself, April and May, 1847; and second, of a Letter to Mr. Gladstone, Nov. 17, 1847.

That Correspondence and that Letter are the key to the whole of my resistance for thirty-one years to every part of the action of the Committee. I have never swerved so much as one hair's breadth from the position then taken. Beginning with 1847-9, I have separated myself absolutely from all connection, direct or indirect, with the Committee of Council on "Education;" and am thankful to say, that I have not from that year had one farthing of the public grant which it administers.

In respect of Mr. Gladstone there are strong and special reasons why I should be very exact and precise as to our relative positions in this matter. And I think I cannot do better than cite here the first two paragraphs of my published Letter. I shall not, as I said above, cite private letters in my possession. The only thing which I will prefix to the paragraphs cited, I prefix because in the contest for Oxford, January, 1853, it became public property in a letter from me as Chairman of Mr. Perceval's Committee, written in answer to a letter from Mr. Gladstone to myself, and sent by me for publication to Mr. Gladstone's Committee. My recollection is that the Committee did not publish it; it would not have served their cause. Mr. Gladstone's letter to me, was to call my attention to the fact, that a letter of mine published in the "Times" a few days before had been generally understood as implying, that he had first gone with me upon the question between the Church and the Committee of Council, and then abandoned me; and that this was the cause of my active hostility to him. He added, that he was sure that I remembered how from the first he had not gone with me in the amount and extent of my apprehensions, and asked me to clear him by a public statement to this effect, from an imputation which was doing him harm in the Contest.

I replied upon the instant, that I would readily do what he asked; that is, that I would state publicly that he had given me no support[d], and would send the letter to

---

[d] In my letter to the members of the Bristol Church Union, dated January 17, 1853, from Mr. Perceval's Committee-room, I say:—

"If Mr. Gladstone had up to this time given any proof of so much as a disposition to offer a steady and uncompromising resistance to the attempt to introduce the 'comprehensive system' into the schools of the Church; or if he had not made himself the colleague of the active enemies of Church Education, I could in some sort have understood men who, though forward and active in resisting the first inroads of the comprehensive system, have voted for Mr. Gladstone in this election.

"But there is no proof of the kind. I have had as much to do with the question as any man, and I affirm positively, that Mr. Gladstone has never, in any one single instance, from the Spring of 1847 up to this time, given me any manner of support in or out of Parliament. I am obliged to go further still, and to say that by his hesitating, uncertain, and most discouraging manner of dealing with the whole question in Parliament, he has done more to damage the cause than any man living. This is not the first time that I have been compelled to think and to speak of him as the chief difficulty in the way of obtaining for the Church of England her RIGHT in this great matter.

"On this account it was with the utmost difficulty, as is well-known to some of the chief Supporters of Mr. Gladstone, that I brought myself to support Mr. Gladstone in 1847, and again in 1852. In 1852, my name was placed on his London Committee without my knowledge, and against my wish. I remonstrated privately; but as the list of the Committee had been published, I did not then think it necessary to take so decided a step as to withdraw my name.

"But now it is a good deal more than a negation of support: Mr. Gladstone is a member of a Cabinet, of which the Whig members—and they are many—are pledged to the 'comprehensive system.' It is their darling project; the only idea of the method and manner of 'Education' of which their minds appear to be capable. Its starting-point is religious Indifferentism: its fruit, wheresoever it has been really tried, is a general unsettling of a People's Faith. It should, I think, have been sufficient to ascertain and fix a Churchman's vote, to see Mr. Gladstone in the same Committee of

his Committee for publication; but that, in writing the letter, I should have to add one thing to which his letter did not advert: that thing was, that it was a letter from himself to me in 1847, the letter adverted to in the beginning of the second of the two paragraphs cited below, which first called my attention to the duty of watching the "Management Clauses" then "recommended" by the Council Office, 1846.

I revert now to the two paragraphs of my Letter to Mr. Gladstone, November 17, 1847:—

"East Brent, November 17, 1847.

"MY DEAR GLADSTONE,

"In the early part of the summer I published a brief correspondence between the Secretary of the Committee of Council and myself, on the subject of some assistance towards the school of this place, which I had proposed to derive under the late Minutes. I was compelled to withdraw my application, and to seek to provide from other sources for the increased efficiency of my school, in consequence of certain grave apprehensions having been forced upon me respecting the character of the scheme then lately propounded by Government. I was unable then to reconcile it with my duty to the Church, and all that has since passed has confirmed me in the belief that I decided rightly, that I should be in any degree a party to a system, which, if carried out in what I judged to be the spirit of those who proposed it—and there was, and is, every indication that it will be so carried out—threatens to inflict a very heavy blow on the integrity of the teaching of Church-schools, and therein on Catholic Truth.

"The substance of this correspondence will be in your recollection, because you wrote to me on the subject, and expressed your opinion that the danger which I feared was a remote one. I was sensible that it was remote in the sense of its being the

Council with Lord John Russell and Lord Lansdowne; who, as they sit in the Cabinet nominally without office, but in effect as *joint Ministers of Public Instruction*, will have ample leisure, and be the better enabled, to devise and mature a scheme for employing the power and influence of the Coalition Government to undermine, *and finally to destroy by Law the Parochial System of the Church of England.*"—(See in illustration of these last words, the Elementary Education Act of 1870, passed by Mr. Gladstone's Government.)

last, as well as the greatest injury, which the undue action of the influence and authority of the State could bring upon us; but I feared then, and am persuaded now, that in point of time it is not remote. There are certain steps to be taken, certain stages to be gone through, before it can be thoroughly developed: but the experience of the last few months has shewn in how determined a spirit that course has been entered upon, which threatens to terminate at no distant day in the establishment of State authority over the schools of the Church."

Now what have thirty-one years witnessed?

On my part, I am exactly where I was when I wrote the Letter, in respect of what was to be feared: but the fear has been realized; the prognostication has become fact; the assault has been consummated; the parish-school has been destroyed. I shall shew further on the steps to this consummation, and the exact nature of the consummation itself.

On Mr. Gladstone's part, what has been the final issue? It was Mr. Gladstone's Government that in 1870 passed the Elementary Education Act, by which all the evils, all the manifest unfairness, all the breaking down of authoritative teaching, which I anticipated in 1847; and over and above these, the "Time Table Conscience Clause," an iniquity of which I had, in 1847, formed no conception, and which, with Education-rate and School Board, was reserved for the final blow — have been inflicted upon the Church by the Civil Power.

I turn to these things with much pain: it is not without much distress, mingled, indeed, with much comfort, that I have searched the correspondence of many years. And for Mr. Gladstone himself—whose seat for Oxford University I did all I could to take away from him in 1853, and should have taken away then if the Low Churchmen had not been afraid of me—I have so deep and abiding a sense of his great personal kindness, especially in 1856, after the Judgment of the Court at Bath against me in the matter of "THE REAL PRESENCE," that I would not have referred to him if I could have helped it. But it is necessary to the clearing of the position that I should so refer; and I think no man will deny that I have earned the right to clear the position so far as is in my power. I do not forget that it was my move against Mr. Gladstone in 1853 which broke up and scattered to the winds that large army, by help of which I had fought my battle from 1847 to 1852. And yet my move *against* him was on the specific ground upon which they had supported me. It was a remarkable instance to what extent high personal character, marked antecedents, personal attachment and love, great abilities, attainments, eloquence, have power to make men contend and vote for the man, but against the principles which have hitherto been assumed to be common to them and to him. My kind friend and helper, John Keble, would hardly speak to me for some time: Pusey wrote to me in terms of very strong reproach. It all came right two years afterwards; but it was a heavy burden at the time.

My letter to Mr. Gladstone adverts further on to the first indication of *open aggressive* attempt on the part of the Committee of Council on " Education." This was later in 1847.

The means adopted were the "Management Clauses," to which Mr. Gladstone had, in his letter to me about the Correspondence on the subject of the Minutes of 1846, called my attention.

It has been upon these " Clauses "—first *recommended* for adoption to founders of Church-schools, afterwards insisted upon and imposed without authority of Parliament or consent of the Church, as a condition of assistance from the Parliamentary grant in founding schools— that the controversy began, and was conducted for several years, till the Church army broke up in 1853, after the Oxford contest. The ugly thing called the " Conscience Clause," and its uglier child, the " Time Table Conscience Clause "—

O matre turpi filia turpior—

came later.

Now, to prescribe to founders of Church-schools new conditions of State assistance, is to provide that every school to be founded shall be of that character which best suits, not the Church but, the State. Both they cannot suit; this is excluded by the nature of the case. The "interests" of "Church" and "State," if they have been identical at any time for the last three hundred years,—which is more than doubtful,—have ceased to be identical for the fifty years last past. The interference with liberty of founders ends necessarily sooner or later, as it has *de facto* issued already, in the State being the "Educator," not the Church; in a State of no particular belief being the "Educator" of the Church's children.

It is a curious Churchmanship which can fall in with such an issue as this, even supposing the State to be exclusively a "Church" State. *A fortiori*, when it is not only not "Church," but of no particular religion,—"Indifferent" in respect of all other "forms of faith." In its "Indifferentism" actively hostile, by the nature of the case, to Catholic Truth and Order.

A State of the character of the State of England in Century XIX., will have first what is called the "comprehensive school;" next, what is called the "combined school." The Church can never, if it would be found faithful, have the "comprehensive school," in that sense of the word "comprehensive" in which the State employs the term. It may, indeed, "comprehend" others than Church children in its schools, as it sees occasion, for missionary purposes; but this exclusively upon its own terms only. The Church may never have the "combined school" in any sense. The State "comprehends" first, not for any spiritual purposes at all but, for temporal purposes only,—political, social, economical. The State ultimately ends as the State of England has ended, in the worst form of the "combined school," to the formal exclusion of all religion, except here and there "natural religion." Ultimately, I believe, it will exclude even this.

The divorce of Statesmanship from Churchmanship lies

at the root of the entire controversy. One would have thought that, when it first assumed a public shape in 1847, it would have called forth the most vigorous and general resistance on the part of Churchmen; but somehow or other it did not. English Churchmen are curiously slow to apprehend and realise assaults upon first principles.

I noted it at the time*, and in proof that I was not making facts out of my own apprehensions and conclusions, and so speaking by way of rhetorical figure only, I adduced the language of James Kay Shuttleworth himself, who, if not the originator and prime mover of the revolution, has certainly done more than any other man, dead or living, to shape, promote, consolidate, and, finally, to complete it.

In his pamphlet, 1847: "The School in its relation to the State, the Church, and the Congregation, being an Explanation of the Minutes of the Committee of Council on Education in August and December, 1846," he says:—

"Little reflection is necessary to shew why a Statesman should prefer a system of combined Education."

Now, it is essential to anything like a true understanding of what the revolution is, to be exact and precise about what is meant by 1. "a system of comprehensive Education;" 2. "a system of combined Education." The "Explanation," indeed, professed to abandon the last for the time, however to be "preferred," as a thing "against which the religious sympathies of the country revolted." But in "abandoning" the "combined system," it clung closely and tenaciously to that which is its natural antecedent, the "comprehensive system." The "comprehensive system" thus grasped firmly by the hand of the Civil Power, prepared the way step by step for the "combined system," and finally ushered it into *de facto* existence, in the shape of the School Board of 1870.

* "Correspondence with the Secretary of the Committee of Council on Education, April and May, 1847." "Letter to Mr. Gladstone, November 17, 1847." "Letter to Bishop of Bath and Wells, January, 1849," &c., &c.

The Secretary was a very able and adroit man, and understood thoroughly what *cedendo imperat* means. Accordingly he abandoned his "combined education" in 1847, only that he might pave the way by successive steps, more or less "unostentatious," for making it an established principle of public policy in 1870.

Now the exact notion of the "comprehensive system" is this: That the school shall be, nominally, a school of one definite religious character, i.e. Church of England, Roman Catholic, or Dissenting, as the case may be; but that it should admit freely children of all "persuasions" or of no "persuasion," leaving it to the parents or friends of the children to decide whether they shall receive any, and if any, what, religious teaching.

The exact notion of the "combined system" is this: That the school shall not have, even nominally, any one definite religious character, but that the children of the Church, and of all "persuasions" or of no "persuasion," shall be admitted alike to the "advantages" of secular instruction. The Clergy of the Church, and the teachers of the several "persuasions," attending at certain hours to give the religious lesson. The schoolmaster, meantime, to continue the secular instruction of such children as are of no "persuasion."

The "comprehensive system" took the form of the school under *the old Conscience Clause*, which made free admission of children of "all persuasions" into the Church-school of the parish, a condition of State assistance; exempting such children, if desired, from the exercise of the Office of the parish Priest in the parish school.

This was a large step, and in many respects full of the worst evil,—one particular of the evil I touch upon below. The supposed compensation rested upon social, political, economical, not at all upon religious, considerations.

The "combined system," *pur et simple*, is not, I think, found in England. A system compounded of the "comprehensive" and the "combined" takes the form of the school under *the new, or Time Table, Conscience Clause*.

By this, the parish Priest is robbed of his Office in the school; being allowed to exercise it only *sub modo*, and for a limited time each day; and "Religious Education" is debased into "religious instruction."

The School Board system, with its "anti-Conscience rate," is the "combined system" with the "religious lesson" left out; not recognising, *as of itself*, so much as the outward show of religious teaching; and, when admitting anything of a religious character, admitting it only in deference to lingering prejudices of the English mind, in favour of what either is, or looks like, religion in a school.

It is obvious that, so far as the preservation by man of the dogmatic teaching of Catholic Truth is concerned, and its necessary connection with Christian Education, all these systems carry with them the same fatal consequences. But the system compounded of "comprehensive" and "combined," that is to say, the system under which schools, nominally "Church-schools," but connected with the State, are administered under the Act of 1870, is the most dangerous, because the most insidious. There is a pretence of "Religious Education" about it, which the "School Board" system has not.

Again, the "compounded system" as applied to a nominally Church-school, is most miserably unfair to the children of the Church, in holding up to them day by day, and under their own eyes and experience, the strongest practical proof that soundness and Unity of Faith is, in the view of those who govern and instruct, reward and punish, a thing of secondary importance: that in the view of these same governors and instructors, the Truth is a thing not external to, and independent of, man's judgment and opinion, but simply what "every man troweth;" and in tempting them to think little of "the Unity of the Faith" themselves, because they see that children, whether trained in the Catholic Faith or not, have precisely the same advantages supplied to them in the pursuit after secular knowledge.

Of the many startling phenomena of this controversy, no one has been, and is, more startling or more sad, than the reckless manner in which care for the children of the Church has been sacrificed to the assumed necessity of bringing the children of the same place, or part of a place, together in the same school. The Faith of the Church being put into one scale, and money, with political and social convenience into the other, the first has kicked the beam. As I go about now, and hear Churchmen talking about their schools as connected with the Committee of Council, I hear commonly of little else, than the number of pounds they get by way of grant: this seems to be the test of a good school. Sometimes I hear it contended, that it is an improvement to have Religious teaching confined to one hour in the day. Is it "Religious teaching?" I say it is not. It may be *a* religious teaching; but it is not *the* teaching of Religion. That is a thing for every hour of every school and home day alike. That is a thing which is an integral part of the Parish Priest's trust and office; and may not be surrendered or compromised at man's bidding, under any pretext, or colour, or difficulty whatsoever.

If Religion were a thing like reading, writing, summing, &c. &c., there might be room for the contention; but it is not. A "religious lesson" for an hour is nothing, or, rather, worse than nothing, if that is all. You may just as well confine the religious life to the time passed in public or private prayer: the whole thing is a very miserable fallacy.

Religion is the beginning, the middle, and the end of all Christian teaching; the golden thread that runs through it all, linking all its parts together in the right use of the gifts of our life, to the saving of our own, the winning of others' souls; and all to the glory of GOD.

When we come to analyse a little, and to enquire, how does it come to pass that in a "Christian country," the prevailing element of the school is, not the religious but, the secular element; and further still, that all the tendencies of the school are to exclude the religious element altogether, however modified? The answer appears to be of the kind following :—

It is assumed, as the primary principle governing the whole case, that the children of the country are to be "taught." The next step is "the school;" that is the assembling together children under the master or mistress, or both, appointed to conduct the school: so far there is no controversy.

I am not stating the case from what is necessarily the Catholic stand-point, but from the stand-point of a people calling itself a "Christian people," whether Catholic, or not Catholic. Whatever is true of such a people generally, is, *à fortiori*, true of the Catholic portion of it, true according to those particular and special principles and rules, which are the inheritance of the Catholic.

What, then, is it that the children are to be taught when they are so assembled? They are to be taught *first* to be good, i.e. to be religious; for in a "Christian country" to be good and to be religious are convertible terms; two names for one and the same thing. They are, *secondly*, to be taught to be useful, that is, to be able and ready to do their part in this world's life: and both those things in inseparable connection, and in mutual interdependence.

So far there is no dispute. This is allowed on all sides accepting the Christian name and profession to be the true idea, the sound theory of the school in a Christian country.

And observe, it implies necessarily that there must be as many *distinct* schools in a given country, as there are *distinct* forms of faith. Otherwise, the particular "form of faith" out of which the distinction has come is an unreality, and a self-contradiction. If men feel "constrained" to separate themselves from their fellow-men, either in respect of doctrine, or discipline, or worship, then I suppose they will, by parity of reason, be constrained to have their own particular school for the teaching of their children, according to their own particular belief, and upon their own particular system. With anything short of this, the belief very soon becomes uncertain and indistinct, and the system collapses, or merges into some general difference, of which nobody can give any exact account; and which is without any influence upon the religious life, whatever influence it may retain upon the social and political life.

So far, then, there is no real controversy; but at this point the controversy begins. For here, in the face of almost numberless "religious divisions," comes in what goes by the name of "the religious difficulty."

Observe, therefore, out of what does "the religious difficulty" come? out of this, that the Faith of CHRIST abiding, the Unity of the Faith does not abide. I am stating facts and issues *simpliciter*, not discussing any of them.

What is to be done with "the religious difficulty?"

There are only two ways of dealing with it, and ultimately, the two resolve themselves into one.

The one is the tentative way, the way of minimising the "difficulty;" the other is the absolute way, the way of leaving it out of the consideration, and getting rid of it summarily, by getting rid of religion summarily out of the school.

By the first way, the school becomes quasi-Christian; by the second, anti-Christian. In the end, according, I believe, to a law of GOD'S retributive Providence, the second absorbs the first.

We have reached both the ways; that is to say, the Christian order of things has been inverted under the pressure of economical, social, and political "difficulties," and according to the world's teaching. The Christian order is, first, Religion; second, usefulness for this world's life; and the two in necessary combination, interwoven with one another throughout.

The quasi-Christian, in the end the anti-Christian, order is, first, usefulness for this world's life; second, Religion.

And the attempt to combine the two in the inverted order being found impracticable in the nature of things, Religion is sacrificed to this world's usefulness. The school becomes in no respect anything but what may be found in a heathen country.

The Christian ship is lightened of her cargo—of the whole of it of any value—by throwing Religion overboard. All that is left is dregs and refuse.

This is some brief account of our own position. The school in England is by a sure and rapid process becoming the school of Julian the Apostate[1].

It is the old, old story; CHRIST against the World, the World against CHRIST; CHRIST'S own people betraying CHRIST and serving the world. Man driven to choose, and choosing the World rather than CHRIST, and all the while satisfying himself about what he does upon this or that pretext.

In what manner the Church people of Century IV. met the school-policy of Julian the Apostate I do not know: I am not read in the history of the time.

Whether it was with the weapon of CHRIST, that is, with "suffering;" or with the weapon of the arm of the flesh, that is, with consent, however reluctantly given, or even with active concurrence and co-operation, I do not know.

But we all know how the school-policy of the Imperial Government of England during the last fifty years of Century XIX., has been met by the Church-people of England.

It has *not* been met by "suffering."

Most Church people appear to think it sufficient to say: "I know it is very bad, and all wrong from beginning to end, but we must have schools."

Certainly you must *if* they be Christian schools, otherwise you must not. Better far have no schools at all, than quasi-Christian or anti-Christian schools.

For the Imperial Government of England, its case is worse than the Apostate's case: the first professing CHRIST, but in works denying HIM; the second not professing CHRIST, and in works denying HIM. There

---

[1] Chap. II., p. 14. See also Appendix.

is a practical hypocrisy about the first, which is not found in the second.

At the root of all, feeding the Upas tree, is the right of private judgment, as against the Divine Commission and Authority of the Church of CHRIST.

It is a problem of which I do not see the solution: how it has happened that so many of my brethren, Priests and Laymen, who say that they are prepared to suffer all things rather than part with Catholic ceremonial (and here they are quite right), should have parted so easily, I may say complacently, with the Catholic school: I should have thought that the school had had an equal claim, to say the least of it.

Does the one parting forecast the other? GOD forbid; but, warned by what I have seen, I have my fears.

For Roman Catholics in England, I told some very dear friends of mine who were once English Catholics, but are now Roman Catholics, that I used to have a great respect for Roman Catholics (though I was never tempted to leave my Communion for theirs) on two grounds: 1. that they were chief guardians of Dogma, and 2. that they had learnt so well to conjugate *non possum* in all its inflections, as against attempts at encroachment on the part of the Civil Power: but now that they were sitting upon "School Boards," I had parted with at least half of the respect.

One thing more for English Catholics: I do not know how many hundred thousands a-year they get as their share of the Education Grant: getting nothing myself for the last thirty years, it does not interest me, personally.

But, whatever the number of thousands may be, it is no use attempting to conceal that they are the price of the surrender of the Catholic school.

Well, this is a terrible thing to have to admit; for the richest Church, in the richest country in the world, to say that if it is to go without the four or five hundred thousands a-year it cannot keep up its schools, is a confession which does not say much for the care and the loving enthusiasm of English Church people for the English Church. It seems to me that Bishops, Priests, and People of the "Establishment," have great need to take a leaf out of the book of the Roman Catholic, the Presbyterian, and the other " persuasions."

Before I enter upon the outline of the history of the school controversy in England, when it had taken its public form and shape, something ought to be said of the previous " school history" of this country, in respect of " the Education of the poor."

The " parish school" of the Church of England, the nursery of the parish church, has been gained and lost within the hundred years last past.

There had been for the not-poor, Church Universities, Church public schools, Church private schools: in many places for all classes Church endowed grammar-schools: it may be, here and there in the parishes, dames' schools.

Nor is it to be forgotten that one of the first objects to which the Society for Promoting Christian Knowledge directed its attention in 1698, was the foundation of schools for the poor; and in an account of that Society, circulated periodically with the Annual Reports of its proceedings, the following notice appears respecting its design, with regard to schools :—

" The first was, to procure and encourage the erecting of charity schools in all parts of the kingdom; and that those schools might answer the true purposes for which they were erected, the Society have not been wanting (in their correspondence with such of their members as have been concerned in the support and management thereof) to recommend at all times that, together with religious and useful instruction, care should be taken, and all proper means used, to inure the poor to industry and labour, that so they may become good Christians, loyal and useful subjects, and be willing, as well as fit to be employed, not only in trades or services, but also in husbandry, navigation, or any other business that shall be thought of most use and benefit to the public. With these views, the

Society printed and dispersed such rules for the good order and government of these schools, as had been approved of by the Archbishops and Bishops, who directed that the same should be observed within their respective dioceses."

The efforts of this venerable Society appear to have met with considerable success, especially in the metropolis. It laboured specially to promote works of industry in schools; and with that view, issued from time to time circulars particularly urging this point on the notice of school managers. It was under its countenance and encouragement also, that the solemn and imposing annual assemblage of children in St. Paul's Cathedral, which is still conducted under the management of the Society of Patrons, took its rise.

Notwithstanding, however, the exertions which had been made, it is quite evident, from sermons and papers printed prior to the year 1811, that the educational destitution which then existed was very great.

There was then, so to speak, no parish school, the nursery of the parish church, seventy or eighty years ago. For the Religious element there was Catechising in the church, as enjoined by Canon 59, 1603-4, upon "every Parson, Vicar, or Curate, every Sunday and holyday before Evening Prayer." But I believe obedience to the Canon to have become a very rare thing, if at any time since the enactment of the Canon it had been general. The children of the poor were not to any appreciable extent provided with the means of being taught reading, writing, arithmetic, sewing. The excrescences of the present day—which is, by a retributive process, gone school-mad,—the number of things stuffed into children, to the great injury of what it would be really of use to them to be taught well, and more or less, to the disparagement, if not the exclusion, of Religion,—all these things I leave to the "Educators" of the time. I am not concerned with them, except as evidence of the prevailing National Lunacy.

The next move of any account in the matter of schools, was made by Mr. Raikes of Bristol, in or about 1780; Mr. Raikes was the founder of the Sunday school. The move was afterwards much promoted in Somerset, and I believe elsewhere, by Mrs. Hannah More.

Then came the "Bell and Lancaster" move, of which the chief feature was the monitorial system; called, from the place where it first came under Dr. Bell's notice, the "Madras system," largely introduced into England, and copied to some extent in other countries. The personal controversy between Bell and Lancaster, is of no importance to my present purpose; the two systems are respectively parts of the history of the National Society, and of the British and Foreign Schools Society.

In 1808 [g], was established in London, a society for promoting the Royal British, or Lancastrian system, for the Education of the Poor: but at the fourth annual meeting of the society, on the 21st May, 1814, the name of the Institution was changed for that of "the British and Foreign Schools Society."

The object of the society, was the promotion of Education amongst the labouring and manufacturing classes of society, of every religious persuasion; and by Rule IV. it was ordered, that all schools supplied with *teachers* at the expense of the society should be open to the children of parents of all religious denominations, and that reading, writing, arithmetic, and needlework, should be taught; the lessons for reading should consist of extracts from the Holy Scriptures; no catechism, or peculiar religious tenets were to be taught, but every child should be enjoined to attend regularly the place of worship to which their parents belonged.

In 1809-11, "the National Society, for promoting the Education of the Poor in the principles of the Established Church," was first founded. It was incorporated by Charter, 1817.

The connection between the National Society and the

---

[g] Date of foundation stated to me variously, 1804—1805.

system of Dr. Bell will be clearly seen from the following extract from the Minutes of the Standing Committee of the National Society, of January 22, 1812. Lancaster was similarly connected with the British and Foreign Schools Society.

" Resolved,—

" 1st. That Dr. Bell be requested to act as Superintendent in the formation and conduct of the central and other schools, under the direction of this Society, with power to engage such persons as Masters and Mistresses, as shall be adequate to carry the purposes of the Society into effect; and to retain, suspend, or dismiss the Masters or Mistresses.

" 2ndly. That Dr. Bell be empowered to engage persons to be trained as Masters and Mistresses.

" 3rdly. That the Trustees of the several schools of Lambeth, Marylebone, and Gower's-walk, Whitechapel, be immediately applied to by the School Committee, to be hereafter appointed, to enable this Society to give Dr. Bell sufficient powers to train Masters in those schools, according to the former resolutions to this effect.

" 4thly. That a Sub-Committee be appointed for the general management of the central and other schools, and to assist Dr. Bell in carrying into execution the foregoing resolutions; and that such Committee do consist of the Lord Bishop of Salisbury, the Right Hon. Lord Radstock, the Right Hon. Sir John Nicholl, the Rev. Dr. Barton, and Wm. Davis, Esq.; three of whom may be a quorum.

" 5thly. That Dr. Bell do report his proceedings from time to time to such Committee, and that such Report be submitted to this Committee."

It was, I believe, about 1830, possibly before it, that the Whig plot for revolutionising the parish school, and "utilising" it, was first hatched by the joint incubation of the then Lord Lansdowne, Lord John Russell, and Francis Kay Shuttleworth,—who the first parent may have been I do not know.

It has been followed up, as was doubtless part of the scheme, by a like revolution in the Public School and in the University; these, too, have been robbed of their distinctive Church character, and have been perverted into "National Institutions." The "World" of England has carried the day as against the "Church" of England.

A "National Institution" in the England of Century XIX., is a thing either of no particular "belief," or, of no "belief" at all [b].

The Church endowed schools have also been robbed, perverted, and utilised. The plundering has been extended to Scholarships at Universities, and other charitable bequests of pious Church-founders, which were devised to be, and, as matter of fact, were, of vast help and encouragement to poor students.

Everything has been "reformed" in this matter; not, be it observed, "re-formed." The word has two very different, and indeed opposite significations, according as it is written.

This, then, has been the Whig plot, concocted for Whig purposes; concocted to please Nonconformists, religious and political, at the expense of the Church; concocted to please those who were then the instruments and servants, but are now the masters of the Whig. The retribution is just; whether it be not severe upon our common country is another matter: and yet, if I must be in the hands of either Whig oligarch or Nonconformist democrat, political or religious, I prefer the latter.

The Whig plot received its final consummation in the Elementary Education Act of 1870, passed by Mr. Gladstone's Government. Universities, public schools, had gone before, so had endowed schools, and other educational Church charities; private schools had followed suit; and "Church Education," with here and there exceptions, conducted by faithful men, has perished out of the land.

The concocters and promoters of the plot faced their

[b] The restoration of "Cathedral Churches" in our day, is commonly spoken of, not as the restoration of "Cathedral Churches" but, as the restoration of "National Monuments."

chief difficulty with a courage, adroitness, fixity of purpose, and act, of which it would be good to find examples on the side of the Church as by law established; and have in that sense deserved their triumph.

They found a great network of Church "Educational Institutions" covering all the land : so long as this remained in substance intact, and was only stimulated into greater reality of exertion by the assault upon it, the assault was hopeless. Again, if they had set about pulling it to bits openly, they would have been met with enforced open resistance. They were wise in their generation, and took another course; they betook themselves steadily and patiently to the sapping and undermining process; to the perverting and utilising process; they set about it quite quietly, and in professed friendship, or, as Mr. Shuttleworth put it, in a moment of unguarded exultation, "unostentatiously."

The weapons of the Downing-street armoury have been chiefly these :—

1. Acts of Parliament, passed, not in Parliament but, in the Council Office.

2. Bribery by way of grants.

3. Snubbing and discouragement; trading upon poverty of applicant by way of no grants.

4. Interference, first suggestive and hortatory, and "unostentatious;" then insisting; lastly, dictating and imperative.

5. "Minutes" capable of many constructions.

6. A large use of the words "My Lords," in the hands of Chief Secretary and his subordinates.

7. The taking every, however minute, advantage presented by the incurable weakness, not to say unfaithfulness, of Establishmentarian defence.

8. Finally, when all the train had been nicely adjusted, and then exploded outside, Acts of Parliament passed in Parliament.

I do not know anything anywhere so clever and so triumphant, as the policy of the Committee of Council on "Education" since 1840, except it be Russian diplomacy, which is undoubtedly the first thing of its kind anywhere upon record. The parallel holds also in respect of the remarkable short-sightedness, weakness, and general unworthiness of the opposing diplomacy, as we are finding now more and more every day to our great confusion of face.

To complete the summary of the Educational position as between Church and State up to 1839, the year of appointment of Committee of Council on "Education," I subjoin the following Precis. Some few particulars relating to Scotland, 1834-8, are added.

Debates and Parliamentary Grants, 1833—1838.

On the 17th of August, 1833, an Act was passed by which a sum of £20,000 was granted in aid of private subscriptions, for the erection of schools for the Education of the children of the poorer classes in Great Britain. To render the application of this sum most generally useful, the Chancellor of the Exchequer, with the concurrence of the Lords of the Treasury, laid down the following rules :—

1. That no portion of this sum be applied to any purpose whatever, except for the erection of new school-houses; and that in the definition of a school-house, the residence for masters or attendants be not included.

2. That no application be entertained unless a sum be raised by private contribution, equal at the least to one-half of the total estimated expenditure.

3. That the amount of private subscription be received, expended and accounted for, before any issue of public money for such school be directed.

4. That no application be complied with unless upon the consideration of such a report, either from the National School Society, or the British and Foreign Schools Society, as shall satisfy this Board that the case is one deserving of attention, and there is a reasonable expectation that the school may be permanently supported.

5. That the applicants whose cases are favourably entertained, be required to bind themselves to submit to any audit of their accounts which this Board may direct, as well as to such periodical reports respecting the state of their schools, and the number of scholars educated, as may be called for.

6. That in considering all applications made to the Board, a preference be given to such applications as come from large cities and towns, in which the necessity of assisting in the erection of schools is most pressing; and that due enquiries should also be made before any such application be acceded to, whether there may not be charitable funds or public and private endowments, that might render any further grants inexpedient or unnecessary.

By the 7th March, 1834, the whole of the grant had been appropriated and exceeded by £484 14s. and the Lords of the Treasury in their report stated, that "reviewing the practical operation of the grant, which must in the first instance have been considered as experimental, and perceiving that, from the papers before them, applications have been received for the establishment of 236 new schools, calculated for the instruction of 55,168 scholars, and that local and charitable funds to the extent of £66,492 6s. have been already tendered in aid of the Parliamentary Grant, they feel that they may safely recommend to Parliament to grant a further sum of £20,000 for the service in the ensuing year."

1834.

In accordance with this Minute, in 1834 a further sum of £20,000 was voted by Parliament for the building of schools. On the 11th of July, 1834, the Lords of the Treasury stated that, in making a selection from the numerous applications before them, from the inadequacy of the funds at their disposal, it is not in their power to comply with the wishes of the memorialists, and they feel it their duty to distribute the sum now remaining in the manner which will most conduce to the object for which it was granted; with this view, they are disposed to give priority to those applications where, by a smaller expenditure, they can forward the education of the largest number of scholars, and having attentively considered the schedule of claims, they are prepared to sanction at once a grant to those schools, where the number of scholars proposed to be educated is in proportion to two to every £1 applied for. Upon this principle £7,978 was appropriated. In August a further appropriation, on the same principle, was made to the amount of £10,481, to the building of schools in such towns and cities where the population exceeded 5,000 inhabitants. Further appropriations of a like nature were made in January and February, 1835, which exhausted the whole of the Parliamentary Grant.

1835.

In 1835, on the 16th of July, the House of Commons voted another sum of £20,000 in aid of the building of schools in England. In distributing the grant, the Lords of the Treasury gave preference to those applications in which the sum required did not exceed £1 for every two scholars; this was the principle adopted in the previous year. By this grant, appropriations were made towards the erection of 278 schools, calculated for the instruction of 45,321 scholars. In the appropriations of this year, the Lords of the Treasury exceeded the vote by £1,669.

A further sum of £10,000 was voted by Parliament towards the erection of model schools for the education of teachers; but up to 1839, none of this grant had been expended.

1836.

In the session of 1836, a further grant of £20,000 was voted by Parliament for the erection of schools in England; and the Lords of the Treasury, in distributing this grant, acted on the principles laid down in previous years, i.e. giving preference to those applications where the amount applied for did not exceed the proportion of £1 for every two scholars proposed to be educated. Appropriations were accordingly made towards the erection of 181 schools, to provide for the education of 37,026 scholars. The proportion of students to the amount of the grants was not so great this year, as the exceeded sum of £1,669 of previous year had to be made up. The actual amount spent over the erection of the 181 schools, was £17,277.

1837.

Of the grant of £20,000 voted this session, I can find no separate account; but from a general report of 1838, the numbers, &c., appear to be as follow: £21,055 was appropriated towards the erection of 196 schools, which accommodated 47,879 scholars. This return shews that the Lords of the Treasury followed the rules laid down in the previous years; of favouring those applications, where the amount applied for did not exceed the proportion of £1 for every two scholars.

1838.

During this session another grant of £20,000 was voted by Parliament for the erection of schools in England. This grant appears to have been appropriated as in previous years, (I cannot, however, find any separate account). On Feb. 12, 1839, on account of LORD BROUGHAM'S proposed new Bills, LORD J. RUSSELL informed the House of Commons that it was not the intention of the Government to propose another grant for the erection of school-houses.

1839.

In spite of what was said on the 12th of February, a grant of £30,000 was voted by Parliament for the purpose of Education in Great Britain; but as the Committee of Council on Education had already been constituted, the appropriation of this grant fell into their hands.

SCOTLAND.

During the session of 1834, £10,000 was granted by Parliament for building schools in Scotland, and model schools in England. In appropriating the sum, the Lords of the Treasury adopted as their guide the regulations, Nos. 1, 2, 3 and 5, (which are given in p. 119.) The whole of this sum appears to have been devoted to Scotch schools. Appropriations were made towards the erection of 27 new schools, calculated for the instruction of 8,040 scholars.

The sum of £10,000 was granted each year till 1838; but I cannot find separate returns of any year except 1836; when it appears that £3,905 was expended in the erection of 14 schools to accommodate 3,530 scholars; £6,000 being set apart in aid of the endowment for schoolmasters in 41 highland parishes; and £83 was deducted to meet excess of previous year.

List of Grants voted by Parliament for the purposes of promoting Education in England and Scotland, from 1833 to 1839.

ENGLAND.

1833 Grant of £20,000 for the erection of schools for the Education of children of the poorer classes in Great Britain.

1834	,,	£ 20,000	,,	,,	,,
1835	,,	,, 20,000	,,	,,	,,
,,	,,	,, 10,000	for erection of model schools for the instruction of teachers, (vote not expended).

1836 „   £ 20,000 for same purpose as that of 1833.
1837 „   „ 20,000   „   „
1838 „   „ 20,000   „   „
1839 „   „ 30,000 for purpose of Education in England; this sum was appropriated by the Committee of Council on Education.

SCOTLAND.

1834 Grant of £10,000 for erection of school-houses and model schools in Scotland.

1835	„	£ 10,000	„	„	„
1836	„	„ 10,000	„	„	„
1837	„	„ 10,000	„	„	„
1838	„	„ 10,000	„	„	„

Dec. 1, 1837, (*House of Lords*).—LORD BROUGHAM presented his two Bills on the subject *of General Education, and the better management of Charities*. In detailing his plan, Lord Brougham said that the Education Bill was in all respects the same as that proposed last session, viz., that a paid Board of Commissioners should be appointed for life, to superintend a general system of Education in Great Britain; that the measure was so formed as not to interfere with the exertions of private individuals; to help, but not to supplant; to aid, but not to control.—The EARL OF WINCHELSEA expressed great satisfaction that Religion was positively included in the plan, but he feared that the Bill was too complicated for adoption.

Aug. 14, 1838, (*House of Lords*).—LORD BROUGHAM postpones the consideration of his Bills till next session.

We come now to 1839, Feb. 12, (*House of Commons*).—LORD J. RUSSELL in presenting some papers, availed himself of the opportunity of explaining his views on the subject of General Education. Considering the different schemes which had been proposed, he could not coincide with any of them. The Government deemed it unadvisable to adopt either the exclusive principle desired by the Church, or the open principle advocated by the British and Foreign Schools Society. It had, therefore, determined to establish a Central Board for considering and arranging the subject, which *Board was to consist of five Privy Councillors, with the President of the Council at their head*. If, as in former years, £20,000 should be voted by Parliament, or as he should prefer £30,000, that Board would have to settle the distribution of the grant. The first duty of the Board would be to establish a normal school to educate masters for the schools, and to allot funds for establishing local schools.

SIR R. PEEL said that before the House was called upon to vote a grant of money, they should have distinct information as to the principles by which the Board was to be guided: because, if they made the vote on the understanding that year after year the Board was to decide what principles should govern them, and how far it should be governed by the principles of the Church of England, that would be giving the widest possible discretion to the Board . . . Sir R. Peel also asked whether the new proposed Board of Privy Councillors was to discharge the functions hitherto performed by the Treasury, with respect to the appropriation of funds voted by Parliament.—LORD J. RUSSELL answered this question in the affirmative.

Feb. 14, 1839, (*House of Lords*).—Papers relating to Education, which had been laid before the House of Commons by LORD J. RUSSELL, were ordered also to be laid before the House of Lords.

Feb. 20, 1839, (*House of Commons*). — MR. WYSE moved that the Queen be asked to appoint a Board of Commissioners of Education for England.—Motion withdrawn.

April 30, 1839, (*House of Commons*).—LORD STANLEY asked that a copy of the Order in Council, by which the Committee of Privy Council on Education was constituted, should be laid before the House. He also asked whether the new Committee was to have the disposal of sums appropriated by Parliament for the purposes of Education, and whether a vote would be asked for that session.—LORD J. RUSSELL said the Order in Council appointing the Committee should be laid before the House. That it was the intention of the new Board to distribute the sums granted by Parliament as they had been hitherto appropriated by the Treasury; and that Parliament, due notice being given, would be asked to vote a sum for the purpose of Education.

May 3, 1839, (*House of Lords*).—The BISHOP OF LONDON

asked that the papers relating to the Order in Council appointing the Committee of Education should be laid upon the table.

June 4, 1839, (*House of Commons*).— LORD J. RUSSELL announced the intention of the Government to abandon their Education scheme, and that there was a new plan *in petto*, and that £30,000 would be asked for educational purposes. This grant would be distributed between the National School Society and the British and Foreign Schools Society.—This mode of appropriation was generally objected to by the Opposition, and after a long discussion, LORD ASHLEY moved for a call of the House on the 14th inst.

June 10, 1839, (*House of Lords*).— LORD BROUGHAM presented petitions in favour of National Education, and asserted that the Established Church had no right to assume the exclusive Education of children.—The BISHOP OF LONDON presented counter-petitions.

June 14, 1839, (*House of Commons*). — On the motion for going into Committee, when LORD J. RUSSELL was to have moved his resolutions on Education, LORD STANLEY moved as an amendment, that an Address be presented to the Queen, praying her Majesty to be pleased to revoke the Order in Council of the 10th April, 1839, appointing a Committee of Council to superintend the application of any sums voted by Parliament for the purpose of promoting public Education. Lord Stanley objected that such a body, exclusively political, should be entrusted with the entire control of the people's moral and religious Education. That the systems of grants to the National Society, and the British and Foreign Schools Society, had answered well, and no complaints had been made; and therefore there was no reason for departing from this system of granting aids to schools, especially also as it had been carried out on a mutual principle.— LORD MORPETH objected to the Amendment, on the ground that it separated the Education of the people from the superintendence of the Government. — LORD ASHLEY complained of this new system, because it left to the Government all the powers it pretended to give up when Lord Brougham's Bills were abandoned; and also on the grounds that it was opposed to the interests of the Established Church.—(Debate adjourned).

June 19, 1839, (*House of Commons*).—MR. WYSE contended

that Lord Stanley, as the introducer of the National system of Education in Ireland, was bound by analogy to support the present proposal for Education in England. He also shewed that it was necessary to take some speedy steps, as Education in England was at a lower standard than in any other country in Europe.—(After a few unimportant speeches, debate was adjourned).

June 20, 1839.—MR. D'ISRAELI maintained that England was indebted to the State for very little of its social advancement, but owed it chiefly to private enterprise. He denounced the plan now propounded, as a centralization injurious to the national character.—MR. GIBSON contended that the schoolmasters should in all matters relating to the Education of children, be quite independent of all Church influence, even though the children were Churchmen's children; and that in the present state of religious feeling in England, the schoolmaster should not be under the control of the Ordinary.—MR. GLADSTONE maintained that if the principles of the Government were to be followed out to its consequences, in recognising as a duty of the State the endowment of dissenting schools, by reason of some abstract right, it would be equally a State duty to endow dissenting chapels. — The CHANCELLOR OF THE EXCHEQUER contended that, according to the arguments of the Opposition, the State should educate the children of the Establishment in the Established Faith, but should leave all other children wholly uneducated.—LORD J. RUSSELL stated that the whole object of the present Government in their proposals was, to afford a better and more general system of Education to the lower classes of the country.—SIR R. PEEL asked the Government why, if it laid down as a principle that it was bound to educate children of dissenters, did it shrink from educating them in the tenets of their particular faith. He objected that in Education religion should be made an open question; so he advised the Government to rescind the Order in Council on the following reasons: (α.) that in the present state of the country a Board of Education could not wisely be constituted; (β.) that any such Board ought not to consist exclusively of members of the Government; (γ.) that in the religious education of children it was unwise to exclude the ecclesiastical authorities, who were properly placed in charge of the religious education of the country;

and (8.) because the petitions against this new scheme were more numerous than those in its favour.

The House then divided: for Amendment, 275; against, 280.—Lord J. Russell, in spite of this small majority, said it was the determination of the Government to proceed with the motion.

June 24, 1839, (*House of Commons*).—Lord J. Russell moved that £30,000 be granted to Her Majesty for public Education in Great Britain for the year 1839. In answering the arguments of the Opposition, Lord J. Russell said that it appeared to be their object to allow Education to the people on no other principles than those of the Established Church. He also stated that the system of the British and Foreign Schools Society was to read the Scriptures during the week, and to allow all children to go to their particular places of worship to receive instruction in religion from the teachers of their own sect. These were the principles upon which the Government proposed to act.—Lord Teignmouth thought that the system of Education proposed by the Government would lead to universal sectarianism.—Mr. O'Connell said that Roman Catholics ought to have a share of the grant, and that it was unfair to make an exception in their case.—House divided: for the Grant, 275; against, 273.

June 27, 1839, (*House of Commons*).—Sir R. Peel, in answer to a question from Lord J. Russell, stated that it was not intended to take the sense of the House on the Education Vote. The vote was thereupon agreed to.

July 1, 1839, (*House of Lords*).—The Archbishop of Canterbury moved an Address to the Queen, praying that certain papers relating to various sums granted for public Education, &c., on Aug. 3, 1833, March 2, 1834, and July 5, 1838, be laid upon the table..

July 5, 1839, (*House of Lords*).—The Archbishop of Canterbury moved that an Address be presented to Her Majesty containing the following resolutions, on the subject of the Ministerial proceedings in respect to National Education:—

(1.) That this House has had under its consideration the various documents presented by Her Majesty's commands relating to National Education.

(2.) That a Committee of Council has been appointed, consisting exclusively of Her Majesty's Ministers, for the purpose of considering all matters relating to Education, and of superintending the application of any sums voted by Parliament for that purpose; also, that a model school for the education of teachers was proposed to be built.

(3.) That the Committee was to have full and every control over schools in respect of management and discipline.

(4.) That these powers are so great, that they should not be committed to any public authority without the consent of Parliament.

(5.) That exception was taken to the proposed scheme of Religious Education.

(6.) That no steps be taken with respect to the establishment or foundation of any plans for the General Education of the people of the country, without giving to this House, as one branch of the Legislature, an opportunity of fully considering a measure of such deep importance to the highest interests of the country.—The House divided: for the Address, 229; against, 118; majority 111.—Address ordered to be presented to the Queen.

July 11, 1839.—Answer of the Queen, in which she stated that she approved of the appointment of the Committee of Privy Council to superintend the distribution of the grants voted by Parliament for Public Education. She promised also that annual Reports of the Committee should be laid before the House.

July 15, 1839, (*House of Lords*).—LORD BROUGHAM moved the second reading of his Education Bill. The principles for which he contended as the basis of his measure, were:—(1.) That all Education should be voluntary. (2.) That it should not necessarily be uniform. (3.) That those who contributed to the support of schools should have a considerable share in the management of them. (4.) That a central Board, under due restrictions, should have a check and control over the local management of the ratepayers.—This Bill, being opposed by the BISHOP OF CHICHESTER, LORD BROUGHAM, upon the suggestion of LORD MELBOURNE, in consideration of the advanced period of the session, consented to withdraw it altogether.

August 26, 1839, (*House of Lords*).—LORD BROUGHAM, on moving for the Charter of the London University, discussed at some length the National Education question, and expressed a hope that the House would pledge itself to proceed with a Bill next session.

There is no authentic record of grants made by Parliament from 1839 to 1851. In 1851, the Committee of Council began issuing a list of grants made.

Upon the return of the Whigs to power, 1846, the Minutes of 1846 were issued.

Many Churchmen, myself included, were weak enough to be caught by the bait of the Minutes. I remember well my good friend Bellairs, then Inspector of Church schools under the Order of Council, August 10, 1840, making private communication to me at East Brent in 1846, touching the coming Minutes, and advising me to apply for assistance under them.

Early in 1847, having opened my eyes to the ulterior purpose of the framers of the Minutes, I withdrew my application; and in 1849, having placed beyond all doubt, by means of a correspondence between the Secretary of the Committee of Council on Education and myself, that the Order in Council, August 10, 1840, was not duly observed on the part of "My Lords" and their Secretary, I refused to allow the Government Inspector to inspect any more the parish school of East Brent.

I said to Bellairs thereupon,—"My dear Bellairs, I love you very much; but if you ever come here again to inspect, I lock the door of the school, and tell the boys to put you in the pond."

He never did come again. The Secretary blustered a good deal, and then subsided, as he could not help doing.

For many years I never set eyes, to my great content, on a Government Inspector. How many years ago exactly it is that my dear friend Tinling, who then held the office for these parts, proposed coming to inspect, I do not recall; I said, "Oh, come by all means. I shall never ask for a sixpence of their money, and I think them quite as mischievous as I ever did; but pray come if you like, always very glad to see you."

Now a thing happened the day of his inspection for

which I have been most unjustly blamed, and my dear wife too; and for which I have even been "taken to," and the song cited, possibly sung, in the House of Commons by some jealous "Educationalist."

About the time when I thought the Inspector would be finishing, I said to my wife, "Let's go and see how they are getting on."

When we got into the school, he was about finishing. He said to me, "Do they sing?"

"Oh, yes," I said, "I believe so. Georgie, make them sing something."

Now it happened that she had been teaching them "Goosey, Goosey, Gander, &c." It amused the children, and they sung it with a will. She said, "Sing, children;" away they went with their favourite song.

I saw Tinling didn't quite know what to make of it; but the thing was done, and I couldn't help enjoying the scene and the song. When they came to—

> "Old father long legs
>   Wouldn't say his prayers,
>   Take him by the left leg,
>   Take him by the left leg,
>   Take him by the left leg,
>   And throw him down stairs;"

calling to mind how apposite all this was to the matter in controversy between the Committee of Council and myself, the fun of the thing overcame me, and I retreated. I had reason to think afterwards that my dear friend thought it was all concocted to throw ridicule on his inspection. I told him more than once that this was in every particular a mistake, and I repeat it here: it would have been very unseemly to concert it; as it happened, it was only funny. I don't like Inspectors certainly; but I hope I could not take advantage of their being my guests to do anything to hurt or annoy them.

Tinling never came again after that day, and East Brent "Inspection" ceased for my time.

In 1847 came the Management Clauses, to which Mr. Gladstone had called my attention, as I said above, in writing to me upon my correspondence withdrawing my application under the Minutes of 1846.

I cite here part of my letter to him, of Nov. 17, 1847, from which I have already cited in these "Notes:"—

"It is unnecessary to revert to the details of the proceedings in Parliament: there is little in them to which the Church can look back with any satisfaction. Suspicions, indeed, that all was not right had begun to creep in long before the vote (for Education) was passed, arising chiefly from the publication of the anonymous pamphlet referred to above[1]. Some faint tones of remonstrance were heard; and many persons who had petitioned in favour of the Minutes, began to wish they had been less precipitate. Some curious instances of the power of expansion and development, so inherent, as it would seem, in Minutes of Council, and which render them so dangerous a substitute for an Act of Parliament, had extorted strong expressions of distrust and disappointment in high quarters; but, on the whole, the 'Education scheme' may be said to have been still regarded as full of promise when the Parliament was dissolved.

"A few months however—not to say a few weeks—have witnessed a most remarkable change. General distrust has taken the place of individual disapproval. Churchmen are, more or less, afraid of the scheme out of which they had hoped so much good might arise. Promoters of schools are refusing Government aid; others are hesitating what to do; hesitating between their necessities, and their fear of committing themselves to a vicious principle, and embarrassing all their future efforts to maintain the integrity of Catholic teaching. The Bishop of this Diocese has addressed a public remonstrance to the President of the Council; a numerous meeting of Clergy and Laity have tendered to him their respectful thanks, and have signified their cordial concurrence in the terms of his remonstrance; the Diocesan Education Board has added its voice to that of the general meeting. There are many signs that similar expressions of distrust will be heard from other

---

[1] "The State, the Church and the Congregation." The authorship was commonly attributed to the then Secretary of the Committee of Council, Mr. Kay Shuttleworth.

Dioceses. The Archdeacon of Durham has, in a late Charge, called the attention of the Clergy of his archdeaconry to the hardships of the circumstances in which the Church is placed. A resolution of remonstrance has been adopted by them, and communicated to the Committee of Council. Another resolution has been passed by the Oxford Diocesan Board of Education, which states very clearly and forcibly the objectionable character of the novel conditions which the Committee of Privy Council are imposing upon the promoters of Church schools, and the great danger of the precedent of State interference, which this course appears to introduce. The Church at large feels that she has been betrayed into a false position, and that she is reaping a very bad return for the confidence she allowed herself to repose in the intentions of the State."

The school at Enmore, near Bridgwater, in this diocese, was one of those in the case of which the Committee of Council made one of their earliest attempts at the 'comprehensive school." The Bishop and the diocese, as represented for the next seven years at the annual meetings at Wells, had become quite alive to the danger, to its character, extent, and imminence. I applied myself to the utmost of my powers to clear, vindicate, and establish the diocesan position, and throughout those seven years I received here, as elsewhere, an amount of cordial, generous, confiding and vigorous support, upon which, now that it is a thing of the past, now that all that we fought for together then has been lost to the Church, now that I may apply to myself,

Solus, et in sicca secum spatiatur arena,

I rejoice to look back upon with great thankfulness of heart.

The solitude and isolation is not a thing of my own making, though it be of my own choosing; I have preferred it, as I must prefer it to the end, to co-operation at the cost of principle.

In the Preface to these "Notes," I have stated my position relatively to those who once supported me in the matter of "religious education." I will not repeat the statement here.

I will add to it this only, that the common and crushing defeat of Churchmen does not lie at my door. The event has placed beyond dispute that, in substance, my contention has been right from first to last; and that therefore, as time went on, I ought every year to have been better supported, instead of worse.

We shall see, as we go on, what the causes were which broke up the High Church army of 1847—1852, and proved the unreality of the tie which had appeared to bind all its members together into one body, which might indeed be defeated by the adversary, but would never assist in promoting the defeat; *as has been generally done.*

I am not saying that "Church Education" in England, at the time when the plot was laid for putting something else into its place, was good education. In all its principle it was good; in very much of its practice it was bad. In all its theory it was right; in many parts of its execution it was wrong.

What was wanted was amendment and improvement; what has come is ruin.

Who is to blame for this issue? The man who has a good thing entrusted to him, knows all about its goodness, and about his duty and responsibility to make the most of it: or the man to whom the good is alike entrusted, but who deliberately prefers something else: or, lastly, the man who believes the thing to be not good, but bad?

The first is the Churchman; the second is the Secularist; the third is the Nonconformist.

I say that the first is most to blame; then the second; I do not see that the third is to blame at all. It is part of Nonconformist belief, that "Church Education" is a bad thing; the belief is wrong, but the action is consistent. The Nonconformist acts "ignorantly in unbelief." The Secularist does not say that "Church Education" is a bad thing; but in all his action he postpones it, or any other "religious Education," to "secular Education:" this world is first with him, not the world to come. The Churchman says that "Church Education" is a good thing, and that it is his trust; and, saying this, betrays it into the assailant's hands.

The Churchman is, by a great deal, the most to blame.

I sum up the case. It cannot be said with any truth of the Archbishops and Bishops of the Church of England that, in the thirty years from 1840 to 1870, they have made one real effort to save "Church Education." So far from it, with some faint show of resistance now and then, they have played more and more every year into the hands of the Civil Power; that is, into the hands of the "Indifferent Power."

Neither can it be said of Priests and People, that they have made any large, steady, consistent effort to save it: any effort worthy of the trust committed to their keeping.

It is the old story of gifts first neglected, then abused; and of the sure retribution that waits upon both.

The history of the educational conflict of this century dates, on the part of the Civil Power, from 1839, the year of the Establishment of the Committee of Council, by majorities of 5 and 2, 280, 275; 275, 273, in House of Commons; and against majority of 111 in House of Lords.

On the part of the Committee of "the National Society for promoting the Education of the Poor in the Principles of the Established Church," the conflict dates from August 10, 1840, when the Concordat was made touching Government Inspection.

The conflict finally closed in 1870: after thirty-one years of steady advance on the part of the Civil Power; of compromising resistance and successive overthrow on the part of "the National Society." It closed in the irretreivable ruin of the educational position of the Church, *as connected with the State*, under the Act of 1870, intituled "the Elementary Education Act," brought in and passed by Mr. Forster, on the part of Mr. Gladstone's Government.

In tracing the course of the conflict, I have before me all the necessary evidence, documentary and other, public and private; a great mass of Papers, Letters, &c.

What I have to do, is to represent as succinctly and clearly as I can, introducing only so much of detail as appears to be required, the broad outlines of the conflict.

The successive aspects of it, all of them parts of the original scheme for "utilising," perverting, and finally subverting Church schools, are as follows:—

1. Minutes of Council, 1846.
2. Management Clauses, 1847.
3. Abolition of exclusive character of Church schools, in respect of admission of children, and of teaching, 1847 to 1870.
4. "Education" Rate attempted. Manchester and Salford scheme, 1851-3.
5. "Conscience Clause," 1850 to 1870.
6. "Time Table Conscience Clause," 1870.
7. Education Rate completed, with School Board, 1870.

I have already said all that is necessary touching the stand-point of the Civil Power in this matter. For the stand-point of "the National Society," founded in 1811, we must first go back to its antecedents.

First in order, then, I cite here the preamble to the Charter, where the reasons for granting the Charter are stated:—

"And whereas it has been represented to us by the humble Petition of the Most Reverend Father in GOD, our right trusty and right entirely beloved Councillor, Charles, Lord Archbishop of Canterbury, on behalf of himself as President, and of the Vice-Presidents and Committee of a certain Society called 'THE NATIONAL SOCIETY FOR PROMOTING THE EDUCATION OF THE POOR IN THE PRINCIPLES OF THE ESTABLISHED CHURCH THROUGHOUT ENGLAND AND WALES,' that such Society has been established between four and five years; and that its sole object was originally declared to be '*to instruct and educate the Poor in suitable learning, works of industry, and the principles of the Christian Religion according to the Established Church:*' That the Committee has, ever since the foundation of the Society, zealously and anxiously laboured to carry into effect the great designs which its Founders contemplated, by educating the children of the Poor, *without any exception*[k], in the doctrine and discipline of the Established Church, &c., &c., &c.

"And it being also represented to us, that the said Society has been instituted principally for the purpose of educating the children of the Poor in the doctrines and discipline of the Established Church, according to the Liturgy and Catechism provided for that purpose.

"We, willing that all due encouragement, &c., &c., &c.

"At our Palace of Westminster, the twenty-third day of May, in the fifty-seventh year of our Reign."

The Terms of Union are of later date, 1839. They are a condensed expression of what I have cited from the charter. See note below[l].

[k] "*Without any exception.*" It would appear that the Founders foresaw that a time would come, when the security which these words provide, against any tampering with the primary purposes of the Society, would be greatly needed.

[l] "*Terms of Union to be subscribed by Parties desirous of uniting their Schools with the National Society for promoting the Education of the Poor in the Principles of the Established Church throughout England and Wales.*

We, the undersigned, being desirous that the School at (or to be established at)   near   in the County of   and Diocese of   should be united to the NATIONAL SOCIETY, declare that

1. The Children are to be instructed in the Holy Scriptures, and in the Liturgy and Catechism of the Established Church.

2. With respect to such instruction, the Schools are to be subject to the superintendence of the Parochial Clergyman.

3. The Children are to be regularly assembled for the purpose of attending Divine Service in the Parish Church, or other place of worship under the Establishment, unless such reason be assigned for their non-attendance as is satisfactory to the Managers of the Schools.

4. The Masters and the Mistresses are to be Members of the Church of England.

5. A Report on the state and progress of the Schools is to be made, at Christmas in every year, to the Diocesan Board, the District Society, or the National Society; and the Schools are, with the consent of the Managers, to be periodically inspected by persons appointed either by the Bishop of the Diocese, the National Society, or the Diocesan Board of Education.

6. In case any difference should arise between the Parochial Clergy and the Managers of the Schools with reference to the preceding Rules, respect-

I return to the antecedents.

In 1811—12, a Sub-Committee of the General Committee of the Society, including Mr. Norris and Mr. Watson, drew up and presented a Report which, after being con-

ing the religious instruction of Scholars, or any regulation connected therewith, an appeal is to be made to the Bishop of the Diocese, whose decision is to be final.

Signed,

Dated, 18

To be signed either by the Minister and Managers in conjunction, or by the Minister alone, *stating that he is sole Manager;* or by the Minister alone, declaring that he is empowered to sign both for himself and for the Managers."

"*Form of Certificate to be filled up and signed when application is made on account of Infant Schools.*

We, the undersigned, being desirous of connecting the Infant School for the benefit of the poor at (or to be established at)   in the County of   and Diocese of   with the NATIONAL SOCIETY, do hereby certify that the Education in such School is to be conducted on the principles of the Established Church, and by Masters and Mistresses who are Members of the same :—and we further declare that we shall be ready to report upon the state and progress of the School from time to time, in the manner usually pursued by National Schools.

Signed by the Managers of the Infant Schools, ...
Countersigned by the Parochial Minister, ...

Dated, 18

N.B.—When a Grant in aid of Building an Infant School-room is solicited from the funds of the National Society, and there is not any *Sunday* or *Sunday and Daily* School in the Parish or District, it is required, as a condition of such Grant, that the INFANT SCHOOL-ROOM shall be used for the Instruction of older Children on the Lord's day, until a separate National School-room shall have been provided; and in this case an application for the Union of such Sunday School must accompany the above Certificate.

In the absence of the Incumbent of the Parish, it is requested that the Officiating Minister who signs the above will state whether the Incumbent approves of the application for Union.

NATIONAL SOCIETY'S OFFICE,
Sanctuary, Westminster."

In 1870-1, the Paper following was added to the documents of the Society. I am given to understand, that the purpose of it was to provide against the transfer of schools in union to a School Board. I am bound to say that I do not see in what distinct, specific and absolute way it does so provide. But if it did, the matter in hand is, not the transfer of a School in union to a School Board, but, of what exact character the School in union is in accordance with the Charter and Terms of Union.

sidered and amended by the General Committee, was finally adopted Jan. 29, 1812.

In that Report we find the words following:—

"*The Committee of the National Society have no desire to dictate to the promoters of Schools the terms on which their Trust Deeds shall be drawn up. All that the Committee require is, that a Clause should be inserted in the usual form, providing for the union of the School with the Society.*"

MANAGEMENT CLAUSE I.

And it is hereby declared that the said School shall always be in union with, and conducted according to the principles, and in furtherance of the ends and designs of the incorporated National Society for Promoting the Education of the Poor in the Principles of the Established Church throughout England and Wales. Provided always, and it is hereby declared that the said [Trustees] shall, and may from time to time, and at any time hereafter, with the consent, and at the request of the National Society for Promoting the Education of the Poor in the Principles of the Established Church throughout England and Wales, testified by writing under their Common Seal, but not otherwise, grant or convey for educational purposes, but not otherwise, to any body corporate or bodies corporate, or person authorized by law to accept the same, the whole of the estate or interest hereby vested in them, or any smaller interest in the said School, in such manner and upon such terms as the said Society shall as aforesaid direct. { *Society's Union Clause.* } { *Added since 1870.* } And subject to the declaration aforesaid, the said School, and the funds and endowments thereof, and the selection, appointment, and dismissal of the School Teachers and their Assistants shall be in all respects under the management and control of a Committee*, to consist of the Minister for the time being of the said Parish or Ecclesiastical District of   , his licensed Curate, or Curates, if the said Minister shall appoint him or them to be a member or members of the said Committee, the Churchwardens of the said Parish, if members of the Established Church, and of
other persons being members of the Established Church, and subscribers of not less than 10*s*. annually to the funds of the said School; and any vacancy which may occur in the said Committee by death, resignation, or otherwise, of any of the aforesaid other persons, shall be filled up by the nomination, on the part of the continuing or surviving members, of another person or persons, being *bonâ fide* a member or members of the Established Church: Provided always, that the religious instruction to be given in the said Schools, and the entire control and management of any Sunday School held in School premises, shall be vested in the said Minister for the time being, or, in his absence, in the officiating Minister. And in case any dispute or difference

---

* It is to be noted here that it is *assumed throughout* that there will always be a Committee of Management. So that the case of a school in which the Minister is *sole manager*, as distinctly recognised by the Terms of Union, (see p. 138, l. 9,) being the precise case contended for by myself and others at the Annual Meetings, is left out in the cold to take care of itself.

"That the Society itself being instituted principally for educating the Poor in the doctrine and discipline of the Established Church, according to the excellent Liturgy and Catechism provided for that purpose, it is required that all the children received into these schools be, *without exception*[m], instructed in this Liturgy and Catechism; and that, in conformity with the directions in that Liturgy, the children of each school do constantly attend Divine Service in the Parish Church, or other place of public worship under the Establishment, &c."

Concurrently with the formation of the Society in London, a number of diocesan and district societies were formed in various parts of the kingdom.

I observe in the account of the formation of two of these societies, Devon and Winchester, the words, "for the united purposes of educating the children of parents of all denominations."

I have not been able to find these words in any record of "the National Society."

But, supposing them to be found there, I observe first, that they are as nothing in the face of the distinct and express provisions touching the teaching and the attendance at public worship of "*all the children received into these schools without exception.*"

And second, that the utmost they can be taken to amount to, is that the idea of the founders of the National

shall arise, on any matter respecting the religious instruction given in the said School, an appeal may be made to the Bishop of the Diocese, whose decision in writing upon the matter in dispute shall be final and conclusive, and binding upon all parties."

[m] In an authoritative statement kindly communicated to me this year from the office of the National Society, I read that, in the report of 1813, the words "without exception" are omitted. Two reasons are assigned for the omission, as giving a probable account of it. 1. That though Infant Schools were not then contemplated, some children might be too young, and therefore require to be "excepted;" or 2. because the expression "all, without exception," was tautological.

I am disposed to believe that neither of these reasons presents the true account of the omission. It looks to me much more like "stealing a march," when defenders were absent or dozing. And I am confirmed in this view by finding that in the Charter of 1817, four years after, the words stand in their proper place.

Society, and their construing of its provisions, extended to the "missionary character" of schools in union; that is to say, that children received into such schools, if not Church children already by Baptism, were to be instructed and cared for throughout, with the express object of their becoming Church children.

Here then we have, ascertained by reference to its own documents, and to the interpretation of them by its founders, "the stand-point of the National Society."

This being the STAND-POINT, what *has been* for many years, and what *is* now the POSITION of the National Society?

Can the POSITION be identified with the STAND-POINT? I say that it cannot. The Charter and the Terms of Union retain their distinctly exclusive "Church" character; the position of the Society cannot be so described. The Society retains also its title; it is still entitled, "The National Society for promoting the Education of the Poor in the Principles of the Established Church." Does it promote "the Education of the Poor in the Principles of the Established Church?" I say that it does not.

I say more, I say that decay of "Education of the Poor in the Principles of the Established Church," lies at the door much more of "the National Society," than even at the door of the Civil Power. For those who hold truth, and profess to make it their primary rule, but conduct themselves as though it were, not primary, but secondary, always do more mischief in the world than those who openly assail truth.

When we come to analyse the position, the result is this,—that "Education" having a religious and a secular element, the order of it is, that the religious element is always, under all trials and difficulties, the principal, guiding, controlling, and everywhere pervading element; the secular, everywhere the secondary and subordinate element.

The temptation is to reverse this order; the temptation has prevailed : the (so-called) "exigencies" of the temporal life have had greater power than the requirements of the spiritual life ; have exacted first, a division of time and attention, in itself necessarily fatal to "Education ;" and second, have exacted for themselves by far the larger share of time and attention.

Then, again, there has been the working of this very fatal fallacy, that whereas the differences between Rome and England are vital, the differences between the Church of England and the sects are not vital. I know of no more transparent fallacy than this, and yet it fits into the common English mind so well, that it has come to be taken as Truth itself; and you find high authorities, ecclesiastical and civil, ministering to its growth and practical development.

The temptation and fallacy in conjunction, began to "do their proper work" early in the history of "the National Society ;" and the accredited position of the Society remaining the same as it has been from the first, the practice of some Managers of schools in union in various parts of the country, with the acquiescence, if not the direct encouragement of the Managers of the Society, episcopal and other, paved the way for the triumph of the temptation and the fallacy. The order of "Education" was reversed ; the secular element became primary and governing, the religious element secondary and subordinate. And the perpetual giving way in respect of the first principles of the National Society, as representing in the matter of "Education" (during the abeyance of the Synods of the Church) the Church of England, has issued by successive and natural steps, as it only could issue,—

1. in the Management Clauses ;
2. in the Conscience Clause ;
3. in the Time Table Conscience Clause ;
4. in quasi Church schools ;
5. in the Education Rate ;
6. in the School Board.

The principle of the Act of 1870 is the School Board ; a thing in its conception and its execution irreligious.

England will see School Boards everywhere, as England deserves to see; when the very feeble barriers that for a time stop, or rather I should say, appear to stop the way, are broken down, and swept out of the course as it marches along.

I know of no instance in which the British rate-payer has paid in a few years so largely for a thoroughly bad article, as in the instance of the School Board. I often wonder how long the payment will go on; at present, it increases steadily year by year.

I am bound to add that what is commonly called now a "Church school,"—what I call a "quasi Church school," —is even a worse article than the School Board School, on this ground; that a thing, about the real character and operation of which there is no disguise, is less mischievous than a thing, about the real character and operation of which there is every disguise.

I return to the summary of details of the conflict, as these have formed part of my personal experience.

It requires no argument to shew, that the stand-point of the Civil Power could not possibly be made to coincide with the stand-point of the National Society, which was, not simply prior in point of time but, diametrically opposed to it in point of principle. That, therefore, negotiation between the two must of necessity issue in the affirmation and application of one principle, to the abnegation and exclusion of the other.

It was abundantly plain from the first, that the Civil Power would not recede from its stand-point by so much as a hair's breadth. All the powers of the world were on its side, as was also the "Establishmentarian" Power.

It was equally plain that the National Society could not recede from its stand-point so much as a hair's breadth without violation of its own principles, as set out in its own Charter; that its obligation and duty to the Church was this, that so soon as conditions of pecuniary assistance out of the Parliamentary Grant were finally insisted upon by the Committee of Council administering such Grant, such conditions being incompatible with adherence to the letter and spirit of the Charter, to break off all relations between itself and the Civil Power, and to throw itself upon the alms of the Church.

Under these circumstances of the time, being unable to find any indication that the Committee of the Society would adopt this course, I felt myself called to endeavour—in conjunction with the Bishop, and many of the Clergy and Laity of this Diocese; with the Church Unions; with members of the National Society in other Dioceses; and with some of the oldest members of the Committee of the National Society itself[a]—to press the truth and exigencies of the position upon the Committee of the Society. The endeavour dates from April, 1847.

I will anticipate here the answer to a remark which has often been made to me, in the sense that I have pressed these things unduly, and that the proof that I have done so, lies in the large increase, since 1840, of schools in connection with the National Society.

It is a characteristic of my countrymen, that there is hardly a question of any kind which they are not in the habit of testing by numbers *pro* and *con*.

And if my endeavours had been concerned with the *quantity* of schools, I should not have had much to say. But as it was wholly concerned with the *quality* of schools, I do not see what the increase in numbers has to do with it. The difficulty is not the covering the country with schools; the difficulty is, the covering the country with " Church schools;" aye, and the preserving to schools already in existence their Church character. You may teach a hundred children where you taught one before; but it does not follow that the teaching of the hundred is worth so much as the teaching of the one.

---

[a] Particularly the Rev. H. H. Norris, a principal founder of the Society. I went to see him by his own request, and had afterwards a large correspondence with him: our judgment upon the position was throughout the same. I had also the concurrence of Mr. Joshua Watson.

It is further said, that the specific claim which I have insisted upon in behalf of the Church school, as against the Civil Power in respect of the Management Clauses, is a claim which cannot reasonably be insisted upon.

This is very easy to say; but when the claim comes to be looked into a little, and dealt with *as it is*, and not as it may suit the politician or the mere Establishmentarian to represent it, it will appear to be not only reasonable, but in exact accordance with first principles of justice and of equity. It will further appear that, as respects the manner of insisting upon it, this is most moderate.

I proceed to demonstrate both these points.

The State comes forward offering to help Churchmen and others towards building schools.

That it is the duty of the State to annex conditions to its assistance, I have never disputed. The whole question is *what conditions?*

There are two necessary and legitimate conditions; and two only:—

1. That the site be legally secured.
2. That it be ascertained, from time to time as the State may appoint, that the school built with its assistance is used for the purposes stated at the time when the application for assistance was made.

This is the whole amount of legitimate condition; anything beyond this, direct or indirect, goes to put the State in the position of dictating to founders of what character the school shall be as the price of assistance towards building it. If the dictation be accepted, the foundation, in its essential nature, passes out of the hands of the founder or founders, into the hands of the State; and it becomes easy for the State to use the school for its own loose purposes, in place of the strict purposes of the founders.

Now, whatever may have been said thirty years ago, when the attempt to "utilise" Church schools for secular purposes was in its earlier infancy, about the "good intentions" of the State, he must be a bold man, and not a very scrupulous or a very wise one, who ventures upon the subject of these "good intentions" now. The flimsy veil which it was convenient to interpose for a few years, having served its purpose, is thrown away, and the purpose of the State in first "recommending," and finally "insisting upon," the Management Clauses stands out in all its native and original deformity.

The purpose was to get the parish school out of the hands of the parish priest. This was the first step necessary towards the ulterior object of latitudinarianising the school, of making it a nursery of Indifferentism instead of the Catholic Faith. This step once taken and secured, all the rest became easy.

Now my claim, and the claim of those who for a few years supported, and then, upon one ground or another, deserted me, was that it is the founders of a school, Church or other, who are the judges of what the character of a school shall be; and that the State has nothing on earth to do with that character, provided always the character be not criminal; and therefore that when the site and the application of the money granted to the purposes for which it was asked were secured, the legitimate action of the State terminated absolutely.

Of course, this conclusion would not have suited the founders of the Committee of Council at all. But, I apprehend that that makes nothing against the reasonableness, justice, equity of the conclusion. If the State wanted to make itself, in all its Indifferentism, the Educator of the People instead of the Church and the sects, the State should have said so. It did want to make itself the Educator, but it was not convenient to say it. By holding its tongue, it succeeded in deluding all classes step by step, till the time came when it could make itself Educator, and say all it meant from the first.

This "holding the tongue" is a chief part of diplomacy. I remember long ago, in the old Oxford time, a man who held a college living with his fellowship, and had been married some years.

A friend said to him, "Why, how have you managed to be married and hold your fellowship?"

He said, "Any man may hold anything so long as he holds his tongue."

The Committee of Council people held their tongue sufficiently for their purpose. English people are very easy to take in: occasionally the Committee or its Secretary were betrayed into incautious language by exultation at the rapid success of the plot, and by their contempt for the shallowness and feebleness of their opponents; but they held their tongue sufficiently, and they "have their reward."

For the moderation of the manner of my claim, I never proposed to interfere with the liberty of my brethren who liked to be servants and instruments of the Committee of Council; to take their clauses and their wages and to do their work, consciously or unconsciously. All I said was, Let there be liberty for those of us who do not find these things pleasant things, who find them against their conscience, against their duty to the Church; who do not want to be held up with entire justice to coming generations, as aiders and abettors in the plot for destroying "Church Education" in England, either as ignorant and silly people, or as knowing and evil-minded people. All I said was, Let not the English Churchmen whose heart and mind and endeavour is to set forth the Church of England as she is, be the only people in England who are ridden over and trampled upon, and cheated of their proper share of the "Education Grant."

I think I have demonstrated the reasonableness, the justice, and the equity of my claim on the part of the Church; and also the moderation of the manner of it. That this was the opinion of the late Lord Derby and his Government in 1852, is matter of public record. I shall have to advert to this farther on. Meantime, I adduce it here in evidence. That nothing came of this opinion of the Government and of the assurance, or rather I should say the pledge, given to me in the summer of that year, makes no difference as to the fact of the opinion. Lord Derby's Government proposed to give me something, not much, in respect of the Management Clauses. Upon the faith of that proposal I acted, with the general concurrence of all concerned, at the Annual Meeting of the Society in 1852; giving up a strong vantage-ground, without, in the end, receiving in exchange what I had been prepared to receive. Looking back upon all that passed, I have no word to say but in acknowledgment of truth and kindliness of purpose on the part of the Government. But they undertook, and I accepted, what in the face of the "Liberal" majority there was no reasonable prospect of carrying through Parliament. It seems to me now to have been a mistake on both sides. But, as in the six months that followed, support on our side melted away under the influence of the active opposition which I had no choice but to give to Mr. Gladstone's re-election for Oxford University, January, 1853, the mistake left the position very much where it would have been without it.

At the close of 1853, I published a letter to my dear and honoured friend Christopher Wordsworth, then Canon of Westminster, now Bishop of Lincoln[*]. That letter was written when all the history of the controversy for the six years next preceding was fresh in my recollection; and as it presents a *resumé* in its substance complete, and only here and there requires illustration, I cannot do better than reprint all such part of it as falls into its proper place in my "Notes."

A LETTER, &c.

My dear Wordsworth,

I address the first portion of this letter to yourself, for a reason which appears upon the face of the letter. The latter portion

---

[*] "The Position and Prospects of 'The National Society for the Education of the Poor in the Principles of the Established Church.' A Letter addressed to the Rev. Canon Wordsworth, D.D., and to the Schoolmasters of the Parish Schools of the Church of England, with Appendix upon the preparation and examination of Candidates for Holy Orders. By George Anthony Denison, M.A., Archdeacon of Taunton." (London: Joseph Masters, Aldersgate and New Bond-street, 1853.)

of it is more immediately addressed to the Schoolmasters of the Church of England[p].

There may be statements and conclusions in the letter in which you do not concur; other statements and conclusions, again, which you deprecate. It is almost needless to say, that the mere fact of publicly addressing this letter to you, does not make you responsible, in any degree, for any portion of its contents. I address it to you, because you were my earliest coadjutor in an attempt, in which, after a struggle of six years, I have been *wholly, finally* and *irrecoverably* defeated.

When, in 1848, I first endeavoured to oppose, by way of Resolution, the policy of the Committee of Council on "Education," you consented, at my request, to second the Resolution which I was about to move at the Annual Meeting of the National Society for that year.

I reprint the Resolution here, with its preamble, containing a summary of the reasons advanced by myself in support of the Resolution.

"Seeing,

- "1. That there is no room for doubt as to what are the views of Government in respect of the future character and constitution of Church Schools.
- "2. That the success of these views is irreconcileable with the maintenance of Church teaching and discipline.
- "3. That the Church has already had large experience of an aggressive policy.
- "4. That the method and means of carrying out the views of the Government are in contravention of the two principles upon which they professed to base the administration of the 'Education' grant; viz.:—
    - "1st. The abstaining from all interference, direct or indirect, with the constitution and management of *any* school.
    - "2nd. Absolute equality and impartiality.
- "5. That the Church *must stop at some point;* and that it is far better to contend in the outset for a principle, than virtually to surrender it, and attempt to supply its place by any arrangement of details.

---

[p] I omit this portion of the Letter. It seems to me a mockery now to ask the Schoolmaster to stand in the breach, when Bishop, Priest, Deacon, Communicant and Churchwarden have run away.

"It is resolved,—

"That it is the opinion of this meeting, that no arrangement, which shall involve the compulsory imposition of any management clause whatever, as a condition of State assistance, or of any condition whatever, except the legal tenure of the site and the right of inspection, as defined and ascertained in 1840, can be satisfactory to, or ought to be accepted by, the Church."

The gist of this Resolution is to affirm the true position of members of the Church of England, *Clergy and Laity*, when applying to the State of England for assistance towards building schools, not as a matter of abstract principle or theoretical right, but as bearing immediately, practically, and powerfully upon the great question—

WITH WHOM DOES IT ULTIMATELY REST TO DECIDE WHAT SHALL BE THE CONSTITUTION AND MANAGEMENT OF THE PAROCHIAL SCHOOLS OF THE CHURCH OF ENGLAND—WITH THE CHURCH OF ENGLAND, OR WITH THE GOVERNMENT OF ENGLAND, *representing and reflecting divers interests and influences, many of them alien from, and hostile to, the Church of England?*

The words which I have printed in italics are the expression of a most important element of the above question, one too obvious to be overlooked by any one who considers the matter, but one, nevertheless, which for all practical purposes has been very generally overlooked.

If the Government of England had been identified with the Church of England, as in other days, there would have been no attempt on the part of Government to interfere with the duties and responsibilities of the Church, and particularly with those of the Clergy, as the divinely-commissioned teachers of the people. Being no longer identified with the Church, the Government, not unnaturally, seeks to make the requirements of the Church fall in with, and adapt themselves to, the altered position of things. It makes no difference to a Government *so constituted* that this *cannot be done*, except at the expense of the principles of the Church, because it is an element of a Government *so constituted* that it has no real regard for, and is not bound by, the principles of the Church.

But though Government could no longer, from the inherent vice of its own constitution—*a vice every year more and more developed*—deal with the Church of England as the one teacher of the People, still it could not but be very desirous to avail itself of the vast machinery ready to its hand in the parochial schools; *provided only* it could so influence and ultimately alter the character of these schools as to suit its own views and purposes; *provided only*, that is, *that it could succeed in converting the parochial schools of* THE CATHOLIC CHURCH *of England into schools of the " Broad Church of Englishmen."*

In using this language, I am not imputing *bad motives* to any one. It was only natural that Government should do as it did, and *as it is doing still;* the only difference between *then* and *now* is, that the policy is a good deal more boldly and openly avowed; as is commonly the case when men find that *they have all things their own way*. But I am not imputing *bad motives* to any one. If a member of a Cabinet be not a Churchman, he cannot be expected to care for Church principles. If he be only half a Churchman, his care for them cannot be expected to be of any consistent kind. If, being a Churchman, he subordinate his care for Church principles to political and party considerations, this is blameworthy. But I wish to be understood as not imputing conduct of this description to any member of the present or of late Governments. It is quite enough to have to resist men's acts, without adding to the burthen by assailing their motives. Neither am I assailing the motives of that large number of my brethren, the Clergy,—whether Bishops, Priests, or Deacons,—who have opposed me in this matter. Nor, again, the motives of that larger number still who have to all appearance taken no interest in it. I cannot hesitate to say *in words*, what I have said *in the acts* of six years, that for the Clergy to have dealt with this question as the great majority of them have dealt with it, has been one of the worst and most fatal mistakes they ever made. For they have—as it would seem, without knowing it—transferred the charge of the school teaching of the children of the Church from themselves to a department of Government—a Government which has *no Creed*. Nor can I refrain from saying plainly that, while it is *only natural* for any Government of England, constituted as English Governments are now, in the palmy days of that most absurd, if, indeed, it be not blasphemous, watchword, "Civil and religious liberty," to deal with the Church, and with all that concerns the Church, in a loose and latitudinarian way, it is *not natural* to the Clergy of the Church to stand by and see this done, and not so much as to make one sign. However, the thing *is done*, and it remains only to pray that the consequences be not measured by the neglect, or by the want of faithfulness *in act ;* I do not say *in purpose*.

With the anticipations of evil, which I have above stated, pressing heavily on my mind, I set myself to resist the first overt act by which Government renewed the attempt originally made in 1839, to establish a system of school teaching throughout the country, of which system the Government and not the Church,—*no, not even so far as her own schools were concerned,* —should, *ultimately*, have the effectual control. The *form* of the attempt was that of making the acceptance of certain Management Clauses framed by the then Secretary of the Committee of Council on "Education," a necessary condition of a building grant.

The danger was imminent; the mischief incalculable, as the result has already proved; and the only opportunity which presented itself for submitting the matter to any public and formal consideration was supplied by the Annual Meeting of the National Society.

Now, it is said, the National Society is not the Church. True enough; but those who make the remark, meaning by it that the Annual Meetings of the Society are not the proper places for discussing such questions as the above, appear to forget, 1st. That in the abeyance of Synods, Church Societies become, very unfortunately, as I think, but doubtless, very unavoidably, Committees upon various Church matters. 2. That these Societies are so dealt with by Government. 3. That Government could hardly do otherwise in the case of the National Society, seeing that its Committee includes all the Bishops *ex officio*, and that it has been incorporated by Royal Charter, "for the Education of the Poor in the Principles of the Established Church," AND FOR NOTHING ELSE.

Again it is said, that the government of the Society is by its Charter vested in the Committee; and the meaning of this remark is, as the Bishop of London put it very broadly at the Annual Meeting of the present year, that it is not for the members present at the Annual Meetings to interfere in any way, whether by remonstrance, suggestion, or advice. Now really, considering that the Society is *wholly* dependent for its resources upon the voluntary contributions of its members, it is a somewhat strange assumption, at least here in England, that when members see that the money they have given themselves, and have asked others to give, for one specific purpose, is in danger of being applied to a *wholly different* purpose, they are not to be at liberty to say a word upon the matter. Does the Bishop really suppose that voluntary contributions will long abound upon such an understanding as this? I say a "wholly different" purpose, because the "purpose" of the Committee of Council, and the "purpose" of the "National Society for the Education of the Poor in the Principles of the Established Church," *are* "wholly different;" and it is almost too plain *already* to require even to be stated, much less proved, that the *ultimate destination* of all money now and henceforth given to the National Society is only to subserve the carrying out the "purposes" of the Committee of Council. THE NATIONAL SOCIETY HAS BY ITS OWN ACT MADE ITSELF A SUBORDINATE AGENCY OF THE COMMITTEE OF COUNCIL. Now there are those, even amongst ourselves, who labour, *Sisyphi more*, to shew that the purpose of the National Society, and of the Committee of Council, is *one and the same* purpose. *It may be so*, if the Catholic Church be *one and the same* with the "Broad Church."

The difficulties in our way in 1848, in respect of the adoption of the Resolution, were very great; arising as well out of other considerations not necessary to mention here, as out of the skill with which Government had combined the obnoxious imposition of the Management Clauses with the proposal of annual grants of various kinds to be made to Church and other schools.

However, we made the attempt; and the Resolution in which I expressed what appeared to me then, *and appears to me now*, to be the only course fitting for the meeting to pursue on behalf of the Church, in so far as it could be said to act in behalf of the Church, was, as I have stated, seconded by yourself.

I moved the Resolution in the hope that it might lay the foundation of some steady and consistent endeavour, on the part of the National Society, to vindicate and preserve from reproach the Catholic character of the Church of England, in respect of the duty and responsibility of her Clergy in the great matter of bringing up her children in her own Faith. This is what I proposed to myself in moving the Resolution; *this and nothing less*. Nothing of any minor or inferior importance, no consideration less broad and vital, would have stirred me to move at all, or to incur the thankless toil, expense, obloquy, and estrangement of six weary years.

For I saw then, I believe as clearly as I see it now, after six years of rapid and almost uninterrupted advance and successful aggression by the Committee of Council on "Education," that if the claim *then* set up on the part of that Committee, in respect of the Management Clauses, were once established, and free scope given to its energies, and its various means and powers of *persuasion*, it would not be many years, at most, before we should see the control of the school-teaching of the country,— *as far, at least, as the Church of England is concerned, for the Roman Catholics and Dissenters take better care of themselves,*— in such sort and to such extent, brought under the direct and indirect influence of the Committee of Council; that the due exercise of the office of the Parochial Clergy in this particular, and by necessary consequence in divers other particulars, would be very generally superseded, and degenerate into *a subordinate agency of a State department.*

I speak principally of the Clergy, because the Clergy are directly and solely responsible for all that is taught in the parish schools; for the matter and the manner of it. For the Clergy are, in virtue of their Office, the "dispensers of the Word of GOD and of His Holy Sacraments;" and it is upon the Word of GOD, and upon His Holy Sacraments, that all Christian Education, in any true sense of the word, must be based, as it is by the due employment of the same great gifts of GOD that it must be guided, extended, and, so far as is possible in this life, perfected.

Now, to admit the principle of the general supervision and control of the Clergy, would have been fatal to the views and purposes of the Committee of Council. Perhaps it was too much to expect *them* to realize the idea. However, as it presented great difficulties, and placed serious hindrances in their way, they invented a distinction between "religious" and "secular" instruction, which has since become very popular, whereby it seemed possible to undermine, and finally to remove the hindrance altogether.

Of this notable distinction I need not say much here,—*it is unknown to the Church Catholic.* Out of it have sprung *such things* as the Irish National School System, and the "Queen's Colleges." Its principle is aptly expressed in some memorable words of a leading article in the "Times" of September, 1853, in which we read of its being "*possible to tone down even the Bible itself to a judicious neutrality.*"

I am no lover of Roman Catholicism, but I will say that I thank the Roman Catholic Bishops with all my heart, for the stand which they are making against a principle which begins with unsettling, and ends with destroying, for all whom it may be allowed to pervade and imbue, the Catholic Faith.

The Resolution of 1848 having been moved, seconded, and discussed, was withdrawn, that its adoption might not *embarrass negotiations then pending between the Committee of the Society and the Committee of Council.* These negotiations had no satisfactory issue; the utmost that was gained by them in the end, during the succeeding twelve months, being some points of detail; and points of detail, however valuable in themselves, become valueless, or *worse*, when they are grafted upon a system of which the principle is radically vicious.

At the Annual Meeting, therefore, of 1849, having previously endeavoured to lay the true state of the case before the Church at large, by a Memorial addressed to the Committee of the National Society, and afterwards published, as well as by other publications, I again moved *the same* Resolution, and it was again seconded by yourself.

The Resolution was upon the point of being carried by the vast majority of the Meeting, when unhappy influences, acting through one who has ceased to be a member of the Church of England, were brought to bear upon the Meeting; and I was only able to save, in any degree, the principle for which we were contending, by insisting upon the addition of a clause at the end of *an unmeaning and worthless amendment.*

The negotiations continued down to December 11, 1849, when they were finally closed by the following letter :—

"*National Society's Office, December* 11*th,* 1849.

"SIR,—I am instructed by the Committee of the National Society, to express to the Committee of Council on Education, their conviction of the propriety of terminating their correspondence on the subject of the Management Clauses.

"The Committee of the National Society deeply regret the resolution finally adopted by the Committee of Council, to exclude from all share of the Parliamentary Grant for Education those Church Schools, the promoters of which are unwilling to constitute their Trust-deeds on the model prescribed by their Lordships. The Committee are by no means insensible to the value of the modifications which have been adopted at their suggestion; but so long as this resolution is maintained, they cannot acquiesce in the hope expressed by their Lordships, that the most material causes of difference between the Society and the Committee of Council are removed.

"The Committee of the National Society entered on the present negotiation from an earnest desire—a desire which they still retain—to act in concert with their Lordships; and to secure this end, were ready to acquiesce in any measure consistent with the principle which they have always maintained, that local views and feelings are to be studiously consulted.

"But since the Committee now find, to their deep regret and disappointment, that if they are to co-operate with their Lordships in constituting school-trusts, they must be prepared to set aside the general principle of local freedom, and to treat the proposed clauses as indispensable to the efficiency of all Church-schools, they consider themselves under the necessity of resuming their original position. Leaving, therefore, to the Legislature the settlement of the terms on which the Parliamentary vote shall be distributed, they see no other course for themselves, under existing circumstances, than to continue to vote Grants according to the Charter of the Society; and without joining in any recommendation of Management Clauses, to leave the promoters of schools either to adopt, or to decline, the proposed Government Clauses, provided they constitute their schools in a manner consistent with the Society's terms of Union.

"I have the honour to be, Sir,
"Your obedient Servant,
"JOHN G. LONSDALE, *Secretary.*

"*To the Secretary,.*
"*Committee of Council on Education.*"

Did, then, the Committee of the National Society, who thought the refusal of that claim for liberty, for which we had contended, so important, that they broke off all negotiation, and closed the correspondence in consequence of that refusal; did the Committee of the National Society take *any* step to bring their case before Parliament; did they shew *any sign* of an anxiety to procure redress of a grievance which they themselves declared to be so great? There is no evidence of any attempt or anxiety of the kind, *but the reverse.* They appear to have satisfied themselves with writing the letter, and to have considered that by writing it they had washed their hands of a very troublesome and inconvenient business. Now the effect of this way of dealing with the matter was simply to say to all parties concerned, and who were looking anxiously to the Committee of the National Society for some steady and consistent defence of Church principles, We have done all we can, i.e., *we have written a letter;* and now we advise you to do as the Committee of Council on Education bids you. It is true that our letter says we advise no such thing; it is true that it expresses great regret and dissatisfaction on account of the injustice done you, but as we see *no objection* to your taking the Management Clauses of the Committee of Council, *and do not intend to apply to "the Legislature" for any redress on behalf of those of you who* CANNOT *take them, our non-advising may not unreasonably be regarded in the light of a recommendation.*

That this is *the true interpretation*, and has been *the effect* of the letter of December 11, 1849, coupled with the subsequent acquiescence in, or, more properly speaking, *approval* of the policy and the acts of the Committee of Council by the Committee of the National Society, is too plain to require to be proved. My conclusion then is that, from the date of that letter, *the National Society became, by its own act, a subordinate agency of the Committee of Council on "Education."*

But, it will be said, the Committee of the National Society, in their letter of December 11, 1849, speak of "resuming their original position."

Now it happens very commonly that a statement represents accurately enough a certain fact in the history of an individual, or of a public body; but that all their subsequent history does not only *nullify* that fact, but converts it into a fact of *the exactly opposite description*.

This is *curiously* and *particularly* instanced in the case under review.

Since December 11, 1849, the position of the Committee of the National Society has, neither *affirmatively* nor *negatively*, been their "original position."

Not *affirmatively*, because they have, since that time, *done absolutely nothing of any kind*, towards establishing the justice of their case as against the aggressive policy of the Committee of Council; not *negatively*, because they have, since that time, *done everything in their power*, almost indeed ostentatiously, to shew that they are *in effect at one with* the Committee of Council, notwithstanding the signal defeat they had sustained, on the part of the Church, *upon a great principle*, one which is, in fact, however it may be misrepresented or disguised, *the turning-point* of the whole question between the Committee of Council on "Education" and the Church of England.

These considerations appear to me effectually to dispose of any force which might *once* have attached to the statement of the Committee, that they "resumed their original position."

The events of succeeding years have established the fact of the new position. It was not so much manifested in 1850, when the attention of Churchmen was greatly distracted by the judgment of the Privy Council in the Gorham case; i.e. by an attempt to persuade the Church of England that she has no Doctrine of the Sacraments; but at the Annual Meeting of 1851, the fruit of the "laisser aller" course, taken by the Committee of the National Society, was displayed in its full maturity.

In the winter of 1851, came the renewed assault of the Bishop of Manchester upon one of the terms of union of that Society, in which he is, *ex officio*, a member of Committee. This assault was all in the sense of the Committee of Council; a great step indeed *onwards;* because it was transferring the war from the outposts to the centre of the camp.

When I saw the assault made, it appeared to me that our opponents had placed a weapon in our hands with which, if we could not recover the ground so unnecessarily and so hopelessly lost upon the Management Clauses, we might, at least, ward off all *direct* injury to the teaching and discipline of the Church. Accordingly, I gave notice of a Resolution on the subject of the teaching of the Catechism to all scholars in the schools of the Church; as well as of a Resolution expressing regret that Government should still refuse our demand for liberty to constitute our schools in any way allowed by the Church, without forfeiting thereby a building grant. In this way, I hoped to provide for a continued Protest on the part of the National Society, against the injustice of the State, and to guard against *direct* injury to the school-teaching and discipline of the Church.

I was thankful to obtain the assistance of Mr. Keble in the matter of the teaching of the Catechism; his memorial was laid before the Committee of the Society and favourably received, and this matter *was supposed* to be in train towards some satisfactory conclusion.

Meantime, Lord Derby's Government had discovered that it was quite true what we had all along maintained, viz., that the Clergy and Laity of the Church of England were placed at a great disadvantage, in respect of liberty to provide for the constitution and management of their schools, relatively to the Clergy and Laity of the Church of Rome; and the Minute of June 12, 1852, was framed to correct this inequality.

It was the first instance of anything like so much as a disposition, on the part of the Committee of Council, to deal fairly by the Clergy and Laity of the Church of England,—*and it has been the last*.

It was small redress, indeed, when set side by side with the demand for liberty; and I was very careful to say as much at the Annual Meeting of 1852. But, as it was an indication of a disposition to do justice; on *this* ground, with the cordial approval of all with whom I had acted for many years, I thankfully accepted it in the spirit in which it appeared to be given.

However, the Annual Meeting was hardly over, when Lord Derby declared in his place in Parliament his intention of "suspending" the Minute.

It has since been "cancelled" by the present Government; and a Minute substituted for it which has effectually demolished the only fragment of justice ever dispensed in connection with the Management Clauses by the Committee of Council on "Education" to the Church of England, *and has re-placed the Church* of Rome in her former position of greater liberty.

It has suited the friends of Lord Aberdeen's Government to represent the Minute of June 12, 1852, as less even than a fragment of justice. I suppose, in order to do away, if possible, with the blame which so justly attaches to that Government for cancelling it. The representation is *unworthy*, because it is *untrue*. I am, however, well content that they should ridicule the act of giving it on Monday, as a means of purchasing *peace*, and taking it away on Friday, when it was no longer wanted for that purpose.

The cancelling of the Minute of June 12, 1852, has finally settled the whole Management Clause controversy in the sense of the Committee of Council.

Who is to blame for this? I answer, The Committee of the National Society are *principally* to blame for it.

Are any others to blame? Yes. All those members of the Society and others, who once supported me in making the demand for liberty, but who have, for some time past, deserted me.

The movement, like all other movements of what is called "the High Church party," which I have witnessed, has been one of *restlessness*, rather than *strength*; as has been well remarked to me of the movement for the revival of Convocation. Men seem to take up causes, great, and having to do with things sacred, and to lay them down again, after a while, as if they were playthings.

If twenty "High Churchmen" come together *now* to consult upon any grave question of Church interest, the chances are that they *divide*, in about the proportion of nine to eleven: first, as to whether *anything* shall be done; second, as to *what* shall be done; third, as to *how* it shall be done.

Some twelve hundred persons were present at the Meeting at Willis's Room, in February, 1850. Clergy of all orders, and a large proportion of Laity. I do not believe that there were twenty persons in the room who were not distinctly and emphatically in favour of the Resolutions passed by the meeting.

Those Resolutions were all of them expository of, or subsidiary to, the claim for "liberty" set forth in the Resolution moved by me in 1848 and 1849.

The Bishop of Chichester having undertaken, shortly after, to bring the matter before the House of Lords, and to ask for an inquiry; and the debate having been adjourned for a week; in the space of six days 1,270 petitions, numbering upwards of 12,000 signatures of Clergy and Laity, were received, and placed in the Bishop's hands for presentation to the House of Lords.

These petitions were all of them in the sense of the Resolution of 1848-9.

Now, those Members of the Church of England, Clergy and Laity, who felt so deeply aggrieved in 1850,—not for their own, but for THE CHURCH's sake,—*have received no redress; no, not a particle of redress; they have not even obtained an inquiry.*

The *principle* for which they contended has been peremptorily set aside. Governments have changed, but there is *the same* denial of justice to the Church of England.

We are in the year 1853. What has become of those who contended in the year 1850, as it seemed, so earnestly and so unanimously, for that principle?

They are *worn out by the vastness of their efforts;* or they are no more of one mind, but of a hundred minds. The question before the Church is *exactly the same* as it was, but I do not believe that it could be possible *now* to get fifty men together even *to affirm* the principle for which, three years ago, they appeared to be ready *to give up so much.*

There seems, indeed, to be a remarkable difference between the public action of members of the Church of England and that of members of *any other* religious body. However great and vital the matter at stake, members of the Church of England content themselves, *at most*, with a demonstration or two, commonly very tame, spiritless, and ineffective; and, having done so much, if defeated in their young attempts—which they always are—*never* persevere. A very small dash of discouragement breaks up all their forces.

Members of other religious bodies do exactly the reverse—they *always* persevere, and this *the rather* because defeated. The result is that *they* vindicate *their* principles, and get redress of *their* grievances; neither of which members of the Church of England, in any collective way, ever do.

The key to the understanding of this startling difference is, that members of the Church of England *come forward* now and then to maintain the principles of THE CHURCH, but when defeated or discouraged, they *fall back* upon *the Establishment.*

Now no man values the Establishment more than I do. But if men will thus put it into the place of the Church, they rob it of that which gives it its true value, and makes it to be a real blessing *to the whole country.*

I have found fault with Government after Government not sparingly for these last six years; *and it is certainly true that Government after Government has dealt with the Church of England in this matter, with an entire disregard for the commonest principles of justice.* Nevertheless, it may be doubted, after all, whether the blame, or by far the greater portion of it, do not really attach to members of the Church of England, and *especially* to the Clergy, *for not knowing their own minds* in a matter of the deepest moment to the well-being of THE CHURCH, rather than to any Government. For a Government may very fairly and reasonably say—when they see men *adeo incerti instabilisque animi,*—"these men are not in earnest, they do not really care for what they talk about. If we take no notice of their complaints they will *defeat themselves.*"

This is just what has been done by the "High Church" party in respect of the "Education" and other questions,—*they have defeated themselves.* Combinations of "High Churchmen" have been *hollow* and *unreal*, and have had a corresponding issue and success. After six years of a puny and pauperised existence, Church Unions themselves have disappeared, except in name; leaving behind them the unpleasing recollection of great profession, little performance, and much *dis*union. I have now no expectation myself, that the Convocation movement will have any better event than the "Education" movement. Men's hearts are not in it; and besides, it has already been overlaid by "policy" and ecclesiastical diplomacy, to a dangerous extent, and is, in consequence, in a rickety and unhealthy state.

The above general remark may be extended to combinations upon Church matters which cannot be called combinations of "High Churchmen." When "the great Conservative party" want to damage the Whigs, they cry, "the Church in danger;" but when they have turned out the Whigs by help of the cry, they adopt and foster the identical Whig policy which they assailed, having cast just so much of dirt and odium upon it as suffices for the occasion. Churchmen go on nevertheless leaning upon their "friends" in Parliament, with an unsuspecting confidence peculiarly their own. To be sure they cannot lean upon Lord John Russell and the Whigs, and most Churchmen seem, after all, to have made up their minds that they must have *something* in the State to lean upon. Some day, perhaps, they will be wiser,—but I fear that the lesson will have to be taught in a very rude way before it is learnt.

The debates in both Houses of Parliament in 1839, upon the occasion of the first appointment of the Committee of Council on "Education," and the subsequent conduct of "the great Conservative party," supply a memorable instance of what I mean. Men began to think that "the great Conservative party" was really going to make a stand in defence of the Church of England as against the Whigs. I well remember the feelings with which I listened, on the night of July 5, 1839, to the debate in the House of Lords, *and especially to the speech of the Bishop of London;* with what thankfulness I came away, fully persuading myself that a great deal was really going to be done towards maintaining and extending, in all its integrity, the teaching of the Church; that the establishment of a latitudinarian school-teaching agency, by way of a Government department, was a thing no longer possible. It was *a weak and silly anticipation*, as was speedily demonstrated by the event. "The great Conservative party" came into office, and not only did not set aside, *but did more then, and have done more since, than the Whigs had done, or have done since*, to confirm and establish the dominant authority of the Committee of Council on "Education" *as against the Church*. I may go farther still, for if common report says true, no man had more to do with consulting upon the *original* scheme of the Management Clauses than the Bishop of London.

The issue of the movement commenced at the Annual Meeting of 1852, about the teaching of the Catechism to all scholars in the schools of the Church, is a very memorable instance of vacillating, and so of divided counsels.

The same men who joined with me in actively promoting that movement in 1852, and the same men who came together in crowds to hail and applaud it, refused to prosecute it in 1853, and many of them went so far as to express publicly their satisfaction with the result of an inquiry, *before they could have any accurate knowledge of what that result was*.

There was, I know, a good deal said at the Annual Meeting of 1853, of prosecuting the movement at *a future time, in case* the result of the inquiry should prove to be less sufficient and satisfactory than was anticipated.

The result has been published: it is most *meagre, insufficient,* and *incomplete,* and therefore most *unsatisfactory. Will the movement be prosecuted in* 1854? The result does in no way disprove the truth of the charge made by the Bishop of Manchester. *Will any one demand a more searching and general inquiry? If any one does, will he be listened to? We shall see.*

Possibly any "inconvenient" discussion may be once more prevented by what I am obliged to call *the trick* of an adjournment before the *real* business of the day begins—an adjournment moved, seconded, and carried *this* year by a coalition curious in the history of Church "politics q."

---

q The only way *towards* repairing the mischief, will be to throw no impediment in the way of a full discussion of the subject at the Annual Meeting of 1854. At present, those who promoted the inquiry in 1852, have had no sufficient answer to that inquiry.

What the true history of this *coalition* may be, I have not been able clearly to ascertain. To be sure, the Oxford Election had fallen between the Annual Meeting of 1852 and that of 1853; but I am slow to believe—all the evidence in my possession notwithstanding—that the Oxford Election can have been allowed to change men's counsels and actions, in respect of the teaching of the Catechism to all scholars in Church Schools. I am slow to do men, with whom I have acted with much confidence, dishonour so great as is implied in any such belief.

But so much is plain, and must be said—men either supported the course taken in 1852 from conviction that it was the right and true course—*the* course, I mean, *demanded* of them by *their duty to the Church*, or they did so upon other and inferior grounds.

If *the last*, they *did wrong*, and had much better have let it alone. If *the first*, five hundred such things as the Oxford Election *ought not* to have had any power to change their counsels or their actions.

But, to say truth, I was not, after all, so much taken by surprise as might have been expected. I have not had a good deal to do with "High Church Party" movements during the last five or six years without learning *something*—and what I have learnt is this, that High Churchmen, *as a party, never go to the bottom of anything*. Their way of acting is *shadowed* out, for I cannot say it is *defined*, in that eminently uncertain and misty periodical, "the Guardian," of which it has been lately well said by one of its contemporaries, that it "is never good at need." At one time it is considerations *political* that interfere with any straightforward course; at another, it is considerations personal; at another, considerations of possible and impossible *consequences*. There is a chimera abroad now, and I have heard it stated in words by some excellent friends of mine, about an approximation of what is commonly called the Evangelical party: the only foundation of this delusion, for it is no less, which I can at all make out upon due and careful inquiry, being that "Low Churchmen" are becoming more like, or less unlike "High Churchmen" in the use of the externals and decorations of Church worship. I think no man pretends to say that they are more like, or less unlike them in respect of doctrine.

But the foundation is the point to examine, not the outer face of the walls. Now how is it *possible* that a school—the theology of which is the expression, by way of adoption, or adaptation, or development, of one or more of the "new and strange doctrines" of the XVIth century—*can* approximate towards a school, the theology of which is expressed by THE CREEDS?

If indeed—as the "Edinburgh Review" thinks, and as the Committee of Council on "Education" thinks, and as some others appear to think, THE CATHOLIC CHURCH OF ENGLAND is about to disappear, and to merge into *the Broad Church of Englishmen*, some such "approximation" is, not only *possible*, but *near at hand*.

For my part, I wait for the Doctrinal test, and do not think much of the Æsthetic test. Indeed, I had much rather *not have the last at all*, unless I can have the *first* to build upon.

All this coquetting and quasi-alliance with a misty Protestantism, coupled with high-sounding words and pretensions to Catholicity, and much observance of outward ceremonial, is only to cast with our own hands our resources into the lap of Rome. If it be true, as it certainly is, that "Low Churchmen" help Rome greatly by denying on every occasion that the Church of England holds and teaches the Primitive Faith of the Church Catholic, it is as certainly no less true that "High Churchmen" help Rome greatly by affirming principles which they do not realise; by encouraging counsels, but deprecating their issue in any act; in a word, by stirring depths which they dare not fathom.

I have ceased to think it *possible* to preserve either the constitution of the schools of the Church, or the matter or manner of its school teaching, through any instrumentality of the National Society.

Having been *entirely* and *irrecoverably* defeated in respect of the whole attempt which commenced in 1847—not through anything done or said by opponents, but through the vacillation and desertion of friends, and through the apparent resolve of the Bishops of the Church of England to let the Committee of Council *have its own way*—I do not propose to expend upon that attempt, so far as the Management Clauses are concerned, any further amount of my time and energies.

Church Societies, *always an anomaly*, become *an evil* so soon as they are subordinated to any other influence but that of the Church itself.

The next assault will be upon the whole system and framework of the parish schools. I look forward to an attempt on the part of the Committee of Council, at no distant day, to introduce generally into our parishes a system analogous to the Irish system, or some system which shall include that climax of all anti-Church policy, an " Education Rate."

Will the Committee of the National Society resist the attempt? if it does so, will it resist the attempt in such manner as to *deserve*, if not to *command*, success? will the Bishops of the Church of England resist the attempt in, or out of Parliament? I have no belief of the kind.

Whether in what I have now said I have at all succeeded in conveying what I myself feel to be the depth and extent of the evil which not only threatens, but has fallen upon, the Church of England, through her acquiescence in the claims and the policy of the Committee of Council on " Education," I cannot tell. To my own apprehension my language appears very inadequate, and the anticipation of future and yet deeper evil is greatly enhanced by the very painful consideration that for the present helplessness of her position, and her prostration at the feet of a State department, it is not those who *do not*, but it is those who *do*, care for the Catholic character of the Church of England, that have principally to answer.

For there were *two* safeguards to look to, so far as man is charged with the *safety* of the Church Catholic in any land; one of them of great power, from its public, collective, and authoritative character; the other of a more private nature, and in its operation necessarily detached and desultory.

The first *was* the firm, and not, as it has been, the *passive*, but the *active* resistance of the Committee of the National Society, by which I mean its *leading the way* in an appeal to Parliament—an appeal, if need were, often repeated—for justice to the Church of England; *in which case* the Committee of the Society would have been so largely and powerfully supported, that there would have been no room for any move or for any " agitation " on my own part, or on that of any other private member of the Society. The other *was* the steady refusal of individual clergy and laity, at whatever cost of " means of efficiency," to fall in with *any portion* of the progressive scheme of the Committee of Council on " Education " for establishing *a dominant authority* in respect of school teaching throughout the country.

Both have been found wanting. When, indeed, the first was

found wanting, it could hardly be expected that the other would abound. For men easily, readily, and reasonably shelter themselves, even though with much secret misgiving, under the cover of an authority, which if it be not that of the Church itself, is yet the nearest to it of which they have any present cognizance.

The battle, which has been LOST *on the ground of the Parish Schools, is now being fought over again on the ground of the University of Oxford; the question, now as before, being between* THE CHURCH CATHOLIC *and the "Broad Church;" the point distinctly at issue being, whether the University shall continue to be the handmaid of* THE CHURCH, *or an agency of its counterfeit*

People write and speak as though the question were primarily one of a choice between the professorial and tutorial systems. The deceit is shallow and transparent; but, doubtless, it serves its purpose. Even when this ground is taken in all honesty and singleness of purpose, it is very narrow. The battle can never be fought upon it.

Of the general issue I have little hope. English Churchmen seem to me, not to be defenders of ALL *which* GOD *has given them to defend, but to be givers-up of one part of it after another, in the vain hope of saving the rest by some art or contrivance of man's device.*

This may be Conservative, but it is not Catholic: it may be Policy, but it is not FAITH.

Believe me, my dear Wordsworth, and my fellow-labourers in the household of God,

Very faithfully yours,
GEORGE ANTHONY DENISON.

EAST BRENT,
Christmas Eve, 1853.

We have here, then, some account of the assault and defence, 1847 to 1853. The assault, commencing formally with the formation of the Committee of Council in 1839, made no public progress during the five years of Sir R. Peel's Government, 1841-6. In 1846, Lord John Russell returned to power, and the assault returned to its public, but still "unostentatious," character in the Minutes of 1846.

In 1847 came the Management Clauses. In respect of these, and I may indeed say, of all else, the battle was virtually lost in 1852, though it was continued against hope for some sixteen years after.

There is some curious evidence supplied by Sir James Kay Shuttleworth himself, that although the Peel Government did nothing publickly to forward the purposes of the Committee of Council, yet that privately it did much.

Let us hear Sir James himself[r]. Considering the speeches and divisions in both Houses of Parliament in 1839, it is a remarkable chapter in the history of "Conservatism." I cite from my Charge, 1853 :—

"In the interval between 1842 and 1846, Sir Robert Peel's Government cautiously extended the administration of the Education Department of the Privy Council. This development was probably the more gradual, because that great statesman was unwilling to subject a Government which had undertaken the responsibility of a vast fiscal reform, to the further risks arising from the controversies which had attended every step towards a system of public Education. Every act of the Committee of Council under Sir Robert Peel's Government was, however, a confirmation of the principles on which the policy of their predecessors had been founded. Every proposal by which that policy would have been endangered (and such proposals were not wanting) was deliberately rejected. The principles on which the department had been originally founded, were practically developed by a process of natural growth. The abandonment of the Education Clauses of the Factories Regulation Bill in 1842, marked the deference paid by Sir R. Peel and Sir J. Graham to the repugnance of a large portion of the middle classes to acknowledge any supremacy in matters of religion. They plainly yielded to the unequivocal rejection of all authority over the conscience, and to the assertion of the right of private judgment in the interpretation of Scripture. Though, therefore, the advance of the Education department appeared, during Sir R. Peel's Government, to consist chiefly in the increase of the public grant, and of the number of inspectors and normal

---

[r] "Public Education as affected by the Minutes of the Committee of Privy Council from 1846 to 1852, with Suggestions as to Future Policy." By Sir James Kay Shuttleworth, 1852, pp. 5, 6.

schools, the principles of a great public policy were in operation, and were silently attracting to themselves, like centres of crystallization, a mass of precedent and authority which was to become irresistible."

The position on both sides could not be more clearly stated,—on the side of real assault and of quasi or sham defence. If there be any one amongst our statesmen, members of the Church of England, who shares with Sir James Kay Shuttleworth the consolidation of the dominant position of the Committee of Council on Education, it is Sir Robert Peel.

The defence began in the diocese of Bath and Wells, and was reduced into shape at the annual meeting of the Diocesan Societies in the autumn of that year, under the presidency of the Bishop. The attitude of the diocese was the same throughout, down to the year 1855, when it was reversed in the course of the first twelve months of Lord Auckland's episcopate. The particulars of reversal will come in the order of time.

The defence was transferred by me from the diocese to the Annual Meeting of the National Society, first in 1848. I had some difficulty in finding a seconder; Clergy and Laity were alike afraid of "committing" themselves. At last I came across my dear friend Wordsworth; I told him that I knew he was with me, and prayed him to second. He said he was sorry, but he had an appointment which he must keep. I said, "I will not let you go, unless you promise to be back in time." He promised he would. I remember well the surprise on the faces of the Bishops present when Wordsworth rose to second me; they did not think much of me, but Wordsworth's opposition was another matter.

In 1849 my supporters had increased largely, and the issue of the meeting was very decidedly in our hands. Then it was that my two most active opponents among the Bishops—my brother, Bishop of Salisbury, and Samuel Wilberforce, Bishop of Oxford—as their last resource put up Manning—then Archdeacon in the Church of England, now Cardinal in the Church of Rome—to move an amendment. I have called the amendment, in the Letter reprinted above, "unmeaning and worthless;" I had better have said "ruinous." From that hour I date the ruin of "Church Education" in England at the hands of Churchmen.

Manning had then a wonderful position, the improvement of which he well understood: when I found him "amending," I knew what would happen. I did what I could; I insisted upon having some words inserted in the amendment, to guard, as far as might be, against the mischief of it. And in this form it was carried[a]. But the Bishops of Salisbury and Oxford, who were ready to vote for it as originally proposed, would not vote for it as by me amended. The parentage of Manning's amendment became abundantly clear.

Most of my supporters congratulated me and themselves, thinking we had done very well. I knew better; I knew that the battle was virtually lost that day, and I reproach myself for having accepted the amendment, however modified at my instance. I ought to have fought it out there and then, and not have concerned myself with the immediate issue; but I was comparatively young then in my experience of these things.

Kind friends collected money for a testimonial: it was applied to the restoration and improvement of windows in East Brent Church. The Committee on Education of June 7 was appointed, and I went back to the diocese of Bath and Wells and the Bristol Church Union, to see whether anything could be done towards retrieving the defeat which so many called a victory.

It was suggested to me about this time, that it would be of incalculable service if I could prevail upon John Keble to take an active part with us. I acted upon the sugges-

---

[a] I have lying before me the correspondence which took place afterwards between us; according to my rule I abstain from publishing it: as also a letter of my own to the Bishop of Bath and Wells, stating the view of the whole proceeding which I was compelled to take.

tion at once, wrote to ask leave to come to him at Hursley, and, receiving his kind answer, armed myself with my documents and went down.

I was shewn into Keble's study. On a table near the door was a bust of John Henry Newman, with its veil of white crape. Keble came in. I laid the case before him as between the Church and the Committee of Council.

He said, with that wonderful childlike simplicity which I never saw equalled, "My dear Denison, it is impossible; I cannot believe any men would be so wicked."

"Well," I said, "here are all the documents; let me leave them with you for a couple of hours. I will go and look about me, see your church, &c., and come back to you."

When I came back he said, "I have read all; I did not think men could be so wicked. I will do everything you ask me to do."

The year 1850 saw the revival of the project for training masters of schools of no particular religious "persuasion." This had been first attempted in 1840, but then withdrawn, as a part of the latitudinarian scheme prematurely pressed. In 1850 it was revived, in the establishment, at the cost of a large outlay of the public money during five years, of Knellar Hall: the present Bishop of Exeter was the first Principal. In 1855 the Committee of Council gave it up, for reasons which, I think, do not appear in their published documents. While it remained, the Committee of June 7 and the Church Unions did what they could to expose its real character.

When the Bishop of Chichester consented to present the petition agreed to at the meeting at Willis's Rooms, presided over by my dear friend, Hon. J. C. Talbot, I went to the House of Lords to see the issue.

Government objected that there was nothing before the House to shew that the grievance complained of in, and the redress sought by, the petition was generally felt and claimed. It was proposed to adjourn the debate for a week, to see what evidence of this could be produced.

It was not a very liberal allowance of time, and people laughed at it. Lord Nelson came to me at the bar, and said, " How many petitions can you get for us by Monday next ? "

" Twelve hundred," I said.

" Did you say twelve hundred ? "

" Yes, I did."

He went away, smiling gently, as is his wont. I went to the Bishop of Chichester, and asked him to authorize me to take charge on the Monday morning following of any petitions addressed to him, and lying in the robing-room.

The next day, the kind exertions of my dear friend Henry Hoare, a name loved and reverenced by us all, obtained for me the use of rooms at the National Club, and with a small army of some fifty clerks we went to work.

Monday morning following I went to the robing-room.

" Any petitions for Bishop of Chichester."

"Yes," the attendant believed there were a few.

I took them, and getting into a cab, went to the Bishop's house in Queen Anne-street. When I got there, I could hardly get into the house for the petitions. Four cabs were called, and the petitions packed into them, carried down to the National Club, arranged as to dioceses, and at 4 P.M. I delivered to the Bishop in a small excess of the number guaranteed, 1270 petitions, all with the same prayer as the petition from Willis's Rooms. We gave Government what they had asked for ; but we might have spared our trouble, so far as they were concerned ; they knew well that by their own steady perseverance, and sham resistance, ecclesiastical and civil, the game was altogether in their hands.

Lord Derby came into power, Feb. 26, 1852.

I was still endeavouring to fight the battle of the Management Clauses, and had given notice of Resolutions for the Annual Meeting, June 11.

I subjoin so much of the report of the proceedings of

that day as is necessary to the clear and exact account of the position in which matters were left when the meeting closed.

But before doing this, I have a statement to make. Three days before the meeting I received a letter on the part of the Government, asking me to come up at once to London.

In London I was shewn the draft of what Government proposed to do in respect of the Management Clauses, and I was asked whether it would satisfy me.

I replied that it gave me something of what I had from the first contended for; and that, therefore, I was so far content to accept it [1].

I was asked next, whether, upon this basis, I would at the Annual Meeting, Friday, June 11, withdraw my Resolution respecting the Management Clauses. I said that I would.

I was asked further, whether I could answer for my supporters. I said that I could.

Upon this understanding, I spoke at the meeting as follows:—

My Lord Archbishop,

I am glad to think that, without subjecting me to any suspicion of disrespect, a very few words will convey all that is necessary or fitting for me to say to this meeting. The Committee of this Society have given their sanction to an inquiry respecting the teaching of the Catechism in schools in union with the Society. I am very sensible that this is the legitimate way of proceeding under the circumstances of the case. I have, therefore, nothing now to state in reference to Resolution 1; but that with much thankfulness, which I may be allowed to express here on my own behalf and on behalf of many friends, I shall, when I sit down,

---

[1] I had previously, with advice and help of able assistants versed in, and faithful to, Church principles, and learned in the law, prepared and printed "Proposals for Amending and giving a distinct Church character to the Management Clauses of the Committee of Council on Education, A, B, C, D, and for completing the series by the addition of Clause E."

It was no part of the Government proposal to give me Clause E; which was *the* thing I had contended for all along.

beg permission of your Grace and the Committee to withdraw it. I perhaps may be allowed, as briefly as I can, to place before the meeting the circumstances under which that decision has been received with such thankfulness by us. It was communicated in answer to a memorial from one whose name only requires to be mentioned in any assembly of the Church of England, John Keble. I will now, with the permission of his Grace and the Committee, read the documents connected with the decision of the Committee.

"London, June 7, 1852.

" REV. SIR,

" May I ask the favour of you to lay the accompanying Memorial before his Grace the President and the Committee of the National Society, at the first convenient opportunity.

" I have the honour to be, Reverend Sir,
" Your obedient Servant,
" JOHN KEBLE.

"*To the Rev. J. Lonsdale.*"

" To his Grace the Lord Archbishop of Canterbury, the Vice-Presidents, and other members of 'the National Society for the Education of the Poor in the Principles of the Established Church.'

"The memorial of the undersigned member of the said Society humbly sheweth :—

" That the Charter of the Society sets forth as its sole object, 'the instruction and Education of the Poor in suitable learning, works of industry, and the principles of the Christian Religion according to the Established Church;' and again, 'the Educating the Children of the Poor, without any exception, in the Doctrine and Discipline of the Established Church.'

" That the said Charter, in a subsequent passage, recites as an essential part of the grounds on which it was granted, that it had been represented to his Majesty that 'the said Society had been instituted principally for the purpose of Educating the Children of the Poor in the Doctrine and Discipline of the Established Church, according to the Liturgy and Catechism provided for that purpose.'

" That the terms of union to be subscribed by parties desirous of uniting their Schools to the Society begin with an engagement, 'that the children are to be instructed in the Holy Scriptures, and in the Liturgy and Catechism of the Established Church.'

"That, in dependence upon these enactments and engagements, a very large body of members of the Church of England has, from time to time, united itself to this Society, and very great efforts and sacrifices have been made in its behalf.

"That public statements have lately been made, professing to rest upon authority which cannot be overlooked, to the effect that in very many schools in union with the Society, the above-mentioned enactments and engagements are deliberately and systematically violated, and the teaching of the Catechism at least partially suppressed, for the purpose of 'respecting the feelings of Dissenters in this particular.'

"That your Memorialist, in common, as he believes, with a great many attached members of the Society, hoping that the above-mentioned statements are grounded not on cases of intended suppression of the Catechism, or of any part thereof, but on certain variations in the manner and order of teaching it which the missionary office of the Church may, in some instances, have seemed to require, is nevertheless convinced that it is essential to the credit and well-being of the Society that some explanation should be given of the above statements, and the evil which they indicate (if it really exist) be abated.

"Your Memorialist desires respectfully to draw the attention of the Committee to this important matter; and to request, with all deference, that enquiry, as exact and general as the case may allow, be made into the grounds of the said allegation, and the result made known to the Society on or before the day of the General Meeting in 1853.

"JOHN KEBLE, M.A., *Vicar of Hursley, in the Diocese of Winchester.*"

"*June* 8, 1852.

"REVEREND SIR,

"I have the honour to inform you that I have submitted to his Grace the President, and the Committee of this Society, your letter dated 7th inst., with the memorial accompanying the same. I am instructed by them to forward to you a copy of the resolution to which the Committee have agreed:—

"'That the Bishops of the several Dioceses be requested to ascertain, if they think fit, through the Diocesan School Inspectors, or in such other way as to them may seem most expedient, what is the practice of schools in union with the National Society within their dioceses, as to the teaching of the Liturgy and Catechism of the Church.'

"I have the honour to be, Reverend Sir,
"Your faithful servant,
"JOHN G. LONSDALE,
"*Secretary.*"

"*The Rev. John Keble.*"

It would be very presumptuous in me to attempt to express my own personal thankfulness for what I have just read. I may be permitted to add, that though this Memorial does not exactly accord with the resolution which has been published as the one which I was about to move, yet it does exactly accord with an amendment of that resolution which I drew myself, and which I should have been entirely prepared to accept as a friendly amendment, if the course of the proceedings this day had obliged me to move the original resolution.

With respect to the second resolution, I am thankful to announce to the meeting that I have a task equally easy and hardly less satisfactory to perform. Her Majesty's Government have consented to introduce certain alternative modifications into the Management Clauses for Church of England Schools. These modifications are not yet officially before the public; but I believe that I betray no confidence when I state that I am aware of what is, substantially, their nature and extent. I find indeed, that the fact of such modifications having been made was yesterday officially announced in the House of Commons by her Majesty's Secretary of State for the Home Department.

Now I am not going to say what I do not suppose any one expects me to say, that those modifications, valuable as they are, are co-extensive with what has appeared throughout to myself and others to be the equitable claim of the Church of England: a claim advanced for no purpose of exclusion or aggrandisement: still less of what some may consider priestly domination; but in the hope of providing for a more enlarged and comprehensive usefulness in promoting the Education of the People. But I apprehend that whether these modifications be complete or no, is not the present question. The present question is rather whether we shall accept, in a kindly and thankful spirit, the acknowledgment of the fact which any such modification supplies; and endeavour, as friends labouring in a common cause, to place before her Majesty's Government in other ways than by resolution here—for I trust resolutions will never be necessary more—those points connected with the Management Clauses, and with the general relations of the Committee of Council on Education to this Society and to the Church at large, which in our judgment will remain yet to be adjusted for the common and mutual benefit of Church and State. Being persuaded myself, and having good reason to know that herein I speak for others too, that the latter view of the question before us indicates what is now our true course of action in this matter, I have only to add with respect to Resolution 2, and I add it in the same spirit of thankfulness for myself and others which I adverted to in speaking of the withdrawal of Resolution 1, that when I sit down I shall beg permission of your Grace and the Committee to withdraw it also.

And now in taking leave, I trust finally, of the task of moving resolutions at our Annual Meeting, I will venture to hope that I neither carry away with me, nor leave behind me one feeling inconsistent with brotherly good-will. I have, I trust, had nothing so much at heart throughout this controversy, as the well-being and efficiency of the Church. Those who have differed from me, have certainly no less claim than I have to the same favourable construction of all they have said or done. I have nothing to complain of in them. I have much of kindness and consideration to remember gratefully. What they may have to complain of in me I cannot doubt they will forget. I beg leave to withdraw the resolutions.

I was much collauded, flattered, bepraised and congratulated that day, by foe as well as friend. At one moment I was in great fear that the Rev. Francis Close, D.D., Dean of Carlisle, was going to kiss me then and there, on the two sides of my face. "I had been much misunderstood." "After all, I was a man of peace," &c. On the other hand, I was much abused by "Liberal" newspaper-men, who were weak enough to think, as for a day or two I was myself, that I had got something, however minute, really worth having for the

Church of England from the Civil Power. A very few days sufficed to dispel an illusion, never to re-appear.

In 1851 I published, "Why should the Bishops continue to sit in the House of Lords?" It attracted a good deal of notice at the time, and went into three editions. Last year I re-published it.

It had for some time appeared to me that the secular position of the Bishops was a great evil, and that it carried with it no compensating advantage; that the nothingness, so to speak, of their affirmation and defence of Church principles was to be traced to that position as to *a* principal cause, though not, as I have since tried to shew in my "Episcopatus Bilinguis," 1874, *the* principal cause. The principal cause is one which, interwoven with the entire fabric of the Establishment, has an especial connection with the Episcopate, as I believe myself to have there demonstrated. For the general case, Religious Institutions fail in exact proportion to their unreality. Now the position of a branch of the Church Catholic as the National Church of a country, which is, not only not Catholic but, of no particular religion, is about the most unreal thing that may be found anywhere.

But I am not going to trouble my readers with a résumé of my published and re-published pamphlet. I refer to it, because it supplies a chief link in the order of these 'Notes of my Life.'

I published it in the summer of 1851. In September of the same year, the Bishop of Bath and Wells made me Archdeacon of Taunton. Many people were astonished, some were amused at the bravery of the Bishop. The Bishop was indeed as brave and straightforward a man as I have ever known, or he would never have made me Archdeacon.

But this is not my point here. My point here is that the pamphlet published before I was made Archdeacon, sets out formally and categorically in the shape of propositions, the precise Doctrine of the Blessed Sacrament, for teaching which I was brought under prosecution some three and a-half years after. I shall have to revert in the order of time to the history of the case, and to the causes which led to an official severance—it was never for a moment more than official—between my dearly loved friend the Bishop and myself.

Meantime I adduce here, from p. 22 of the pamphlet as re-published in 1877, the words following :—

"I understand THE DOCTRINE OF THE SACRAMENTS to be this :

"I. That man is 'made a member of CHRIST, the child of GOD, and an inheritor of the kingdom of heaven' in and by Holy Baptism.

"II. That man, 'made a member of CHRIST, the child of GOD, and an inheritor of the kingdom of heaven' in and by Holy Baptism, is renewed from time to time in Holy Communion.

"III. That 'a death unto sin and a new birth unto righteousness,' is GIVEN to every adult and every infant in and by the outward visible sign or form in Baptism, Water, in the Name of THE FATHER, and of THE SON, and of THE HOLY GHOST.

"IV. That the GIFT may be RECEIVED, in the case of adults, worthily or unworthily; but that it is ALWAYS RECEIVED.

"V. That THE BODY and BLOOD of CHRIST are GIVEN to every one who RECEIVES the Sacramental Bread and Wine.

"VI. That the Gift may be RECEIVED worthily or unworthily, but that it is always RECEIVED."

In the summer of 1851 I was asked to preach two sermons in St. Peter's Church, Derby[a]. I mention this because it was, I think, in publishing the Sermons that I first adverted publickly, in Advertisement prefixed, to the "Manchester and Salford Education Scheme," embodying Conscience Clause and Education Rate.

Afterwards I had much public controversy with Mr. Entwistle and other chief promoters of it, and much communication with Members of Parliament in both Houses upon it. Among them, with Mr. Gladstone. The scheme

[a] "The Church and the School." (London: Masters, 1851.)

has now received its final accomplishment, and a good deal more, in the Elementary Education Act of 1870. Twenty years before, public men generally were "not prepared" for it. In conjunction with two very powerful allies, one in the south of England, one in the north,—the Rev. Henry Newland, and W. Romayne Callender, Esq., afterwards Member for Manchester,—I did what I could to stay the plague.

It is difficult to convey the idea of the amount of labour and care bestowed by Mr. Callender upon the attempt to avert the evil of the scheme. He came to see me at East Brent about it, and his letters in my possession are very many, filled with everything that was to be adduced, statistical and other.

I asked Mr. Newland to write the articles which originally appeared against the scheme in the columns of the "English Churchman," and gave him the outline of the argument, as it is stated p. 45 of Mr. Shutte's Memoir of him (London: Masters, 1861). The articles told very powerfully at the time.

They are both gone to their rest: kinder, more earnest, and abler friends no man ever had. For my share in the controversy it has all been published, and need not be reproduced here.

September, 1851, having no hope left that the National Society and the Church at large would save themselves from becoming ultimately nothing but subordinate agencies of the Council Office, I converted the larger half of the Vicarage-house of East Brent into a training and a middle school. I was kindly and largely helped; and the schools, opened in January, 1852, prospered exceedingly. In 1854, under the pressure of the prosecution in the matter of THE REAL PRESENCE, I was obliged to close them.

I have anticipated the history of the Parish Schools' question during 1852: the battle was lost; but some few of us kept our faces to the foe. Our army finally broke up in 1853, as I state more in detail further on.

Meantime the Whig plot, coiled in its many folds in Downing-street, kept uncoiling itself slowly, laying hold tenaciously of every inch of ground within its reach and grasp.

I often used to think, and I often think now, how the people in Downing-street must have kept laughing at the people in the Broad Sanctuary. Weakness, especially in high places professing highest principles, is as ridiculous as it is painful and dangerous. Milton has made Satan saying to Beelzebub,—

> "Fallen Cherub, to be weak is miserable,
> Doing or suffering."

In the autumn of 1852, in conjunction with my dear friend, Rev. Francis Charles Massingberd, afterwards Chancellor of Lincoln, I got together at Swindon the meeting for considering how best to promote the revival of Convocation. The meeting adjourned to London, and issued, after much discussion, in the Representation, entrusted to my kind friend Dr. Spry, to introduce into the Lower House of the Convocation of the Province of Canterbury. Her Majesty's Government having decided to offer no further obstacle to the assembling of Convocation, the Representation was so introduced, Friday, November 12, 1852, and was referred by vote of the House to a Committee; but the Committee never met. It was another bit of unreality.

The goodness of GOD has given me many friends of my public life; all so kind, tender, and forbearing towards me, that I hardly like to particularise. But I believe I shall hurt no one of them when I recall the unfailing evidences of the wise, gentle, and loving spirit of Francis Charles Massingberd. I could add many other names to his in a like tribute of remembrance; but if I began, I should hardly know where to close the record.

Others of our brethren had anticipated Massingberd and myself in preparing the way for revival of Convocation. We came in taking up their work, and, so far as might be done, giving effect to it in a formal shape when the opportunity arose. I shall have to return to the general action of Convocation further on.

At the close of 1852 came the coalition between Mr. Gladstone, representing the Peelites, and the Whigs, the prelude to his "Liberal" leadership. In January, 1853, came the contest for Oxford University, when I proposed Mr. Dudley Perceval.

My good friends of the Bristol Church Union, and many others, thought that it was party politics that moved me to do what I could, in the last fifteen days' poll of election history, to unseat Mr. Gladstone, and passed a resolution of the Union against mixing up Religion with Politics. The resolution was abstract in form, in substance it was aimed at me.

My good friends and late coadjutors made a mistake. I was not concerning myself with "Politics" at all; I was concerning myself with "Religious Education." I was thinking of the "Religious Education" of this and coming generations,—of the battle which my good friends and I had been for some years fighting together. They clung to the man who, though he had never helped us in or out of Parliament, was to them so identified with English Churchmanship, as to make them not only condone, but defend everything he did then, or might do thereafter. I clung to the principle for which we had fought in common, and for it gave up the man. And so we parted, after seven years of what had seemed to be a real union, for the maintaining of "Religious Education;" but which, when it came to be fairly tested, turned out to be only a rope of sand.

The Coalition meant to me "Conscience" Clause, Education Rate, School-Board. No school truly Church— ten thousand schools quasi-Church. That is to say, it meant to me then what all experience since has conclusively and finally proved it to have been.

For this cause, then, I did what I could in 1853 to unseat Mr. Gladstone. I knew very well what "Conscience" Clause and the rest of it meant; I knew very well that they meant the Indifferentism of this generation; the Socinianism of the next; the pervading Rationalism of the coming century.

And so I did what I could, with all my regard and respect for the man, and with a deep and abiding sense of his great personal kindness to me, to take away his seat. It was not the seat that I cared about, as giving and securing a vote this way or that, a vote of special influence: what I cared about was the principle of the seat; what it meant, and what it must needs help to do one way or the other.

But, what with the friends who indicated that I was a traitor, and the many others who had no more liking for me than they had for Mr. Gladstone, I was for a time defeated.

I say "for a time," for when we come to 1865, I believe I can shew that I had more to do with the unseating of Mr. Gladstone than any other elector for the University.

I have no vote now: I have taken my name off the books a good many years. The representation of the University has no charm about it for me now. A vote, indeed, anywhere now is nothing to me; it cannot, however remotely and infinitesimally, help the Church, because the Church is, not simply as matter-of-fact, but cannot be as matter of possible combination, ever helped by Parliament.

As for "Conservatives" and Liberals," it is six of one and half-a-dozen of the other; if, indeed, the "Liberal" be not the less dangerous of the two. There is only one point of disagreement between them, and about that point I have ceased to care; the point is, the "Establishment." Now I am persuaded that for a long time past, possibly for all time, the "Establishment" has been doing so much injury to true Religion, that, though I am as little of a "Liberal" as any man, I have joined the Church League for the separation of "Church" from "State."

Nevertheless, I have no belief that the separation is coming soon; not, that is, as matters stand at present. England likes her "Establishment;" it suits the tone of her mind; for England is not Catholic. And it has, no doubt, temporal and social advantages many and great. The Whigs, too, like it better since it became the servant and instrument of the Civil Power.

The Education army, as it had been used to muster in London for five years, having been broken up in 1853 by the Oxford Contest, the Diocesan army of Bath and Wells broke up in 1855, under the episcopate of Lord Auckland, who succeeded to the see in 1854.

I have known no man to whom, coming to be personally acquainted with him late in life, I have been more affectionately attached, and for whose character I have had a higher respect, than Lord Auckland, Bishop of Bath and Wells, 1854—1869. We did not agree upon educational and other matters, but nothing ever interfered with his frank, kind, hearty way of meeting and talking and dealing with me.

However, it was clear that, sooner or later, we should be formally at issue upon the Schools matter; and this came to pass, January 10, 1855.

Extracts from Minutes of Diocesan Education Board.

"Jan. 10, 1855. The LORD BISHOP read a correspondence which had taken place between himself and Rev. J. G. Lonsdale, Secretary of the National Society, on the subject of the grant made by this Diocesan Board to the parochial school of Tiverton; also a report upon the system of religious Instruction pursued by the Rev. G. Buckle, the Vicar at that school.

"(Subject, 'The Church Catechism not taught,' I believe.) £20 voted, October, 1854.

"Ven. Archdeacon GUNNING moved, 'That in future no pecuniary aid be rendered by the Board to any school, in any case, except where the school is, or proposes to be, in union with the Diocesan Association; and (except as provided otherwise) this Committee adopt the papers of the National Society in dispensing the funds confided to them.'

"Amendment by Ven. Archdeacon DENISON; seconded by Rev. Prebendary BEADON:—

"'That, considering that a Resolution was passed by a majority of this Board, at the Quarterly Meeting, Oct. 4, in the terms following,—

> "'Some misunderstanding having arisen respecting the relations between this Board and certain schools in which the Rules of the National Society are not enforced; it is hereby declared that this Board desires to extend its operations to every Church of England school in the Diocese, where its assistance may be useful.
>
> "'That every Church of England school in the Diocese has a *primâ facie* claim to assistance from the Board.
>
> "'That every school receiving assistance from the Board shall receive the Diocesan Inspector.
>
> "'Considering that the resolution above recited requires to be very carefully guarded and defined,—
>
> "Resolved, That it appears to this Board that no school is *properly* a Church of England school, in which the acquiring a knowledge of the text of the Church Catechism by the scholars, and the 'further instruction' of them therein by the teachers, are not made to be *primary* and *principal* portions of the work of the school; and of which it is not also a rule that the scholars attend the service of the Church, except upon reasons to be approved as good and sufficient by the Managers of the school : That it be, therefore, a condition of a grant by this Board, that the normal and settled practice of a school applying for aid be that which is set down in this Resolution in respect of the Church Catechism, and in respect of the attendance of the scholars at the service of the Church."
>
> "The numbers, upon a division, having been equal, 19 to 19, the amendment was rejected by the casting vote of the Chairman[1]."

Upon this division, shewing unmistakeably, not simply that the Diocesan Board was no longer with me as it had been for eight years, but that it had sanctioned a rule of distribution of funds placed at its disposal with which it was impossible for me to have anything to do directly or indirectly, I ceased to attend meetings of the Board for exactly ten years, Jan. 10, 1855, to Jan. 10, 1865, and took no further interest in its proceedings.

[1] Two of my supporters missed their train.

In 1859, 63, 64, I attended the anniversary meetings of the Diocesan Societies, as under.

In 1865, several members asked me to return to the Board for the specific purpose of moving a resolution on the subject of the Conscience Clause, as under.

I told them that my coming was of small use or comfort to myself, or to anybody else; for that I had been taught by experience how the support of one year (or even of many consecutive years) became the opposition of the next.

They assured me that this would not happen; and I went and carried the Resolution, which was seconded by my dear and excellent friend, John Horner.

I was also present, April 18, the same year, upon a like occasion.

Extracts from Minutes of Diocesan Education Board.

"October, 1859 and 1860. ARCHDEACON OF TAUNTON attended Anniversary: seconded First Resolution to adopt Reports.

"September, 1863. Anniversary. Seconded Resolution 2: Expression of approval of munificence of Revs. F. Smith and E. Lance, in erecting new churches.

"October, 1864. Anniversary. Moved Resolution 3 :—

"'That this Meeting deprecates the legal enforcement of a "Conscience Clause" as a condition of State aid, because it believes that the religious education of all the children will be weakened, from the fact that two or more systems of religious training are at work in the same school.'—Carried.

"January 10, 1865. Quarterly Meeting. Moved by the ARCHDEACON OF TAUNTON, seconded by Rev. Prebendary HORNER :—

"'That a Petition on the subject of the Conscience Clause be presented to both Houses of Parliament.'

"Amendment by E. A. FREEMAN, Esq.; seconded by ARCHDEACON OF BATH :—

"'That no petition be presented.'

"It was agreed, on a division, That petitions be presented; and a Form, submitted by the Archdeacon of Taunton, was, after amendment, finally approved.

"Attended a meeting held April 18, for the purpose of considering the Duke of Marlborough's Government Education Bill (read a second time in the House of Lords).

"Motion by Rev. G. FAGAN, seconded by Rev. T. BRANCKER:

"'That the Bath and Wells Board adheres to its recorded opinion, that to insist upon a so-called Conscience Clause as a condition of a grant out of the common taxation of the country distributed by Parliament, on the denominational system, to schools of the Church, is unjust to the Managers of such schools, and tends to fetter and discourage the extension of the education of the people.

"'That this Board, therefore, earnestly desires to see the present Bill amended by the omission of all reference to a Conscience Clause.'"—Carried.

I do not remember having been at the Board again up to 1870. After 1870, being unable to take part in any manner of proceedings which imply connection of any kind, direct or indirect, with the Civil Power in the matter of Schools, I have ceased to attend the Board as of necessity.

I revert at this point to other chief parts of the "ultra-Protestant" or "Indifferent" assault upon the Catholic position of the Church of England prior to 1852. There is the assault positive, and there is the assault negative; the last including the feebleness, the vacillation, the unsoundness, and the consequent speedy and final collapse of the defence.

These parts are,—

1. The appointment by Lord John Russell of Dr. Hampden to the Bishopric of Hereford, 1847-8.
2. The declaring the Doctrine of Holy Baptism to be an open question in the Church, as by law established, by Court of Final Appeal in the Gorham case, 1850.

Earl Russell represents so much more than any other man living the position of the assailant, and is so largely identified with all the success of the assault, as to make some more particular reference to him and to his action, so to speak, a necessary ingredient of these "Notes."

That the house of Bedford, largely enriched out of the plunder of Century XVI. by the spoliation commonly called sacrilege, should not be instinct with Catholic instincts is nothing wonderful : it is only retributive justice. But this may be, as it has been in the case of other members of the family, the true account of the general family position, and yet not be accompanied throughout a long and distinguished public life by the most pronounced and successful "ultra-Protestant" action, as in the particular case of Earl Russell. In him, social position, high personal character, eminent ability, have been only so many ingredients of anti-Church power.

No man has had a greater share than Earl Russell in the ruin, under the Establishment, of "Church Education;" of Church constitutional and possessory right; no man has used his position as leader of the House of Commons, more violently and more persistently,—witness the history of the establishment of the Committee of Council on "Education" in 1839; and, as Minister, in the intrusion of Dr. Hampden into the See of Hereford, 1847-8. There is nothing, from repeal of Test and Corporation Act, 1828, downwards to this day, in respect of which he has not, as a true Whig, seized and grasped firmly every opportunity of dealing a blow, through the Establishment, upon the Catholic position ; and certainly he has not been without his many triumphs.

On the other hand, look at the opposing forces, and the method and the amount of resistance. It is instructive to note that where he has been met by the "Establishment Power," he has always defeated it ; where he has been met by the "Church Power," it has defeated him.

Contrast, for example, his success in the Hampden case with his defeat in the "Ecclesiastical Titles Act" case. In the first he was confronted as the Establishment is wont to confront ; and the result was triumph on his part, rapid and complete. In the second, he was met simply by the passive resistance of the Church Power, "not established," and his defeat was speedy and ignominious.

I know of nothing more painful to the true son of

the Church of England, than the feeble and timid counsels of the defence in the Hampden case, save the tone and manner of the Archbishops and Bishops of the Church of England in siding with Earl Russell in his vain attempt to resist what was called at the time, "the Papal aggression." Here were Archbishops and Bishops— who had acquiesced in the destruction of ten of the Irish Bishoprics; who had not hesitated, save in one or more rare instances, to acquiesce in the un-Catholic invention of the Jerusalem Bishopric—denouncing, and that in very unfitting language, the See of Rome, because that See, which never parts with, or consents to the infringement of, what it holds to be its inherent and inalienable right and possession in trust, took its own opportunity of insisting upon and asserting that right and possession by way of formal public decree and act. Since that time, "Liberals" and "Conservatives" have both found out what the Roman Catholic power in Parliament is. It is not "convenient" to either of them to run their heads against a wall, which not even their united efforts could prevail to shake. They have learnt the lesson, stereotyped in 1829, that State policy requires all to be done that may be done in the face of the "ultra-Protestant" mind, to soothe Roman Catholic authorities in England as in Ireland; that the soothing process be carried out at the expense of the Church of England, and of what used to be called "the United Church of England and Ireland," this is a small matter, and need be no obstacle in the way of the State policy.

The then Archdeacon of Bristol, my dear friend Thomas Thorp, President of the Bristol Church Union, was charged with collecting the signatures of Clergy to a Protest against the intrusion of Dr. Hampden; and with one other of the Secretaries of the Union I went with him to London, early in 1848, for that purpose. As far as my recollection serves me, and in this particular I have no documents to refer to, the signatures collected did not exceed eighteen hundred; and this, although thirteen of the Bishops had, in the previous December, addressed Lord John Russell against it.

The move on behalf of the Church shared the fate of all other like moves before or since. The Civil Power comes into conflict with the Church as by law established: the Civil Power goes its own way, that way not being the Church's way: the Church remonstrates feebly, if at all, and then succumbs; and goes its way just as if nothing had happened at all.

It was either in 1847 or 8, I think in 1847, that I received a kind message from Henry, Bishop of Exeter, asking me to come and see him at Bishopstowe. I had had no previous personal acquaintance with the Bishop. For nearly twenty years I had the honour of intimate and confidential intercourse and correspondence with him; and, so long as his health permitted him to receive visitors at Bishopstowe, used to be with many others, his guests, there every autumn. I recall thankfully the profit and the enjoyment of the gatherings at Bishopstowe. I shall have to return to some details of intercourse and correspondence in their place.

We come now to the "Gorham" case. I was present with my dear friend Lord John Thynne, at the delivery of the Gorham Judgment, March 8, 1850. As we came down the steps of the Council Office, I said to him, "Well, what do you think will come next?"

He said, "I suppose you mean something about the other Sacrament?"

"Yes," I said, "and it will come very soon!" I did not think, when I said it, that it would come in my own person within four years from that day.

Looking back upon the fifty years from 1828 to 1878, the assault is found to have been directed in all its substance against the teaching of the Church. It is common to represent this otherwise; but the representation is a fallacy engendered either of ignorance, or of shallow assumption, or of wilful blindness. It suits our weakness and want of stedfastness, defects of character very natural to a people so steeped up to the lips in the spirit of compromise, as to have imported it into their method of dealing with God's Eternal Truth, to be always running off upon details and side issues, as if the matter in hand were one of such subordinate things, and not a principle, which, if we hold at all, we may not surrender or compromise directly or indirectly. All my experience has taught me the extreme difficulty of bringing Churchmen in England to look at a question as what it really is, and as to what it involves *ex necessitate rei*. There is perpetually some detail or side issue imported into the discussion; and as in this way great facilities are given for escape from coming to definite conclusions upon the primary matter in hand—all such conclusions being very inconvenient things, except to such as have made up their minds to action, and not to talking only—the discussion commonly goes off upon one or more of such things. I speak from a large experience of Church meetings, and Resolution making; of Convocation for twenty-five years, and as Chairman or member of many of its Committees.

This is, I believe, some account of the fact that so many of us are always shrinking from what I have just stated above—viz. that in its substance, it is nothing else than the *teaching* of the Church against which the assault of fifty years has been directed; and, if resisted for a time by individual action of Churchmen, acquiesced in sooner or later by all that is corporate or quasi-corporate in the Church.

The teaching, stated in its broadest outline, is, 1. in the School; 2. in the Church. We have seen what has become of Church teaching in the School, at the hands of the Civil Power and of the Establishment. For teaching in the Church, this, if it have any substance and unity in it, resolves itself into the teaching of the Doctrine of the Sacraments, the beginning, the middle and the end of the life in CHRIST here. Well, the whole purpose and vigour of the assault, the ground having been first cleared by sweeping away the Church School, is directed against the teaching of the Doctrine of the Sacraments. Has there been any corporate resistance worthy of the name on behalf of the Church? I say, there has been none.

And if there has been here and there individual resistance, there has been at the least quite as much individual encouragement of assault. People may shrink from the conclusion, but they cannot escape from it. The country raves about Ritual; Bishops stimulate the raving. What is "Ritual?" Surely the English people are not so far gone in ignorance or passion, or both, as to suppose that it is outward ceremonial only which the assault is furious to destroy *quocunque modo;* which the defence is resolved to maintain by Grace sought and given; content to leave the temporal and temporary issues in man's hand. Does not everybody know, whose knowledge is worth a straw, that what is really assailed under the name of "Ritual," is the public teaching and exposition in the Church of the Doctrine of the Sacraments, and especially of the Sacrament of the BODY and the BLOOD?

Now the Judicial Committee of Privy Council, the so-called Court of Final Appeal, dealing with the Statute Law after a fashion peculiar to itself and Century XIX., as if there were no such thing in England as the Law of the Church Catholic and the Judgment of the Spiritualty in matters Spiritual, the Judicial Committee of Privy Council has done what it could, first in the Gorham case then in the Bennett case, to ruin the teaching of the Doctrine of the Sacraments. It has not succeeded, to be sure, and it is the failure which has made men so mad against "Ritual," because they see that it is the only battle-ground now remaining to them: it has not succeeded, to be sure, in ruining the teaching of the Doctrine of the Sacraments; on the contrary, it has promoted that teaching to an incalculable extent. But it has tried to succeed to the best of its power; and it is not a very pleasing consideration for those who love "Church and State," to see the Court of Final Appeal in Causes Ecclesiastical doing all it can in the name of the Sovereign to destroy the teaching of the Doctrine of the Sacraments.

The Protests following having been read in East Brent Church, as stated at the foot of each, some notice was taken of them in the House of Commons. I subjoin particulars as recorded in Hansard, with my letter to Lord John Russell, enclosing statement read by him in the House.

[PROTEST A.]

In the name of the most holy Trinity.—Amen.

Whereas the Universal Church alone possesses, by the commission and command of its Divine Founder, the power of defining in matter of doctrine; and, subject to the same, the Church of England alone possesses, within its sphere, the power of interpreting and declaring the intention of such definitions as the Universal Church has framed;—

And whereas a power to interpret formularies of the Church by a final judicial sentence, the Synods of the Church not being, in practice, admitted to declare the doctrine of the Church, becomes in effect a power to declare and make such interpretations binding upon the Church;—

And whereas by the suit of Gorham *v.* the Bishop of Exeter, as well as by the case of Escott *v.* Mastin, in the year 1842, it appears that the Crown, through a Court constituted by Act of Parliament alone, claims and exercises a power to confirm, reverse or vary, by a final judicial sentence, the decisions and interpretations of the courts of the Church in matters of doctrine;—

And whereas in the present state of the law nothing hinders but that an interpretation which shall have been judged to be unsound by the Courts of the Church may be finally declared to be sound by the said Judicial Committee; or that a person who shall have been judged to be unfit for cure of souls by the spiritual tribunal may be declared to be fit for cure of souls by the civil power;—

And whereas the existence of such state of the law cannot be reconciled with the Divine constitution and office of the Church, and is contrary to the law of CHRIST;—

And whereas the exercise of power in such matters, under such state of the law, endangers the public maintenance of the Faith of CHRIST;—

And whereas the existence of such a state of things is a grievance of conscience;—

And whereas no judgment pronounced by the Judicial Committee of Privy Council, in respect of matters of doctrine, can be accepted by the Church;—

I, George Anthony Denison, Clerk, M.A., Vicar of East Brent, in the county of Somerset, and Diocese of Bath and Wells, do hereby enter my solemn Protest against the state of the law which empowers the Judicial Committee of the Privy Council to take cognizance of matters of doctrine, and against the exercise of that power by the said Judicial Committee in each particular case; and I do hereby pledge myself to use all lawful means within my reach to prevent the continuance of such state of the law, and of the power claimed and exercised under the same.

(Signed)   GEORGE ANTHONY DENISON.

EAST BRENT,
4th Sunday in Lent, March 10, 1850.

[Read in the Vestry of the Parish Church of East Brent, in the presence of the Churchwardens and other witnesses, and copies delivered to the Churchwardens, and transmitted to the Bishop, Sunday, March 10, 1850.]

[PROTEST B.]

In the name of the most holy Trinity.—Amen.

I. Whereas the Church of England is a branch of the One Catholic and Apostolic Church, and, in virtue thereof, holds, absolutely and exclusively, all the Doctrines of the Catholic Faith.

II. And whereas George Cornelius Gorham, Clerk, B.D., Priest of the Church of England, has formally denied the Catholic Faith in respect of the Holy Sacrament of Baptism.

And whereas the Judicial Committee of the Privy Council has—in the case of Gorham *v.* Bishop of Exeter—reversed the judgment of the Church Court, and has pronounced, by final sentence, the said George Cornelius Gorham to be fit to be instituted by the Bishop to a benefice with cure of souls;—

And whereas such sentence is necessarily false;—

And whereas such sentence gives public legal sanction to the teaching of false doctrine, and therein and thereby has a great and manifest tendency to lead into error of doctrine, or to encourage to persevere in error of doctrine, or to plunge finally into heresy, all such as are tempted, in one degree or another, to deny the Faith of CHRIST in respect of the Holy Sacrament of Baptism;—

And whereas such sentence does injury and dishonour to CHRIST and to His Holy Church ;—

And whereas all, who, with a full knowledge of the intent, meaning and purpose of such sentence, are, or shall be, concerned in promulging or executing it, and all who, with a like knowledge, shall approve of, or acquiesce in, it, are, or will be involved in heresy ;—

And whereas it has become necessary—in consequence of such sentence—that the Church of England should free herself from any participation in the guilt thereof by proceeding, *without delay*, to make some further formal declaration in respect of the Holy Sacrament of Baptism ;—

I, George Anthony Denison, Clerk, M.A., Vicar of East Brent, in the county of Somerset, and Diocese of Bath and Wells, do hereby enter my solemn Protest against the said sentence of the Judicial Committee of the Privy Council, and do warn all the Christian people of this parish to beware of allowing themselves to be moved or influenced thereby in the least degree; and I do also hereby pledge myself to use all lawful means within my reach to assist in obtaining, without delay, some further formal declaration, by a lawful Synod of the Church of England, as to what is, and what is not, the doctrine of the Church of England in respect of the Holy Sacrament of Baptism.

(*Signed*)   GEORGE ANTHONY DENISON.

EAST BRENT,
Fourth Sunday in Lent, March 10, 1850.

[Read in the Vestry of the Parish Church of East Brent, in the presence of the Churchwardens and other witnesses, and copies delivered to the Churchwardens, and transmitted to the Bishop, Sunday, March 10, 1850.]

(*Copy.*)
22, *Great George-street, Westminster,*
March 18, 1850.

MY LORD,

I have taken the great liberty—I trust you will think it a pardonable one—of addressing direct to your Lordship the enclosed formal statement in reference to the allegation that I deny the Supremacy of the Crown as the Head of the Established Church, contained in Mr. Hume's notice of a question to be put by him this evening in the House of Commons.

I have the honour to be, my Lord,
Your Lordship's obedient faithful Servant,
GEORGE ANTHONY DENISON.

The Lord John Russell, &c.

Statement read by Lord John Russell in the House of Commons, Monday, March 18, 1850:—

I have not denied, and do not deny, that the Queen's Majesty is Supreme Governor of this Church and Realm; and is, in virtue thereof, supreme over all causes Ecclesiastical and Civil; judging in causes spiritual by the Judges of the Spiritualty, and in causes temporal by temporal Judges, as enacted by the Statute Hen. VIII. c. 12.

And I have not impeached, and do not impeach, any part of the Royal Supremacy, as set forth in the Second Canon and in the Thirty-seventh Article of our Church.

But I humbly conceive that the Constitution does not attribute to the Crown, without a Synod lawfully assembled, the right of deciding a question of Doctrine; and this—although disclaimed by the Lords of the Judicial Commitee of Her Majesty's Privy Council—is what, as appears to me, has been done, indirectly indeed, but unequivocally, in the late case of " Gorham *v.* the Bishop of Exeter."

(*Signed*) GEORGE ANTHONY DENISON.
22, *Great George-street, Westminster,*
March 18, 1850.

March 18, 1850, (*House of Commons*).—Mr. HUME said that he held two documents in his hand which purported to be Protests against the late decision of the Judicial Committee of the Privy Council in the case of Gorham *v.* the Bishop of Exeter, signed by the Rev. G. A. Denison, Vicar of East Brent, and dated the 10th of March. Mr. Hume, having read the two Protests, said he thought it was incumbent on the Government, if they wished to have the decisions of one of the highest tribunals in the kingdom respected, to take notice of such language; and the question he wished to put was, what notice the Government intend to take of the Protest of Mr. Denison, published in all the papers yesterday, impugning the judgment of her Majesty's Council in the case of Gorham *v.* the Bishop of Exeter, and denying the Supremacy of the Crown as Head of the Established Church?—LORD J. RUSSELL: I think it just to Mr. Denison that I should read to the House a statement which he sent to me, which I received this morning, and which professes to be a statement of his opinion as regards the Supremacy of the

Crown as connected with this case. (He then read the statements, and said,) Now, I have no hesitation in saying that I think Mr. Denison is entirely mistaken in this opinion which he has given, and that the judgment given by the members of the Judicial Committee of the Privy Council is entirely within their jurisdiction, and such as they were authorized by law to give. I believe it is likewise a decision which has generally given satisfaction. But as the hon. Member for Montrose asks me further what notice the Government intends to take of the Protests of Mr. Denison, I must say that, though it may be necessary for the Government at a future time to take some steps, if it should appear that any measures adopted hereafter on the part of those who think with Mr. Denison required them, —though I guard myself with saying that this may be necessary,—yet I should be most reluctant to take steps against any men who give what they conceive to be the conscientious expression of their views with regard to the Church, and should fear any such act on the part of the Government would only tend to disturb still further the harmony of the Church. And therefore, entirely dissenting from Mr. Denison, and thinking it may be doubtful, particularly after the letter I have read, whether he means to deny the authority of the Judicial Committee of the Privy Council, or whether he intends that he ought to use every lawful means to alter the law, the Government, as at present advised, is not prepared to take any steps with regard to the Protests.

In the course of the summer of 1850 the following Resolutions were agreed to in London, and signed. Of the fourteen persons signing, six shortly after left the communion of the Church of England for the communion of the Church of Rome. Finding that nothing was done, or attempted to be done, in any authoritative way for the re-affirmation of the Doctrine of Holy Baptism, impugned by the "Gorham Judgment," they lost faith in the position of the Church of England.

I took an active part in bringing those who signed together, and in all the discussion that ensued; but, having made my own Protest public in the March preceding, I did not append my name upon the first issue of the Resolutions: afterwards, it appeared to me to be due to myself and others that I should append it. The Resolutions, as I read them now, I do not like much.

"RESOLUTIONS.

"I. That whatever, at the present time, be the force of the sentence delivered on Appeal in the case of Gorham *v.* the Bishop of Exeter, the Church of England will eventually be bound by the said sentence, unless it shall openly and expressly reject the erroneous doctrine sanctioned thereby.

"II. That the remission of original sin to all infants in, and by the grace of, Baptism, is an essential part of the Article, 'One Baptism for the remission of sins.'

"III. That—to omit other questions raised by the said sentence—such sentence, while it does not deny the liberty of holding that Article in the sense heretofore received, does equally sanction the assertion that original sin is a bar to the right reception of Baptism, and is not remitted except when GOD bestows regeneration beforehand by an act of prevenient grace, (whereof Holy Scripture and the Church are wholly silent,) thereby rendering the benefits of Holy Baptism altogether uncertain and precarious.

"IV. That to admit the lawfulness of holding an exposition of an Article of the Creed, contradictory of the essential meaning of that Article, is, in truth and in fact, to abandon that Article.

"V. That, inasmuch as the Faith is one, and rests upon one principle of authority, the conscious, deliberate, and wilful abandonment of the essential meaning of an Article of the Creed, destroys the Divine Foundation upon which alone the entire Faith is propounded by the Church.

"VI. That any portion of the Church which does so abandon the essential meaning of an Article of the Creed, forfeits, not only the Catholic doctrine in that Article, but also the office and authority to witness and teach as a Member of the Universal Church.

"VII. That, by such conscious, wilful, and deliberate act, such portion of the Church becomes formally separated from the Catholic body, and can no longer assure to its Members the Grace of the Sacraments and the Remission of Sins.

"VIII. That all measures consistent with the present legal position of the Church ought to be taken without delay, to obtain an authoritative declaration by the Church of the doctrine of Holy Baptism, impugned by the recent sentence, as, for instance, by praying licence for the Church in Convocation to declare that doctrine ; or by obtaining an Act of Parliament to give legal effect to the decisions of the collective Episcopate on this and all other matters purely spiritual.

"IX. That, failing such measures, all efforts must be made to obtain from the said Episcopate, acting only in its spiritual character, a re-affirmation of the doctrine of Holy Baptism, impugned by the said sentence.

H. E. MANNING, M.A., Archdeacon of Chichester.
ROBERT J. WILBERFORCE, M.A., Archdeacon of the East Riding.
THOMAS THORP, B.D., Archdeacon of Bristol.
W. H. MILL, B.D., Regius Professor of Hebrew, Cambridge.
E. B. PUSEY, D.D., Regius Professor of Hebrew, Oxford.
JOHN KEBLE, M.A., Vicar of Hursley.
W. DODSWORTH, M.A., Perpetual Curate of Christ Church, St. Pancras.
WILLIAM J. E. BENNETT, M.A., Perpetual Curate of St. Paul's, Knightsbridge.
HENRY WILLIAM WILBERFORCE, M.A., Vicar of East Farleigh.
JOHN C. TALBOT, M.A., Barrister-at-Law.
RICHARD CAVENDISH, M.A.
EDWARD BADELEY, M.A., Barrister-at-Law.
JAMES R. HOPE, D.C.L., Barrister-at-Law.
GEORGE ANTHONY DENISON, M.A., Vicar of East Brent."

April 8, 1850, my dear friend, the Rev. Mayow Wynell Mayow, addressed a remarkable letter to the Secretaries of the Church Unions.

In that letter he refers first to his anxious desire to bring forward at the meeting of Committee of Conference in London, 18th and 19th of March, the proposal to " hold a public meeting in London, for the one specific purpose (and of persons friendly to that purpose alone) of agreeing to an address to her Majesty, begging her to call together the Convocations of the Provinces of Canterbury and

York, for the re-affirmation of the Doctrine of the Church of England on the subject of Holy Baptism, impugned through the result of the late appeal to the Judicial Committee of Privy Council in the case of Gorham *v.* the Bishop of Exeter."

The letter goes on to say that the time of the Committee was so urgently occupied with other matter, that he had no opportunity of bringing forward the proposal.

This was the first indication of the difficulties which had to be met and overcome before the meeting was finally held, July 23, 1850.

Mr. Mayow proceeds to give his reasons in detail. The force of these reasons soon became so generally admitted that I need not transcribe them in this place. He adverts further on to the specific character which ought to attach to any such meeting, and "give it a *differentia* from all ordinary meetings," and particularly to the rule which was adopted for the conduct of the meeting, "that the usual manifestations of approval should be altogether withheld."

My recollection is, that upon receipt of this letter I put myself at once in communication with him upon the matter, and that, by our joint efforts, the proposal was ultimately brought to bear, and carried out in two meetings, held simultaneously in St. Martin's Hall and Freemasons' Tavern; the first presided over by J. G. Hubbard, Esq., the other by Lord Fielding.

I have a very clear recollection of the difficulties we had to encounter between March and July. The battle for the meeting was fought principally in the Committees of the London and the Metropolitan Church Unions, and I had a good deal to do with it in both Committees. I remember that one day, being wearied out with opposition and delays, I said that if the Committee did not decide that day to hold the meeting, I should do what I could the next day to hold it myself. I remember also my infinite amusement when it leaked out that a great many members of the Committee were afraid of my taking a part as one of the speakers at the meeting.

I said to them, "Make yourselves, my dear friends,

quite easy. I have no purpose of speaking. I have had quite enough difficulty in getting the meeting held, and have said already publicly, long before this, all that I have to say."

After the meeting was over, one of those who had hesitated came up to me on the platform in St. Martin's Hall, and said, "Well, I am bound to say to you, that you have been altogether in the right in this matter."

"Thank you," I said, "I never doubted about that from the first; it was to me a plain case of duty, not to be put aside upon any considerations."

The Bishop of Bath and Wells, Richard Bagot, was the only Bishop present at the meeting; first at St. Martin's Hall, then at Freemasons' Tavern. He issued afterwards a Pastoral Letter to his diocese, affirming the Doctrine of Holy Baptism, which, with the Address to him of the Scottish Bishops, I have inserted in the Baptism Register of the parish of East Brent.

It is to me matter of deep thankfulness that I took the course I did upon this occasion, in conjunction with my dear friend. I believe entirely that if it had not been for our standing quite fast, the meeting would never have been held.

Now a meeting, however remarkable in its character, is not in itself much. But as I believe that, in the absence of anything like a move of the Church Corporate, the meeting did much towards clearing and settling the minds of English Church-people touching the true Doctrine of Holy Baptism, I look upon it as a great mercy, vouchsafed at a time of extreme confusion and distress.

I may mention here two other instances, parts of my own personal experience, of the good of "standing fast."

As soon as I became Archdeacon of Taunton in 1851, I asked the opinion of the Clergy of the Archdeaconry upon three points connected with the Archdeacon's Visitation:—1. Omission of Sermon; 2. Celebration of Holy Eucharist; 3. Inviting Churchwardens to dine with the Clergy, and talk over matters of common interest.

I think I am correct in saying that, at the time of

which I speak, there was no Celebration of Holy Eucharist at any Visitation in England and Wales, Episcopal or other. Now it is usual.

It had long seemed to me a strange thing that, upon the only day in the year when Clergy and representative Laity come together for Church purposes, the one great bond of Christian fellowship and unity should be wanting, the Celebration of the Blessed Sacrament.

From all the four deaneries of the archdeaconry the answer to my circular letter was favourable, more or less, in respect of Nos. 1 and 3; from three of the deaneries, in respect of No. 2 also.

In the deanery of Dunster, a considerable body of the Clergy were against No. 2. It was not so much the thing, as the man that they objected to; they were afraid of me and of my ways. Among the objectors was my dear kind old friend Thomas Luttrell, Vicar of Dunster, in whose church the Visitation for that deanery used to be held.

Under these circumstances, I did not like to insist upon my right as Ordinary to cite[2] the Clergy and Churchwardens to Dunster, and moved the Visitation to Stogumber. A good many of my friends began to be alarmed, but I "kept never minding," according to one of my dear old Tutor's rules.

On the day came open opposition : a large attendance, but some absences, and some protesting. At last I said, "If another word is spoken out of the proper order of the business of the day, I adjourn this Visitation to this day fortnight." Some word more was spoken; I adjourned the Visitation, and left the church.

The Churchwardens were very generally with me: though

---

[1] I have a list of the Archdeacons of Taunton from 1106 to 1851,—745 years : forty-five Archdeacons, among them Thomas Cranmer, 1522; Archbishop of Canterbury, 1533.

[2] The old citation is curious. It begins with saying that the Archdeacon proposes to visit "for the encouragement of the virtuous, and the extirpation of the vicious, with charity and clemency." Truly a discipline of a profound and searching character. Its restoration is, as the Prayer-book tells us, "much to be wished."

they did not propose to Communicate themselves, they could not understand the Clergy declining to Communicate.

The opposing Clergy sent two of their number to London to consult Dr. Haggard, the eminent Doctors Commons' authority, as to whether they were bound to come to my citation. He asked them two questions :—

"What does the Archdeacon say he will do to you if you don't come?"

"He says he will put every one of us into the Ecclesiastical Court the next morning."

"Is he a man who does what he says?"

They thought I was such man.

"Then," he said, "I advise you by all means to go; for if you don't, you will certainly be in the Court, and I cannot tell at all when you will get out of it."

So they all came and answered to their names, but stood in the porch at the time of Celebration.

The whole thing has ceased now for some twenty-five years to carry any trouble with it. Indeed, it has been a chief comfort that, even at the moment, it had no effect in disturbing, for so much as one day, the relations of cordial good-will subsisting between me and the opposing Clergy, in the midst of all their fear of me and my ways. I dined and slept that day and the next at the houses of two of the leading opponents; and we have always been, and, where living still, are, best friends[a]. At no place has the Visitation dinner been better attended throughout my time than at Dunster, both by Clergy and Laity.

Afterwards, I thought it best to go back to Dunster Church for the Visitation; but not to Celebrate there, till I could do so with the same hearty and general concurrence with which I had been met in the other deaneries.

This state of things remained till Lord Arthur Hervey became Bishop, when his uniform practice of Celebration at his own Visitation removed all difficulty. Meantime, I was repeatedly asked by many of the Clergy of the Dunster deanery to Celebrate for Dunster deanery, as for

---

[a] I find among my letters one from dear Bishop Bagot congratulating me, and expressing his great satisfaction with the entire issue.

the other deaneries. My answer was, that I thought it better to wait for that quiet settlement of the difference which I knew must one day come.

One more instance of the good of "standing fast." Some time after 1854—the exact year I forget—I proposed a meeting at Taunton, open to all comers, against the Abolition of Church-rate. A panic seized upon the diocese, from the Bishop downwards. The diocese made up its mind that there would be a great disturbance, which is almost always a sufficient argument with the Establishment against taking any steps for affirmation and maintaining of principles. The Bishop wrote to a dear mutual friend to say, "Can't you stop Denison? It's no use my trying: do you try." Our dear friend knew me too well to try. However, the panic found its way to me. I took no heed: drew my resolutions, made them as strong as I could; and published them in the local papers a fortnight before the day of meeting.

The meeting was crowded; Clergy and Laity, many Nonconformists also present; some of them spoke. I opened the meeting; put the resolutions, as published, moved, seconded, and spoken to from the chair; and carried each and all *nem. con.* Opponents saw it was no use opposing.

When the meeting was over, and I got into the market-place, a good many "supporters" came and thanked me. "My dear friends," I said, "if you had thrown all this warm water over me yesterday, instead of the cold water of the last three weeks, it would have been more comfortable."

In a few years "Church-rates" followed the common rule of "Conservative" and Establishmentarian resistance, and the small minority of the meeting had their revenge.

When, in 1850, the Bishop of Exeter convened the Synod of Exeter, he communicated to the officials of his diocese the Declaration following. It was a private document but not unnaturally it found its way into the newspapers before the Synod came together. I preserved it, seeing all its historical value :—

"DECLARATION.

"Adverting to the circumstances of the times in which we are called to minister in this reformed branch of the Church of Christ, we deem it necessary to declare our firm and immovable adherence to that great article of the faith—'One baptism for the remission of sins,'—affirming it as it is authoritatively set forth in the Nicene Creed, II. Œcumenical Council, and as it is taught unequivocally by our own Church in its authorised formularies, especially in the offices of Baptism, and in the Catechism; and we are the rather induced to make this Declaration, because we hope that many who are now divided from us may be brought to agreement by thus knowing the real meaning and extent of the doctrine which we hold.

"I. Acknowledging 'one baptism for the remission of sins,' we hold as of faith, that persons duly baptized are not only baptized once for all, but also are baptized with the one baptism of Him who 'baptizeth with the Holy Ghost,' and who thus maketh us 'to be born again of water and the Spirit,' delivering us thereby from the guilt and bondage of all sins original and actual.

"We hold as implied in the aforesaid article of the Creed all the graces ascribed to Baptism in our Catechism. For 'by one spirit we are all baptized into one body,' even the body of Jesus Christ. We are all made to be 'His body,' members in particular of 'His body,' 'members of Christ;' and being thus baptized into them, we are 'baptized into His death,' who 'died for our sins.' We are 'dead with Him,' 'dead unto sin,' 'buried by baptism with Him, wherein also we are risen with Him,' 'quickened together with Him,' 'set together in heavenly places in Christ Jesus.' Believing that by the Holy Ghost so given us in baptism by Jesus Christ, we are in Him 'created anew;' we believe, also, that we are children of God in Him, and 'if children, then heirs—heirs of God, and joint-heirs with Christ,' inheritors of the kingdom of heaven.

"II. We hold accordingly that all infants presented either in church or privately, according to the Book of Common Prayer, and baptized with water, 'in the Name of the Father, and of the Son, and of the Holy Ghost,' become spiritually engrafted and incorporated into His mystical body; original sin being so far from an obstacle to the right reception of baptism, that as St. Augustine says, 'Infants, because they are not as yet guilty of any actual sin, have the original sin that is in them remitted through the grace of Him who saveth by the washing of regeneration.' And as our own Church declares, the baptized child, 'being born in original sin, and in the wrath of God, is by the laver of regeneration in baptism received into the number of the children of God, and heirs of everlasting life; for our Lord Jesus Christ doth not deny His grace and mercy unto such infants, but most lovingly calls them unto Him.' And in accordance herewith, the 27th Article expressly says that the baptism of young children is most agreeable with the institution of Christ.

"III. Without presuming to define whether it may not please God to give a larger measure of grace in baptism to some infants, in answer to the more earnest prayer of those who bring them, we hold that if any shall affirm that the imparting of the aforesaid graces in the baptism of young children is hypothetical, depending either on the sincerity of those who present them, or any other conditions (whereupon it follows, that in cases in which the said conditions do not take place, both the form of baptism itself, and the article 'One baptism for the remission of sins,' must be understood, not as true, but as false and unreal), he doth greatly err, contradicting an article of the Creed, and also the commission and promise given to the Apostles by our Lord Himself.

"IV. Lastly, we hold, and would earnestly impress upon all Christians, that the foregoing statements, rightly understood, so far from disparaging the need of conversion and amendment, are a most powerful incentive to holiness of life, and especially to fervent prayer for renewed or continued grace, as long as the term of this life shall last. For baptism, being the ordinance and instrument of Christ, by which we are born again of the Spirit, John iii. 3, 5, it binds us to do that which it enables us to do, 'to walk in the Spirit, and not to fulfil the lusts of the flesh: for if we live after the flesh we shall die, but if through the Spirit we do mortify the deeds of the body, we shall live.' Baptism makes our bodies to be temples of the Holy Ghost, which is in us, which we have of God, and if any man defile the temple of God, him shall God destroy, for the temple of God is holy; wherefore it follows that they, who having in baptism received the Holy Spirit to dwell in them, live not after the Spirit, but after the flesh, do thereby draw on themselves greater damnation, unless by the grace of God they arise again and amend their lives."

It would have been well if the Synod had affirmed the Doctrine as it stands in this Declaration. Alterations were made in it in its passage through the Synod, which, I proceed to shew, very seriously impaired its value.

Thirty years ago theology in England was, comparatively, a rare thing. The current of religious thought had long been sluggish, and its channel a shallow channel. The special dangers of the time were beginning to quicken the current and deepen the channel; but this could not be readily done. The marvel is, that under the good Providence of GOD in caring for HIS Church, it has been done so quickly.

There are, besides, elements of the general English mind which are, so to speak, anti-theological. It is independent and self-reliant,—excellent gifts, but carrying with them, like all other gifts, their own special trial and temptation.

Again, the general tendency of English life is that of compromise and adjustment; excellent things again in their place, but not in every place. In the principal place inadmissible altogether. The Faith of CHRIST admits of no compromise or adjustment, of any degree or kind whatsoever: it is always eternally the same, whatever the mental condition upon which it falls: it is eternally ONE LORD, ONE FAITH, ONE BAPTISM [b].

Again, of the objective and the subjective, the latter fills a much larger space in the general English mind than the former; and the necessary issue is, a shrinking from what is out of the province of the reasoning faculty to deal with at all, save only as accepting it as delivered by Divine authority. This shrinking very commonly de-

---

[b] The "Times" newspaper, as cited in my Letter to Wordsworth, spoke of its being "*possible to tone down the Bible itself to a judicious neutrality.*" I suppose there to be hardly more blasphemous words anywhere upon record.

generates into resistance; then comes cavil, then scepticism, finally unbelief. It has been well said, that there is nothing more reasonable than to submit our reason unto GOD. In other words, that it is the highest exercise of reason to reduce itself within its own proper limits; and not to presume to lay hands upon the mysteries of GOD.

But the general English mind is very slow to accept this. And it may be said of it, that in no people is there a greater habitual confusion between the *right* of private judgment, which is rebellion against GOD, and the *duty* of private judgment, which is His Will.

Now, when the Synod of Exeter came to the consideration of the Doctrine of Holy Baptism as set out in the above Declaration, it was more or less under these influences. I am only stating what is, I submit, a simple historical fact: I am not accusing or charging my brethren. I shall produce, before I have done, two chief testimonies to the truth of my account of this matter.

The Declaration, as it came from the hands of the Bishop, set forth the Gift conveyed to "persons" in and by Holy Baptism, whether infant or adult, to be a thing absolute, and independent of anything in the receiver.

The Declaration, as it left the Synod, affirmed this in respect of infants, but made it conditional in respect of adults.

Here is the confusion, so often found in English theology, between the Gift and the Blessing of Sacraments. In the case of Holy Baptism, making "Regeneration" or the "New Birth" to be not *given* in the case of an adult baptized in hypocrisy; nullifying, that is, in his case, the Sacrament, by taking from it its "inward and spiritual grace." The case of the infant is not in controversy here. We are proceeding, in respect of the infant, upon the basis laid down for us, "It is certain by GOD's Word, that children which are baptized, dying before they commit actual sin, are undoubtedly saved [c]."

---

[c] There is no bar to the Blessing in the infant case.

Now the adult has the "New Birth" conveyed to him in his Baptism, just as the infant has. If he receive the Gift "worthily," he has then and there the blessing also; if "unworthily," then he has not the blessing; rather does he make it to become a curse, just as in the case of the Sacrament of the BODY and the BLOOD.

The same truth may be put in another way. The *opus operatum* is true as respects the *Gift* conveyed; it may not be true as respects the *Blessing*. Sacraments follow the rule of all other the works of GOD.

Now it ought to have been of itself sufficient to prevent an error like this, to note that, as Holy Baptism may not be repeated, then, if the fact of the Baptism of an adult is conditional upon his repentance, and faith, and charity; in all cases where these are not, he is not, and cannot be afterwards, baptized at all.

I do not presume to enter upon discussion of the theory of a suspended Blessing in Holy Baptism, any more than into that of the withdrawal of the Presence, in the case of one unworthily receiving, in Holy Communion. I have no mind for unauthorized subtleties, distinctions, and speculations such as these, beyond what is written, and, as such, delivered by the Church Catholic. All such things are best left where they are, among the Mysteries of GOD.

As soon as I saw the Declaration as it left the Synod, I wrote to dear John Keble about it. His answer was brief, as his letters commonly were, but distinct and emphatic: "It is very sad about the Synod of Exeter. The first thing the next Synod will have to do is to rectify."

Another of the best and wisest men I have known, a layman, said to me, "I can understand very well your Doctrine of the Sacraments, but I find it impossible to understand the Doctrine of the Synod of Exeter. They have made two Baptisms."

At the time I published what I had to say upon the

matter; and some correspondence ensued. I do not publish it, as by my rule in these "Notes."

At the close of the year 1850, upon the occasion of the "Papal aggression,"—which, in itself, I held all along to be a thing to be resisted strenuously upon "Church" grounds, but the resistance to which, in the shape it took in Bishops' and others' hands, I have all along deplored, —the following correspondence took place. Mr. Sanford was a very good personal friend to me then and since: a man, as long as he lived, much respected and loved. But he was a Whig. "Hinc illæ lacrymæ."

"CORRESPONDENCE.

"I.   (*Copy.*)

"*East Brent, Cross, December* 2, 1850.

" SIR,

" I see in the 'Times' of Saturday a summary of the proceedings at Taunton on Thursday last, from which it appears that you have thought it right to make certain reflections upon my conduct, and upon my fitness to discharge the trust committed to me in this Diocese.

" It appears further that Mr. Miles very kindly said what he felt himself able to say in my defence.

" Now I am unable to accept the defence, i.e. I cannot acquiesce in the suggestion that I have changed my mind, that I have departed from the principles laid down in my first letter to the 'Times,' or that there is any inconsistency between what I say in that letter, and my proposing the address to the Bishop of the Diocese adopted unanimously at the Wells meeting of the Clergy of the archdeaconry; and as I am anxious, on others' account even more than on my own, that my position in this matter should not be misunderstood, I beg to place in your hands the following short statement.

" Perhaps I may, without offence, ask you to give it the same publicity with the observations which have called it forth, by sending it to the 'Times,' with a request that it may be published.

" In my letter to the 'Times' I deprecated—

" 1. The uniting with the Protestant sects against Rome; I hold all such union to be opposed to Church principles, and to be full of the utmost danger to those principles.

" 2. The putting aside, in the excitement of our present alarm, the fact of the extreme peril to which the Church of England is exposed from the aggressions of the Civil power.

" 3. The appealing to the Civil power to interpose between the Church of England and the Church of Rome; I have no belief that the Legislature will find itself in any position to do what it is being asked to do in this matter.

But I never said, or implied, or thought, that it is not the duty of every member of the Church of England to resist the invasion of the English dioceses by the Church of Rome. This I always supposed to be self-evident; the question was simply as to the method and manner of resistance: and accordingly, as soon as the opportunity was given me—which it was the day after I wrote to the 'Times,' and before my letter was published —I expressed my readiness to take part in such resistance, and at the Wells meeting proposed an Address [d] to the Bishop of the Diocese. Into that Address, as it is before the public, I need not enter; I may be allowed, however, to refer to what is reported to have fallen from Mr. Miles, viz. that it was such as he thought no persons present at Taunton would have hesitated to sign.

" I did not concur in, though I did not oppose, the Address to the Crown proposed and carried at Wells; I have not attended any other meeting, or signed any other address besides that to the Bishop of the Diocese.

" I think, therefore, that you will allow that my position in this matter is at once consistent, and removed from any reasonable suspicion of unfaithfulness to the Church of England.

" I believe, as I have always believed, that the connection between the Church and the State is essential to the well-being of this country; I see no security for that connection except in a combined, steady, and patient resistance to all attempts to divest the Church of England, step by step, of her Catholic character, by refusing to her the exercise of her inherent and inalienable right of self-government, and by substituting vague generalities of doctrine for the Catholic Faith.

[d] The Address is printed at the close of the Correspondence.

"All my affections are with the Catholic Church of England, always have been, and I will venture to add, always will be. Those who charge me with unfaithfulness to her, have nothing to found their accusations upon but suspicions as groundless as they are unworthy.

"I am, Sir,
"Your obedient Servant,
"(*Signed*) GEORGE ANTHONY DENISON
"E. A. Sanford, Esq."

"II.   (*Copy.*)

"*Nynehead Court,* 3rd *December,* 1850.

"SIR,

"I have the honour to acknowledge the receipt of your letter of yesterday's date.

"The opinions expressed in it do not surprise me, as they are in accordance with those you have already put forth; and in alluding to them at the county meeting, which, allow me to repeat, I did with sincere regret, it was far from my intention to attribute to you any inconsistency; but as a Protestant Layman in Communion with the Church of England, considering it dangerous that a Minister of our Church, holding the opinions you had professed, should be entrusted with the examination of young men destined for the Ministry, I felt that as a Churchman I was at liberty to comment on those opinions, as you had thought fit to publish them: the present question, in my opinion, not being one of Catholic or Non-Catholic, but rather one between Protestants and Romanists, between the cause of the Reformation and Popery.

"In compliance with your wish, I shall forward your letter and my reply to the 'Times,' that it may be published should they think proper.

"I have the honour to be, Sir,
"Your very obedient Servant,
"(*Signed*)   E. AYSHFORD SANFORD.
"*The Rev. G. A. Denison.*"

"III.   (*Copy.*)

"*East Brent, Cross,* December 5, 1850.

"SIR,

"I have the honour to acknowledge the receipt of your letter of 3rd instant.

"I beg to observe that I have not complained of your having

imputed to me any inconsistency, but of your having stated publickly that I am unfit to discharge the trust committed to me in this Diocese; and that my unfitness to discharge that trust is evidenced by my published letter.

"I am sorry to see that in your letter of 3rd instant you virtually repeat the charge.

"Now a charge of this description is a very grave matter, and one that cannot be rested upon the fact of a difference existing between your method of viewing, and dealing with, the late aggression of the Church of Rome, and my method of viewing and dealing with it.

"And yet, as far as I can see, it has, up to this time, nothing else to rest upon.

"There is *a* ground indeed upon which a charge of this description may very properly be rested, viz. distinct proof either of unfaithfulness to the Church of England, or of teaching, habits, and practices which may tend to produce such unfaithfulness.

"I now therefore call upon you, as you have made the charge, and have not withdrawn it, to proceed to *prove* it.

"I call upon you to adduce any one single instance in which, either in respect of my parochial ministrations, my public or private teaching, or the discharge of my office as Examining Chaplain, I have at any time done, or propounded, or maintained, or suggested, anything which has not been in strict accordance, in letter and in spirit, with the doctrine and discipline of the English Branch of the one Holy Catholic and Apostolic Church, as set forth in her Liturgy, Articles, and Canons.

"If, indeed, it is meant that no Priest of the Church of England, who is careful to do nothing which may compromise her Catholic character, is fit to discharge the duties of such an office as that committed to me; notwithstanding that he shall have—as I have done upon this occasion, and am ready to do again upon any like occasion—publickly declared what is the true position and character of the Church of England, and what is the schismatical character and position of the Church of Rome; and shall have, at the same time, protested against the corruptions of Rome, and the danger of her popular practice—if *this* be what is meant, I would submit that it would be well that it should be openly and distinctly stated.

"But I cannot believe that this *is* what is meant; and I have still a just confidence that it will appear to you that you have done me grievous wrong: and that you will not be slow to repair it.

"I beg to add, that I propose to publish this letter with your reply.

"I have the honour to be, Sir,
"Your obedient Servant,
"(*Signed*)   GEORGE ANTHONY DENISON.

"*E. A. Sanford, Esq.*"

"IV.   (*Copy.*)

77, *Pall Mall, 9th December,* 1850.

"SIR,

"Having left home before your letter arrived, it has been forwarded to me, I have therefore to apologise that it has not received an immediate reply.

"You are quite correct in supposing that the opinions published by you in your letter dated "All Saints' day" were the reasons why I considered you unfit for the charge that has been committed to you; in reference to yourself, I alluded to nothing else at the county meeting.

"You hold a highly responsible position in the Reformed Protestant Church of England, at a time when it has been violently assailed by the Church of Rome, and when we have to deplore so many seceders from our own Church; you publish opinions that I, as a member of that Church, consider to be dangerous; I therefore felt that I had full right to express my opinions.

"I quite agree with you that this is a grave matter; and if I imagined that I had done you a grievous wrong, you would find no one more ready to make every atonement in his power than myself.

"Your letter, I suppose, was intended to produce some effect on the minds of the Church; I thought that effect likely to be productive of evils, and therefore felt it to be my duty to endeavour to counteract it by such feeble means as I possessed. If, therefore, a grievous wrong has been done to you, it has been occasioned by your own publication; had that never appeared, I should not have presumed to allude to you; but if a Clergyman of our Church thinks proper to volunteer and publish opinions, a Layman of the same Church may surely be permitted to remark on them at a legally convened public meeting.

"I have also seen your second letter to the 'Times;' it may possibly be some mitigation of, but, in my opinion, does not counteract the evils likely to be produced by the first.

"I have the honour to be, Sir,
"Your obedient Servant,
"(*Signed*)   E. AYSHFORD SANFORD.
"*The Rev. G. A. Denison, East Brent.*"

"V.   (*Copy.*)

"*East Brent, December* 11, 1850.

"SIR,

"I have the honour to acknowledge the receipt of your letter of 9th instant.

"It appears from that letter that you have *no proof* to offer in support of your charge against me of unfitness for the office which I hold in this Diocese.

"But that, in your view, it is a sufficient justification to say that 'as a Member of the Church of England,' you 'consider' the 'opinions' published by me, a Minister of the Church of England, in my first letter to the 'Times' 'to be dangerous.'

"*In what the danger consists you have nowhere stated.*

"There is not a word in my first letter to the 'Times' which I have any desire to retract (as I have taken care to state in my second letter), or which *can be shewn* to be inconsistent with the duty of a Minister of the Church of England to publish at this crisis.

"My second letter to the 'Times' is not, therefore, in any sense, a qualification or modification of the first.

"I am now compelled to call public attention to what appears to me to be the issue of this Correspondence—viz.

"1. That a Lay member of the Church of England, holding a high position in this county, has made publickly an injurious charge against a Minister of the Church, placed by the Bishop in an office of trust and confidence.

"2. That he is unable to support the charge by any evidence.

"3. That nevertheless he not only refuses to make reparation, but repeats the charge.

"I very deeply regret that at a moment when the Church of England calls upon *all her Members* to assert her true position —which is at once Catholic and Reformed — and to unite upon this basis, in fresh exertions to increase her efficiency, as the *only real* security against the aggressions of Rome; unfounded charges of disloyalty and unfaithfulness, such as that you have endeavoured to fasten upon me, should tend powerfully to promote division, and mutual alienation and distrust.

"I have the honour to be, Sir,
"Your obedient Servant,
"(*Signed*) GEORGE ANTHONY DENISON.
"E. Ayshford Sanford, Esq."

Address moved by the Rev. G. A. DENISON and seconded by the Rev. RICHARD A'COURT BEADON, and unanimously adopted, Wells, November 14, 1850:—

"*To the Hon. and Right Rev. Richard, Lord Bishop of Bath and Wells.*

"We, the undersigned Clergy of the archdeaconry of Wells, desire to offer to your Lordship the assurance of our dutiful attachment to your office and person, with our respectful thanks for your late Pastoral Letter.

"The schismatical act of the Church of Rome, in publishing its decree for the establishment of the Roman Catholic Episcopate in this kingdom, and ignoring therein and thereby the very existence of the Catholic and Reformed Church of England, calls imperatively for our solemn Declaration and Protest; and for our anxious and patient consideration, under the counsel and guidance of our Bishop, as to the best means of resisting the aggression, and of meeting any evil consequences which may attach to it.

"We do therefore hereby Declare—

"1. That the English branch of the one Holy Catholic and Apostolic Church, which has reformed herself, taking primitive Christianity as her model, has a claim upon the undivided and faithful allegiance of the whole English people.

"2. That the position of the Church of Rome is, and always has been since the Reformation, schismatical in these islands; and that by the publication of the late Papal bull for the establishment of the Roman Catholic Episcopate in this kingdom, a fresh and most injurious instance has been supplied of the determination of the Church of Rome to persevere in, and to aggravate, the schism.

"3. That the Church of Rome has, by formal decrees and other authoritative acts, added to, and taken away from, the Faith of CHRIST.

"4. That her popular practice is very dangerous to true religion.

"We do, therefore, further Protest:—

"1. Against the assumption of the See of Rome to exercise Episcopal authority in this kingdom.

"2. Against her manifold corruptions of the Faith of CHRIST.

"3. Against her popular practice, as very dangerous to true religion.

"And, finally, we do hereby Declare—That, by GOD'S help, we will co-operate with our Bishop in maintaining the Catholic Faith of the Church of England, and her Catholic position in this kingdom."

The substance of considerations following upon the subject of preparation for Holy Orders was first published as an Appendix to my Letter to Wordsworth, in 1853:—

Of all the many things which want mending in England, there is certainly no one which requires *more* mending than the professional training of Candidates for, and the conditions of their admission to, Holy Orders.

And not only *more* mending, but *more immediate* mending; and this for a *special* reason, which has only of late years begun to operate, but which *is operating* very powerfully already, and will operate every succeeding year more powerfully.

What I have in my mind is this,—

1. The fact that, while the schoolmasters, the teachers of the young, are now receiving *much professional training, and will receive more*, the great majority of Candidates for Holy Orders, who are to be *the teachers of the teachers and of all*, are receiving *none*.

I am not forgetting here the great advantages of what is commonly called "a general education;" but I am remembering that these are not peculiar to those who propose to take upon themselves the office of the Ministry; it is shared by them with all those who propose to enter into the other learned professions. I am speaking of *professional training*. "General education" is, moreover, being rapidly superseded by "particular instruction." Nevertheless, even such instruction with a view to Holy Orders is, comparatively, a very rare thing.

2. The fact that, while the competency and general fitness of the schoolmasters are, not *assumed* but, ascertained with very considerable pains and exactness of inquiry *before* they are admitted to enter upon the discharge of the duties of their office, the competency and general fitness of Candidates for Holy Orders is, as a general rule, *not so ascertained;* it is *rather assumed*, and this very commonly in the face of much *adverse* evidence.

Now the fault of admitting men to Holy Orders, after examination had, who are found unprepared and unfit, is a very grave fault! Is it an uncommon fault? I fear not at all uncommon. Many get ordained upon a *minimum* continually. There are two chief causes in operation producing this result. Their combined effect is to lower, and to keep low, the standard of admission to Holy Orders. One of these is the large amount of private patronage, supplying excuse for laxity on the Bishops' part; the other is, the having *no* system of professional training, by help of which men might present themselves to be examined less unprepared and less unfit. The first does not fall within my present scope.

For the second, without some such system, brought into general operation for the whole Church, the history of such admission can hardly be other than it is. For it is contrary to natural justice for a Church to say to her members—as the Church of England *in effect does say*—"Those of you, who propose to take upon you the office of the ministry, may be examined with a view to that office after an amount of professional training, *very little absolutely*, and *relatively to that demanded with a view to other callings none*," and then to turn round upon individual Candidates and reject them, because their proficiency is of a corresponding character.

I have felt this so strongly that, although my own examination has had the repute of some considerable stringency, I have only rejected *two* Candidates in the course of *eight* years, on the score of ignorance of the subject-matter of the examination. If, therefore, I am charged, on account of anything I have said above, with using language of indiscriminate censure, all I have to say is, that I blame no one more than myself. But the truth is, that it is not so much the officers of the Church who are to be blamed, as it is the system, or rather no system, under which they work.

One result of these facts is a false position relatively to one another, on the part of both Clergy and Schoolmasters; a false position, to say the least of it, unseemly and unfitting in itself, and full of deep mischief to minister, schoolmaster, and parishioners,—in a word, to the whole Church.

It seems to me madness *to be* multiplying training Institutions for Schoolmasters, and 1st. *not to be* multiplying, *pari passu*, Institutions for the training of Candidates for Holy Orders. 2nd. Not to be making the conditions of admission to the discharge of the latter function better able to bear to be contrasted and set side by side with those of admission to the former, than they are *now*.

It is further still to be borne in mind, that the schoolmaster, if he be *afterwards* found to be incompetent or generally unfit for his work, may be, without much difficulty, displaced; but that no amount of incompetency or general unfitness suffices to displace a beneficed Clergyman; on which account those whose office it is to "send" the Clergy to teach the people, are the more bound to be most careful and exact in "sending" those whom they cannot recall.

I have been desirous, during the last year, to bring this matter immediately under the notice of Convocation, as being emphatically a practical question, and one concerned with the remedy of a very great and pressing evil; but it seems that Convocation *is* indeed to be permitted, once a-year, to echo, in general language, the "Gravamina et reformanda" of the Church, but is not to be permitted to deliberate touching the application of any remedy.

In the absence of anything approaching to a general system of professional training of Candidates for Holy Orders, it is becoming every day more difficult to know what is to be done.

Having held the office of Examining Chaplain in the Diocese of Bath and Wells for eight years, during which time a six months' notice has been required of Candidates for Deacon's orders; and a list of books and subjects has been given to each as the subject-matter of examination, I wish to state, that the result of my experience is *against a six months' notice, and against any list of books and subjects*.

I need hardly say that it is with no view of making the examination *less* stringent and *less* searching that I say this.

I say it because,

1. I have found that to ask a six months' notice is, in effect, to tell men that six months is a *sufficient time* for preparation, by way of study, for Deacon's orders*.

2. I have found that to give men, besides the Bible and the Prayer-book, a list of books and subjects to "get up" in six months, has, practically, *this* result—that men come to be examined, knowing *something* of these books and subjects, but *very little* of the Bible and Prayer-book. This happens because they *assume* that they *know* the last; but are quite clear that they *do not know* the first.

I say "assume," because, as matter of my experience as Examining Chaplain, Candidates know very little of the Bible, less again of the Prayer-book, and yet, without some real knowledge of both, how is a man to be "apt to teach?" The basis must be laid in the Bible and the Prayer-book, other books come in to help the building-up.

If, therefore, I had to begin again, I should propose:—

1. To require only so much notice as would suffice to enable the Bishop and his officers to make the necessary inquiries into the previous life of the Candidate, and to examine his testimonials.

2. To have *no* list of books or subjects either for Deacon's or Priest's orders.

3. To let it be publicly known that every Candidate for Deacon's orders would be examined in the Bible and the Book of Common Prayer, and Administration of the Sacraments.

4. When the Candidate had passed his Examination for Deacon's Orders, and the Examining Chaplain had ascertained, as well *vivâ voce*, as from his papers, all particulars respecting his abilities, his knowledge, and the extent of his reading, up to that time; *then*, to tell each Candidate, *accordingly*, that his Examination for Priest's Orders would include, together with the Bible and Prayer-

---

* There is, besides, an objection of another kind to a six months' notice, which is, that unless there are *four* ordinations each year in a Diocese, it is very difficult to *carry out* the rule; and if a rule is to be continually dispensed with, it had much better be given up.

book, such book or books, subject or subjects, as may appear to be most required for, or best adapted to, each separate case.
5. To make notes of all this, and to examine each Deacon for Priest's Orders *accordingly*.
6. The subject-matter of the Examination being thus limited, and exactly specified as judged to be most suitable in each case, the Examinations themselves to be *very particular, searching, and stringent*.

I understand that the requirement by the Bishops *generally*, that Candidates for Holy Orders, being members of the University of Cambridge, shall produce a certificate of having passed the "Voluntary Theological Examination," *has lowered the standard of that examination, and so tended to mar the main purpose of it*. I am grieved to hear this, but I cannot say I am surprised.

CHAPTER VIII.

EAST BRENT. 1853—1858.

Prosecution for teaching the Doctrine of The Real Presence.

I COME now to the preliminaries of the "legal proceedings" taken against me in the name, but not at the instance, of the late Rev. Joseph Ditcher, Vicar of South Brent in this Diocese, 1854—1858.

The primary movers of the "legal proceedings" were the leaders of the "Evangelical Alliance," a body occupying at that time much the same position in its substance with that occupied now by the "Church Association." The intermediate mover was the Rev. Henry Law, then Rector of Weston-super-Mare, Archdeacon of Wells, since Dean of Gloucester.

The ostensible mover was his official, the Rev. Joseph Ditcher, Vicar of South Brent.

The *causa provocativa* was the fact of my having been compelled, in the discharge of my duty to the Bishop of the Diocese as his Examining Chaplain, "in every case with his distinct previous knowledge and approval," to reject certain Candidates for Holy Orders, whom I found not to hold "Regeneration," or "the New Birth," in and by Holy Baptism; and the opportunity now supplied by the preaching and publishing of my two Sermons upon "THE REAL PRESENCE" in 1853, was eagerly seized upon as a favourable opportunity for trying Sacramental conclusions.

I return to the immediate preliminaries. These were:—

1. The relations, during the earlier part of 1853, between Bishop Spencer (late of Madras), acting as the Commissary of the Bishop of Bath and Wells under a particular commission, and myself.
2. The relations, from June 4, 1853, between Bishop Bagot and myself.
3. The preaching in the Cathedral Church of St. Andrew, Wells, August 7 and November 6, 1853, my Ser-

mons on THE REAL PRESENCE, Nos. I., II.; with Mr. Ditcher's letter to me thereupon, asking me to retract, January 16, 1854; and my reply, refusing to retract anything, the same day.

I take No. 2, first,—

On the morning of Saturday, June 4, 1853, not long after the publication by Bishop Spencer of the Correspondence between himself and me, I was, as I had been for nearly eight years, the Examining Chaplain of my Bishop, and very dear old friend, Richard Bagot, Lord Bishop of Bath and Wells.

When the day began, I had not only no ground for *thinking* that there was the smallest difference of judgment between the Bishop and myself, but I had the most certain ground for *knowing* that there was close and exact agreement, with distinct and express approval by the Bishop, of all that I had said or done in the particular matter between Bishop Spencer and myself.

In the afternoon of the same day I had resigned my Examining Chaplaincy, and had demanded a public enquiry.

The act of resignation and of demand rested *exclusively* with myself. The causes which compelled both on my part were not of my making.

It was a day not only of overwhelming surprise to me, but it was also one of the very saddest days that I have lived to see; but I have never seen cause to regret the step I took that day.

I am going now to break the public silence of twenty-five years. I imposed that silence upon myself at the time; I imposed it of my own mind and act. I could not help anticipating what afterwards came very naturally and generally out of this silence, I mean the imputation that I had taken advantage of the Bishop's failing health and enforced absence from his Diocese, to act in a manner which, as soon as he came to know it, he was compelled to disapprove; that is to say, to act, and this in a case of the utmost gravity, without first communicating everything to him, and receiving his distinct and express approval and sanction.

I looked this imputation in the face. I thank GOD that it did not prevail with me.

I say "public silence," because it was an understanding between those who acted for Bishop Bagot and myself, an understanding offered on my part, accepted on his, that I should not make public the letters that had passed between the Bishop and myself; but that I should be at full liberty to shew them to private friends, as I saw to be either necessary or advisable.

Once only, between 1853 and 1878, I thought it probable that I should be compelled to make all public.

When the pro-Diocesan Court was sitting at Bath, June, July, August, 1856, under the Presidency of the then Archbishop of Canterbury, I said to my Counsel that, if any allegation was made or insinuated against me in the course of the proceedings, that I had acted unfairly or improperly in any particular by Bishop Bagot, I should be compelled to clear myself then and there, as I had it in my hands to do definitely, completely, unanswerably.

No such allegation was made or insinuated; and I kept public silence, as I have kept it for twenty-five years. I have no choice now, in publishing "Notes of my Life," but to state all that is necessary to establish my case. I owe this to others as to myself. A good name is a very precious thing. I believe also that it is best for the memory of my dear old friend, the Bishop, that I should shew exactly what the difference between him and myself really amounted to. I did not know this the day that I resigned my office: I had no means of knowing it. All my information then pointed directly to a difference upon the Doctrine. This proved afterwards not to have been what the Bishop meant.

I remember well that, when I told my dear friend, Charles Stephen Grueber, privately—the able, loving, and indefatigable helper of many years—how the case really stood, he was moved to tears, and said, "In Heaven's name why do you not make all this known publicly? the one ground why I have hesitated about you in this matter is, that I could not help having misgivings, as others of us had, that there might be room for the imputation. You will be as ready to forgive me, as I am rejoiced to know what you have now told me."

And, no doubt, when I resigned my office so suddenly, and said no word about the special circumstances under which I resigned it, men, not unnaturally, thought of me that I had taken some such advantage.

I had in my hands then, as now, evidence shewing distinctly, expressly, unanswerably, that I had done nothing of the kind—nothing which by any colouring could be made to look like it.

But, in my great love for my dear old friend, I was content to bear the burden which the fact of our sudden official severance, though *exclusively* my own act, naturally and almost necessarily laid upon me.

I knew very well that nothing but the fast-failing health and energies of my dear old friend, and his being persuaded to yield up his own better knowledge and judgment to ill-advised, or uncertain, or timid counsels, or to all of them together, could have imported this burden into the case between us.

The following summary of the case is all that is necessary to be stated here.

In 1853, Bishop Spencer (late of Madras) was Confirming and Ordaining for the Bishop of Bath and Wells under Commission, Oct. 4, 1852.

Bishop Spencer had either never read, or had forgotten the terms of the Commission.

The Commission authorized him to ordain those whom I presented to him; it did not authorize him to take any part in the examination of the candidates, or to interfere with it in any way, directly or indirectly. This was reserved to myself, under a special form of "direction and authority" from the Bishop of the diocese, Dec. 19, 1852.

At the Christmas Ordination, 1852, Bishop Spencer states that I "invited" him to "speak to the candidates," i.e. speak *privately*. My recollection is clear and distinct that I did not "invite," but only assented to, when proposed by him. I felt that it was *extra vires*, but made no objection, as, strictly speaking, I ought to have done. A "Charge" to the candidates is a wholly different thing; no objection was ever made by me to that. See my letter, May 9, 1853.

In speaking to the candidates, the Bishop travelled out of the limits of his Commission, expressing to them his "willingness to listen to any question which might then be proposed."

Accordingly, Jan. 27, 1853, the Rev. W. F. Fisher—ordained Deacon Christmas, 1852—wrote to Bishop Spencer about his understanding of what I had said to the Deacon candidates upon the subject of the Holy Eucharist.

Mr. Fisher had wholly and very strangely misunderstood what I had said, and had assumed that it was my purpose to impose a new test of admission or rejection of candidates upon my own authority.

A little accuracy of recollection would have satisfied him that I had stated no such purpose; a little reflection, that it was absurd to suppose that I could state such purpose; a little knowledge of Bishop Spencer's position as Bishop Commissary, and of my position as Examining Chaplain, that he was altogether in the wrong in writing to Bishop Spencer in the matter, or in any matter connected with the examination.

The accuracy, reflection, and knowledge, and I am sorry to have to add, common courtesy, were all lacking; but it is plain that Bishop Spencer was much more to blame than Mr. Fisher, in having "invited" communication, than Mr. Fisher in making it.

Bishop Spencer wrote two letters in reply to Mr. Fisher, one soon after Jan. 27, 1853, the other Feb. 12, 1853. In the second he states his view of the Doctrine of the Holy Eucharist.

Into this Correspondence with a Deacon of the diocese, preparing for his examination for Priest's Orders, the Bishop—being Bishop Commissary, and, as such, having nothing to do, directly or indirectly, with the examination of candidates—allowed himself to enter; and not only this, but he did it without one word of communication to me.

It was not till May 10, 1853,—that is to say, some three months and a-half after the date of Mr. Fisher's first letter to Bishop Spencer,—that Bishop Spencer mentioned to me the name of Mr. Fisher, and the fact of his Correspondence with him. And yet he began his letter to me of April 23, the first of our correspondence, with the words, "I feel it due to us both to write to you with perfect frankness[a]."

This was the position when I went to Wells, April 25, to examine the candidates. Bishop Spencer, acting in entire ignorance of what his position and authority was, had told me of his purpose to examine the candidates, with the view of declining to ordain any of them holding the exposition of the Doctrine of the Holy Eucharist contained in my letter to him. My reply to this was, that it was impossible for me to admit such "counter examination."

The case had become grave and complicated, and, according to my invariable practice, I proceeded while there was yet time to place it before the Bishop of the diocese.

I had all the Correspondence between Bishop Spencer and myself copied out in the office of the Bishop's Secretary, and enclosed it, April 27, in a letter from myself to the Bishop at Brighton. I received, April 30, the Bishop's reply, containing these words :—

"*Brighton, April* 29, 1853.

"I entirely approve of *everything* you have said and done in this disagreeable business. You are right in Doctrine, and it is the Doctrine of the Church; and you are also as clearly right in your view of what should pass between a Bishop and his

---

[a] For all the above facts, see "Letter of Bishop Spencer to the Bishop of Bath and Wells." (Rivington, 1853.)

And "Correspondence between Rev. W. F. Fisher and myself," being a Supplement to the above Letter, published by my direction. (Masters, 1853.)

Examining Chaplain. Pray do not, above all things, publish anything, unless Bishop Spencer publishes; it is much to be avoided on every account.

"R. BATH AND WELLS."

I was with the Secretary at the Palace when the letter came. I gave it to him, saying that I had been so sure before it came about what it would say, that, if it had been delayed, I should have gone on with my part of the Ordination just the same.

Bishop Spencer, having ascertained that his powers under the Commission were confined to what I had told him, ordained the candidates as presented by me to him, May 1; then resigned his Commission, and published the Correspondence.

June 4, 1853, being at East Brent, and about to go to Wells that morning to see the Bishop upon other diocesan business, I received a letter from him containing the words following:—

"*Wells, June* 3, 1853.

"It is very extraordinary that, till my passing through London yesterday, I had never met with the published Correspondence between Bishop Spencer and yourself. On my way down yesterday I read it through, and it pains me to say that I cannot hold the Doctrine of the Real Presence to the extent that you there go.

"R. BATH AND WELLS."

Being unable to put any construction upon these words, except that of a difference *upon Doctrine*, now *for the first time* made known to me, I went to Wells, and resigned my Examining Chaplaincy that same day.

No word passed at my interview with the Bishop to so much as lead me to think that it was not a difference *upon Doctrine* that was meant by his letter of June 3; and that I left him with that and no other understanding of his letter in my mind, is plain from the facsimile of a letter of mine to Mr. Davies, his Secretary, two days afterwards, June 6, 1853:—

"*East Brent, June* 6, 1853.

"DEAR DAVIES,

"Will you, throughout this business, bear carefully in mind the following facts:

"That the Correspondence which I sent to the Bishop, April 27, and which was in his hands when he wrote the letter to me of April 29, contains,—

"1. Bishop Spencer's exposition of the Doctrine of the Real Presence.

"2. My exposition of the Doctrine.

"That I have made *no* statement anywhere of the Doctrine of the Real Presence which is not *fully* and definitely set out in Letter E.[b]

"That, therefore, the exact point at issue between Bishop Spencer and myself was fully and plainly before the Bishop when he wrote his letter to me of April 29. (See above, pp. 227, 8.)

"That I now understand *for the first time*, from the Bishop's letter, dated June 3, 1853, that he *dissents from* the exposition of the Doctrine made by me.

"These are the facts. I send a copy of this letter to Mr. Pinder.

"Yours truly,
"GEORGE A. DENISON.

"*Edmund Davies, Esq.*"

Afterwards, in July, 1853, it became clear to me, through my dear friend John Horner, that what the Bishop had meant to pronounce against was, not my exposition of the Doctrine at all, but only against its being imposed upon the candidates as a *sine quâ non;* and that this had been said by the Bishop in a letter to Lord John Thynne.

Upon this, I wrote to the Bishop, July 1, 1853, to ask him to confirm this to me under his own hand.

---

[b] The statement is, in all its substance, and almost in every word of it, *identical with* that published by me in 1851, in my "Why should the Bishops continue to sit in the House of Lords?" *before* I was made Archdeacon of Taunton in the same year.

The same day Lord John wrote to me to say that the Bishop had said to him : "I never condemned George D. ; but I do not think he should require it of all candidates."

In reply to my letter of July 1, the Bishop writes to me :—

"What you heard from Horner is correct,—that when I said I could not go so far as you did with regard to your statement of the Doctrine of the Real Presence, what I meant was, against its being imposed upon the candidates as a *sine quâ non*."

Now all that is necessary to say here upon this point is this ; that not only had I never imposed it, but had never so much as thought of imposing it of my own authority.

The purpose was saddled upon me by Bishop Spencer and his correspondent, Mr. Fisher ; but all the facts of the case are wholly irreconcileable with the allegation.

There was, therefore, here a very remarkable confusion ; and, looking back upon all that passed, it is clear to me that, if the matter had been put upon this ground to me at Wells, June 4, I should not have resigned my Chaplaincy : but it was never so put till it was too late.

In 1854, the Bishop's advisers, not a great many days before his death, with the object of getting rid of legal proceedings, by being able to produce some sort of Judgment of Bishop Bagot in the case, persuaded him to put his hand to a vague sort of quasi-censure and admonition, endorsing the strange blunder and jumble of 1853, touching my having imposed, or purposed to impose, of my own authority a new test upon candidates for Holy Orders. The reason, no doubt, was to see what could be done to "get rid of" the whole business, and the threatened legal proceedings, by shewing that all that could reasonably be asked for by my opponents had been done already *ex cathedrâ*. I knew that it was very kindly meant as towards myself personally.

But then the "business" was one which was not a personal matter ; one also which, in my hands, could not be "got rid of," so long as life and strength of mind and body remained to me.

A test of truth. of Doctrine is one thing; *that* it was my clear right and my duty to propound. A test of admission or rejection of candidates for Holy Orders is another thing; *that* is for the Bishop to impose, not for the Examining Chaplain. Neither Bishop Spencer, nor his correspondent, Mr. Fisher, nor indeed dear Bishop Bagot, or rather, I should say, his advisers, appear to have grasped the distinction.

It was an official severance, it was never anything more, full of great personal sorrow and distress. Beyond the personal sorrow and distress it caused to my dear old friend, dear Lady Harriet Bagot, and all theirs, as to ourselves and all ours, I have nothing in it to regret.

The same year I preached in Wells Cathedral, and published my Sermons on THE REAL PRESENCE; challenging, and eventually compelling, the public enquiry which I had demanded.

Sermon I. was preached August 7, 1853; Sermon II., November 6, 1853; Mr. Ditcher's letter asking me to retract, and my reply to it refusing to retract anything, the same day, January 16, 1854; Sermon III.; May 15, 1854.

I am not going in these "Notes" into any *résumé* of the history of the "legal proceedings" of four years; I shall touch some salient points here and there. But the history, both on my own and others' part, has long ago been published; and there is no room for, or if there were, no advantage in, republication of details; neither am I going into any discussion of Doctrine.

But, in order to make my position clear, I must go back a little to what was, and had been for some time, in my mind before the difference arose between Bishop Spencer and myself.

I had felt then, for some time, that in one grave particular my position as Examining Chaplain was an unreal and contradictory position. I was required to accept and to act upon definite and exclusive Doctrine in respect of

"Holy Baptism;" I was not required to accept and to act upon definite and exclusive Doctrine in respect of Holy Communion. More than this, it was assumed that it was wrong for an English Churchman, in an official position, so to accept and act in respect of "Holy Communion."

This position of things seemed to me, the longer I lived, to be false, and very dangerous to the holding of the Truth. The Doctrine of "Holy Communion," like all other Doctrine, was, I knew, one and indivisible; but in the Church of England it had been made, for three hundred years, not only more than one, and divisible, but many and wholly contradictory Doctrines.

I began to see that this was what lay at the root of the weakness of the Church of England as a Church, and of the unsoundness of the position of her Episcopate; and it forced itself upon me more and more year by year, that I must needs do what I could towards the recovery and specific affirmation of The "One Faith" in respect of the Sacrament of THE BODY and THE BLOOD; and, if I found that the Bishop, whose Examining Chaplain I was, was not prepared to assert this for his own diocese, in that case to withdraw from my official position. I had never "known" any Doctrine but one of the Sacrament of THE BODY and THE BLOOD, and I recoiled from my own position as that of a Priest who was, in his official position, doing what he was not doing in his parochial position, i.e. largely ministering to the growth of the "Indifferentism" so widely prevailing already in respect of that Doctrine. And I used to say to myself, If belief touching the Sacrament of THE BODY and THE BLOOD be a thing indifferent in the Church of England of the last three hundred years, what is the meaning of talking about "*the Doctrine*" of the Church of England? If this is so uncertain upon a primary point, why not upon all other primary points? It was nothing to say in reply, that the Prayer-Book and the Articles delivered expressly the Doctrine of THE REAL PRESENCE. Thousands of Priests, every Bishop, so to speak, used the Prayer-Book in common with myself and others; but by some strange and curious process of interpretation, managed to read it differently.

And again, there was a specific demand upon belief in respect of one holy Sacrament, and no such demand in respect of the other: one was to mean one thing, and one only; the other was to mean almost anything a man pleased either to invent for himself, or to choose from among the "isms" of Century XVI. The historical account of this curious difference is no doubt to be found in the fact that the controversy of Cent. XVI., so far as it was "religious," centred in the Holy Eucharist; very little, if at all, in Holy Baptism.

My whole position, with all its surroundings, personal and other, was beginning to weigh upon me heavily, when Bishop Spencer's public charge against me in respect of a specific portion of the Doctrine of the Sacraments as stated to him by me,—that such portion "*is not the Doctrine of the Church of England*,"—brought the matter to an unexpected issue; and I became free to contend earnestly for the Faith as best I could. I accepted the freedom as it was sent to me: it involved the pain of official severance from one whom I had always loved, and loved to the end with all my heart, and whose memory is to me and to my most beloved wife a very precious thing. But the official severance (it was never anything more) was to be; and I might not shrink from completing it; but I am bound to confess here, that if it had not been for Bishop Spencer's assistance, I should have gone on as I had done. I had said something to the candidates, at the Christmas Ordination of 1852, of what was in my mind; but not only had I not carried my conclusions into effect, but I had not matured my arrangements for making the attempt. The condition of the Bishop's health, and his frequently-enforced absence from the diocese, were elements of extreme difficulty. I paused, and hesitated.

After Mr. Ditcher's letter to me, January 16, 1854, and my reply to it the same day, the legal proceedings dragged their slow length along.

On or about February 9, 1854, the Bishop of Bath and Wells, in answer to Mr. Ditcher's representation, called upon him to state his "specific charges" in a formal shape.

On March 3, 1854, I asked to be furnished with a copy of such charges.

On March 8, 1854, I was informed that "no specific charge" had, up to that date, been placed in the Bishop's hands.

On March 20, 1854,—two months and four days after the date of Mr. Ditcher's letter to me,—having heard nothing further as to any "specific charge," I communicated to the Bishop the Paper following:—

Propositions first published by me March 22, 1854, being a condensed and formal statement, under eight heads, of what I had affirmed and proved in Sermons I. and II.

I set out below, in VIII. Propositions, THE DOCTRINE OF THE HOLY EUCHARIST maintained in my two published Sermons [e], intituled THE REAL PRESENCE.

> I maintain this DOCTRINE: I have not anywhere, at any time, maintained any other DOCTRINE.
>
> I. That the Bread and Wine become by the Act of Consecration the outward part or sign of the LORD's Supper; and, considered as objects of sense, are unchanged by the act of Consecration, "remaining still in their very natural substances."
>
> II. That "the Inward Part, or Thing signified" is "the BODY and the BLOOD of CHRIST."
>
> III. That the BODY and BLOOD of CHRIST being Present naturally in heaven, are supernaturally and invisibly, but Really, Present in the LORD's Supper, through the Elements, by virtue of the Act of Consecration.

---

[e] Sermon III. contains *no* statement of Doctrine which is not contained in Sermon I. and II. It is an exposition and historical illustration of the true meaning and bearing of Article XXIX.

IV. That, by "the REAL PRESENCE of the BODY and the BLOOD of CHRIST in the LORD'S Supper," is not to be understood the Presence of an influence emanating from a thing absent [d], but the supernatural and invisible Presence of a thing present; of HIS Very BODY and VERY BLOOD, Present " under the Form of Bread and Wine [e]."

V. That "the outward part, or sign," and "the Inward Part, or Thing signified," being brought together in and by the Act of Consecration, make the Sacrament [f].

VI. That the Sacrament—i.e. "the outward part, or sign," and "the Inward Part, or Thing signified"—is given to, and is received by, all who communicate.

VII. That "in such only as worthily receive the same (the Sacraments of the BODY and the BLOOD of CHRIST), they have a wholesome effect, or operation: but they that receive them unworthily, purchase to themselves damnation, as St. Paul saith [g]."

VIII. That Worship is due to "the BODY and BLOOD of CHRIST," supernaturally and invisibly, but "Really Present in the LORD'S Supper" under the form of "Bread and Wine," by reason of that GODHEAD with which they are personally united. But that the elements, through which "the BODY and the BLOOD of CHRIST" are given and received, may not be worshipped [h].

The above Propositions, although first published by me March 22, 1854, i.e. nine months before the sitting of the Commission at Clevedon, as setting out *the exact substance* of the Doctrine of the Real Objective Presence, as maintained by me in my Sermons, were not included in the

---

[d] "Thus much must we be sure to hold, that in the Supper of the LORD there is no vain ceremony, no bare sign, no untrue figure of a Thing absent." —Homilies, Book II., first part of the Sermon concerning the Sacrament.

[e] Note at end of First Book of Homilies.

[f] "Accedit Verbum ad elementum, et fit Sacramentum."—S. Aug.

[g] Article XXV.

[h] "The Sacrament of the LORD'S Supper was not by CHRIST'S Ordinance reserved, carried about, lifted up, or worshipped."—Article XXVIII. Doubtless, *the Sacrament* may not be worshipped: one of the two parts in the Sacrament is "the outward part or sign," the "Bread and Wine," which may not be worshipped.

charge against me, either at Clevedon or at Bath; nor were they at any time, so far as I am aware, adverted to on the part of the prosecution. Possibly it was not convenient to advert to them.

They were drawn up, after repeated consultation with men of high place and chief authority as theologians.

It was objected at the time to my act in publishing them, that I was doing what I could to force on an enquiry. It was quite true; I was determined to have an enquiry, if it could be had.

The Bishop afterwards sent me, April 16, 1854, his Opinion or "Judgment" upon the case (referred to above, p. 230), and having done this, declined to promote "legal proceedings."

The "Judgment" (extra-judicial) acquitted me of having maintained any Doctrine either condemned or censured by the Church of England, but pronounced that there were certain errors in my manner of teaching; and with respect of such errors, passed a sentence of admonition upon me, and enjoined me to be more cautious in future[j].

Some letters passed between the Bishop and myself[k]. I was compelled to demur absolutely to the "Judgment" or "extra-Judicial opinion."

My dear old friend died not many days after the date of his last letter to me, May 11, 1854.

Under all the circumstances, and with the knowledge of facts I had at the time, it is impossible for me not to state here, that I do not believe that any one of the letters of the Correspondence was dictated by himself; written by himself I knew they could not be. His name was used by the writer of the letters, the framer of the "Opinion" or "Judgment," I am obliged to say I think not legitimately. The letters themselves bear no mark of the

[j] See published Protest to Archbishop of Canterbury, Sept. 22, 1854.

[k] "Correspondence between the Hon. and Rt. Reverend Richard, late Lord Bishop of Bath and Wells, and the Venerable George Anthony Denison, M.A., Archdeacon of Taunton." (Masters, London.) March, April, May, 1854.

Bishop's mind and hand, both for so many years familiar to me.

I recognise the motive that caused them to be framed and written; the desire, as I said above, to "get rid of the business." I do not *think* the motive, however kindly conceived, a justifiable motive. I *am sure* that the positions taken in the Correspondence are not entitled to the credit of either theological depth or accuracy.

After Bishop Bagot's death, May, 1854, Lord Auckland became Bishop of Bath and Wells; and, having been applied to by the promoters, declined to proceed by way of letters of request.

Upon this the prosecutor, Mr. Ditcher, applied to the Archbishop to issue a Commission under the Church Discipline Act.

Notice of issuing the Commission was given me, October 31, 1854; issue served upon me, December 21, 1854.

The Commissioners assembled at Clevedon, January 3, 1855.

January 10, 1855, the Commissioners found that "there is sufficient *prima facie* ground for instituting further proceedings."

After divers delays touching method and place of conducting further enquiry, the proceedings in the pro-Diocesan Court, presided over by the Archbishop of the Province at Bath, commenced July 22, 1856, and were continued the five days following.

The following is a summary of proceedings from Jan. 10, 1855, to June 5, 1856.

The Commissioners having made their Report to the Archbishop of Canterbury, and the Bishop of Bath and Wells having been again applied to, and asked to take proceedings upon this

Report by sending the case to the Court of Arches, and having declined to do so, Articles were prepared and deposited both in London and in Wells, on the part of Mr. Ditcher, and the Archbishop was pressed to constitute a Court, and to hear the case, under Section XI. of 3rd and 4th Vic., ch. 86.

The Archbishop declined to proceed further in the matter; upon which steps were taken in the Court of Queen's Bench to compel him to proceed. The following are the dates of the several steps taken :—

Rule nisi	November 22, 1855
Rule absolute.	January 24, 1856
Rule peremptory	April 19, 1856
Citation to the Archdeacon to appear in London	May 5, 1856
Return to Rule quashed.	May 26, 1856
Appearance to Citation.	May 27, 1856
Requisition to appear at Bath	June 5, 1856.

Divers legal objections were taken by my Counsel; but were, one after the other, overruled by the Court.

The question having been argued upon its merits, the Court adjourned to August 12, 1856, when the Archbishop made his Declaration. The Declaration was found afterwards to require modification (see below, p. 240).

The Archbishop then allowed to October 1 for "revocation of errors" by me.

September 30, 1856, I delivered into the Registry of the Diocese of Bath and Wells a Paper stating the grounds upon which it "was not in my power to make the revocation required of me by the Court."

October 21, 1856, the Court re-assembled.

The following is the substance of what took place, October 22, 1856.

Dr. Lushington said, he was expressing the desire of his Grace, when he said that, even at that moment, if Archdeacon Denison would make the revocation required by the statute, his Grace would be ready to receive it.

Dr. Phillimore said, it would be impossible for him to reply without entering into some discussion as to what was required by the declaration and by the statute. He thought the Court had included in that declaration a proposition which it could not intend Archdeacon Denison to revoke. The Archdeacon was called on distinctly to deny a denial of Transubstantiation. He (Dr. Phillimore) could not advise him to do so.

Dr. Lushington would state the two propositions contained in the declaration which Archdeacon Denison was called upon to revoke :—

"That to all who come to the Lord's Table—to those who eat and drink worthily, and to those who eat and drink unworthily—the Body and Blood of Christ are given ; and that by all who come to the Lord's Table, by those who eat and drink worthily, and by those who eat and drink unworthily, the Body and Blood of Christ are received."

The error contained in that passage his Grace required to be revoked.

Dr. Phillimore said the Archdeacon did not conceive that that stated his doctrine. He had never intended to say *simpliciter* that the wicked did eat the Body and Blood of Christ ; what he stated was, that they received the Body and Blood of Christ to their damnation. It was rather hard that he should be represented as stating *simpliciter* that the wicked received the Body and Blood of Christ. He had stated that he was quite ready to deny that the wicked did receive the Body and Blood of Christ *simpliciter*, but he was not prepared to deny that they received it to their damnation.

Dr. Lushington said, the question was not whether they received it to their damnation, but whether they received it at all. The other proposition was, " It is true that worship is due to the real, though invisible and supernatural presence of the Body and Blood of Christ in the Holy Eucharist, under the form of Bread and Wine."

Dr. Phillimore asked whether the words in the Homily were objected to?

Dr. Lushington said the whole of what he had stated was objected to, as not being consistent with the doctrine contained in the Articles.

Dr. Phillimore would confer with his client upon the subject.

Dr. Lushington said, his Grace would be happy if, after a conference with the Archdeacon, the learned counsel was prepared on his behalf to make such a revocation as was required.

After an absence of about an hour, his Grace re-entered the Court, attended by his assessors; but Dr. Phillimore, not having returned from the conference with the Archdeacon, a further pause ensued.

Dr. Phillimore then entered the Court, and said, that he had had a conference with his venerable client, and he hoped that his Grace would be of opinion that, inasmuch as the declaration was modified by what fell from the Court, he had not occupied any greater length of time than was necessary. His venerable friend was anxious that he should read to the Court his answer to his Grace's proposition, which was as follows:—

"In respect of the receiving of the Body and Blood of Christ by the wicked,

"I find in Article Twenty-five the words following: 'They that receive them (the Sacrament) unworthily purchase to themselves damnation, as St. Paul saith.'

"I find in the Catechism, 'That a Sacrament has two parts—the outward and the inward. That the inward part or Thing signified of the Sacrament of the Lord's Supper is the Body and Blood of Christ.'

"I am, therefore, unable to deny that the Body and Blood of Christ, the inward part or Thing signified of the Sacrament, are received by the wicked to their damnation, and I disclaim the receiving of them in any other sense.

"In respect of the worship due:—In the notice appended to the First Book of Homilies, and referred to as of authority in the title-page of the Second Book, there are the words following:—

"'Of the due receiving of His Blessed Body and Blood under the form of Bread and Wine.'

"My proposition is,—

"'It is true that worship is due to the real, though invisible and supernatural, Presence of the Body and Blood of Christ in the Holy Eucharist, under the form of Bread and Wine.'

"I have, in the only two places in which I have spoken of the worship due, expressly denied that worship is due to the consecrated elements. I am unable to deny that Christ Himself, the

Thing signified of the Sacrament, is to be worshipped in and with the Sacrament. I say that, apart from and without the Sacrament, wheresoever He is, He is to be worshipped. I disclaim any other worship.'

Dr. Lushington said, it was perfectly clear that that statement, so far from being a retractation, was a reiteration of what had been said before. The learned Judge then proceeded to deliver the Judgment of the Court: depriving me of my Vicarage and Archdeaconry.

Notice of Appeal to the Court of the Province was given on my part, and time allowed for such appeal to December 5.

Early in 1857, the Court of the Province reversed the Judgment of the Court at Bath upon the first legal objection.

The Prosecutor appealed to "the Court of Final Appeal in Causes Ecclesiastical."

On February 6, 1858, the Court of Final Appeal rejected the appeal of the prosecutor, and the "legal proceedings" of above four years came to a close.

It had been a curious spectacle, and a complicated transaction.

Two Diocesans of the Diocese of Bath and Wells, not of the same school either in Politics or Religion, refusing to have anything to do with "legal proceedings," the second refusing twice. The Archbishop of the Province, seven months after the first move of the prosecutor, issuing a Commission,—a Commission got together, after many failures, with extreme difficulty, and composed exclusively of men opposed to the person charged with false doctrine. The Commission brought together four months later. The person so charged refused a hearing before the Commissioners. The Archbishop, upon report of Commission, January 10, 1855, proceeding only under compulsion by *mandamus*, June 5, 1856. A Court of first instance presided over by the Archbishop at Bath, composed as the Commission had been composed at Clevedon. An Assessor — nominally "Assessor," really "the Court"—formerly Judge of the Court of the Province, overruling in succession "legal objections" to the proceedings *on his way to "the merits;"* the first of which objections was, upon appeal, sustained against him as fatal to the entire proceedings at law, and his sentence of Deprivation quashed, first by the Court of the Province, finally, upon Counter Appeal of the Prosecutor, by the Court of "Final Appeal in Causes Ecclesiastical." An Assessor, in his eagerness to arrive at the prestige of condemnation by a Court presided over by the Arch-Bishop, condemning Bishop Andrewes, whose words had been adopted as his own by the person charged with false doctrine. All these things have their use and warning: they do not present a pleasing picture of "legal proceedings" in a theological case.

For myself, I was at no period of the proceedings troubled about the final issue as respected myself, although I was a good deal troubled about the cost of time and labour and money to kind friends, and the interruption of work at home and elsewhere. I have, however, great cause for thankfulness, in the knowledge that the long discussion of the case contributed very materially to a much more general, and a much sounder knowledge of the Doctrine of the Sacraments.

For others' anxiety on my account I could not but feel deep concern.

I despised throughout the imputation that I was shielding myself under "legal objections," when, if I had been an honest man, I ought to have waived all such things and gone at once to "the merits." I despised the imputation as dishonest: I laughed at it as ridiculous. If there had been so much as the shadow of a shade of a decently fair tribunal, rather I should say, if there had been *any* tribunal in England recognised by the constitution in Church and State as competent to pronounce in matter of Doctrine (the same has to be said now in respect of matter of Worship), I might possibly have considered about taking the case *simpliciter* upon its "merits." But fairness and competency were alike lacking.

I was proceeded against under a penal Statute, involving the highest penalty known to our time. It was no secret that the promoters of the prosecution were straining every effort to procure a conviction. Proceeded against under Statute, I defended myself under Statute. I knew well that I had other highest interests in my hands, beyond and beside what might befall me personally. I knew well that what was aimed at in my person, was the branding with "heresy at law" the Catholic Doctrine of the Blessed Sacrament. I knew that the prosecution had left, were leaving, and would leave, no stone unturned to get condemnation of me.

Being charged with "false doctrine," it seemed no doubt, upon the surface-view of the case, unworthy to be fighting about points of law. I shrank from it myself at first, but a very little consideration sufficed to shew me that it was my plain duty, under the circumstances, to myself and to others. And indeed, where could a decision upon the merits be had, entitled to the smallest respect? From the packed Commission? From the packed Court? As for the Courts of first, and of Final Appeal,—the first in its subordination to the second, the second in its own nature,—were devoid of legitimate authority in matters of Faith and Worship.

And besides, I knew very well that the utmost of what could be looked for "upon the merits," from the so-called Court of Final Appeal, would be a condonation of myself, but a condonation disparaging and vilifying Catholic Truth.

All these things combined to make me despise the imputation as dishonest, and laugh at it as ridiculous.

I was therefore not sorry when the supposed tragedy, but real farce, was played out, and I was left to go back to my proper work.

If by any combination of circumstances I had been "finally deprived," and the choice allowed me still, whether I would recant or lose my Vicarage and Archdeaconry, everybody who knows anything of me, knows very well what my choice would have been. The exclusion of Catholic Truth would have robbed the Establishmentarian position of all the inducement to continue to minister in the Establishment, just as at the present time the exclusion of Catholic Ceremonial, if carried out in my person, would leave me without any desire remaining to continue so to minister. There is a worse thing than the being deprived, and the suffering worldly loss; and that is, the betraying CHRIST and His Church rather than suffer worldly loss. The one has its penalty here; in its measure it has its reward here also[1]; the other has its present satisfaction here; it has its penalty here and hereafter.

I turn away from the darkness of vital difference among Christian people touching the Truth of CHRIST, to the bright light of loving-kindness which, even where difference has been deepest, runs like a thread of gold through all the conflict of my life. At no time has it shone more brightly, and been more carefully tended by so many hands, sympathizing and opposing, than in 1853—1858. Not even in my illness, twelve years after, when I look back upon it with comfort and thankfulness, greater than words can tell. It is always present to me; the loving and self-denying help of family and friends, and very many personally unknown to me; the reluctance, and the positive refusal of opponents to take any part against me. My dear brother, Robert Phillimore, brought to bear upon the case from first to last, with unsparing and self-denying hand, all the power of his great abilities, varied and sound knowledge, and acute perception. One other name I

---

[1] St. Mark x. 29, 30: "And Jesus answered and said, Verily I say unto you, There is no man that hath left house, or brethren, or sisters, or father, or mother, or wife, or children, or lands, for My sake, and the Gospel's, but he shall receive an hundred-fold now in this time, houses, and brethren, and sisters, and mothers, and children, and lands, with persecutions; and in the world to come eternal life."

must specify here. No man has done more then and since—few men so much—for the cause of Catholic Truth, than my dear friend, Charles Stephen Grueber. I shall have to record presently, one remarkable and exceptionable instance.

Here, then, I leave what could not be measured by many words, and which no one will think that I measure by the few I give to it. If, besides time and labour unpaid and not to be repaid, the money-cost of four years' conflict was great, it was not, much of it, my own money. If the cup of loving-kindness was day by day put into my hand, however I might drink of it, it was always full.

Concurrence in the position taken by me in respect of the Doctrine of the Holy Eucharist, and approval of the test applied to what was meant by THE REAL PRESENCE, was at first a very much rarer thing. I was not surprised nor disappointed. For three hundred years there had been a recognition of teaching in the matter of the Holy Eucharist, not only not Catholic teaching but directly opposed to it, as being admissible in the Church as by law established, side by side with Catholic teaching. This could hardly issue in anything but that in which it had issued: negation of the Doctrine of Rome—without any but a surface apprehension of what that Doctrine is, and with unlimited confusion of authoritative theological statement with popular practice—and no specific and distinct affirmation of the Doctrine of the Church of England. It had come to be generally received that the only *quasi-positive* statement that an English Churchman had need to make was, that he was not a Roman Catholic or "Papist." The whole teaching was in a misty and confused and intricate position. There was nothing of that simplicity about it which is always a sign and an incidence of Truth. It had come to be assumed that the Prayer-Book leaned very much one way, the Articles another. No doubt there are expressions in the Articles which seem to deliver the anti-Catholic Doctrine; and there is one such in the Prayer-Book; but the weight of evidence from both is incalculably on the other side. The man who is outside the Church of England, who is therefore neither Catholic nor neo-Evangelical, the intelligent and well-read Nonconformist, is the best judge of the plain natural sense of Prayer-Book and Articles in this respect; and his judgment has many times been given on the Catholic side. The Nonconformist has little sympathy with the Catholic; he has less than little with the Evangelical: but he respects the first, as teaching according to the documents and authority of his Church; he mistrusts and does not respect the second, because he finds him narrowly exclusive, without any intelligible ground for his exclusiveness; inasmuch as he thinks very little, if anything, more of the Sacraments than the Nonconformist himself. He finds that the Evangelical has always on his lips "Prayer-Book and Articles," "the Doctrine of the Church of England," and the like; but that his preaching, which is to him the chief part of his Office, is anti-Prayer-Book and Articles; and his understanding of "the Doctrine of the Church of England," a negation only; a vague and misty thing.

This is the "Evangelical" of our day. He ought to be at one with the Nonconformist; he is farther away from him than the Catholic. The Nonconformist sees plainly enough that of those who hold the benefices of the Church of England, no one has so little right to hold them as the modern Evangelical.

And indeed, apart from Nonconformist judgment, the modern Evangelical has given sentence against himself here. Who is it of English Churchmen who is calling for alterations in, and eliminations from, the Prayer-Book? It is not the Catholic. He feels quite safe with what has been so marvellously preserved to him by the Providence of GOD: he regrets, no doubt, the loss of many things, and with patience waits till it please HIM to repair the loss; but he is against all change in the Church's formularies, because they include all the essential parts of Catholic Truth, and deny no part of it; and because he knows very well what the character of any change at this time would be. The modern Evangelical would have a "Reformed" Prayer-Book, and accept it even at the hands of a Legislature of "all persuasions" and of "no particular persuasion," provided only that the "Reform" would leave the Prayer-Book stripped of the Catholic character now stamped upon it throughout.

The old Evangelical was a man of another stamp. He was nearer to Wesley's time, and his holding of the Doctrine of the Sacraments was as Wesley's was: the same Gift always given in and by the outward sign; the Blessing or the Curse according to the state of heart and mind in receiving the Gift.

I was not, therefore, without expressions of sympathy and concurrence from the old Evangelical in and out of England. He could not understand his modern brother's desire and endeavour to cast me out.

"High Churchmen," with some exceptions, at first looked coldly on; that class especially of "High Churchmen" which is represented by the "Guardian" newspaper. But as the prosecution went on, and especially after the Declaration of the Archbishop at Bath, of what is not, and what is, the Doctrine of the Holy Eucharist in the Church of England, they gathered round me, no less from deep and earnest desire to do what might be done towards maintaining The Truth, than from a clear and indignant sense of the iniquity of the manner and method of the prosecution.

I think that the prosecution did not see at first that in putting the Declaration into the Archbishop's mouth, it had placed itself in a self-contradictory position. It had escaped it in the very act of declaring itself, and in the teeth of its own statement of the position, in its haste to get what condemnation it could, that it is no part of the Power Judiciary, any more than it is of the Power Legislative, to define what is or is not true Doctrine; all that it can do is to say (the question of the right to say *anything* in the matter is quite another and a preliminary question) whether such and such statements can be reconciled with the Church's formularies [m]. Accordingly, the Assessor used these words: "The *only question*, then, "his Grace has tried, *or could try*, with reference to the "law was, whether these sermons did or did not contain "doctrines opposed or repugnant to the Thirty-nine Articles of the Church of England." Now in the teeth of this, there was the definition of what the Doctrine of the Church of England is, made and "declared" by the Archbishop; and when the Court came to pass sentence upon me, October 22, 1858, it had no choice but to "declare" it again; as it had been previously declared, August 12, the same day upon which it had been acknowledged that the Court had no power to declare it at all.

When the Court came to *file their Declaration* (the *filing* is dated *the same day* as the *delivery*), the words, "*The only*," down to "England," were found to be inconvenient to insert, because not compatible with the added statement of what *is* "the true and legal exposition of the 28th and 29th Articles," therein repeated. This was retained; the words stating that it ought not to be there were left out.

Again, there is the significant difference that, in the "Declaration *as delivered*," it is "true legal;" in "the Declaration *as filed*," "true *and* legal." "True legal" means, if it mean anything, "legally true;" here the Statute-law is the dominant, and the Truth the subordinate, element. "True and legal" means, "True prior to, and independent of, Statute-law;" the Truth being afterwards embodied in and by Statute. The Declaration *as filed*, August 12, 1856, goes a very long way indeed beyond the Declaration *as delivered the same day;* but it takes no account of the progress: it would not have been "convenient."

---

[m] See Declaration of the Court, *as delivered at the Court*, Tuesday, August 12, 1856. "Proceedings at Bath," pp. 129, 135.

DECLARATION OF THE ARCHBISHOP OF CANTERBURY at the Court at Bath on August 12, 1856, as filed by the Court [a].

Dr. Lushington stated that his Grace the Archbishop of Canterbury desired him to read the following declaration :—

That his Grace has taken into consideration the Articles filed in this proceeding on behalf of the Reverend Joseph Ditcher, Vicar of the Parish of South Brent, in the County of Somerset and Diocese of Bath and Wells, against the Venerable George Anthony Denison, Vicar of East Brent, and Archdeacon of Taunton, in the County and Diocese aforesaid, the evidence adduced in proof of the said Articles, the arguments of counsel and the authorities cited, and with the assistance of his Assessors, he has come to the following conclusions :—

That the eight first Articles filed against the said Archdeacon are proved so far as is by law necessary.

That the 9th, 10th, 11th, 13th, and 14th of the Articles, filed in this proceeding on behalf of the said Rev. Joseph Ditcher, are proved, and that the charges therein made are established so far as is hereinafter mentioned : Whereas it is pleaded in the said 9th Article filed in this proceeding that the said Archdeacon, in a sermon preached by him in the Cathedral Church of Wells, on or about Sunday, the 7th of August, 1853, did advisedly maintain and affirm doctrines directly contrary and repugnant to the 25th, 28th, 29th, and 35th of the Articles of Religion, referred to in the statute of the 13th of Elizabeth, chap. 12, or some or one of them; and, amongst other things, did therein advisedly maintain and affirm, "That the Body and Blood of CHRIST, being Really Present after an immaterial and spiritual manner in the Consecrated Bread and Wine, are therein and thereby given to all, and are received by all, who come to the LORD's Table;" and "That to all who come to the LORD's Table, to those who eat and drink worthily, and to those who eat and drink unworthily, the Body and Blood of CHRIST are given ; and that by all who come to the LORD's Table, by those who eat and drink worthily, and by those who eat and drink unworthily, the Body and Blood of CHRIST are received." His Grace, with the assistance and unanimous concurrence of his Assessors, has determined that the doctrine in the said passages is directly

[a] "Proceedings against the Archdeacon of Taunton, 1854-56," pp. 136-9.

contrary and repugnant to the 28th and 29th of the said Articles of Religion mentioned in the aforesaid statute of Queen Elizabeth, and that the construction put upon the said Articles of Religion by the Ven. the Archdeacon of Taunton, viz. that the Body and Blood of CHRIST become so joined to, and become so Present in°, the Consecrated Elements by the act of Consecration, that the unworthy ᵖ receivers receive in the Elements the Body and Blood of CHRIST, is not the true or an admissible construction of the said Articles of Religion. That such doctrine is directly contrary and repugnant to the 28th and 29th Articles; and that the true and legal exposition of the said Articles is, That the Body and Blood of CHRIST are taken and received by the worthy receivers only, who, in taking and receiving the same by faith, do spiritually eat the Flesh of CHRIST, and drink His Blood; whilst the wicked and unworthy, by eating the Bread and drinking the Wine without faith, do not in anywise eat, take, or receive, the Body and Blood of CHRIST, being devoid of faith, whereby only the Body and Blood of CHRIST can be eaten, taken, and received. Whereas it is pleaded in the said 11th of the Articles filed in this proceeding, that divers printed copies of the said sermon or discourse in the 10th Article mentioned as written and printed, or caused to be printed, by the said Archdeacon Denison, were, by his order and direction, sold and distributed some time in the years 1853 and 1854, within the said Diocese of Bath and Wells; and whereas the said sermon or discourse contains the following, amongst other passages: "That the Body and Blood of CHRIST, being Really Present, after an immaterial and spiritual manner in the Consecrated Bread and Wine, are therein and thereby given to all, and are received by all, who come

---

° The proceedings of the Court abound in instances of inaccuracy and unfairness; e.g. in this and other places, no manner of notice is taken in respect to the use of the word "in," of my note to Preface of Sermon II., as in all editions.

The note is this: "Having been advised that the use of the word 'in' in this context, though not uncommon in the writings of our own Divines, might appear to some to savour of some *material* Presence, I have carefully avoided such use in my further statements and arguments. In the present Preface I could not do so, because I am here quoting previous statements and answering objections taken to such statements." Preface to Sermon II., Third Edition, 1855. (Masters, London.)

ᵖ Note here the confusion between "unworthy receivers" and those "receiving unworthily."

to the LORD's Table;" and "That to all who come to the LORD's Table—to those who eat and drink worthily, and to those who eat and drink unworthily—the Body and Blood of CHRIST are given; and that by all who come to the LORD's Table—by those who eat and drink worthily, and by those who eat and drink unworthily — the Body and Blood of CHRIST are received." His Grace, with the assistance of his Assessors, has determined that the passages aforesaid contain a repetition of the erroneous doctrine charged in the Ninth Article filed in this proceeding, and that such doctrine is directly contrary and repugnant to the Twenty-eighth and Twenty-ninth of the Articles of Religion mentioned in the aforesaid Statute of Queen Elizabeth.

Whereas it is pleaded in the said 14th of the Articles filed in this proceeding, that divers printed copies of a Sermon or discourse in the 12th Article mentioned as written or printed, or caused to be printed by the said Archdeacon, were by his order and direction sold and distributed in the years 1853 and 1854 within the said Diocese of Bath and Wells; and whereas the said sermon or discourse contains the following, amongst other passages: "That to all who come to the LORD's Table, to those who eat and drink worthily, and to those who eat and drink unworthily, the Body and Blood of CHRIST are given; and that by all who come to the LORD's Table, by those who eat and drink worthily, and by those who eat and drink unworthily, the Body and Blood of CHRIST are received;" and "It *is not* true that the Consecrated Bread and Wine are changed in their natural substances, for they remain in their very natural substances, and therefore may not be adored. It *is* true that worship is due to the Real, though invisible and supernatural Presence of the Body and Blood of CHRIST in the Holy Eucharist, under the form of Bread and Wine." His Grace, with the assistance of his Assessors, has determined that the doctrines in the said passages are directly contrary and repugnant to the 28th and 29th of the said Articles of Religion mentioned in the aforesaid Statute of Queen Elizabeth.

Here, then, it is said, are two modes of one and the same belief; the "true and legal," the false and illegal — (it should have been, as in the order of the thought conceiving, "legal and true;" but let this pass for the present). Is it one and the same belief? Nay, but it is two beliefs. If two beliefs, then, not one Faith, but two faiths; if two faiths, then, not one Religion, but two religions.

The neo-Evangelical is beginning, in his extremity—for indeed he is fallen very low—to find this out. He is beginning to talk about two religions; speaking of his own religion and the Catholic Religion: his own religion, that is to say, one of the thousand developments of "Protestant" religion, and called "neo-Evangelical."

Now, beyond all dispute, the neo-Evangelical is right here. It is two religions; not two modes of one and the same religion.

For Religion is a compound thing, made up of two parts: one of these objective, *quod animo objicitur;* the other subjective, *quod animo subjicitur:* one GOD'S Gift, the other man's acceptance. Both compounded make up Religion. But in their nature they are things distinct, and may not be confounded. Gift is not acceptance; acceptance is not Gift. The Gift is one eternally, as the Giver is One eternally; the acceptance is of many kinds, and may be temporal or worldly only,—many false kinds, one true kind. The kind of acceptance does not alter the Gift; that remains one eternally; but it alters the Religion. If the one true acceptance, then the one true Religion; if a false acceptance, then a false religion. It is just as GOD'S Predestination and man's free-will; both compounded make up GOD'S Providence unto life. There is good free-will unto life; there is bad free-will unto death. The Predestination is one and eternal; the free-will is good or bad: but it is always free-will, as it is always Predestination. Can we comprehend this? No, not any part of it. But if, nevertheless, we do not make it the rule of our life, we walk through this world in the darkness that may be felt. Make it the rule of our life, and then, without comprehending, there is love, rest, peace, joy in believing.

The neo-Evangelical is, then, right in his conclusion from his premises,—it is "two religions." What lies at the root of his premisses, which are false, is some intrusion, more or less, into the province which is, not man's, but GOD'S only. He confounds Gift with acceptance, acceptance with Gift.

Now, then, let us apply a little.

Let it be granted that "Catholic" and "neo-Evangelical" accept alike Incarnation and Atonement. The divergence begins and culminates about the manner of application of Incarnation and Atonement to man's soul.

To the "Catholic," this is by the Sacraments; he knows of no other way, because no other way has been revealed, and this way has been revealed. Sacraments are *the* channels by which GOD is pleased to dispense the Gift.

The neo-Evangelical has another order: he does not accept GOD'S Sacraments as the channel of Grace; he prefers man's preaching. And so he makes a religion; but it is not CHRIST'S religion, not, that is, the Catholic Religion.

Neo-Evangelicalism is only one form of many-headed "Protestant" error; the Declaration of the Court at Bath, with its significant jumble of "true" and "legal," is the expression of it. It should have been, as I said above, "legal" and "true;" "Law" first, Truth after. For the neo-Evangelical wants man's law, the law of a Legislature and a Judiciary of all religions and of none, in place of God's Revelation by His Church; he wants his own particular heresy to be dominant and exclusive, instead of tolerated, as by the precedent first established in Century XVI. His wants are natural; they follow the nature of his belief.

But he cannot have his wants, however much the "policy" of the time—social, political, economical—may be on his side. GOD guards His own. Why do "the People imagine a vain thing?"

In 1855 I published "Saravia on The Holy Eucharist, the Original Latin from the MS. in the British Museum, then printed for the first time." The translation on the opposite page is my own; there is also Notice of the Author, and Appendix. (Masters, London.)

It is a very interesting treatise, as well from its own great value, as from the character and position of its author, and his close connection with Hooker.

In the treatise, the precise teaching charged against me as false doctrine and a depravation of "the Articles," is illustrated, unfolded, and definitely taught.

I find that I state in the Preface that, in the discussions of Saravia's time, as in those of earlier and later time, the reception by the ungodly of "the Inward Part or Thing signified" of the Sacrament, is found to have assumed at once the character of *a test* of the right understanding of "THE REAL PRESENCE;" and that I am persuaded, as I had stated elsewhere, that it is the soundest and the safest test.

One day, during the sitting of the Court at Bath, Grueber came to me with a letter in his hand, which he gave to me to read. It was a letter from Keble.

Before I give the contents of the letter, I should explain that, at the beginning of the case in 1854, it had been proposed that Pusey, Keble, and I were to be a Committee for receiving contributions to meet the expenses of the Defence.

I found afterwards that there was a difficulty somewhere about carrying out this arrangement, and ascertained, after a little time, that Keble was not then fully prepared to endorse my position touching reception by the wicked.

Upon this, knowing well that it would be much against Pusey's wish that he should act in the matter where Keble did not, I wrote to Pusey at once, to say that I should be glad if he would let the matter of receiving contributions rest for the present in my hands only. And so it remained till after Judgment given at Bath; when other kind friends formed a Committee, and, so long as the case lasted, relieved me of all further care about money.

Meantime, Grueber had published many tracts, &c., upon the case, having grasped it in all its depth, extent, and fulness from the first. His deep and accurate knowledge of the subject-matter, his clearness of statement and power of argument, touching this and all other great Church questions of our time, are well and widely known amongst us.

As he published the successive parts of his Argument, he had always sent a copy to Keble: Keble's letter, mentioned above, was a letter of acknowledgment of the publication last received.

The letter went on to say that he had a special reason to be thankful to Grueber, in that it was principally to Grueber's publications that he was indebted for the full persuasion which enabled him to put his hand to a proposition about which he had hesitated two years before.

I reproduce here the Protest, to which Keble signed his name in the autumn of 1856:—

"THE BATH JUDGMENT.

" Protest.

" The following Declaration has been signed and issued. It has been thought better not to wait for a general collection of signatures.

" We the undersigned, Priests of the Catholic and Apostolic Church, called by God's Providence to minister in the Province of Canterbury according to the Common Prayer, do hereby, in the Presence of Almighty God, and in humble conformity with the tenor of our Ordination vows, as we understand them, make known and declare as follows:

" 1. We believe, in the words used in the Book of Homilies, that we 'receive the Body and Blood of our Lord Jesus Christ under the form of Bread and Wine;' and, with Bishop Cosin, 'That upon the words of Consecration, the Body and Blood of Christ is really and substantially Present, and so exhibited and given to all that receive It; and all this, not after a physical and sensual, but after an heavenly and incomprehensible manner;' of which statement Bishop Cosin says, ' It is confessed by all divines.'

"2. We believe, in the words of Bishop Ridley, 'that the partakinge of CHRIST'S BODYE and of HIS BLOUDE unto the faithfull and godlie, is the partakinge and fellowship of life and of immortalitie. And again, of the bad and ungodlie receivers, S. Paul plainlie saieth thus : " He that eateth of this breade and drinketh of this cuppe unworthilie, he is guilty of the BODIE and BLOUDE of the LORD." He that eateth and drinketh unworthilie, eateth and drinketh his own damnation, because he esteemeth not the LORD'S BODIE; that is, he receiveth not the LORD'S BODIE with the honoure which is due unto HIM.' Or, with Bishop Poynet, 'that the Eucharist, so far as it appertains to the nature of the Sacrament, is truly the BODY and the BLOOD of CHRIST, is a truly divine and holy thing, even when it is taken by the unworthy; while, however, they are not partakers of its grace and holiness, but eat and drink their own death and condemnation.'

"3. We hold, with Bishop Andrewes, 'that CHRIST Himself, the inward part of the Sacrament, in and with the Sacrament, apart from, and without the Sacrament, wheresoever HE is is to be worshipped.' With whom agrees Archbishop Bramhall : 'The Sacrament is to be adored, says the Council of Trent, that is (formally), the BODY and the BLOOD of Christ, say some of your authors : we say the same ; the Sacrament, that is the species of bread and wine, say others : that we deny.'

"We, therefore, being convinced—

"1. That the Doctrine of THE REAL PRESENCE of 'the BODY and BLOOD of our SAVIOUR CHRIST, under the form of Bread and Wine,' has been uniformly held as a point of Faith in the Church from Apostolic times ; and was accepted by General Councils, as it is also embodied in our own Formularies ;—

"2. That the interpretation of Scripture most commonly held in the Church has been that the wicked, although they can 'in no wise be partakers of CHRIST, nor spiritually eat HIS FLESH, and drink HIS BLOOD,' yet do in the Sacrament not only take, but eat and drink unworthily to their own condemnation the BODY and BLOOD of CHRIST, which they do not discern ;—

"3. That the practice of Worshipping CHRIST then and there especially Present after Consecration, and before Communicating, has been common throughout the Church ;—

"And, moreover, that the Thirty-nine Articles were intended

to be, and are, in harmony with the Faith and teaching of the ancient and undivided Church ;—

" Do hereby Protest against so much of the Opinion of his Grace the Archbishop of Canterbury, in the case of Ditcher *v.* Denison, as implies, directly or indirectly, that such statements as we have cited above are repugnant to the Doctrine of the Thirty-nine Articles.

" And we appeal from the said Opinion, Decision, or Sentence of his Grace, in the first instance, to a free and lawful Synod of the Bishops of the Province of Canterbury ; and then, if need be, to a free and lawful Synod of all the Churches of our Communion, when such by GOD'S mercy may be had.

BARTHOLOMEW, C. C., M.A., P.C. of St. David's, Exeter.
BENNETT, W. J. E., M.A., Vicar of Frome.
CARTER, THOMAS T., M.A., Rector of Clewer, Oxon.
GRUEBER, C. S., Incumbent of St. James', Hambridge.
HEATHCOTE, W. BEADON, B.C.L., Precentor of Salisbury Cathedral.
HENDERSON, T., M.A., Prebendary of St. Paul's ; Vicar of Massing.
KEBLE, JOHN, M.A., Vicar of Hursley, Winchester.
NEALE, J. M., M.A., Sackville College.
POPHAM, J. L., Prebendary of Salisbury ; Rector of Chilton Folliatt.
PUSEY, E. B., D.D., Regius Professor of Hebrew, Canon of Ch. Ch., Oxford.
SCOTT, WILLIAM, B.D., Perpetual Curate of Christ Church, Hoxton, London.
STUART, E., M.A., Incumbent of St. Mary Magdalene, Munster-square, London.
WILLIAMS, ISAAC, B.D., Stinchcombe, Gloucestershire.
WOODFORD, J. R., M.A., Vicar of Kempsford, Gloucestershire.
YARD, G. B., M.A., Rector of East Terrington with Wragby, Lincolnshire."

Two things appear to me to be specially noteworthy here : first, the humility and frank simplicity of such a letter, written to a man so far younger than himself. But this was Keble all over. No letter of any other kind ever came from him.

Besides this, the evidence which his statement seemed reasonably to supply touching the condition at that time amongst us of acceptance of the Doctrine of the Sacraments. If Keble hesitated, how many were there who had not so much as begun to think.

I have spoken above of the *test* of what is meant by THE REAL PRESENCE, supplied by "reception by the wicked." It is curious to note that, among other results of the discussion of it during the four years of my prosecution, there was this result,—that when the late learned and good Bishop of Brechin was called to account in Scotland for his teaching in respect of the Holy Eucharist, very soon after the close of the assault upon the Doctrine made in England in my person, "reception by the wicked" was not included among the counts of indictment. It had become clear that the charge of false doctrine here could not be sustained.

When I had filed my Answer at Wells to the Court at Bath, Sept. 30, I sent one of the first copies to my good, kind friend the Bishop of Exeter, with whom I had very frequent communication, by interview and by letter, since the opening of the case.

I allow myself to make an exception here to my rule of not publishing letters, and publish the Bishop's reply, now lying before me:—

"*Bishopstowe, Octr.* 3, 1856.

"MY DEAR ARCHDEACON,

"Accept my best thanks for sending me a copy of your 'Paper filed at Wells.'

"Accept also my warm congratulations on the victory that Paper must achieve, whether the fight be continued or not.

"I think I never read a Paper which did its work more satisfactorily.

"Dr. Phillimore has promised to be here to-day; Mr. Beresford Hope is already here. I fully expect that a case will be made out ensuring prohibition; but this would not have been entirely satisfactory, if it were not preceded by your victory on the merits.

"Yet I am bound in candour to say this, though I decline discussion and even mention of particulars, that I do not accord with you in all your statements.

"Believe me always,
"Very faithfully yours,
"H. EXETER."

"*Ven. Archdeacon Denison.*"

I believe the Bishop to have had in his mind, in the concluding paragraph of his letter, something of what was, not uncommonly, urged against me at the time; which I laboured throughout to shew to be groundless, and I think with success,—that I speculated and dogmatized about *the manner* of THE REAL PRESENCE.

It was an objection which, when first stated to me, took me more by surprise than any other thing connected with the case; for I had shrunk throughout from so much as venturing to *think* about *the manner*, and had expressed myself to that effect many times. There had been at one time some correspondence upon the subject between the Bishop and myself.

I am the more disposed to take this view of the concluding paragraph of the letter, because I find, ten years after, a letter of mine to the Bishop, with his reply, upon this specific point. From those letters — the last that passed between us—it appears that if there had been a suspicion of difference in his mind, it had ceased to find a place there :—

"*East Brent*, March 10, 1866.

"MY DEAR LORD,

"I need not make many words about my affectionate respect for you.

"I want only to say—what I know I may say—that it is of deep comfort to me to find set out now in your own words (Appendix A. to Archdeacon of Exeter's book) what I have often heard from your own lips.

"This is what I have always held and maintained touching *the manner* of THE PRESENCE.

"Believe me, my dear Lord,

"Yours always most truly,

"GEORGE A. DENISON.

"*The Lord Bishop of Exeter.*"

"*Bishopstowe, Torquay, 19th March*, 1866.

"MY DEAR MR. ARCHDEACON,

"Though I am obliged to use another hand, yet I cannot forbear thanking you for the expression of your acquiescence in the statement I have made in the matter of "the Real Presence" in the Eucharist.

"Believe me always,

"Most faithfully yours,

"H. EXETER.

"*The Ven. Archdeacon Denison.*"

In 1857 my Churchwarden, Mr. John Higgs—a constant Communicant, and near and dear friend—came to me to suggest having every year a "Harvest-home" at East Brent. I entered into the proposal immediately and heartily. It had long appeared to me that we wanted recognised holidays for the working-men, women, and children; and here was a step in that direction, specially recommended by one of its leading features, that it was not only a holiday for all classes alike, but a holiday which all classes kept and enjoyed, in close contact one with another.

The proposal was generally welcomed as soon as made, and we held our first Harvest-home Sept. 3, 1857.

At that time there was, I believe, nothing of the kind in this part of England. I understand that there had been Harvest-homes in the eastern counties, but I do not know enough about them to be able to give any account of their little history.

The East Brent Harvest-home has become a Somerset institution; and though it has long ceased to retain all its original character in respect of gathering together here many chief people on the Harvest-home Day who came to see what we were about, and whether it would be good to follow suit at home, it has retained, and more than retained, it has increased, all its original popularity; and I am enabled to say, having watched every one of them from year to year,—with rare intervals, every year has had its Harvest-home, beginning with 1857,—that each one has been an improvement upon its predecessor.

The original scheme has in all its substance remained intact. Alterations and improvements have come in matters of detail.

I have kept a book from the first, which I bequeath to the Vicar, my successor. In it I find some account of the scheme in letters of mine, published in the local papers, 1859.

"The Harvest-feast with us is a feast given by the farmers and their wives, with such others of us as are in a position to subscribe, to the entire population of the parish.

"We provide also, 1. for the guests of the parish, whom it is left in my hands to invite; two tickets are given to each of these, with liberty to purchase others: 2. for the friends of the several subscribers, for whom they purchase tickets. Men, and boys above fourteen, dine; women, and children under fourteen, have tea.

"Our festival is given not to the Harvesters only, but to the entire population of the parish, which is, I am persuaded, the only principle upon which such gatherings can be expected to do good."

I have read and heard of (and have seen) other schemes of Harvest-home arrangement; but of no one which was, I think, so good as our own.

There have been, as I said above, alterations and improvements not a few as time went on, but the principle of the thing has remained the same.

The East Brent Harvest-home seed has grown into a tree.

In 1857, the total funds were £63 18*s.* 5*d.* balancing the total expenses; 300 at dinner, 500 at tea. In 1877, total funds £165 17s.: total outlay, £146 14s. 5d. Dinner 500, tea 1000: one day, two evenings. Total numbers present, from 2000 to 2500. Population of the Parish, about 750.

There are two Celebrations on Harvest-home Day; the first at 8 A.M., the second at 9. Matins at 7.30 A.M.; Harvest Service and Sermon, 11.30; Evensong, 6 P.M.

In 1868, I put together a short form of Harvest Service, which we have used always since, and which is much approved.

Sentence, Confession, Absolution, LORD'S Prayer, Suffrage, Psalm CIV., First Lesson, Deut. xxiv. 19, 22, Te DEUM, Second Lesson, 1 Thess. v. 14, 23, Benedictus, Creed, Suffrages, Collects 1, 2, 3, Anthem, Prayer for all Conditions of men, General Thanksgiving, Prayer of S. Chrysostom, Grace, Short Voluntary, Sermon, Harvest Hymn, Blessing.

This, putting the Sermon at "not exceeding twenty minutes," a length amply sufficient, does not occupy more than one hour.

We are most fortunate in respect of place for holding our Harvest-home. On the east side of Brent knoll, on the last slope of the hill, in front of the Vicarage, adjoining the Churchyard, divided from Vicarage-lawn by iron hurdle fence, is a very pretty field of some four acres.

The general management and direction of the Festival has always been most kindly left in my hands.

My experience of twenty-one years is all in its favour; and I believe my verdict will be endorsed by almost every one who has had to do with it. It would have been absurd not to expect drawbacks, and untrue not to admit them; but these have gradually diminished in number and extent. On the other hand, I have noted with very great thankfulness a very marked progress in all that makes such gatherings not simply pleasant, but, much more than this, useful and good things to have. Of the courtesy and kindness of all, parishioners and others, towards myself I cannot say too much. All those who make themselves responsible for the carrying out the several parts of the Festival work with a will.

When the "legal proceedings" first indicated January 16, 1854, formally taken at Clevedon, 1855, and at Bath, 1856, had been set aside by the Court of the Province, 1857, and finally quashed and reduced to nothing by the Court of Final Appeal, February 6, 1858,—the Parishioners of East Brent were not slow to express their great satisfaction with the issue.

I think often of that day; I have had differences since, some fourteen years after it, with some of those who were then of the same mind with all the rest, in welcoming me and my dear wife with warmest and heartiest welcome. I had preached earnestly to my people the Doctrine of the Sacraments, from 1845 to 1858. For the last four years of that number I had been before a Commission and a Court, held under, and by, the Archbishop of the Province, upon a charge of false doctrine, in respect of the Holy Eucharist. I had been deprived of all my preferments by the Court; the sentence of deprivation had been set aside, not upon the merits, but upon a point of law.

None of these things had shaken the regard and confidence of my people. Fourteen years after, when I had become persuaded, not of the advantage only, but of the duty, of aiding the teaching of the ear by the teaching of the eye q, and had accordingly introduced into my Church some more Catholic Ceremonial of no elaborate kind, in exposition and illustration of the precise Doctrine for which I had been deprived at Bath,—of which condemnation my parishioners had taken no account, except to welcome me back again among them, with all the honours of affectionate regard, as having defeated the attempt to eject me from my Vicarage and Archdeaconry; fourteen years after, some, not many, of the same people, who had had no word to say against me on the ground of my teaching the Catholic Doctrine of the Blessed Sacrament, separated themselves from me on the ground of

---

q "I have heard of Thee by the hearing of the ear: but now mine eye seeth Thee." Job xlii. 5.

the Ceremonial of the Sacrament,—on the ground vulgarly called "Ritual."

> "Segnius irritant animum demissa per aurem
> Quam quæ sunt oculis subjecta fidelibus."

It has made me at times very sad. But an improved Ceremonial was not only in the natural order of things, and, however for many years neglected, was so strictly in accordance with the Prayer-Book, and the entire framework and constitution of the Church of England, that I could not, certain antecedents of mine notwithstanding, hesitate to introduce it. And not only have I had no true cause to regret having done so, however great the troubles that have come of it, but I am deeply thankful for having done it.

I shall have to revert to this matter further on.

In 1858, my parishioners were all with me. We were in London, when I received a letter from a gentleman then living in the parish, to say that it was the general desire to give us a public welcome on our return home.

I had no right to discourage the proposal; and I am not going to pretend that I wished to discourage it. Genuine, spontaneous, hearty kindness and good-will is not a thing any man has a right to discourage, even if he wished to escape from the public expression of it. All the circumstances considered, I had no such wish.

Accordingly, we were met at Highbridge Station by, as I was told, every man, woman, and child of the parish that could come. The Address below was there read to us, and we were carried off to East Brent. As we got nearer home, it was a small army. At the bounds of the parish, the horses were taken from the carriage, and men's hands drew us a mile and a-half to the church, to which I had asked to be first taken, that I might return thanks with my people. Coming out of church, I said what I could to them from the old Cross in the churchyard. They drew us on to the Vicarage, and there, with a few hearty cheers, left us to ourselves.

I have had large experience of kindness,— kindness delicately and considerately done. I have no experience of greater kindness and truer delicacy, than that which governed all the actions of my parishioners towards us that day. I found afterwards that they had added to their kindness by taking precautions against any manner of excess, lest there should be any blot upon the recollections of the day.

An Address to the Venerable Archdeacon Denison, from his Parishioners, East Brent, February 26, 1858. Presented on behalf of all the Parishioners, by S. A. Goldsworthy, Esq., at Highbridge Station.

"REVEREND AND DEAR SIR,

"Upon your return from the successful termination of a suit that has not been more vexatious to yourself than painful to your parishioners, the whole population of East Brent have felt most desirous to testify to you their gratification in receiving you back amongst them, not only as a victor, but as their beloved pastor, freed from those anxieties which have been heaped upon you during more than four protracted years. Not only has it been a sincere pleasure to us to welcome you and your revered Lady at the nearest Station, and to lead you in triumph, in the midst of your parishioners, to your Vicarage; but we wish, if possible, to express to you more calmly, our deep sense of gratitude that you have not been dragged from amongst us. Many years of kindly intercourse have endeared you to us. In you we have ever had the earnest Priest and the sympathizing Vicar. Your instructions in the church have been exemplified and enforced by your private virtues and public charities; and in the quiet offices of benevolence, our poor have learnt to feel that you were nobly seconded in your pious labours by the help of Mrs. Denison; therefore, had we been deprived of you as our Vicar, the Church would not only have lost a zealous servant, but we should have lost our friends of many years, and our examples of those Truths so earnestly preached from the pulpit. We heartily rejoice that our language upon your return is that of congratulation, and not of condolence. Anxiously, though quietly, we have watched the case. We regretted it ever arose; we regretted its long-protracted infliction; but now that you stand freed by the highest Court in the land, we can never regret the display of Christian fortitude and Christian forbearance you have manifested to us during those four years and a-quarter. Not one of your parishioners can tax his memory with having heard you use an unchristian, an unkind, or an ungentlemanly expression, against those who unfortunately were your accusers. Meekly have you borne the Cross, meekly may you wear the Crown. It must be gratifying to you, Reverend and dear Sir, to be informed that the feeling of pleasure by us expressed, is a feeling shared by every one of your flock in East Brent; therefore, we request you to accept the unanimous and hearty congratulations of your parishioners of thirteen years' standing; our respect for your character can never be greater, but permit us to express the hope that for very many years the Church will be adorned by your earnest labours, and we shall be blessed by your continuing to occupy the position of our Vicar, and that health and happiness will be granted to Mrs. Denison, to cheer and second you in all your plans for the spiritual and temporal good of East Brent. May you be supported and blessed in the future, and be a blessing to

"Reverend and Dear Sir,
"Your attached Parishioners
"of East Brent

"*To the Venerable Archdeacon Denison, Vicar of East Brent.*"

The day following, I sent my servant with a note to Mr. Ditcher at South Brent, to say that we should be thankful to be allowed to resume our old friendly relations. I received a kind answer of full accord, but adding that it was right I should be told that a history of proceedings in the case would shortly be in the publisher's hands. Upon this, I said to my wife, "We will go to-day; perhaps, if we wait, it might not be quite so easy." We went, and were very kindly received.

From that time, to Mr. Ditcher's death in 1875, there was much friendly intercourse, and some united action between us,—particularly in respect of maintaining the position of the Athanasian Creed, and also in the matter of the Bishopric of Exeter, 1869[r]. In my illness in 1870,

[r] In both these, my dear and loving friend and neighbour, Prebendary Stephenson, R.D., writes to me that Mr. Ditcher, he, and I were entirely one; and that we met at my house to consider what we should do.

among a host of kindest neighbours and friends, no one was kinder than Mr. Ditcher.

When he died, November, 1875, his widow asked me to preach the Sunday morning after the funeral in South Brent Church. The request moved me greatly; and my compliance with it was a compliance of deep thankfulness.

I return to three particulars belonging to the time, 1852-8. With two of them my personal connection is close and intimate; the third is a matter of public policy, with its natural sequel at the present time, to which it would have been out of place to refer in these "Notes," were it not for its bearing upon the religious character of this country. I hated the policy at the time, and have hated it ever since. It is now receiving its just reward.

My dear wife's father, Mr. Henley, has, at the age of eighty-five, retired from public life. Much has been said, and well said—it could not be said too much and too well—of his thirty-seven years in the House of Commons.

But every notice that I have seen has passed over in silence one part of the action of those years, very remarkable in itself, and which, at the time it was taken, attracted general notice and admiration. I remember well hearing what was everywhere said of his speeches in 1855-6, when he opposed Sir John Pakington and Lord John Russell, and defeated them by a majority of 102; and that the then Speaker (Lord Eversley) had said that it was the most crushing defeat he had ever witnessed, or words to that effect.

It has not happened to me to come across anywhere any notice of this part of Mr. Henley's public life, among all that has been said about him this year.

What is the probable account of the omission? I suppose it to be this. The general public, and *therefore* the newspapers, is, for the present, so besotted with admiration of that very inferior, but very high-priced, article which they call "National Education," that resistance to its onward course, however generally admired, approved, and supported twenty years ago, is now only regarded as an inconvenient fact, to be kept as much as possible out of sight.

And, no doubt, if religious principle is to go for nothing, and civil policy of indifferentism for everything, as is the order of the day, this is intelligible and consistent enough : but I know of no other ground upon which it can be reasonably assumed to be either one or the other.

I need say nothing about the interest I took at the time in Mr. Henley's opposition; interest, personal and public. I remember well his telling me what it was that gave him his majority in 1856. Before I say what this was, let us see a little how things stood *then*, and how they stand *now*. Twenty years ago, Nonconformity in and out of the Houses of Parliament was not altogether what it has become since. It had not arrived, at least not in Parliament, at the proposal to do away with "the Establishment" altogether; it was content to prepare the way in detail. It had two flags, but it kept one of them, the "no Establishment" flag, for the present, folded up; the other was the "Conscience" flag, which they kept waving in the eyes of England, till England began to think there must be some truth in the "Conscience" plea. On the reverse side of the "Conscience" flag was "Good for religion," "Better for the Church herself," with other little sentiments of like character.

I am not blaming the Nonconformist here: it was all in keeping with the history of three hundred years. And I have a respect for consistent people. The people I have no respect for, are the people who say they have got the best thing in the world, and let it be taken away from them bit by bit, till there is nothing of the substance of it left. The great Conservative party, for example.

What I want to note is, the change in Nonconformist tactics, which the near prospect of final success has brought about. Nonconformity, like all other sections of the body politic, has its three elements,—the religious, the social, the political. The triumph of the second is achieved; the triumph of the first is on its way, and not far off. The third element is so obscured by its own internal entanglements, and by the contradictions between its several parts, that it is very difficult to say what it really amounts to positively; negatively, it is a negation of everything Catholic—Greek-Catholic, Latin-Catholic, Anglo-Catholic. But, whatever it may have amounted to in time gone by, this is now wholly absorbed in the political element.

Twenty years ago, Nonconformity recoiled still from "State Education," on the specific ground of the danger involved in it to all definite religious teaching. Mr. Henley said to me, "The Nonconformist leaders came to me in the lobby, and told me they were going to vote with me upon that ground."

Fifteen years after, the vote of 1856 was reversed absolutely. When I made my final attempt, by the meeting at Willis's Rooms, 1868, the Hon. C. L. Wood in the chair, I asked Mr. Henley whether it would be of use to attempt anything in Parliament. He said, "No use at all; those who gave me a majority in 1856, would not give it now."

I subjoin a *précis* of the debate of 1855-6 :—

March 17, 1855, (*House of Commons*).—SIR J. PAKINGTON moved to bring in a Bill for the encouragement and promotion of Education in England and Wales. His Bill was to be a permissive one, and would not interfere in any way with existing Educational establishments. He proposed to create districts, and if in any district a majority of the inhabitants wished to avail themselves of the new measure, they could elect a *board of Education*. These schools should be free to scholars of all classes, and should be under the superintendence of the Committee of Council on Education, with a view to obtaining grants in aid of their support. He also proposed a scheme by which in no case religious and secular teaching was to be separated.—MR. HADFIELD objected to the levy of a compulsory vote for Educational purposes.—LORD STANLEY, MR. ADDERLEY, LORD PALMERSTON, &c., spoke in favour of the Bill.

May 2, 1855.—Sir J. Pakington moved the second reading of his Education Bill. He urged that in principle it was designed to combine the most extended religious Education with the widest tolerance of sectarian distinctions. The funds required to carry out his system were to be provided by grants of public money administered under the supervision of local boards.—Mr. Henley moved as an amendment that the Bill be read a second time that day six months. His objections were founded chiefly upon the apprehension that the Bill would diminish the certainty that all Education receiving public support should include the religious element, and that it might tend to foster and extend the range of the voluntary principle as regarded our educational institutions. The British people was undergoing a rapid improvement, which he considered attributable in great measure to the working of our existing institutions.—Mr. R. Phillimore seconded the amendment, and contended that the measure would degrade the Church of England from her position as the centre of religious Education in this country.—Mr. Miles said that denominational schools having worked so well, it was necessary now to extend them; such means were afforded by this new Bill.—(Debate adjourned.)

June 11, 1855.—Mr. Adderley said there were at present three courses before the House, either to be content with the existing system of Education, as recommended by Mr. Henley; or else to adopt the Bills of Sir J. Pakington and Lord J. Russell, the principles of which were to supplement private patronage by public grants and local taxation; or else to adopt Mr. Gibson's proposal to sweep away all existing schools, and to map out the country with new schools, ignoring all religious instruction. He himself should support Sir J. Pakington's measure.—Mr. E. Denison complained that in all three measures there was no provision to enforce attendance.—Sir J. Pakington answered Mr. Henley's speech of May 2, and said that the latter avoided all the strongest points upon which he relied for making out his case. He said one of his objects, in proposing free schools supported by rates, was to provide Education, not only for children of labourers, but also for those of farmers and tradesmen.—(Debate adjourned.)

June 25, 1855.—Debate again adjourned till July 2.

July 2, 1855.—After explanations from Sir J. Pakington and

Lord J. Russell, who complained of the session being nearly at an end without anything being settled on the Education question, the three Bills, viz. Sir J. Pakington's, Lord J. Russell's, and Mr. Gibson's were withdrawn.

Feb. 2, 1856, (*House of Commons*).—Sir J. Pakington remarked on the omission from the Royal Speech of any allusion to the Education question, and stated his regret at the decision of the Government not to bring in a Bill, but to pass a Resolution on the subject of Education.—Sir G. Grey said it was the intention of the President of the Council to introduce a Bill for extending Education, although it did not embrace the idea of a national measure. It was also the intention of the Government to introduce a measure for placing all matters relating to Education, Science and Art, under the responsibility of a minister of the Government, with a seat in the House.—Lord J. Russell said he had adopted the course of introducing a Resolution on Education rather than a Bill, as the progress of the latter was attended with so great difficulties.

Feb. 22, 1856, (*House of Commons*).—Sir J. Pakington asked Lord J. Russell whether he could give him any information with respect to his Education Resolutions.—Lord J. Russell said the Resolutions would be laid upon the table, but he should propose deferring their consideration till the 6th of March.

March 6, 1856, (*House of Commons*).—Lord J. Russell in introducing his Education Resolutions said, According to statistics, there were at present four millions of young persons between the age of five and fifteen, and that of these two millions were entered on school-books, and 1,750,000 in actual attendance. In his Resolutions he proposed an increased number of inspectors, who were to report to the Committee of Council on Education, as to districts where the provision of schools was needed. With regard to religious instruction, as it was impossible to separate religious from moral instruction, he proposed that the Holy Scriptures should be read daily in the schools, but that parents or guardians, if they wished, could withdraw the children when the Scriptures were being read. He did not see it possible to compel people to send their children to school: although a partial attendance might be required of all children under fifteen who were in employment, the masters bearing the expenses of the schooling. The cost of these improvements he considered would be about £3,240,000 a-year; and it was for a vote to this amount that he should ask the House.—MR. HENLEY approved generally of Lord J. Russell's scheme, but doubted the plan of appropriating charities, (Lord J. Russell having proposed to give to the Charity Commissioners power to divert charities which were now useless).—MR. MILNER GIBSON said it was not true that a secular system of Education was impossible in this country.—(Debate adjourned.)

April 10, 1856, (*House of Commons*).—When the first Education Resolution was put, "that in the opinion of the House, it is expedient to extend, revise, and consolidate the Minutes of the Committee of Privy Council," MR. HENLEY moved as an amendment, that the Chairman do leave the chair. He said he found in Lord J. Russell's Resolutions all the objections that were in Sir J. Pakington's Bill. 1. As to inspectors, he objected to the appointment of them, as there were many schools which would not admit of inspection, and any attempt at compulsion he believed would ruin the scheme. (2.) That school districts would destroy the parochial system, and the influence of the Clergy in the schools. (3.) He objected to the diversion of Charitable Trusts, giving to Education what was intended for the relief of the poor. (4.) As to the levying of rates for the sustenance of schools, he considered the scheme inadequate to secure that end. (5.) As to the subject of religious Education, he considered the plan proposed by the Bill would not answer. (6.) He also did not agree to the clause which compelled employers of children to pay for the Education of such children.—MR. ELLICE and MR. LIDDELL were in favour of Mr. Henley's amendment; and SIR J. GRAHAM said, On the question of rating and of religious instruction, he entered a strong protest, and laid down this axiom,—that if ever they resorted to compulsory rating, they must establish secular Education. He objected to a scheme of National Education, as it was unnecessary, and would, if established, dry up all the streams of charity.—SIR J. PAKINGTON said he should give a general support to Lord J. Russell's resolutions.

April 11, 1856, (*House of Commons*).—LORD J. RUSSELL defended and explained generally his Resolutions, and proposed to withdraw the latter half of his series of Resolutions, which appeared to be mostly objected to.—MR. HENLEY thereupon offered to withdraw his amendment, extending his assent only to the first resolution.—Mr. GLADSTONE objected to this sudden termination of the discussion; and Sir S. NORTHCOTE having severely attacked the remaining Resolutions, the House divided on Mr. Henley's amendment, which was carried by a majority of 102.

June 12.—Sir G. GREY moved that £151,000 be voted for public Education, in addition to £300,000 already voted.—(Motion carried.)

In 1857 came the indelible stain of the Divorce Act; a just judgment for the sin of many years in passing through Parliament, by authorities Ecclesiastical and Civil, private Divorce Bills for the wealthy and great people of the land. I did, as many others did, what little I could to stay the plague; but the people were "set on mischief[a]." I believe the national sin committed in and by the creation of the Divorce Court, to be a sin in respect of which there is no "place of repentance;" and if, as is commonly said now, morality in England is very low, I believe there to be no ingredient of the national life more powerful to pollute, corrupt and poison, than the Divorce Law.

The point of public policy and action referred to above is the Crimean War. I have never forgotten the day when I saw the Cross and the Crescent on the same flag in the streets of London. Twenty-one years have passed, and the same spirit is abroad again. It is said by men from whom we should least expect to hear it, that "British interests," i.e. material "interests," are the one rule of British policy; we have heard the expression of the teaching of the flag reflecting the deep worldliness of the England of Century XIX. We see in the expression itself, and in the welcome it receives, how powerful and how triumphant are the temptations which beset a people who have a world-wide empire to maintain; and we recognise the prophetic truth of Bacon's aphorism: "It is in the declining age of a State that mechanical arts and merchandise most do flourish[b]."

[a] Exod. xxxii. 22.   [b] "Advancement of Learning."

With whom remained the honour of the Crimean War? I might add, with whom the substantial success? I believe both to have remained with Russia; all the marvels of bravery on the side of the allies notwithstanding; the fall of Sebastopol notwithstanding. On one side was Russia, on the other, England, France, Italy, Turkey: Russia could not save her city, but she saved her honour, and was content to wait, and bide her time.

Europe, and especially England, has put the time into her hands. For a hundred years before the peace of Paris, the protectorate of the Christian subjects of Turkey was a Russian protectorate. By the peace of Paris it became an European protectorate; it was exercised effectually neither by England nor by the other great powers. Russia saw her opportunity, and made her demand upon Turkey; she knew very well how little likely it was that any other power would interfere between Turkey and herself. She knew that she could crush Turkey: all the other powers knew it too, or ought to have known it; but after a show of discussion at Constantinople, and a futile attempt to persuade the Turk to give in, the Turk thinking all the time, and *having every reason to think it*— all the much-paraded but not overtrue neutrality of England notwithstanding—that in the end England would come to the rescue, refused to listen, went to war, and has been finally crushed.

Russia having gained her success at the cost of a hundred thousand lives of her best soldiers, and many millions of her treasure, and having by herself fought her own battle, by herself imposes her own terms of peace. A more equitable proceeding could not be.

Then England—whose business it was to have joined with Russia in compelling the Turk to something like decent government of his Christian subjects—England, who had stood by, and let Russia do what it was quite as much England's duty to do as it was Russia's— England, who had not risked one life, nor spent one farthing—England, who might have prevented all the waste of blood and treasure, all the horrors of the entire war—England comes in, and demurs to the peace of San Stefano.

It is very little use in England to say a word which is not wholly for "British interests;" and the fact has no doubt its advantages, though they be not always of the highest character. Still, there are occasions on which there is something eminently ridiculous in British self-complacency and self-exaltation, and the present is one of them. It might be as well if English people, who are so given to think that a thing must necessarily be good and right simply because it is English, were to try to look at the matter just a little from the stand-point of people who are not English. Russia laughs of course at England; Russia does more than laugh, she laughs bitterly. The rest of Europe laughs at England, more or less bitterly; but it all laughs in its sleeve, whatever fine flattering words it may use.

If England were to go to war with Russia, which some people say she will, I want to know, with vast numbers of my countrymen, what we are going to war about? How we are going to war; and what we are going to get by it? All that I can think of is, many pence in the pound Income Tax; possible great mishaps, certain loss of many lives, and, after all, humiliating disappointment. But indeed I never had any belief that the war-cry was anything but a pretence.

Since the above was published, we have the Berlin Congress and "Peace." Pending the issue of the Congress, the secret Anglo-Turkish Convention and the annexation of Cyprus. I see nothing in all this but added ground for mistrusting and shrinking from the "British interests" policy.

CHAPTER IX.

EAST BRENT. 1858—1870.

Convocation.

FROM 1852 Convocation had been winning its way slowly and painfully from ridicule to respect. A form of consideration had come into the place of the popular contempt so largely expressed in the "organs of public opinion," the "Times," especially, and other like "organs." I say "a form of consideration," because it has never been the one true form of consideration; nor, for anything that I can see, is it likely to be.

The ridicule and contempt were not undeserved. They were nothing else than what a Church had reason to expect, which had, for nearly a century and a-half, seen itself robbed by the Civil Power of the inherent right and constitutional position of the Spiritualty to exercise its proper function, as Council of the Crown in things spiritual, when assembled, together with the two Houses of Parliament, by Royal Writ for the despatch of divers and sundry weighty matters concerning the well-being of "Church and State;" and had submitted to be robbed without effort to resist or to recover, and almost without remonstrance.

It is a curious and instructive chapter in the history of "the Establishment," a sign of the lack of spiritual life; of the prevailing deadness in things spiritual, which is the general characteristic of Century XVIII. Not only no progress of the Church at home, but ground lost, as must always happen in matters spiritual where progress is not. No missionary effort at home or abroad bearing any proportion to the resources of England, and the steady advance of English power. Churches shut up from Sunday to Sunday; opened on Sunday to scanty, mutilated, and barren forms, and cold moral essay teaching. The united daily morning and evening prayer of a family and household a rare thing.

I would not have it thought that I am presuming to pass an indiscriminate censure. All I affirm is, that the light which still shone by the mercy of GOD, the true light of CHRIST, in homes and churches, in themselves doubtless many, but relatively very few, served to shew how deep was the general slumber and prevailing darkness.

The Roman Catholic was more than holding his own; the Presbyterian in Scotland had well-nigh undisputed sway. Presbyterianism in England was rapidly assuming the form which it has since definitely taken, there as elsewhere,—the form of Unitarianism. Other Nonconformity was incessantly developing its thousand shapes, or creating these anew. And it is no exaggeration: it is only to state facts as the best reply to the self-complacency and gratulation about our own religious condition, so common amongst us, to sum up the condition thus:—

"The Reformed Religion of the Church of England" in these islands began with claiming for its own in Century XVI. the entire People. This was the claim; what is the fact? It never had Scotland: it never had Ireland: it has lost three parts of Wales, and half England.

Let us lay our hand on our mouth, and confess that it is the mercy of GOD which has spared us to awake and to recover by Grace. It is, indeed, high time for the English Catholic to awake, lest he should awake only to find the Church of England gone the way of the Church of Laodicea which was in Asia.

The abeyance of the assembly of the Spiritualty was at once effect and cause of the lack of spiritual life; it was also an evidence and sign of the pervading growth and influence of " Establishmentarianism " *pur et simple.*

It is not difficult to trace the formal cause of the abeyance. In every " Establishment," and specially in the English " Establishment," the combination of the Crown, or of what represents the Crown, and of the Bishops, the nominees of the Crown, is all-powerful. The hands, and well-nigh the voices, of the Priests are tied.

Now it suited the Crown, or the Whigs who governed the Crown, to shut up Convocation. It suited the Bishops, the nominees of the Crown, that it should be shut up; though, upon a surface consideration, they seemed to be losers by the transaction. For as a "Church," a National Church especially, could not be without some colour of public representation as part of the body politic, so long as the true, genuine, and authentic representation was taken away, the Bishops in their Diocesan, and, more practically still, in their State position as Peers of Parliament, became the sole "accredited representatives" of the Church.

It is out of this position of the Episcopate, so eminently false, that has come by far the greater part of the hindrances which have beset, and are besetting every day, the revival of the spiritual life of the Church of England.

When, after 135 years of abeyance, Convocation was allowed to re-assemble in 1852 "for despatch of business," it was a tardy acknowledgment, wrung from the Civil Power more by the general demand of the entire People for increased freedom of thought and action, than by anything else, of the unjust measure dealt out to the Church for so many years. There were those Churchmen who had laboured long and earnestly for this issue,—foremost among them my dear friend, Henry Hoare, — but the general public, Ecclesiastical and Civil, were either indifferent or contemptuous. The Bishops stood by and looked coldly on.

As a stroke of Court policy, it has its reverse side. People who cared for Convocation, did not look upon this side at the time in the gladness of their heart; but for some twenty years last past they have not been able not to look at it. The reverse side is not a thing pleasant to look upon. It represents the Spiritualty of the Church of England re-assembling by Royal Writ "for despatch of business," in sundry and divers matters of importance to the well-being of "Church and State;" assembling and talking, but doing nothing.

This is what the Civil Power proposed to itself as a quietus to the revival agitation when it unlocked the door; and it has been as the Civil Power proposed to itself, has been,—is,—and will be, all manner of "Reform" of Convocation notwithstanding,

He is a man of really too simple and confiding a character for the business of life[a], who supposes that the House of Commons, the depositary of the Imperial Power, is going to admit an *Imperium in Imperio;* an *Imperium* especially, which, whatever it may have been once, is now, and must continue to be more and more as years go on, of a character opposite in principle to the character of the constitution of the House of Commons. Now, it is true that it is not a *legislative Imperium,* in the sense of Statute law-making, which could belong to Convocation. The Crown in Parliament is the one Statute law-maker. It is not the province or function of Convocation to make law for Church and State; but it is its province and function to advise the Crown in things spiritual *how law, if need be, should be made, and with the view to its being made.*

But the recognition of even so much as this is no part of the present or future purpose of the House of Commons. It is idle to talk about such a thing.

The progress, therefore, of Convocation to consideration and respect, such measures of both as, under the circumstances, it can look to attain to, is slow, and it is also painful. Slow, because it has great obstacles to overcome; painful, because there is no prospect of overcoming; and more than this even, because, the position being unreal, members of Convocation, with those who send them there, whether "ex officio," or representative members, are, by the fact itself of their being sent, and coming as sent, parties to the unreality. Now, a position

---

[a] μακαρίσαντες τὸ ἀπειρόκακον, οὐ ζηλοῦμεν τὸ ἄφρον.—Thucydides, v. 105.

of patent unreality in any matter, and especially in matters spiritual, is a painful position. It is a bad thing no doubt to be robbed *ab extra;* but there is reality about being robbed *ab extra*, and no complicity. To consent to be robbed, the robber giving back, or pretending to give back, what he has robbed you of with one hand, and taking it away again with the other,—to consent to this, without resistance in the shape of a perpetual protest formally repeated every time of assembling, this is painful: it is complicity in the wrong, and hurts the conscience.

The relative position of the Houses of Convocation aggravates the unreality of the case. If the Houses were at one, there would be something of a front on the part of the Church; but the Houses are not at one, nor in the way to be at one. There is a good deal too much "State" in the Lower House, and not enough "Church." In the Upper House there is more of "State" than of "Church." All the real weight of the Bishops' House, whensoever a real point of difference between "Church" and "State" arises, goes into the "State" scale.

Under these circumstances of the case, Convocation though it has commanded unwilling respect by the learning and ability shewn in its debates, and more effectually and permanently still by the reports of its Committees, has failed wholly, as was to be expected, in so much as the laying the foundation of truer relations between the Church and the Civil Power. The Church of England requires, not only for the growth and increase, but for the preservation of her spiritual life, what the Civil Power of England will not—rather I should say, under the present or any probable future conditions of the country cannot—so much as entertain. I go further and say, that if the Civil Power would and could entertain, it would be neither wise nor safe in Convocation to ask it to do or say in any case, least of all in a case of Doctrine, or Discipline, or Worship.

This has been my definite and unmodified conclusion

for many years last past. For several years after the revival of Convocation, I took part in proposals for going to Parliament. But for many years last past have resisted, to the best of my ability, every manner of application to the Legislature for legislation in Church matters. If members of the Legislature can persuade the Houses of Parliament, or either of them, to touch Church questions with the view to legislation, that is the affair of the Houses of Parliament. It is my persuasion that wise Parliament men, knowing the dead-lock that has come between "Church" and "State," deprecate nothing more—nothing perhaps so much—as the bringing any Church questions before Parliament; and above all other, questions of Doctrine, Discipline, Worship. They see clearly enough what must come of it: I wish it might be that Convocation saw it as clearly. Convocation persists in aiming at the "impossible;" in so doing, it provokes the "dangerous," if not the "fatal." It is the old story of men, good and wise men too, looking at a matter from their own stand-point only, and assuming it is the stand-point of a body irreconcilable with themselves upon first principles. I often look back now with astonishment at my own blindness, which made me go with others along the road which seemed to lead to some remote spot, where Parliament would be found busy with promoting the spiritual interests of the Church of England. The vision has long since faded away, and I marvel at the weakness which once accepted it for a reality.

But it takes time to apprehend the whole extent and bearing of a revolution, such as that which has been conceived, planned, developed, completed within the last fifty years in the relations of "Church" and "State." It is a part of the apprehension when it comes, at least it has been in my own case, to be unwilling any longer to spend time and labour upon the subordinate details of the position. It seems to me to be only to promote and perpetuate the delusion, to be busying oneself formally about details of the Church's life, all the time acquiescing helplessly in the disregard, or the formal rejection, on the part of the Civil Power, of the principles of the Church's life. I used at one time to say a good deal about the narrow limits of time allowed for Sessions of Convocation; but, if the time was extended, I do not see now what we should do with it. Nothing comes of debates in Convocation, of Committees and Reports, except sometimes a great deal of compromise, or of direct playing into the adversary's hand. The Lower House resisted in the matter of the Athanasian Creed; having successfully resisted, it fell into a panic about its own success, and began to pare away all the life of the resistance by a Declaration declaring what it meant. The true resistance of a Churchman against meddling with the Verities which the Church has committed to his keeping; against meddling with the Verities themselves, or with the manner of their statement by the Church, is to resist simply and absolutely; not to go about explaining, qualifying, modifying. All these things seem to me to indicate want of faith in the position; or a desire to conciliate what cannot be conciliated in the nature of things; or an unworthy fear of being thought uncharitable: and, with the view of avoiding such unpleasantnesses, the *Depositum Fidei* is allowed to suffer, not in itself, that cannot be, but in respect of the acceptance of it by those to whom it has been principally entrusted to keep and to deliver.

For the Church-rate matter, I do not believe that the action of the Houses of Convocation, though more than commonly unanimous, delayed the final catastrophe at the hands of Mr. Gladstone's Government. For the matter of the Schools of the Church, I am certain it did not; nay, rather it helped it forward.

For many years after 1852, some three-fifths of the Lower House used to support me in all that I tried to do to save the Church School. The Upper House dealt with the matter much as the Committee of the National Society had dealt with it; it was the same men, only in another place. After a time there came over the Lower House what I call "the High Church weariness,"

I remember laughing to myself the last time, I think, that I spoke upon the subject at any length, at seeing the Prolocutor and many others fast asleep; they used to be awake and alive enough before, but I suppose they had given it up, and thought they might as well take a little rest.

I trust I may not appear to be using harsh words towards many dear and loving personal friends, nor again towards other members of the Lower House, whose great and tried kindness in word and in act towards myself I can never think of, as I often do think of it, without my eyes "filling with pleasant tears," when I say here that I believe they did not look fully in the face what they were doing, when they abandoned themselves to the power of the "High Church weariness" spell.

But I may not "extenuate" in such matters as that now before me, any more than I may in any matter "set down aught in malice."

What is it, then, that they have done?

They have made themselves parties to the ruin of the "Church School" in England. They have got what is still *called* the "Church School," but what *is not* the "Church School." A school conducted on the principle of the "Time Table Conscience Clause," is not a "Church School;" what gives it the name is called toleration; what it is, consciously or unconsciously, is betrayal of trust. It is called an "equitable compromise;" what it is, is the bartering away a Trust for State help. It is called a place of "Education in Church principles," what it is, is a place of "Instruction in the principles of Indifferentism." As for the School Board School, the ultimate purpose and effect of the Act of 1870, as respects the entire country, I have no more words to waste upon it.

The Religion of CHRIST is not a thing that can be tampered with after this fashion without grievous loss and harm to all those who tamper with it, and through them to the present and to coming generations. If it comes to be a question with "High Churchmanship," whether the "High Churchman" is to stand fast at all costs, or to see what he can save, or rather what he thinks he can save, for in reality he saves nothing, by making his Trust matter of bargaining between an "Indifferent" Civil Power and himself; then I say, the sooner we give up being "High Churchmen," the better for ourselves and for everybody else.

Two of the worst sins that a people can commit, have been committed by the passing of the Act of 1870. Sins of rebellion against God and of bitter cruelty to man; especially to the poor man.

1. A system of School-teaching irreligious in principle, more or less irreligious in detail, but in no case a truly religious system, and tending inevitably, *facili descensu*, to a Godless system of School-teaching, has been made the law of this land.

2. The poor man, however his religious conscience revolt against it, is compelled under legal penalty to hand over his children to be "taught" under this system.

"The National Society for promoting the Education of the Poor in the Principles of the Established Church;" nay, not "the National Society" only, but "the Church of England as by law established," the Church of England generally, Bishops, Priests, People, have put their hands and seals to this system. Practically, Convocation has endorsed it.

This is my case, and here I leave it; repeating only what I said above, that my dear kind friends can hardly have looked fully in the face what they were about when they made themselves parties to the system of the Act of 1870.

I am not saying—it would be foolishness—that more "standing fast" on the part of the Priests would have stopped the Bill of 1870; though I believe I know how the parish Priests, in conjunction with their parishioners, might easily have made the Act a dead letter.

If the Bishops, as a body, had led the Priests against the Bill, as it was their duty to the Church to have done, that would have been another matter. But why discourse or speculate *de impossibili in rerum naturâ*. Everybody knows that Bishops and Priests of the "Establishment" do not, as matter of fact, "pull together" for the maintenance of "Church principles;" no, nor Priests either among themselves. The Civil Power of England would have harder work by a good deal than it has, in dealing with the Church of England, if they did. It is a very apt illustration of *divide et impera*. How far it may have been a part of the original policy of Century XVI., if not to ensure internal division, yet to take advantage of it when ensured, for the ultimate purpose of domination by the Civil Power, I do not know; nor whether it was formally part of that policy at all. But doubtless, the issue in Century XIX. looks very much as if it had been; and consciously or unconsciously, the effect has been the same.

It is true that, now and then, the Priests unite to "pull up" the Bishops; and, so far, there is what seems to be unanimity of purpose; but, when we sift a little, it is "Establishmentarian" rather than "Church" unanimity.

I instance in the "Burial" matter. The possessory rights of the Clergy, both as freeholders and as trustees, are loudly and generally vindicated on the part of the Priests. The Bishops follow, *non passibus æquis*, but follow they do.

Now there is that about the vindication which marks it for "Establishmentarian" rather than "Church." If it had been "Church," it would have put in the foreground, and have insisted upon as a thing *in limine*, the restoration *within the Church* of Discipline as respects the use of "the Order for the Burial of the Dead."

Put it as you will, it is immeasurably a less evil, though it be a great evil, that a "Nonconformist body" should be buried in a churchyard with Nonconformist Service, than that a "Church body," which by every rule of the Church ought to be refused burial with Service of the Church, should be buried in the churchyard with that Service as matter of legal right, just the same as if there had been nothing to say against such burial, but everything for it. The one is an unrighteous invasion, the other is an unrighteous complicity and an hypocrisy.

For the general question of Church Discipline, I believe there to be nothing for which there lies upon the entire Spiritualty of the Church of England a heavier responsibility, and especially upon the Ordinaries, from Archbishop to Archdeacon, than the utter confusion, neglect, and disrepute into which, in this, as in other particulars, they have allowed the Church to fall. Our Homily says that Discipline is one of the three notes of a true Church[b]. One note, then, of the truth of our position is altogether gone. Discipline now, where there is anything which is, after all, not it but only its counterfeit, means discipline of Clergy only, not of people at all; and commonly degenerates into harassing and persecution of Clergy at the instance of precisely that portion of the community who not only have the least claim, moral or religious, to be consulted or considered, but are themselves the fittest subjects for discipline. The last and worst example is the "Public Worship Regulation Act," a thing in its conception, enacting, executing, of almost inconceivable infamy.

There is a fact in the history of the matter of "spiritual censure," the chief element of true Discipline, of which not many men seem to be aware, and which aggravates the case as against the Spiritualty.

The Act 57 Geo. III. c. 127, the existing law, provides for "discontinuing excommunication" in certain cases; it provides no less for its due continuance and execution in certain other cases.

The second section of the Act is as follows:—

"Provided always that nothing in this Act contained shall prevent any Ecclesiastical Court from pronouncing or declaring persons to be excommunicate in definitive sentences, or in interlocutory decrees, having the force and effect of definitive sentences, such sentences or decrees being pronounced as spiritual censures for offences of ecclesiastical cognizance, in the same

---

[b] "The true Church hath always three notes or marks, whereby it is known: pure and sound Doctrine; the Sacraments ministered according to CHRIST'S holy Institution; and the right use of ecclesiastical Discipline." —Second part of the Homily concerning the HOLY GHOST. (Oxford, 1840, p. 413.)

manner as such Court might lawfully have pronounced or declared the same, had this Act not been passed."

Section 3 provides for enforcement of such spiritual censures. The Act of 2 and 3 Will. IV. c. 93, made further and more stringent provision for such enforcement.

If, then, the practice of "spiritual censures" may .be said to have ceased to exist in the Church of England, the jurisdiction of the Courts to pronounce or declare remaining the same, I want to know where the fault of this state of thing, as great a fault as may be, lies. It does not lie clearly with the Legislature; it remains that it lies with the Bishops, Priests, and People of "the Church of England as by law established." It is a remarkable instance of the operation of the "Establishment," in bringing the Spiritualty to be even less careful for Church Principle than the Civil Power has shewn itself to be.

I dealt with this matter in my Charge to Clergy, Churchwardens and People, 1857. The Charge attracted some notice at the time, particularly from Nonconformists.

Three times in the twenty-seven years that I have held the office of Archdeacon of Taunton, persons in the Archdeaconry have communicated with me, touching presentment to be made to me at my Visitation Court of grievous offences, cognizable by the Court Ecclesiastical. My answer has been that, upon such presentment being made, I should cite the accused to appear before me.

In all the cases, the courage of the accuser failed him, and "insuperable difficulties," (a thing everybody pleads as an excuse for not doing his duty to the full extent of his power, whether likely to "succeed" or to "fail,") were alleged against proceeding in any formal way.

I have often been asked by Clergy, what they can do in cases where their conscience is greatly troubled at being required to read "the Order for the Burial of the Dead" over the body of a notorious evil liver, living in open habit of deadly sin, and dying so that no man is able to testify to his repentance.

My answer has been, by process of enquiry :—

"Have you presented such person, while living, to the Ordinary to be judged? if found guilty, to be first admonished; and, upon failure to repent and amend his life, to be excommunicated?"

"No, I have not."

"Then, in that case, the desecration of the Church Service, and the grievous scandal of such a burial, rests with yourself. You have no justification to allege upon the merits, as you have certainly none in law, for refusing to read all the Service."

If, on the other hand, such presentment had taken place, and it had been, that when in the hands of the Visiting Ordinary, the Visiting Ordinary had got rid of it by taking no account of it, then the burden has been shifted from the shoulders of the parish Priest presenting, to those of the Ordinary indifferent and recusant. It is not easy to conceive a worse or a heavier burden.

I am bound to add here that though, in my capacity of Visiting Ordinary, I have been ready always to judge upon presentment; in my capacity of parish Priest, not resident within the limits of my own Archdeaconry, I fall under my own censure, and have to bear all the burden myself. For I have never presented any one: I ought to have presented not a few.

Spiritual censure, the authority exercising, the manner of its exercise, are among the first principles of the Faith of CHRIST. This is not the place to discuss these things. I assume them as self-evident and vital, insomuch that a Church either rejecting them, or confessing them in words, but in its practice denying them, is so far forth not a "true Church."

It was this consideration that prevailed with me upon the publication of "Essays and Reviews" in 1860; and two years after, of Bishop Colenso's book, to do what I could towards procuring a "Synodical Condemnation" of the two books. The difficulties in the way were many and great in both Houses. Eventually, I became Chairman of both Committees, and in that capacity presented the Reports.

"Essays and Reviews" was first published in 1860. The honour of the first move in the direction of Synodical Condemnation of the book belongs to my dear friend Canon Jelf, who brought the matter before the Lower House, Feb. 26, 1861.

Meantime, the Archbishops and Bishops of both Provinces had censured the book; I think "unanimously."

Session Feb. 26, 1861, Canon Jelf moved for "an Address to His Grace the President, and their Lordships the Bishops, on the subject of a volume lately published, entitled 'Essays and Reviews.'"

The whole matter is so important, and my personal share in it so large, that it is well to present some historical summary of the successive steps taken in connection with it. And this the more, because I am sorrowfully compelled to think that, however great the difficulties in the way of Synodical Condemnation, that is to say, of the exercise of the duty of the Church, by way of spiritual censure in 1861-4 of an heretical book, and in 1863-8 of the excommunication of the heretic also, the difficulties in the way *now*, in any like case, would be greater still, if indeed not insuperable.

The Lower House was not unanimous in agreeing to Dr. Jelf's motion for suspension of standing orders, to enable him to introduce the matter of his resolution. There were many "Noes," and it was necessary to take a division.

Canon Jelf having moved, and having referred to the fact of the Episcopal censure, as not only not superseding, but as enhancing the necessity of Synodical Condemnation, was seconded by Dr. McCaul.

The debate closed in the rejection of "the previous question;" in the withdrawal of Canon Jelf's resolution; and in the carrying by a large majority the following amendment of the present Bishop of Lincoln, seconded by myself :—

"That the Clergy of the Lower House of Convocation of the Province of Canterbury, having regard to the censure which has been already pronounced and published by the Archbishops and Bishops of the Provinces of Canterbury and York on certain opinions contained in a book entitled 'Essays and Reviews,' entertain an earnest hope that under the Divine Blessing, the faithful zeal of the Christian Church in this land may be enabled to counteract the pernicious influence of the erroneous opinions contained in the said volume."

This was all that was to be got from the Lower House that day. I shall surprise nobody when I say that, though I seconded it, I was wholly dissatisfied with it, and thought it very unworthy of the occasion.

Session March 14, 1861, I presented the following Gravamen :—

"*The Gravamen of George Anthony Denison, M.A., Archdeacon of Taunton, and of other members whose names are attached.*

"That a book entitled 'Essays and Reviews' was published in London in the year 1860, containing, as they believe, doctrines subversive of the Inspiration and Authority of Holy Scripture, and, in other respects also, contrary to the Liturgy and Articles of the Church of England.

"That six out of the seven Essays or Reviews comprised in the said book, are written by Clergymen of the Church of England.

"The undersigned humbly pray that his Grace the President and the Bishops of the Upper House will be pleased to direct the appointment of a Committee of this House to make extracts from the said book, and to report thereon to this House."

This Gravamen having been taken up to the Upper House, the late Bishop of Winchester, then Bishop of Oxford, moved, Session March 14, 1861, and was seconded by the Bishop of Chichester :—

"That the Upper House, having received a petition from certain members of the Lower House as to a book entitled 'Essays and Reviews,' and thinking fit to comply with the prayer of the said petition, his Grace the President be requested to direct the Lower House to appoint a Committee to examine the said book, and to report therein to that House, in order that the Lower House may communicate to this House its opinion whether there are sufficient grounds for proceeding to a Synodical Judgment upon the book."

The President and twelve Bishops were present. On a division, the Resolution was carried by 8 to 4.

There is one point especially calling for notice in the debate in the Upper House, issuing in this division.

The point is, the language employed by the late Bishop of St. David's. The language is very remarkable, both because of its decision and power, and because the subsequent language of the Bishop in this same matter was of a very different, indeed, of an opposite character. The Bishop appears afterwards to have looked at the question with some particular personal reference to myself, and his action became wholly adverse, instead of distinctly favourable, to the course which I felt it to be my duty to the Church to take, and which finally issued in the Synodical Condemnation for which I laboured.

The personal question is a very small matter, and I have no clear recollections about it. The Bishop's language, March 14, 1861, is not a small matter; he said,—

"It is not with a view to any effect upon the writers of this book, or upon those who sympathise with them, that I should desire that Synodical action should be taken on this question. It is simply because I think it is something which is absolutely required for maintaining the character, I should almost say the very being, of the Church as a Church, that it should have a distinct opinion upon these matters; that it should have an organ by which it can express that opinion; that, if that organ is not stifled by material force, if it is free to act, that it should act and exert itself, and declare what the mind of the Church is upon the point. My own view of the obligation which is imposed upon us by the circumstances of the case is so strong, that I do not disguise that I should have been disposed to take a step of a very different nature from that which is proposed, notwithstanding my full perception of the difficulties and inconveniences that might attend it. I should not have shrunk even from taking the initiative in this matter, and of joining in a request to his Grace the President to direct the Lower House to form such a Committee as they have agreed to."

Remarkable words in themselves, especially remarkable as coming from the Bishop of St. David's. I have often cited them in conversation, and was not surprised to find my citation received as proceeding upon some mistake of mine ; but there is no mistake in the matter.

Upon the resolution of the Upper House being communicated to the Lower House, Session March 15, 1861, the Committee was named, and I was appointed Chairman.

All my experience of Committees had shewn me that the thing to be done with a view to avoiding desultory and confused proceeding in Committee is, that the Chairman should be ready with a draft Report upon the first day of assembling of the Committee. That is to say, that there should be something definite, and connected in its several parts throughout, for the Committee to go to work upon, instead of attempting to construct the Report bit by bit from day to day.

There is, I know, another way of Report-making in common use ; the way of beginning with a blank sheet, and after discussion, collecting opinions point by point, and waiting to draft Report till all this has been done. I believe the other to be the much better way. The second is very apt to issue in desultory talk, discussion of side issues, and a disjointed production. The man who moves for the Committee is the proper Chairman of it, because it is reasonable to assume that he has most fully considered the matter in hand before he moves, and is therefore in the best position to put into shape the substance of what, in his view of the case, has to be said upon it. Then it rests with the Committee to accept in whole or in part, or to reject in whole or in part, to amend when they see cause, and to shape ; but I have never been able to see that a member of a Committee ought to move to set aside the Chairman's draft, unless he be prepared with a substitute also complete in all its parts.

In accordance with this view of a Chairman's duty, I gave all my time before the assembling of the Committee to the preparation of an Analysis of "Essays and Reviews," shewing the logical connection of thought and order of Number one with the other six, and dealing with each in succession. This I read to the Committee as my draft Report the first day of our assembling.

It was too strong and decided for a good many members of Committee; and it was agreed that we should proceed independently of it. Many members expressed a hope that I should publish it; and some wanted me to make it an Appendix to the Report we might agree to. This last I declined to do, as unusual and inconvenient, and open to other grave objections: but I did publish my Analysis, on my own account; and in 1869 it was republished. One of the members of the Committee, now a Bishop, said afterwards that he had arrived at the conclusion that, when the Committee declined to adopt the substance of my draft, they put aside the only thing which was of value. Another member, my dear, kind friend Dr. McCaul, said to me that my Analysis was the only perfectly clear statement of the contents and connection of parts and of tendencies of the book which he had seen.

However, the Committee more than hesitated; and so we went to work in another way.

The Committee sat twelve days,—sixty-six hours, besides as many passed in the work of Sub-Committees, &c. I liked my own Analysis best, but I very thankfully admit the great value of the Report, as it was presented by me on behalf of the Committee: I did all in my power to assist in preparing it.

The Report was presented, Session June 18, 1861. Having presented it, I gave notice of the Resolution following:—

"That, in the opinion of this House, there are sufficient grounds for proceeding to a Synodical Judgment upon the book entitled 'Essays and Reviews.'"

The debate was adjourned to Session June 20; lasted two days; and, after the rejection of many amendments, my resolution was carried by 31 to 8, June 21, 1861.

The Report had passed the Lower House, but the act of Synodical Condemnation was far away still; the Report had passed the Lower House, but in the face of circumstances, both of support and opposition, of a very saddening character.

First, for the numbers of the Lower House in respect of the spiritual censure of a book, every page of which is steeped in heresy. The numbers in the Lower, as even more distinctly in the Upper House, are conclusive proof, either of a widespread indifference, or of a confusion between the spiritual and the temporal jurisdiction, or of some participation in the heresies of the book: I believe of all three. And if it be said of me that I am a man who allows himself to censure without stint, that is no bar to my saying here, that I am unable to recognise any element in the opposition besides one or other of the three which I have just stated.

Then for the support. The support was such as I can never think of without deepest thankfulness to GOD. But look at the numbers: the Lower House has one hundred and forty-seven members; when I carried the Report, there were only forty members present.

Afterwards, in 1864, when the Synodical Condemnation was finally completed, so far as the vote of the two Houses is concerned, I remember well that upon the first day of the three days' debate, I had to telegraph to twenty men to come up to vote. Fifteen came to my call, and that gave me the majority of twenty in a house of not more than sixty members—39 to 19.

Now I turn to the numbers of the Upper House. Twelve Bishops only, besides the President—twelve out of twenty-one—were present when the late Bishop of Oxford carried his Resolution in answer to our Gravamen, directing the appointment of the Committee of the Lower House, by 8 to 4.

The next step is, what was done with the Report carried in the Lower House, and communicated to the Upper House.

The confusion between the spiritual and the temporal jurisdiction prevailed here. The late Bishop of Chichester moved, July 9, 1861, and the Bishop of St. Asaph seconded, and carried without debate or division—so that I have no means of knowing how many Bishops were there—the Resolution following. Many people thought it plausible enough at the time; but how a Churchman can extend any manner of approval to it, is beyond me to comprehend.

"That his Grace the President be requested to communicate to the Lower House, that this House, having taken into their consideration the communications of the Lower House touching a book entitled 'Essays and Reviews,' have resolved,—

"That whereas, since this House formerly considered this question, a suit has been commenced against one of the writers of the said book for his contribution thereto; and whereas his Grace the President of this Synod, and the other Bishops, Privy Councillors, may, in the course of Appeal, have to decide on the said suit judicially; and whereas it appears to this House inexpedient, either to proceed with the consideration of this subject in the absence of the President and such members of this House, or to embarrass them as to hereafter sitting as Judges in the pending suit, by their having joined in a Synodical Condemnation of the book, it is expedient to adjourn the further consideration of this subject pending the course of such suit."

The opportunity was supplied for the resolution of the Upper House, July 9, 1861, by the instituting of the suit, Bishop of Salisbury *v.* Williams, in the Court of Arches. The delay in recovering the Catholic position of the Church of England in respect of spiritual censure of heretical books, incurred by the resolution, is a thing very deeply to be regretted.

I must also say here that I am not able to understand how the distinction between the old Court of Arches *under the "Establishment,"* and the Court of Final Appeal, was anything but an abstract, and, so to speak, metaphysical distinction. I say, "the old Court of Arches," because it is quite unnecessary to waste time and words upon its absurd and unconstitutional counterfeit created under the Public Worship Regulation Act.

The old Court of Arches had become, in the abeyance of the Consistorial Court of the Diocese, a Court of first instance. Its decisions, in matters of Doctrine, Discipline, Worship, however sound and good, and proceeding upon the spiritual basis, were liable to be reversed by decisions of the Court above, neither sound nor good, and proceeding upon the temporal basis only: and this has been the history of the actual relations between the two Courts. The distinction between them was, I repeat, *under the Establishment* only abstract and metaphysical, all the appointment of the Judge in the Court below by the Archbishop of the Province notwithstanding; and to go into the Court of Arches upon a question of Doctrine, but to refuse to go, upon appeal, into the Court above, was what I could not at the time, and have not been able since, to understand.

The true course was, to go into neither Court. I am quite aware that it will be said here, "Why, did you not yourself propose to go into both; and, as matter of fact, did go into both in 1856 and 1858, first by way of appeal on your own part, next by way of appeal on the prosecutor's part?" It is quite true; but it is to be noted that I did not originate the suit in my case; I was not prosecutor, I was defendant. I was assailed under Statute, and had to defend myself under Statute: I am not chargeable with the form of procedure. I cannot conceive myself, then or since, originating proceedings in matters of Doctrine, or Discipline, or Worship, in the old Court of Arches, much less in its counterfeit, knowing that the Court of Final Appeal is in prospect.

What was wanted was, that the Bishop of Salisbury should have judged Dr. Rowland Williams in his own Consistorial Court; having found him guilty of heresy, have admonished him; and, upon refusal to repent of his error, have excommunicated him by sentence from his own Altar: this would have been an instance and example of the true use of the power of spiritual censure by spiritual judges, *recognised* by the Act 57 Geo. III. cap. 127, and still law of this Church and Realm. The other was, after all said and done, only a proceeding in temporals; and in its issue necessarily weakened, rather than strengthened, the spiritual position. How great the loss of precedent incurred was forced upon the sight even of men who most wished to keep their eyes shut, by what took place in 1863 in the matter of the Colenso heresy; when the act of excommunication was dealt with by those at whose hands any such dealing was least expected, as a matter ultimately of Statute-law only.

But, however these things may be, what happened in 1861 was, that, under the benumbing influence of the spell cast upon the Church by the Resolution of the Upper House, the Synodical Condemnation of "Essays and Reviews," to use the words of the late Bishop of Oxford in the Upper House, April 20, 1864, "slumbered since July 9, 1861." The Lower House had had its answer that day; I suppose no one of us was surprised by the answer, however deeply we might regret it. All that was left to us was to watch and wait.

Meantime, in 1863, came the Colenso case. The first move in this case was on Feb. 11, 1863, when,—having presented Petitions from 101 Clergy of my Archdeaconry, praying that enquiry might be made respecting a book lately published, and entitled "The Pentateuch and the Book of Joshua critically examined," by the Right Rev. John William Colenso, D.D., Bishop of Natal, and that Convocation might proceed to deliver Synodical Judgment thereon,—I moved, according to notice:—

"That the standing orders be now suspended, in order to the moving of an Address to the Upper House, praying the Upper House to direct the appointment of a Committee to examine a book lately published in London, within the Province of Canterbury, entitled 'The Pentateuch and Book of Joshua critically examined,' by the Right Rev. John William Colenso, D.D., Bishop of Natal, Parts I. and II., and to report whether any, and if any, what opinions heretical or erroneous in Doctrine are contained in the said book."

This was seconded by Dr. McCaul, and after one day's debate, carried by a great majority.

Two days after, Feb. 13, 1863, so that the Upper House had ample notice, the prayer of the Resolution of the Lower House was debated in the Upper House.

On that occasion *five* Bishops were present besides the President. It shocked a great many good men at the time, that indifference so marked, should have been shewn by Bishops in such a matter as this. But the good Providence of GOD overruled, and the prayer of the Lower House was affirmed by three Bishops to two. The President observing, after declaring the vote, that he

"should certainly have thought it rather a harsh measure, as he understood the relations between the two Houses, if the Upper House had refused a request of that sort. That it would have seemed very like stifling enquiry, and denying the Lower House the exercise of a liberty which they had reason and right to ask for."

It was in the course of this debate that the present Archbishop of Canterbury, then Bishop of London, made the most extraordinary and wholly unfounded statements touching what had been done by the Lower House in the matter of "Essays and Reviews." The Bishop was corrected at the time, and made a quasi-apology, but accompanied with language of causeless offence and disrespect. I did not think it worth while to take any notice of all this at the time; but when the Bishop reiterated these statements in the Upper House, April 21, 1864, and this in a manner even more unfitting, it seemed necessary to write to the Bishop, and publish the Correspondence.

I subjoin the Correspondence, as published at the time.

"22, *Great George-street, Westminster, April* 22, 1864.

"My Lord,—A statement which your Lordship is reported to have made in your place in Convocation yesterday makes it necessary that I should write this letter.

"Your Lordship is reported to have said that you deeply regretted that the Bishop of Oxford should have founded a motion upon such a paper as the Report upon 'Essays and Reviews'—which came from the Lower House—which was in fact the report of 'one individual.' I abstain from citing here the epithets which your Lordship lavished upon the Report.

"Now the facts are these :—

"As Chairman of the Committee appointed in obedience to the direction of the Upper House, March 15, 1861, I prepared a draft, and submitted it to the Committee at their first sitting, April 22, 1861. The Committee did not adopt that draft, and proceeded to frame a report different both in arrangement and in statement. My draft was published later in the year under the title, 'Analysis of Essays and Reviews,' and the differences between it and the Report of the Committee are easily to be ascertained.

"Having carefully preserved a record of the acts of the Committee, I find that the Committee sat 12 days, in all 66 hours, and that at least as many more days were employed upon different parts of the Report by Sub-Committees and by individual members, as well as by the Chairman.

"The Report was not, therefore, in any sense, 'the Report of one individual;' it was the very careful and considered Report of a Committee comprising many honoured names. I give the list below as printed in p. 1 of Report. The numbers attending on the 12 days varied from 15 to 10. On the last day the Report was finally settled, passed by the Committee, and ordered to be signed by the Chairman on behalf of the Committee.

"I think that if your Lordship had ascertained the facts of the case, and what the care and the labours of the Committee had been, you would not have allowed yourself to use the language which your Lordship is reported to have used. That language has caused deep regret and pain to many members of the Lower House—I believe I might say, to all members of the Lower House who are cognisant of it. For myself, suffer me to assure your Lordship that no expressions of disapproval, or ridicule, or contempt move me, or make me less 'ready with all faithful diligence'—'The Lord being my Helper—to banish and drive away all erroneous and strange doctrines contrary to GOD'S Word.' I do not want any measure for myself which I am not giving to others; but I do want facts, and not mis-statements.

"Your Lordship is also reported to have used, in the course of the same debate, other expressions amounting to a denial of the ancient and undoubted privilege of every member of the Lower House, whether singly or in conjunction with other members, to lay before the Upper House in the form of *gravamina*, by the hands of the Prolocutor, the grievances which press upon themselves and other members of the Church.

"I have the honour to be

"Your Lordship's faithful servant,
"GEORGE A. DENISON.

"*The Lord Bishop of London.*"

"P.S. I beg to add, that I propose to make this letter public, with any reply that your Lordship may give to it.

"Members of Committee.—Archdeacons: Buckingham, Berkshire, St. Alban's[c], Taunton (Chairman), Worcester[d]. Doctors of Divinity: Jelf, Jeremie, Jebb, Leighton, and McCaul. Bachelors of Divinity: H. Browne and Woodgate. Masters of Arts: Best, Fendall, Joyce[e], Prevost, Thompson, and Vincent."

"*London House*, 25*th April*, 1864.

"MY DEAR MR. ARCHDEACON,—I have this day received your letter of the 22nd inst. Believe me, I am very sorry that words used by me should have caused pain to yourself and other good men.

"You assure me that the Report on 'Essays and Reviews,' which came nearly three years ago from the Lower House of Convocation to the Upper, was not the production of one individual. I have no recollection of having said that it was; but as the newspapers represent me as having said so, I fear, and greatly regret, that I used words calculated to convey this impression. What I desired to be understood as specially al-

---

[c] Unable to serve.

[d] Unwell; unable to attend, but communicated his judgment in writing.

[e] Unable to attend, but communicated his judgment in writing.

luding to, in the passages of my speech to which you refer, was Schedule B, sent to the Upper House (I think on 21st June, 1861) along with the Report. Our discussion of Thursday last was naturally given in the *Times* in an abridged form, and the part of the discussion to which your letter relates was, in fact, somewhat interrupted and conversational. I was endeavouring to ascertain whether this Schedule B had been sanctioned by the Lower House of Convocation, or by a Committee of that House, or whether it spoke, in fact, merely the sentiments of one or more individuals. I hope all the eminent persons whose names you give me are not responsible for that Schedule. Of course, I at once accept your statement as to the authorship of the Report; but, after all the attention I have given to your letter and to the records of Convocation, I am unable as yet to feel assured that this Schedule, or indeed even the Report itself, was ever adopted by the Lower House.

"I certainly adhere to my expressed opinion that this Schedule B is an unfortunate document, likely to do much mischief, which, for the sake of the truth it was designed to defend, I was very sorry to see brought again under public notice after I had hoped it was forgotten.

"Respecting the privilege of individual members of the Lower House to lay their 'gravamina' before his Grace the President and the Bishops, I should be much misunderstood if I were thought to deny their right of exercising this privilege. What I contended for was, that their 'gravamina' should always be taken for what they are really worth, as expressions merely of individual opinion.

"I remain, my dear Mr. Archdeacon,
"Your faithful servant,
"A. C. LONDON.

"*Ven. Archdeacon Denison.*"

"22, *Great George-street, Westminster, April* 26, 1864.

"MY LORD,—I beg to thank you for your letter. Schedule B had precisely the same authority as the Report itself—that is to say, it was approved and passed by the Committee after long and careful preparation by many hands.

"It is not our practice to ask the assent of the Lower House to every part of a lengthened Report; but after placing it, in a printed shape, in the hands of members by vote of the House, to found a resolution upon it. This is what was done in the case of the Report upon 'Essays and Reviews,' with its Schedules. It was placed in the hands of members, June 18, 1861. On June 20, I moved and carried by vote of the House, in the face of many amendments, the resolution which was communicated with the Report and its Schedule to the Upper House:—

"'That, in the opinion of this House, there are sufficient grounds for proceeding to a Synodical Judgment upon the book entitled "Essays and Reviews."'

"I have the honour to be,
"Your Lordship's faithful servant,
"GEORGE A. DENISON.

"*The Lord Bishop of London.*"

It was in the same debate, April 21, 1864, that the late Bishop of St. David's gave his reasons for pursuing an exactly opposite course to that which he had so powerfully advocated, when the subject of "Essays and Reviews" first came before the Upper House in 1861. I have often tried to understand his ground of change, but have not found my mental power equal to the task.

The only solution I can offer of mis-statement of facts apologised for, but repeated *in eadem materia*, of much disrespect of the Lower House, apologised for, but repeated *in eadem materia*, is that the advocates of the anti-Church policy of Indifferentism in religion, or, of what practically comes to the same thing, of subordination of the Church policy of Synodical Condemnation of heretical books to the State policy of Indifferentism, having flattered themselves that they had got rid of Synodical Condemnation in the case of "Essays and Reviews" by the three years' delay, when they found that this was not in the way of being done, were transported, in their disappointment, beyond all just bounds. It is the only solution I have to offer; I believe it to be the true solution, and therefore offer it.

Feb. 13, 1863, the Committee of the Lower House in the Colenso case was appointed: I was Chairman of it.

May 19, 1863, the Report of Committee was presented to the Lower House. Our present Prolocutor then moved :—

"That a copy of the Report be forwarded to the Upper House, together with a respectful request from this House that their Lordships will be pleased to consider the matter therein contained, and take such action thereupon as they may think expedient."

This was seconded by the present Bishop of Montreal, and carried without debate. The same day the Report was communicated to the Upper House.

May 20, 1863, the Resolutions following were moved by the Bishop of Winchester (Dr. Sumner) :—

"We, the Archbishop and Bishops of the Province of Canterbury in Convocation assembled, having considered the Report of the Committee of the Lower House, appointed on the Address of the Lower House to examine a book entitled, '*The Pentateuch and the Book of Joshua critically examined*,' by the Rt. Rev. J. W. Colenso, Bishop of Natal, Parts I. and II., and now transmitted to this House by the Lower House, resolve,—

"That the said book does, in our judgment, involve errors of the gravest and most dangerous character, subversive of faith in the Bible as the Word of GOD.

"That this House, having reason to believe that the book in question will shortly be submitted to the judgment of an Ecclesiastical Court, decline to take further action in the matter; but that we affectionately warn those who may not be able to read the published and convincing answers to the work which have already appeared, of its dangerous character.

"That these resolutions be communicated to the Lower House."

The first Resolution was carried, with one dissentient, the late Bishop of St. David's.

The second Resolution amended by the insertion of the words "*at this time*," next after the words, "decline to take further action in the matter," on the motion of the late Bishop of Oxford, was also carried, with one dissentient,—the late Bishop of Salisbury, who expressed his " regret that the House should have declined to take any further action in the matter, in consequence of the belief that the question of the book would be submitted to the Ecclesiastical Court of the Metropolitan of South Africa," and whose objection was not removed by the addition of the words "*at this time.*"

The Bishop of Salisbury was clearly right. The second Resolution was only another form of the hesitation of the Upper House to make "spiritual censure" more than words only; and all the words about "reading published and convincing answers," are not only deplorably weak in themselves, but do in effect exalt private judgment into the place of the Authority of the Church. The Resolution indicated very clearly what would be the course of future Episcopal policy in England in the matter, when, as happened afterwards, it found its way to the Court of Final Appeal at home.

The message from the Upper House placed me in a great difficulty. I regretted the second Resolution upon every ground, more than I can express, and would have nothing to do with it. For the rest, I knew I could get nothing more here in England; and I turned my eyes away from the home Episcopate to that great man, the greatest man by far I have lived to know, the wisest, the humblest, the most faithful, the most truly gentle, Robert Gray, Bishop of Capetown, Metropolitan of South Africa. I looked to him for all that would be done in the great distress and trial which had fallen upon the Anglican Communion. I never doubted, and was thankful I could not doubt, how it was that he would act, whatever might be the action of the collective home Episcopate.

I know of nothing more moving than the patient sorrow of the Bishop of Capetown, as it comes necessarily, and as it were unbidden, to the surface in the published "Life," when he found that the decided support of those of his brethren, Bishops here in England, upon whom he had most relied, failed him; and that considerations of the "legal" position, considerations, as I believe not so much as "legally" valid, were interposed, Feb. 21, 1868, staying acceptance of the sentence of excommunication on the part of the Church of England. The Lower House had done its duty, after a close and severe struggle: for the motion to convert Gravamen into *Articulus Cleri* was carried, in point of suspension of standing orders, by 5 only,—34 to 29. The *Articulus Cleri* was adopted without division; but only after amendment of the Dean of Ely, negatived by 45 to 26.

Meantime, I had to decide at once what I should propose to the Lower House. I eschewed and avoided carefully all recognition of the grounds of delay of action contained in the second Resolution of the Upper House; of all the importation of "published and convincing answers" into the place of the Authority of the Church—as if *this* was for the unlearned, unscientific, and unphilosophical *only*—and proposed as follows, May 20, 1863:—

"That this House, having received the message of the Upper House in the matter of the book entitled '*The Pentateuch and the Book of Joshua critically examined*,' by the Rt. Rev. John William Colenso, D.D., Bishop of Natal, Parts I. and II., do hereby accept and concur in the Judgment of the Upper House, that the book involves errors of the gravest and most dangerous character, subversive of faith in the Bible as the Word of GOD; and that this House do further concur in the affectionate warning of the Upper House against the dangerous character of the book.

"That the Resolution be respectfully communicated to the Upper House."

This was seconded by the late Dean of Canterbury, my kindly and generous opponent, and was carried without debate.

I now see that the Resolution ought to have stopped at "the Word of GOD." The "affectionate warning" of the Upper House had been so damaged by the grounds upon which it was placed, and by its limitation to the unlearned, that I am sorry I touched it at all.

In 1864, the "suit" in "Essays and Reviews" had been "finally" determined; the argument had reached its foregone conclusion. Once more, under colour of administering the Law of this Church and Realm, the Court above had condoned heresy; had "established" Indifferentism; had made every man's private interpretation of Holy Scripture the rule of the Englishman's religious life. Englishmen generally looked complacently on: they had nothing to say against a rule so flattering to their self-conceit, so encouraging to the temptation of "the pride of life," so favourable to the growth and prevalence of individual dogmatism.

No doubt, as I have said above, those members of the Houses of Convocation of Canterbury, who were either defenders of "Essays and Reviews," or who belonged to that large section of Church people, Bishop, Priest, Layman, whose motto is, "It will last my time," had persuaded themselves that the three years' delay had disposed of "Synodical Condemnation," and were proportionably angry when they found themselves to have reckoned without their host.

And yet how nearly did they "succeed," as men count "success." Ten Bishops present, April 21, 1864; divided, 5 to 5: Convocation was saved by the casting-vote of the President. It was worse even than in the "Colenso" case, where it had been saved by 3 to 2. These are facts that pass easily out of men's recollection; but no man can say that they are not as keys unlocking the condition of the ecclesiastical mind.

The steps which had preceded the division in the Upper House, April 21, 1864, were these:—

I had received information upon which I could depend, that it was proposed to revive the question in the Upper House.

On April 19, the late Bishop of Oxford presented a Petition, praying the Upper House to proceed to Judgment; and moved,—

"That this House take into its consideration the message of the Lower House, June 21, 1861, for the purpose of considering whether the House shall accede to the prayer of the Petition."

This was on Tuesday, April 19. The debate was fixed for Thursday, April 21; *thus giving ample time for full attendance of Bishops.*

April 20, the late Bishop of Oxford presented another like Petition from members of the Church of England, lay and clerical.

The same day I presented the Gravamen following, in the Lower House :—

"That a remarkable instance of the injury which is caused to the Church by the confusion of jurisdictions now involved in the Constitution of the Appeal Court, in respect of questions of alleged false doctrine, is found in the present position of the endeavour made by this House, June 21, 1861, to procure a Synodical Condemnation of the book entitled 'Essays and Reviews:' inasmuch as the Upper House (which had directed the appointment of the Committee of this House) in acknowledging, July 9, 1861, the communication of the Resolution of this House, founded upon the Report of the Committee, declared it 'expedient to adjourn the further consideration of the subject pending the course of a suit instituted against one of the writers in the said book, on the specific ground that the President of this Synod, and other Bishops, Privy Councillors, might in the course of Appeal have to decide the said suit judicially."

"That the suit having now been brought to a close, the injury done to the Church by the delay of Synodical Judgment, may be in part repaired by proceeding to such Judgment.

"GEORGE A. DENISON,
"*Archdeacon of Taunton.*"

In introducing the Gravamen, I said that it was my anxious desire that it should go to the Upper House as *Articulus Cleri;* but that if there was any objection to the suspension of the standing orders, in order to making it *Articulus Cleri,* I would request the Prolocutor to communicate it as my Gravamen, and that of other members of the House willing to sign it.

The old, threadbare, and in this particular case, eminently foolish, objection was taken by one member, about dealing with questions "suddenly and abruptly;" the fact being, that it was a return to the decision of the House, after a forced suspension of nearly three years. There were about fifty members present, and I could at once have carried the *Articulus Cleri;* but after what I had said in introducing it, I was bound to send it up only as that of myself and other members. It was signed by myself and thirty-nine other members.

The late Bishop of Oxford, proceeding upon the basis of the Gravamen and Petitions, moved, April 20, 1864:—

"That this House, having received June 21, 1861, from the Lower House their resolution of June 21, 1861, that, in the opinion of the Lower House, there are sufficient grounds for proceeding to a Synodical Judgment on 'Essays and Reviews,' and having July 9, 1861, adjourned the consideration of the subject pending the course of the then existing suit; and that suit being now concluded,—

"Resolved that this House resume the consideration of the subject; and that a Committee of the House be appointed, first, to consider the communications made on this subject by the Lower House; secondly, to consider the book referred to in such communications; and thirdly, to report thereon to the House."

The debate was then adjourned, as previously arranged, to the day following, Thursday, April 21, when the Resolution was carried, upon a division, 5 to 5, by the casting-vote of the President.

The Church of England has indeed great cause to be thankful for the Presidency which gave the casting-vote; thankful to ALMIGHTY GOD for overruling the attempt to stultify Church Authority; to make the Church the slavish instrument of an Indifferent Civil Power; to render unto Cæsar the things of GOD.

The Archbishop and Bishops of the Province of Canterbury were the Committee, i.e. it was a Committee of the whole House.

June 21, the Report was presented to the House. A debate ensued, in places of an excited and personal character, in the course of which I was, not to my surprise at all, roughly handled, and this without any particular regard to the facts of the case. The Report was received and adopted without division.

The late Bishop of Oxford then moved :—

"That the Upper House of Convocation, having received and adopted the Report of the Committee of the whole House appointed by them to examine the volume entitled ' Essays and Reviews,' invite the Lower House to concur with them in the following Judgment :—

"That this Synod, having appointed Committees of the Upper and Lower House to examine and report upon the volume entitled 'Essays and Reviews,' and the said Committees having severally reported thereon, doth hereby Synodically Condemn the said volume, as containing teaching contrary to the Doctrine received by the United Church of England and Ireland, in common with the whole Catholic Church of Christ."

This was seconded by the Bishop of Gloucester, and carried with two dissentients,—the Bishops of London and Lincoln.

One step only now remained,—the concurrence of the Lower House.

The Resolution of the Upper House having been communicated to us the same day that it was passed, June 21, 1864, I moved :—

"That this House respectfully and heartily tenders its thanks to his Grace the President and the Bishops of the Upper House, for their care in defence of the Faith, as manifested in the Report upon the book entitled ' Essays and Reviews,' now read to this House; and that this House does thankfully accept and concur in the Condemnation of the book by the Upper House, which has been based upon the said Report."

After three days' debate, my resolution as amended below was passed, by 39 to 19 ; but, as I have stated above, in order to my majority of 20, I had to telegraph to 20 men to come up to vote; 15 of the 20 answered to my call.

"That this House respectfully and heartily tenders its thanks to his Grace the President and the Bishops of the Upper House, for their care in defence of the Faith; and that this House does thankfully accept and concur in the Condemnation of the book by the Upper House, to which their concurrence has been invited by the Upper House."

It had taken three years, one hundred and nineteen days, to bring about the Synodical Condemnation of "Essays and Reviews." Thankfulness for the issue more than overcomes all the pain of coldness, neglect, indifference, frivolous or irrelevant objection. For hostility direct and indirect, everybody who takes such things in hand is of course prepared; but it is only by painful experience that he becomes cognisant of, and in the end familiar with, the fact that a "friend" is sometimes much harder to deal with than a "foe."

Among many able and learned, kindly and generous helpers, I have special cause to name the honoured name of McCaul, the dear good friend of my later life. I rejoice to think, even more than of the public support, of the close private friendship which had its first beginnings and its consummation in the contention against the book.

Up to the time of the first move, Feb. 26, 1861, our relations had been always kindly, but, I think, in all cases antagonistic. From that time they became, as it were, bound up into one purpose, and counsel, and mutual help. McCaul brought to the work learning and knowledge which I did not myself possess; our intercourse became very frequent, and our deliberations had a common issue. It remained still to supply convincing evidence of personal regard, and he was not slow to supply it by the means ready to his hand.

One day in 1861, he said to me, "I wish you would come and dine with us; we shall only be ourselves, and one or two near friends, and we shall be very glad if you will come." Up to that day, I had never had any personal acquaintance with any member of the family except McCaul himself.

I need hardly say how glad and thankful I was to go. As I was going in to dinner, Mrs. McCaul said to me, "Well, Archdeacon, what odd things happen!"

"Yes," I said, "a good many. I suppose you mean something about me?"

"That's just it. If, a little time ago, I had thought who it was who was the least likely to take me in to dinner in my own house, I should have said it was you. Now, I don't know anybody with whom I would rather go in to dinner."

It is not so often that one comes across free and affectionate frankness such as this is, as to be able to refuse it its due place in the "Notes" of a life. It moved me greatly at the time; and I thought of the Goodness which had brought new love out of old contention, upon the common ground of Defence of the Faith.

From that day, no opportunity was neglected of manifesting the same loving-kindness towards me; and when dear McCaul died, early in 1864 (for he did not live to see our joint work completed), on the day that he died one of his sons wrote to me to announce his death. In my answer I said, that if it was not asking too much, I should be very thankful to be allowed to follow his body to the grave. I was received as one of the near friends, and with them went from the house to the grave. Among the many moving memories of my life, no one moves me more. Reference to what passed in the Lower House, Feb. 5, 1864, is all that I need add here.

There are other things closely bound up with "Essays and Reviews," with which I had much to do, and which find here their natural place.

First, there is the final resistance to the Jowett endowment at Oxford, in 1864. Second, the Oxford Declaration touching the Inspiration of Holy Scripture and Eternity of Punishment, the same year. Third, the opposition to the Consecration of Bishop Temple to the See of Exeter, in 1869.

For the prevailing scepticism, amounting in some cases to pronounced infidelity, at Oxford (I leave the sister University to its own members), especially among the younger portion of the Tutors and Professors, which has been a principal fruit of "Essays and Reviews," at once their cause and their effect, I have had nothing to do with this in any formal or special way, except that it has destroyed my interest in Oxford, and made me take my name off the books.

It presents itself in a very dangerous time to young minds, in their most dangerous time, under seductive shapes: — Science; Scholarship; Criticism; Independence of Authority; release from inconvenient moral and religious restraint; absolute freedom of thought and action; Philosophy.

There was a time in England, a sounder and truer, and therefore a better time than our time, with all its material and (so-called) mental development, when "free thinker" was a term of reproach; of more than reproach, of just general condemnation: now it has become a term of praise. It seems to be accepted, not only as indicating generosity, but as a primary element of the generous mind.

For "Philosophy" and "Philosophers," in connection with the "delivery" of the Religion of CHRIST, it may be worth while to observe that the words are found, each of them, only once in Holy Scripture, and that in a bad sense: Colossians ii. 8, "Beware lest any man spoil you through philosophy and vain deceit;" Acts xvii. 18, "Then certain philosophers of the Epicureans and of the Stoicks *encountered him.*"

In the passage of Colossians, S. Paul characterises "philosophy" as condemned above, with its exponent, *v.* 18, "intruding into those things which he hath not seen, vainly puffed up by his fleshly mind."

For "Science," the term is found twice in Holy Scripture; the Greek is γνῶσις, in both places. Daniel i. 4, "understanding science," γινώσκοντας γνῶσιν; 1 Tim. vi. 20, "avoiding profane and vain babblings, and oppositions of science fasely so called," ἐκτρεπόμενος τὰς βεβήλους κενοφωνίας, καὶ ἀντιθέσεις τῆς ψευδωνύμου γνώσεως.

There have been times in the world's history, in which the warning, positive and negative, here conveyed, has been specially needed. Surely among these, no time rather than our own, no place rather than our own country, where "the pride of life," and the sense of the present and the material are conjointly struggling to occupy all the ground of thought, and word, and act, which belongs first and foremost, as that to which all other ground of thought, and word, and act has to be referred, as being secondary and subsidiary to it, i.e., to the Faith of CHRIST[1]. Every professing Christian affirms this account of the matter, if his profession be true. The Churchman adds to the words, "the Faith of CHRIST," the words "as committed to His Church to keep and to deliver."

For the election of the Rev. Benjamin Jowett to the Regius Professorship of Greek in the University of Oxford, we go back to the year 1855, when Lord Palmerston was Prime Minister.

In 1861, a Statute relating to the endowment of the Professorship by the University was introduced into Congregation. I cite here from the speech of the Dean of Westminster upon that occasion:—

"In recommending this measure, let me first recapitulate the exact facts of the case. The Regius Professorship of Greek fell vacant in 1855, exactly at the time when the professorial system was being put on a new footing. The present Professor was appointed with the understanding that he was to perform the work which the University would require of him, and with the expectation, grounded on the recommendation of the University Commissioners, and on the general conduct of the University in all such cases, that the Chair would be endowed."

[1] Cf. Job xxxvii. 24; St. Luke x. 21; 1 Cor. i. 17—29.

The Dean proceeds to refer to "the work done by the Professor," to "the pay received by him," and to the efforts made to bring about some correspondence between the work and the pay up to the time of his speech; also to the successive failure of these efforts.

What had caused the failure? The case, as put by the Dean, seems a case in which there ought to have been no hesitation about endowment, so far as there were means; and yet the proposal failed time after time. Why did it fail, down to its final rejection in 1865, ten years after the appointment? It failed because of an element of the case which the Dean laboured to eliminate, and which, upon his principle, he was justified in eliminating. It failed because of the refusal of the majorities concerned to have anything to do with the endowment of a professor holding and maintaining opinions, in the matter of the Religion of CHRIST, such as Professor Jowett held and maintained.

This was the ground in morals. For the ground in law, I refer to the "Cases" submitted to the Queen's Advocate, and to his "Opinions" thereon.

In part, all this was antecedent to the publication of "Essays and Reviews;" in part, subsequent to it.

In 1864, Dr. Pusey having pronounced in favour of endowment, and the proposal being again formally before the University, I wrote to him and published a letter, from which I cite here in brief:—

"*East Brent, October* 10, 1864.

"MY DEAR PUSEY,

"In your book 'Daniel the Prophet,' lately published, for which the Church owes you a great debt, I read (Preface, p. vi. note) :—

"'Continued study of Professor Jowett's Essay makes one think sadly, what does there remain of Christianity which the writer can believe?'

"The book of which Professor Jowett's Essay forms a part[g], has been condemned, since the vote in Convocation March 8

---

[g] Professor Jowett's Essay (Essay VII.) is the complement and climax of the entire series of arguments contained in the book.

of the present year, by the Synod of the Province in which it was published."

After citing the Synodical Condemnation as given above in these Notes, p. 310, I go on to say:—

"This is the man whom you are proposing to endow by the act, and at the charges, of the University of Oxford.

"I say, 'whom you are proposing to endow,' because the responsibility of the proposal rests with yourself. Without your assistance, the proposal could not have reached Convocation in March last: without your assistance, it cannot reach Convocation now. I understand from you that, so far as your own judgment goes, you are disposed to renew the attempt; and that it is, with you, only a question of what others may say upon it, and of the time when this may be most conveniently done.

"First, then, let me set down what cannot be your reasons for taking this course, though they be the reasons of many who support you in it. Second, what appear to be your reasons for taking it, to the deep distress of nearly all those with whom you acted in this matter up to this time last year.

"It cannot be among your reasons, that no notice is to be taken of the Condemnation pronounced in June last by the Synod of the Province. It was said in March last, that Professor Jowett's alleged heresies had received no formal Authoritative Condemnation. Who can say this now?

"And although no Synodical Condemnation of a book or writing has any power to deprive the author of it of preferment or endowment,—and in a National Church established by law, ought not to have any such power—yet to bestow preferment or grant endowment in the face of such Condemnation cannot be among things which you approve. You, of all men, will not deny that this is not the way to support the Synod of the Province in its anxious striving to defend the Faith. Those whom you are helping, would gladly see anything done which would be a disparagement and a contempt of the Synod; but it is a strange and startling thing, that your hand should be the hand to do it. After an enforced silence of a hundred and fifty years, the Synod has, under Grace, discharged its primary duty; and has, as in a case which demanded its interference, judged and condemned certain heretical writings. In the year in which this has been done, to see the University of Oxford asked by one of its most honoured sons—twice asked, once before the Condemnation, and once after it—to endow a principal writer of the heretical writings so condemned, and this under a proviso which nullifies the authority of the University, and sets aside its primary duty of insisting that all its Professors be of sound religion—nothing surely has happened in our time more confounding or disheartening than that the name of Edward Bouverie Pusey should be associated with such an act as this.

"I pass by other enumeration of impossible reasons, and ask 'what then are your reasons?'

"There appear to be two.

"That to endow Professor Jowett, is the only way to counteract the prejudice against the teachers of the Truth which at present exists in the minds of many of the younger members of the University, who, having been won by the labours and the popular powers of Professor Jowett, conclude, *more juniorum*, that not to endow him is to rob him.

"That to endow Professor Jowett is the only way to prevent Government or Parliament, or both, from taking up Professor Jowett's case, and compensating him with some preferment.

"Forgive me if I say, that it is impossible to have worse or weaker reasons."

I need not cite the rest of the letter. I pass on to the P.S.

"P.S. I understand that on Saturday last, 8th inst., the Vice-Chancellor in his speech at the opening of term, expressed his regret that the attempt of March last had been defeated, and his hope that the decision would soon be reversed. This challenge has been publicly made by the chief resident officer of the University; it is high time that those who 'contend for the Faith' should prepare to answer it.
G. A. D."

The issue came Tuesday, March 8, 1864, when the proposition to endow was rejected by a majority of 72, 467—395.

Some amusement came out of a miscounting by the Proctors, and their first announcement "*Majori parti placet;*" I knew it was only a mistake, and laughed a little at the blank faces about me: a more correct summing up shewed where the majority was.

Afterwards, it was arranged that Christ Church should endow; a course advocated, among others, by E. A. Freeman, Esq. I leave Christ Church to answer for its own sins: at least, the University had not fallen into the pit.

Concurrently with the Jowett matter came the Oxford Declaration, called forth by the "Judgment" of the Judicial Committee upon appeal, R. Williams, *v.* Bishop of Salisbury, touching Inspiration of Holy Scripture and Eternal Punishment, and condoning heresy thereupon. I proposed the Declaration at a meeting held in the Music Hall, Oxford, and a Committee was appointed to carry it out: I undertook, with the present Dean of Ripon, the work of Committee. The Declaration received some eleven thousand signatures of Clergy, and was in the course of the summer presented to the Archbishop of Canterbury at Lambeth.

The last thing in the order of time, in connection with "Essays and Reviews," ended something less unhopefully than it had begun; but, both upon Canonical grounds and upon ground of avoidance of public disparagement of the Faith, it was, under the special conditions of the case at the time it was done, one of the worst things in its conception and execution within my experience.

In 1869, Mr. Gladstone being Prime Minister, Dr. Temple was designated Bishop of Exeter.

It was more than five years since the Synodical Condemnation of "Essays and Reviews;" and the book was in 1869 in its 12th Edition: the first Essay in the book was Dr. Temple's. Notwithstanding all that has been said to the contrary, I retain my original opinion, that the first Essay carries with it the burden of the whole book; and that it was placed where it is by whoever it was that edited the book, as containing the germ of the entire Argument, developed in the six succeeding Essays in the natural order of its subject-matter.

I am not going to repeat here the reasons for this definite conclusion; having stated them publicly more than once, and having neither heard or read anything to make me hesitate about the soundness of that conclusion.

Up to the time of his designation, followed by his Consecration, St. Thomas's Day, 1869, Dr. Temple had, so far as I know, made no sign of retractation, or of regret, that he had to do with the book at all. Indeed, the fact of the editions through which the book had passed since 1864, appears to dispose conclusively of all such retractation and regret. Year after year Dr. Temple's Essay had held its original position, forming the first part of a book, to the whole of which it is the key. It is to be noted also that Dr. Temple, having been urgently entreated by the Bishop of Lincoln, and by others his brethren, to make satisfaction to the Church previous to his Consecration touching his share in the book, had refused so to do.

Under these circumstances of distress it was my plain duty, having regard particularly to my special connection with the proceedings issuing in the Synodical Condemnation, to enter my Protest against the act of the Queen's Government, and against the occupation of the See of Exeter by Dr. Temple. I knew well that I should effect nothing; but there is a precept of Holy Scripture about "not partaking in other men's sins."

Accordingly, I first made public Protest at Morning and Evening Prayer in my parish church of East Brent, fourth Sunday in Advent, 1869, against the Consecration of Dr. Temple to the Office and Work of a Bishop in the Church of GOD. Eight Bishops of the Province had signified their Protests in writing to the Bishop of London, Commissary of the Archbishop of the Province, against the Consecration.

Further, in a public Letter to the Prolocutor, December 22, 1869, I notified to him my purpose to move in the matter at our first Session in 1870.

Convocation met Feb. 9, 1870.

Late in the day, the Archdeacon of Exeter said that he was "authorised by friends of the Bishop of Exeter to make known in Convocation and elsewhere, that his Essay in the volume entitled 'Essays and Reviews,' would not hereafter appear in any future edition of that volume, should such be published."

Upon this, I at once withdrew from all action in the matter. I had the authority of the Dean of Norwich, who was acting with me, to act for him as for myself. We had received on behalf of the Church, if not exactly as we had wished to have it, yet in substance what we wished to have; and it would have been ill done not to accept it frankly, heartily, and with thankfulness to GOD. It was stated by the Dean of Exeter, that he had reason to believe that no edition of "Essays and Reviews" would appear again.

I cannot satisfy myself to pass away finally from this part of my "Notes," without some brief notice of the Bishop of Exeter's subsequent personal kindness towards me. I remember well his coming up to me at the Joint Committee of both Houses in the matter of the Athanasian Creed, at Lambeth, December, 1872, and making personal acquaintance. I have met him more than once since, and it has always been a very pleasant meeting.

In 1862, I had made my last attempt, as Editor of the "Church and State Review," to promote the placing of the relations of Church to State, and State to Church, upon a truer footing.

The Review was written chiefly by great hands; but was too sound and straightforward to suit the taste of a compromising generation. Too little abusive and scurrilous, to say nothing about "free handling," to be pleasingly exciting to the general public; accordingly was pronounced to be heavy, dull, stupid, and lived only a very few years.

The Church of England as by law established had now seen, 1863, 1864, her office promoted and *sub modo* discharged in respect of Spiritual Censure of heretical books; her duty in this particular recognised by her principal Provincial Synod, and her power to act not interfered with.

In the case of "Essays and Reviews," so far as the two Houses of the Synod were concerned with the Synodical Condemnation in itself, the act was complete. It lacked that which does not appear to have been sought, confirmation by the Crown; but as this really means in our time confirmation by the House of Commons, I suppose that the absurd unreality of the position, to say nothing of other influences, sufficed to prevent the application; and there was besides, the pronounced antagonistic position of the Judicial Committee of her Majesty's Privy Council. Under these circumstances it was a "defect" which could have no proper weight with any Churchman.

In the "Colenso" case there were many difficulties interposed; with incompleteness of result.

The Provincial Synod of Canterbury was bound to expressly declare, by joint act of the two Houses, 1. its concurrence in the excommunication of Bishop Colenso by the Metropolitan of South Africa; the proposal of such concurrence proceeding in due order from the Upper House. 2. Its counsel (asked but not given) to proceed without loss of time to the election and consecration of a new Bishop. It did neither of these things. The Upper House accepting the deposition, but not the excommunication, July 1, 1868. For the second it gave advice as to how it might be done, but it threw the responsibility of doing it upon the Church in South Africa. I have adverted to delays and hindrances in speaking of the Metropolitan of South Africa; these were, indeed, heavy blows and great discouragements dealt upon this faithful man, —of all the Bishops of our time, the greatest Bishop [h].

[h] The Resolution of the Upper House concurred in by the Lower House in 1866,—"It is the opinion of this House that the Church of England holds Communion with the Bishop of Capetown, and those Bishops who lately with him in Synod declared Dr. Colenso to be *ipso facto* excommuni-

I am not leaving out of sight here anything that was done in either or in both Houses, including the following Address carried by the late Bishop of Oxford without division, June 28, 1865,—and all previous and subsequent steps down to 1868,—to the Archbishop of Canterbury as President of the Synod, praying him—

"to convey to the Metropolitan of South Africa, and to the Bishops assembled with him to try a Bishop of the Province accused before them of heresy, the expression of the hearty admiration of the courage, firmness, and devoted love of the Truth of the Gospel, as this Church has received the same, which have been manifested by him and them under the most difficult and trying circumstances. Thanking them for the noble stand they have made against heretical and false doctrine, and trusting that even out of the present difficulties and embarrassments with which they are surrounded, it may please GOD to provide some safeguard for the maintenance of the Faith once for all committed to the Saints."

In 1868, February 19, 20, my very dear friend Canon Seymour carried in a House of only 63 members, by 34 to 29, the suspension of standing orders, to enable him to move that his Gravamen praying the Upper House to declare on the part of the Church of England at home, that it accepts as valid the excommunication of Dr. Colenso. I was his seconder: the scanty attendance and the bare majority are painful things to have to record, (see p. 305).

February 20, the *Articulus Cleri* was adopted without division in a house of 71 members; an amendment of the present Bishop of Carlisle, then Dean of Ely, having been negatived by 45 to 26[1].

February 21, the Upper House, on the motion of the late Bishop of Oxford demurred to accepting sentence of

---

cated,"—is only an evasion of the real question, in the shape of a truism very clumsily put; betraying therein and thereby a false position, and uttered with bated breath. It was concurred in moreover in a house of only thirty-eight members, by 23 to 15. See "Chronicle of Convocation," Lower House, February 12, 1867.

[1] See "Chronicle of Convocation," pp. 1275, 6; February 20, 1868.

excommunication; and a Committee was appointed "to enquire into the Canonicity of the deprivation referred to in the *Articulus Cleri*, and to examine and report on the more recent writings of Dr. Colenso." The Resolution goes on to state grounds of caution and delay.

Upper House, July 1, 1868. The Report of Committee was adopted, the only dissentient being the present Archbishop, then Bishop of London.

The Report concludes as under :—

"With regard, however, to the whole case, with its extreme difficulty, the various complications, the grave doubts in reference to points of law yet unsettled, and the apparent impossibility of any other mode of action,

"We are of opinion,—
1. "That substantial justice was done to the accused.
2. "That though the sentence, having been pronounced by a tribunal not acknowledged by the Queen's Courts, whether Civil or Ecclesiastical, can claim no legal effect, the Church, as a spiritual body, may rightly accept its validity."

It is important to recall all this, especially at this time, when Dr. Colenso, as some say invited, as others say not invited, but intending to present himself, is said to be coming to the Lambeth Synod of 1878.

Now it has to be noted carefully on the one hand, that the *Articulus Cleri* spoke not only of the deposition of Dr. Colenso from the Bishopric of Natal, but of the excommunication of Dr. Colenso, as two things it desired to have recognised as spiritually valid by the Church at home.

On the other hand, that neither the reference to the Committee of the Upper House, "Chronicle of Convocation," p. 1296, February 21, 1868, nor the Report of Committee pp. 1349, 50, takes any notice of the matter of the "excommunication," but only of that of the deposition or deprivation.

The last is conclusive against the admission of Dr. Colenso into the Lambeth Synod of 1878. It is much to be regretted that the other also did not find its proper place in the reference and in the Report.

The President having expressed his great satisfaction with the Address, it was communicated the same day to the Lower House for its concurrence.

I moved the concurrence the same day. There was considerable debate upon it; occupying some eighteen pages of the "Chronicle of Convocation." I carried the concurrence; but it is a fact of a very melancholy character, that it was carried in a house of only 16 members, by 11 to 5.

It is impossible to refrain from saying here, that it is a pity that some portion of the qualities, for which the Address so commends the Metropolitan of South Africa and his brother Bishops, did not find its way into the Houses of Convocation of Canterbury, and bear some fruit worth the trouble of gathering it.

In 1867-8 the position in respect of Dr. Colenso was much debated in both Houses; many Gravamina and Petitions presented.

Feb. 29, 1868, my dear good friend Canon Seymour having, as stated p. 321, moved suspension of standing orders, with a view to making *Articulus Cleri* Address to the Upper House, praying for formal acceptance of excommunication of Bishop Colenso, this was seconded by myself, and carried by 34 to 29. The *Articulus Cleri* was adopted Feb. 20, and communicated to the Upper House.

It is with much pain that I here revert to the fact that, Feb. 21, 1868, the prayer of the Lower House that the Upper House would now proceed to declare Dr. Colenso excommunicate, was put aside in the Upper House upon the motion of the late Bishop of Oxford, upon what appeared to me at the time and since always to be, not only purely technical grounds, but grounds based upon an account of the relations of the Church to the Civil Power in the matter of spiritual censures, which I hold to be quite erroneous in point of the position as recognised by 57 Geo. III. c. 127.

The injury done to the Church by this shelving of the Excommunication question — for it was nothing else — cannot be over-estimated. Something, but not much, came of the Committee of the Upper House appointed the same day. For the present the whole question was delayed in Convocation by this vote of the Upper House, Feb. 21, 1868. It is one of the saddest things upon record in the proceedings of the revived Synod.

It is commonly reported at the time I am writing, that Dr. Colenso has been invited to the second Lambeth Synod, and that he will attend. A Lambeth Synod with Dr. Colenso would indeed be a mockery beyond compare; and I should not be surprised if the invitation and the attendance—most of all the invitation—were to prove a little too much for the "moderation" of even "moderate Churchmen."

However, a man must be very blind who is taken by surprise in our time by anything however incongruous, self-contradictory, violent and anti-Catholic. We have seen a man who denies the Eternal GODHEAD of THE SON, not only made a Member of Committee for Revision of Translation of the Bible, but invited in that capacity to join in Holy Communion in Westminster Abbey. What more do we want to teach us what the character of our time is? It is branded, stamped, and sealed all over with "Indifferentism."

If the report of the invitation of Dr. Colenso be true, it is not unlikely that the Archbishop of Canterbury may defend himself by saying, that the sentence of Excommunication by the Metropolitan of South Africa has not received the formal concurrence of the Synod of Canterbury. There would not, to be sure, be much force in the defence; because, if the Upper House passed by Sentence of Excommunication, Sentence of Deposition was accepted by both Houses: it is true that the Archbishop, then Bishop of London, was the single dissenting Bishop in respect of the Sentence of Deposition.

With respect to "Essays and Reviews," the disregard (to use the lightest term) of Synodical Condemnation in two prominent cases by men of highest repute among English Churchmen, by Pusey and by Gladstone, ought to startle and confound, and to make men open their eyes a little to the real position of things. Pusey in 1864 promoting the endowment of Professor Jowett; Gladstone in 1869 nominating Dr. Temple to the Bishopric of Exeter. Do these things prove nothing? They prove a good many things; and among them the decay and ruin here in England of the principle of Church Authority. The strongest and best Churchmen are found to push it aside when it comes in their way.

And as *malum in pejus* is a very certain rule to go by, I am constrained to repeat my belief here, that if I had had to deal with "Essays and Reviews," and with the book of Dr. Colenso at this time, and with proceedings against him personally as a heretic, instead of some eighteen years ago, I could not carry the condemnation through the Lower House: I need say nothing of the prospect of it in the Upper House.

From 1839 the Russell, Lansdowne, and Kay-Shuttleworth policy had marched on steadily and rapidly to its final issue. I prefer saying "issue" rather than "triumph," because I cannot bring myself to believe that even the prime promoters of the policy fully realized what that final issue would and must be. The policy began with "utilising" the schools of the Church of England for Education which is not the Education of the "Church school," nor indeed, in the true sense of the word, Education at all. In its progress it left no "Church school" in England for high or low, rich or poor. Its final issue is, by the law of retributive justice, schools, first with no religion properly so-called, last with no religion at all. In Century XIX. the Imperial Government of England is steadily and rapidly marching on to the reproduction of the philosophic infidelity of Julian the Apostate.

In all the grief and distress of what I have lived to see, let me try to be fair in apportioning the blame of what it is impossible to me to regard in any other light than that of, not only a great national calamity but, a great national sin.

First, then, politically: the Whig laid the foundation and builded the house, but the Conservative carried the stones and mortar (see p. 168). The Whig went about his work openly, the Conservative with a veil over his face. The Whig, bold and confident, and with only so much of reticence and diplomatic pretext as seemed to him most advisable with a view to his success; the Conservative halting, and trembling, and protesting; but, by a kind of fatal fascination, attracted towards the building, and putting his hand to the work so far as he was trusted to share in it.

Then, ecclesiastically, the founders and builders were, or at least some of them, Churchmen. But to say that their work was Church-work is, both on *à priori* and *à posteriori* ground, simply silly. They founded and they builded themselves; but among their work-people there have been from the first, and are still, a great many whose rule it is to have nothing to do with work which is not Church-work, and yet have fallen into the snare of taking active part, *reluctante animo, negante conscientia*, in what is, beyond all dispute, *not* Church-work.

But if the Whig founded and builded, and the Conservative and the Churchman carried the stones and mortar, who was it that cleared the ground, and made all things ready for the laying of the first stone?

It was the Bishops, Clergy, and People of the Church of England as by law established. Primarily and principally the Bishops and Priests; for, as the Bishop and the Priest of a Church is, so is the People.

The claim of a People to be taught to read follows, slowly it may be, but naturally, fitly, surely, upon the gift of the printing power. The correlative claim for writing and reckoning power cannot be detached from the claim for reading power. In a Christian country, all this has to be taken in hand as subordinate and subsidiary to the claim to be taught and exercised in the Religion of CHRIST. The greater the temporal gift, the greater the need that it be made to minister to the spiritual gift. In a country where there was—in the National Church—the gift of national recognition of the Catholic Faith, the fulness of gift had been received.

Now, as a rule of the National life, England may be said to have had, with the exception of the Endowed Grammar Schools, no schools for the poor up to the earlier part of this century. The Parish School did not exist, except, here and there, in the "dame's School." For the not poor,—and in some degree by exhibitions and scholarships, founded to aid the poor man's child, but by the policy of our time swept into the net of competitive prizes for the rich man's child,—there were public Schools and Universities. There were also many private schools.

But the question remains. Were these all places of Education in its true sense? That is to say, were they *primarily* places for the growth of the Religious Life? They were, so to speak, exclusively in the hands of the Church. Were they made to minister to the true and steady growth of the acceptance of the Doctrine, Discipline, Worship of the Church? They had all been devised and planned and endowed for this end, by pious and devoted hearts and hands. What and where was the fulfilment of the trust? There was everywhere, more or less, the form; but where was the power? There was everywhere the body, but where was the life? The only answer that can be given is an answer of humiliation and distress. I am speaking, of course, of the general and normal condition of the case; and I say that it has been the neglect of the Church-people of England, and principally of Bishops and Priests, which cleared the ground for the "monster building," in more senses of the term than one, of Century XIX.

April 19, 1864, I moved for Committee upon the relations between the Church of England and the Committee of Council on "Education." I moved for it with the concurrence of certainly not less than two-thirds of all members of the Lower House in the habit of attending; and also with the expression of the satisfaction of the Committee of the National Society with the proposal for the Committee [j].

The Committee was agreed to without division; and on Feb. 14, 1865, the Report was presented by me as Chairman to the Lower House [k]. The same day I gave notice of Resolutions upon it. May 22, 1865, I moved and carried the Resolutions seriatim [l]. Feb. 6, 1866, I moved, and carried Feb. 7, the Resolution following :—

"That it is the opinion of this House that to insist upon the insertion of the 'Conscience Clause' in the Trust-deed of a Parish or other School of the Church of England as a condition of assistance out of the Parliamentary Grant is not just; and that to accept the 'Conscience Clause' on the part of such school is neither just as respects future managers of the school, nor is it safe as respects the teaching of the Church [m]."

I see that my speech, Feb. 6, fills twenty-six pages of the "Chronicle." I do not wonder that my dear friend the Prolocutor, with many others, slumbered peacefully on that occasion.

The terms of the Resolution, especially of the latter part of it, and the carrying of it with no resistance of any account, suffice to shew what the mind of the Lower House was in the matter up to 1866. Four years after, Convocation and the National Society lay prostrate at the feet of the Committee of Council on Education, under the Act of 1870, Mr. Gladstone being Prime Minister. The Upper House had never given me any support. With the Lower House, it not only lay prostrate now, bound and fettered by the manacles of an indifferent Civil Power, but hugging its chains; and vainly imagining that a compromise of a Divine Trust is going to have a Blessing upon it. If the

---

[j] "Chronicle of Convocation," 1864, pp. 1483, 4.   [k] Ibid., 1865, pp. 1861-9.   [l] Ibid., pp. 2223, 2261.   [m] Ibid., 1866, pp. 30, 57—69, 103.

"school secular" could have been got rid of in this way, as some seemed to have thought it could be (the truth being that it has been much helped forward by the compromise), that would have been no justification of the compromise.

In 1865, at the Norwich Congress, I had fifteen minutes in which to state seventeen reasons against the "Conscience Clause," any one of them conclusive by itself. Seventeen conclusive reasons published for one penny; as I had before published for twopence, twenty-two reasons equally valid and unanswerable why Church-rate ought not to be abolished. But against popular ignorance and passion, and ultra-Protestantism, the best reasoning the world ever saw has no power.

I give the heads of the anti-Church action, in respect of Schools, on the part of the Civil Power, 1839—1870, thirty-one years.

1839. Establishment of administrative and irresponsible power by appointment of Committee of Council on Education.

1846. Introduction of bribery-power, Minutes of Committee of Council.

1852. Consolidation of compulsory interference with constitution of Church Schools by the Management Clauses.

No. 3 really settled the whole question *for* the Civil Power as *against* the Church. All that followed—"Conscience Clause," "Time-table Conscience Clause," School Board, Education Rate, are only complements of No. 3. In 1852 I saw that the battle was finally lost; but I could not satisfy myself that I was not bound to persevere. I did persevere, in Convocation down to 1870, in Church Unions, in Church Congresses, down to 1868, when I held my last meeting for maintenance of Church Education at Willis's Rooms, Hon. C. L. Wood in the chair,—primary subject, "Education Rate."

Considering the ground of "Conscience" upon which "Church Rate" had been abolished, the "iniquity" of filling up the "Rate" vacancy with "Education Rate" is as great, not only as any upon record, but as any that can be conceived.

I take leave of the struggle of twenty years with an episode, 1865-6.

In the autumn of 1865 I had a good deal of Conference with my dear friend, Lord Carnarvon, upon the "Educational" position; and he undertook to call the attention of the House of Lords to it.

In 1866, nothing having yet come publicly of the understanding between us, came the day of the Annual Meeting of Secretaries of Diocesan Boards of Education in the Committee-room of the National Society's office. It was, and I suppose may be still, an important gathering, because composed of Bishops and representative Priests.

I was neither Bishop nor Secretary, but I was kindly allowed the *entrée* of these meetings.

The late Bishop of Oxford had given notice of some Resolutions, the gist of which was some "Concordat" in the matter of the "Conscience Clause." I went to the meeting for the express purpose of seeing what could be done to defeat the Resolutions.

There were four Bishops present, forty-two Secretaries and others, and I. The Bishop of Oxford in the chair; his Resolutions being entrusted to the present Bishop of Gloucester and Bristol.

I got there late. When I appeared the Bishop of Oxford said: "Here he is, and now we shall carry nothing."

"Not," I said, "if I can stop you."

He gave me a place near him, and the debate began.

The Bishop of Gloucester and Bristol moved; the Bishop of Lincoln (London) seconded: I moved an amendment.

Forty Priests, one Bishop, voted for amendment; two Priests, two Bishops, voted for Resolutions.

I said to the Bishop of Gloucester and Bristol, "I think you have had enough of this."

"Yes," he said, "quite enough; I am going away."

The Bishop of Oxford said to me: "Come and sit by me, I have something to say to you." He went on:

"I see that we must come to what you said seventeen years ago."

"What was that?"

"You said we must give up the Grant."

"Yes, I did say so, and I say so still; but now let me say a word: here we are for the first time after so many years in accord: mind, I have not come a hair's breadth over to you."

"No," he said, "I quite know that."

"Well," I said, "may it not be worth while to try a little to see what can be done by joint action."

He said: "I think we ought to have a great field-day in the House of Lords, after the manner of 1839."

I told him that this was what I had been trying to arrange with Carnarvon the last seven months, and I went on to say, "I saw him yesterday, and asked him about the delay. Shall I tell you his answer?"

"Pray do."

"He said, 'I cannot find so much as one Bishop to help me.'"

"Tell him," said the Bishop of Oxford, "that I will back him with all my strength."

"You mean me to tell him this?"

"Yes, I do."

"Well, give me a sheet of paper, and I will write to him now." I wrote my letter, and shewed it to the Bishop, asking him whether that was what he wished me to say.

"Exactly," he said: "add, if you please, about my seeing him to-morrow upon it."

On the morrow the Bishop and Lord Carnarvon met and conferred; all was arranged, speakers agreed upon, resolutions drafted.

Not many days after—I am not sure it was not the next day—out went the Whig Government. In came the Conservatives,—Carnarvon took office. The Bishop said no more to me: the high contracting parties diverged and separated; and the prospect of a field-day in the House of Lords vanished away from before my confiding eyes.

It made me laugh; I hope not bitterly. It was the last occasion upon which I wasted my time and energies upon the attempt to get Statesman or Bishop to fight for the Church in Parliament. Looking back upon it now, I say of myself what I said of others above:—

μακάρισας τὸ ἀπειρόκακον, οὐζηλῶ τὸ ἄφρον.

For Church Congresses, having taken part in them all from the first at Cambridge in 1861 down to 1870, when my illness prevented my going to Southampton, I have no belief that they are really helpful towards the growth of Church-life. Rather, I believe them to be opportunities only of friendly and social intercourse, employed, in their collective public aspect, principally in paring away vital differences, till you come to a surface smooth perhaps to look at, but crumbling away into rough bits, big and little, as soon as you come to handle it.

I used to spend labour upon the attempt to get the time of Congress employed upon a few subjects nearest to, and most moving, men's minds; instead of shirking these, and ringing yearly changes upon matters, important no doubt in themselves but, of secondary moment and interest, and worn threadbare by annual recurrence of discussion: but I had, so to speak, no success. Failing here, I used to advocate triennial instead of annual Congress, as amply sufficient for the secondary arrangement: I failed here again.

With regard to the School question, the touchstone of what English Churchmen *meant to do*, Congress has been very like the Lower House of Convocation of Canterbury. It has talked and virtually protested, and has applauded me divers and sundry times in the "School" matter as in the "Church Rate" matter, the managers all the time thinking me a great nuisance; but all the fire has gone out, and there is not so much as any smoke remaining.

Whether, then, annual or triennial, I am not able to realise the solid benefit of a Church Congress. It is a comfortable week of compromising tendency; and that is, I believe, about the amount of what has to be said for it. I have ceased to attend; my last appearance was at Plymouth, 1876.

For "Church Unions," I suppose I have had, from 1845 to this time, as much to do with them as any man; and I cannot be sufficiently thankful that the English Church Union, having come into the place of its local predecessors, has now planted its foot upon the solid ground of absolute rejection of secular regulation in matters spiritual. It is the only ground upon which it is possible to fight the battle of the Church as against a professing indifferent, but really and actively hostile, Civil Power.

I was in the chair in Mr. Trower's rooms in Victoria-street in 1860, when the English Church Union was first formed. Not long after, I ceased to be a member. My recollection is that my retirement had something to do with the St. George's-in-the-East business, but I cannot recall the facts with sufficient accuracy. I continued, nevertheless, to have frequent and friendly intercourse with the administrative powers, and some years ago became again a member. I believe the Union to be doing very real and very good work, and indeed to be the *only public body* which is stedfastly maintaining the first principles of the Church's life.

Convocation has gained one thing of great importance, as I regard it, and towards which I have laboured for some years. It has gained Celebration of the Blessed Sacrament upon first days of assembling each year: I wish it may be upon every day. But, so far, it is matter of great thankfulness.

I had all my life believed of Mr. Gladstone that he was entirely satisfied, and that without misgiving, upon all the successive actions of his memorable life; that he had, at each step, what were to him the most solid grounds upon which to take his stand. I could not, like many others, follow the process[n] in respect of concurrence in public policy; but I believe myself to know, in its broad outline, what the process has been, and I am in possession of curious private evidence tending throughout to establish the belief.

I speak, then, of Mr. Gladstone in all the honour of half-a-century. In all the difference of judgment—difference, upon many points of first importance, extreme—up to the first days of "the Eastern question." Here I find myself, for the first time since he published his famous book[o] upon the relations of the State to the Church, in exact accord with Mr. Gladstone; though I am bound to add, that I cannot reconcile his having done so little when in power to exercise effectually the European Protectorate of the Christian subjects of Turkey, established at the close of the Crimean war, in lieu of the Russian Protectorate of a hundred years before it; that I cannot reconcile his having left Turkey free to do as she pleased for twenty years in the matter of her Christian subjects, nor even his share in the Crimean war, which was my abomination, with his present position. All I have to say is, that I think his present position the right, and true, and Christian position. I have moreover a very grateful sense of personal kindness towards myself.

But twelve years ago I was in no manner of public accord with Mr. Gladstone. I had had very solid and sufficient grounds for trying to unseat him for Oxford University in 1853: I had the same solid and sufficient grounds for the like attempt in 1865.

If I use the words, "In 1865 I succeeded in my attempt," I am not magnifying myself: I am only stating the fact, that I had more to do than any other man

---

[n] See the memorable letter to Dr. Hannah in July, 1865, cited in Irving's "Annals of our Time," pp. 704, 5. Dr. Hannah had shewed me the original letter, as I came back with him from the Norwich Church Congress.

[o] "The Church in Connection with the State." (2 vols. 8vo. Murray, 1841.)

with the defeat of Mr. Gladstone at Oxford. I proceed to shew this.

In April, 1864, I was crossing St. James's Park, when I fell in with my good friend, Granville Somerset. He had, as I had, voted for Mr. Gladstone more than once, but had given him up as I had.

I said to him, "Well now, about Gladstone. I think you are playing a very foolish game. You keep on saying that, when he resigns, you will put up Stafford Northcote to fill his place: now he is not going to resign; has not the smallest intention that way. Stafford Northcote will not stand against him; and the end will be, that when election time comes, you will have no candidate ready, and Gladstone will walk over the course. *We must have a man ready now to put up against him.*"

Somerset quite agreed with me.

"Well, then," I said, "let us lose no more time. Do you get together one or two others, four of us will be quite enough to begin with; and let us lay our heads together. Who shall it be?"

We agreed upon Sotheron Estcourt and Hon. Mr. Lygon.

"When shall it be?"

"Next Wednesday."

"Where shall it be?"

"In the Library of the House of Commons."

Wednesday morning I had been with my brother, the Speaker. He had said to me, "What are you going to do about Gladstone?"

I said, "We are going to turn him out if we can." I did not tell him that we were going to meet that afternoon in the Library of his domain.

When we met, I said to Estcourt and Lygon just what I had said to Somerset. They concurred, just as he had.

"Now," I said, "Estcourt, you are the biggest man among us, and have been a Cabinet Minister: we owe it to Stafford Northcote to tell him what we are about, and to ask him whether he will let us put him up from this time as against Gladstone. He won't say 'Yes;'

but, all the same, we owe it to him to ask him. Will you undertake to do it?"

He consented, and we adjourned for a couple of days.

When we met again, Estcourt reported that Northcote would not stand against Gladstone.

"Now then," I said, "let us get together a good meeting in London, from London, Oxford, &c." The meeting was fixed for that day week.

It was largely attended by members of the House of Commons, and others. I was sitting in the chair of Committee in the Jerusalem Chamber, and adjourned the Committee, that I might go with my dear friend, the Warden of All Souls, to the meeting.

I got there only just in time. Mowbray was in the chair. When I got into the room, he said, "Oh, Archdeacon, I am glad you are come; I am just going to put a resolution to the meeting, and I should like you to see it before it is put."

He gave it me. It was like a heavy blow in the face, and confused me for a moment: then I got so angry, that I am afraid I was very rude. The resolution began: "In the event of Mr. Gladstone's retiring," &c. The precise foolishness which I had got the meeting together to get rid of, once for all.

I threw the resolution on the table, saying, that I could have nothing to do with it, except to oppose it; adding what I fear was rude enough, but I could not help it, "Gentlemen, I have not the honour of knowing many of you, but I think, and must say, that it seems to me you are mad. If this is all that we are come together to do, we had better have stayed at home."

There was a silence in the room.

I don't remember to have been more angry any day of my life. I sat myself down by Sir Brook Brydges (Lord Fitzwalter). He said, "What would you recommend?"

"Please give me a bit of paper."

I wrote my amendment:—

"That it is the opinion of this meeting that the return of Mr. Gladstone for the University of Oxford is to be opposed."

"Now, Mr. Chairman, please to put that to the meeting as my amendment."

In three minutes everybody, I think, in the room held up their hands for it.

We had now got out of the slough of despond in which we had been floundering since 1853, eleven years; and had planted our feet upon the solid ground, where we could stand and walk. We were now in a position to fix upon our candidate, and to take measures for going to him in such force as to make it difficult for him not to say, "Yes." The meeting was not long in fixing upon Mr. Hardy, and in laying the foundation of Committees in Oxford and London to collect names to a requisition to him. By the end of the Long Vacation we had more than a thousand names; and Mr. Hardy consented to be our candidate, as against Mr. Gladstone.

Nothing of this could have been done, or even reasonably taken in hand, if the meeting had passed the original resolution. We should have collapsed; have fallen back into the precise position of self-stultification, out of which it was *the one* purpose of those who got the meeting together to escape. You can fight no battle upon an "if" dependent upon the action of an adversary, which action you have not only no ground at all to anticipate, but every ground not to anticipate. This is what we had been doing for some years; it was out of this that we were seeking to escape. You could not go to any man, and ask him to make arrangements affecting his Parliamentary position upon an hypothesis without a basis. I have never been able to understand to this day how the original resolution came to be so much as thought of by the meeting. It became clear enough, when my amendment was put, that the meeting was not sorry to be rid of its puny and feeble infant.

I have always believed, and I think all men who know the facts of the case, and whose judgment is worth having, believe the same, that if I had come into the room three minutes later, Mr. Gladstone would have been Member for the University now. With all the energy, and labour, and time which belongs only to definite and settled purpose, and well-considered pre-arrangement, we had in 1865 not much majority to spare.

I have already referred to the meeting at Willis's Rooms, 1868: the last meeting upon "the Schools matter" with which I had anything to do.

The same year I published a letter to Mr. Hardy; I cite the opening sentences:—

"*London, Feb.* 18, 1868.

"My dear Hardy,

"I see we are to have a Government Bill for National Elementary Education.

"I am told, what I can hardly doubt is true, that the Bill contains, or recognises a 'Conscience Clause.'

"Now the proposal for a 'Conscience Clause' rests upon two assumptions; both of them, to say the least, violent.

"1. That 'Secular Education' is a necessity; but that 'Religious Education' is not.

"2. That 'Secular Education' being a necessity, if the religious scruples of Church-people come in the way of giving it, or allowing it to be given, in Church schools, the religious scruples of Church-people must be put aside, if such Church-people are to have any share in the Parliamentary Grant.

"A 'Conscience Clause' is thus a principal instance of combined secular, financial, religious tyranny, and violation of Conscience.

"I have expected this issue some twenty years. Now that its consummation appears to be imminent, I have nothing left to do but to try to persuade as many as I can to have no hand or part in it. Actively, to save themselves from all complicity by vote in Parliament, and by petition out of it; passively, to relinquish what is *their own*, rather than accept it under the conditions of the Bill, as above anticipated, &c.

"G. A. D."

Seven days later the Whigs were out, and Mr. Disraeli was Minister. Then came the Gladstone ministry, Dec. 9, 1868; the crush of 1869, and his Disestablishment and spoliation of the Irish Church. The final ruin of the

"Church school," was reserved for 1870; also under his Government.

I had done what little I could against Mr. Gladstone's Irish Church policy; but it became clear in the course of 1869, from answer to appeal, and labour, and outlay of London Committee, that, *paries cum proximus ardet* notwithstanding, English Church-people did not care much about the Irish Church: and certainly, if I had realised then what I realise now about it, I should not have toiled as I did in the furious heat of the summer of 1869, in the attempt to save its position.

The two remaining questions of the time with which I have been publicly concerned, are the "Ritual" question, and the "Confession and Absolution" question. My share in the first dates from 1864; but it is, I think, more conveniently reserved for the next chapter.

June 20, 1870, I fell into sudden and dangerous illness; was ill six months, and did not wholly recover my strength till late in 1871. The mercy of GOD, which restored me, filled every day of my weakness with all the cheer and comfort of most tender and loving care, kindly interest and sympathy; cheer and comfort which cannot be forgotten, and cannot be told.

CHAPTER X.

EAST BRENT. 1870—1878.

"*Ritual.*" *Confession to, and Absolution by, the Priest.*

IN respect of Catholic Ceremonial in Churches and Chapels of the "Establishment," vulgarly called "Ritual;" and, particularly, of that portion of it which belongs to the Celebration of the Blessed Sacrament of the BODY and the BLOOD, I have to plead guilty to what I cannot plead guilty to in respect of Doctrine,—I have to plead guilty to having changed my mind. What the change has amounted to, we shall see presently.

In the course of 1864, 5, 6, 7, 8, I had much private communication upon many points of great interest to the Church, with the late Archbishop of Canterbury. The Archbishop's uniform kindness to me had always been very great, and encouraged me to write freely to him.

In July, 1864, in reply to a letter from me to the Archbishop, asking to be told what the exact scope and object of the proposed Royal Commission was, the Archbishop writes, July 19 :—

"There is no Commission going to be issued for the Revision either of *Burial Service*, or Rubrics; both are excluded from its purview. The only points to be discussed, according to present arrangements, are the Table of Lessons, and the possibility of finding any means of relief for the scrupulous consciences of the Clergy in the matter of the Burial Service, without *any change* in the Service."

The italics are the Archbishop's.

I replied that I could not see how it was possible to do anything towards "relieving" the Clergy, without virtually and in substance altering the Rubrics, unless it were by some restoration of "Godly Discipline."

In 1865, after the Norwich Church Congress, I received from the Archbishop the letter following :—

"*Addington-park, Croydon, Oct.* 30, 1865.

"My dear Archdeacon,

"Let me thank you for your 'Seventeen Reasons against the admission of a "Conscience Clause" in the Trust Deeds of our National Schools.' Anything which may imperil the teaching of the distinctive Doctrine of the Church of England in our Schools is certainly most earnestly to be deprecated, and most resolutely to be resisted.

"I am glad of this opportunity of saying how much I approve your Letter on Vestments.

"It is sad to think, when we are contending for the very essence of the Faith, and need to stand shoulder to shoulder in a spirit of cordial unanimity, that the torch of discord should thus recklessly be thrown among us, and our enemies encouraged to assail our position with fresh vigour. Would that the supporters of this innovation could imbibe a little of the spirit of him who has taught us that there may be things lawful which are not expedient.

"Believe me, my dear Archdeacon,
"Very sincerely yours,
"C. T. Cantuar."

I subscribed "ex animo" to the general issue of this letter, though I could not see any more then than I can now how, under the conditions of the Church of England as by law established, anything approaching to a "spirit of cordial unanimity" could be hoped for. I could not assent to the "recklessness," being satisfied then, as I am now, that, though I was not in accord with the promoters of the revival of Catholic Ceremonial, they were not men to whom the term "reckless" could with any justice be applied; nor could I accept "innovation," because all that made it appear to be "innovation" was only long-established neglect; and the concluding sentence of the Archbishop's letter itself is most reasonably construed as admitting the "lawfulness."

However, it is quite true that, in substance, the Archbishop's letter truly represented my conclusions at that time.

February 8, 1866, the first move in the Lower House, in the matter of Ritual, was made by the present Bishop of Carlisle, then Dean of Ely.

By this time, what I am obliged to call the one-sidedness of the proceeding had forced itself upon my mind; and though I did not for a good many years after become a "Ritualist," and having then no notion, as I said in beginning my speech[a], that I ever should, I could not stand by and see brethren among the most earnest and indefatigable members of the Clergy of the Church of England, contending for what they affirmed deliberately to be the Law of the Church of England, ridden over, and "put down" by the strong hand; and this without so much as a hint, or it would seem a thought, that the people who were really to blame, and ought to be corrected,—we will not say "put down," the term stinks in an Englishman's nostrils,—were just either the opposite men, who were some neglecting, some breaking the law, or putting long vicious practice in the place of law, and comforting their consciences by abusing their less easy brethren. Bishops and Priests, High and Low, were commonly adopting the motto, "Surtout, point de zéle."

It was beginning also to dawn upon me, though my antecedents did not dispose me to high Ceremonial, that after all I might be quite wrong upon first principles of Worship; and, more than this, that probably I was quite wrong; inasmuch as a costly and magnificent Ceremonial, besides all its Divine precedent in the Jewish Church, and all seen of St. John in prophetic vision of the Adoration of Heaven, was the natural accompaniment and exponent of the teaching of the Doctrine of THE REAL PRESENCE. The Presence; the Representation and Pleading of the One Sacrifice; the Adoration.

First, then, upon the ground of Catholic inheritance; next, upon the social ground of ordinary equity in administration of law, as between Catholic and Protest-

---

[a] "Chronicle of Convocation," Feb. 8, 1866.

ant; next, upon ground of actual law of this Church and Realm; lastly, upon ground of helping oneself and others to the knowledge of the Truth,—my mind was passing through a great change when the subject first came before Convocation in February, 1866.

I took, therefore, objection to the Resolutions proposed by the Dean of Ely and seconded by Archdeacon Grant, and moved an Amendment, for "a Committee for the purpose of drawing up an Address to the Upper House on the subject of Ritual observances."

An objection being taken to this in point of order, I proposed, and the Warden of All Souls seconded, as he had the first Amendment,—

"That it is not desirable to proceed in this matter by way of Resolution in this House."

The debate was adjourned.

Feb. 9, in the Upper House the subject came up upon two petitions: one of them from Plymouth against "Ritual," addressed to Convocation; the other addressed to the Bishop of Oxford, against certain changes in the Prayer-Book, at that time, as since, much advocated, with a view of "putting down" Ritual.

Feb. 9, in the Lower House, the Dean of Ely having consented, after an interview with me, to propose an addition to his first Resolution, taking away the one-sidedness which had principally called forth my opposition, and I having consented on that condition to withdraw my Amendment, the House consented to such amendment of Resolution, and to the withdrawal of my Amendment.

The debate was then resumed upon the amended Resolution; this was carried without division. Archdeacon Randall then proposed, in lieu of the Dean of Ely's three remaining Resolutions,—

"That this Resolution (the one just agreed to) be communicated to their Lordships of the Upper House, with our humble request that they will take the subject into their consideration, and favour this House with their judgment thereupon."

Canon Woodgate moved "the previous question," which was negatived, and Archdeacon Randall's Amendment was carried without division.

Meantime, the same day, in the Upper House, a debate, or rather a conversation, was taking place upon the same subject, when the Resolutions of the Lower House were brought up.

The Bishop of Oxford moved :—

"That this House desires to concur with the Lower House in the Address presented by it, and that with a view to granting its request, the Lower House be directed to enquire by a Committee as to such measures as may seem fit for clearing the doubts and allaying the anxieties to which the Address alludes, and to communicate to this House such report, and also the judgment of the Lower House upon it."

Resolution put and agreed to.

We had thus got the Committee, proposed by my first Amendment to the Resolutions of the Dean of Ely, Feb. 8, 1866, but which I had been precluded from moving for upon a point of form. The Upper House had directed its appointment *motu proprio;* the Committee was appointed in the Lower House, with the Dean of Ely Chairman. The Dean was unable, from a domestic affliction, to occupy the chair at the last two sittings, and at his suggestion I became *pro tempore* Chairman in his place.

It seems to me to be important to present in broad outline, and as briefly as is consistent with clearness and connection of statement, what took place in Convocation on the subject of "Ritual" at that time. To myself privately, because it enables me to mark the successive steps of my own position; to the Church at large, because I think no man can say that the true position in this matter was either then or has been since taken by Convocation; nor, indeed, *any* position decided and conclusive.

There is further this essential consideration, that this

question, as, indeed, all other principal questions of Church concern, resolves itself ultimately into the question of the "One Faith," and many faiths. For it is, I may take it for granted, not necessary for me at this time of day to recur to what has often been contended for against me, but which may be said now to be allowed on all hands— I mean, that "Ritual" is by its nature closely and inseparably bound up with Doctrine; is the natural, and sooner or later in every case, more or less according to local circumstance, the necessary development and exponent of Doctrine. The declared opponent, the ultra-Protestant, whether outside the Church, or inside the Church in the shape of the neo-Evangelical, has said so from the first; has put it in the forefront of his battle array. "High Churchmen" generally, whose tendencies are for "Ritual," but whose voice and action is, for one reason or another, against it, have tried to put the conclusion aside; but the simple truth of the case has been too strong for them, and, as I have said, it is not necessary for me now to make any more words about it.

Let me, then, review the contending forces, and what that is which is contended for on either side. On the "Ritual" side are men who in such sort believe in THE REAL PRESENCE, that they are "constrained" to express the belief by all the Ceremonial of Worship. These are as yet a small minority, Priests and People; but their numbers increase steadily. Among all classes, high, low, rich, poor, belief in THE REAL PRESENCE marches on, and by its side its handmaid, "Ritual." Let me add here, that without those of us who saw their way in this matter from the first, of whom I was not one, this result would not have been attained. Truth of Belief, and its outward manifestation by act of Worship, are, sooner or later, inseparable things. The familiar instance of kneeling in prayer is a sufficient illustration. The man who really prays, sooner or later, publicly as privately, meekly kneels upon his knees to pray; others look on and kneel too, and by outward act of kneeling are oftentimes led on and taught to pray truly with their heart. *Mutatis mu-*

tandis, it is just the same with all the Ceremonial of Catholic Worship.

On the other side is popular passion, stimulated by ignorant, and therefore unreasoning, fear of Rome; Protestantism, inside and outside the Church; fear lacking no encouragement at the hands of the Civil Power, and its nominees, the Bishops; a seeming incapacity to grasp the truth, (to which the Roman Catholic himself bears ample and repeated testimony, by anger and ridicule combined,) that it is the "Ritualist" who, more than any other, has it in his power to prevent, and as matter of fact does prevent, secession to Rome; timid or half-informed Churchmen, of whom I was, not so many years ago, one myself,—for, if I cannot say of myself that I was timid, I must needs confess that I was half-informed; lastly, all "Establishmentarianism" *pur et simple*.

It is an unequal combat, as the world looks at these things; but the race is not to the swift, nor the battle to the strong. It is minorities which, sooner or later, govern the world. The general account of this being, I suppose, —certainly the account since the day of the hundred-and-twenty in the upper chamber,—that it is, not in majorities, but in minorities of men, that the Truth first asserts its place and power.

Then for the thing contended for. The "Ritualist" contends for his Catholic, and therefore *lawful*, inheritance,—an inheritance dating its existence from long before Statute, or even Common Law of England. Next, he contends for his *legal* inheritance; for the law of this Church and Realm as committed to his keeping, and sworn to by *all* Priests at their Ordination. He confesses all the neglect of many years, which has enabled Bishops and others to speak of Catholic Ceremonial as being "innovation." He confesses his own neglect, which operated in causing delay in respect of his own personal adoption and promotion of "Ritual." It may be that he has to confess to some inadequate, or uncertain personal belief in his earlier time, touching the root of the matter.

the Doctrine of THE REAL PRESENCE. But, however these things may have been, he has been enabled to make up his mind once for all now. He contends for Catholic Ceremonial as he would contend for his life, for all that is most dear. He contends for it at all costs. If he is to suffer such penalties as the World in our time can inflict, he is content, yea, and thankful, to suffer the penalties. He has got a thing of his Master's to keep and to deliver, and he is not going to surrender it in any manner or measure, nor to cease from delivering it at the World's bidding.

On the other side, the thing contended for is new law; new law for the Church, new law for the Realm. And there being great difficulty and probable disruption in any proceeding, by way of Act of Parliament, to deal directly with Ceremonial itself, the method of proceeding by way of Courts of Judicature constituted by Act of Parliament, has been and is resorted to; and the process not being quick enough, or decided enough, to satisfy the anti-Ritualist, a new Court of Judicature has been created by Act of Parliament, at the instance of the present Archbishop of Canterbury, for the express purpose, declared by the present Prime Minister in his place in Parliament, of "putting down" the "Ritualist."

Looking back twelve years at the Report of the Committee of 1866, I find in it things which I either originated or accepted then, but could neither originate nor accept now. Other things of both kinds to which I adhere. I shall touch these in the summary of my own position as I proceed. It takes some digging to get at the foundations of "Ritual," and I had only just begun to dig.

And when you have come to the foundations, there are many stones of it which are being handled with the view of pulling them out, with a view to the ruin of the entire building, either by the hand of that popular ignorance which belongs to a democratic time, or of that cognate confusion of "Roman Catholic" with "Catholic," which seems to be a kind of necessary accident of "the Establishment;" and which, when pushed to its logical issue, ends in preferring every manner of denial of the Faith to the Roman Catholic maintaining of the Faith[b]. The Nonconformist rejects "Catholic" altogether: it is no rule in any sense to him. Many of the sections of the Establishment virtually reject it, while professing to regard it, more or less.

"Ritual" is "Catholic," if it is anything worth having. It is the natural sequel and outcome of the Doctrine of the Sacraments; and especially of the Doctrine of THE REAL PRESENCE. The revival of the Doctrine of the Blessed Sacrament has been accompanied in due course by the revival of the "Ritual" of the Blessed Sacrament. Attempts have been made to affirm and maintain, not only that there is no *necessary* connection in practice between high Doctrine and high Ceremonial,—which may be true as respects this or that individual man, though it be difficult to understand how it can be true in all the extent claimed for it,—but that there is no *natural* and *proper* connection between the two: in other words, that "Ritual" is only another name of decency, order, reverence. Reverence for what? The answer is not easy. But the days of surface-reasoning upon this subject seem to be gone by. The Ritualist knows very well that it is all nonsense; so does the direct anti-Ritualist. The man neither "Ritualist" nor "anti-Ritualist" has found out that his account of the matter will not hold water; but for some years it had much currency among "High Churchmen."

It does not fall within the scope of these "Notes" to give the details of the "Ritual" history of the last twelve years, except so far as to elucidate my own position in relation to it. It is, as I have said, the one question of my life, as Priest of the Church of England, upon which I have changed my mind. I had begun to build upon a foundation which proved to be unsound, as when, e.g. I moved and carried my "preamble and clauses" in the Lower House, June 28, 1866; especially

---

[b] Jew, Turk, Atheist,
Anything except a Papist.

that part which recognises the authority of the Bishop to prohibit, or to dispense with, *ex cathedrâ*, the Priest's action in a matter which is the law of this Church and Realm; confounding therein between the legality, and the caution and charity which may not be put out of sight in every revival, especially in one where the whole difficulty has arisen out of long-continued and indefensible neglect on the part both of Bishop and Priest. I read that preamble and those clauses now, having carried them, with general concurrence, as the issue of much discussion between the Dean of Ely and myself; I read them now as a remarkable illustration in my own case of the old and very true saying, "a little knowledge is a dangerous thing."

I went on, gradually seeing more light, but stumbling all along over the stones of the old foundation, which I had helped to pull out, till my illness in 1870-71. I then for the first time grasped all the principles of the case. But I have still confession to make.

I have satisfied myself with affirming and maintaining the principles; without carrying them out fully in my practice. My adoption of "Ritual" has been partial only. I have never worn the Vestments; I have never used incense in any shape, nor what is properly called "Wafer-Bread." I have confined myself to the Eastward Position, the Altar Lights, the mixed Chalice. I do not know that I have much to say in defence of this partial adoption. I am glad always to be present at the highest and most complete Ceremonial, including Processions and the richest and most costly decoration; but my habit at home has been, is, and will continue to be, partial only. Something, perhaps, may be allowed to my antecedents; but, as I said, I do not attempt to defend myself.

Then as to the course to be taken by the Priest in the case of "Prohibited Ceremonial." I have lying before me in "Private Proof," what I submitted to friends as late as January, 1875, but did not publish. My conclusion then was, that rather than sever himself, or be severed, from his people, the Priest should cease from the use of such Ceremonial as Courts of Law did not allow.

I dissent *in toto* from this conclusion now. If I am to be ejected from ministering in my Parish Church, and ultimately from my Benefice and Cure of Souls, because I refuse to surrender Ceremonial as prohibited by Courts of Law, Courts of Law must eject me by their own act and arm: I will neither by word nor by act of any kind be, directly or indirectly, a party to the wrong. Putting into one scale severance from my people, my one remaining ground of hesitation in 1875; into the other, surrender of one particle of Catholic Ceremonial at the bidding of the Civil Power: the first scale kicks the beam.

I say, "at the bidding of the Civil Power." Now, suppose a National Synod were to abrogate and take away any part of such Ceremonial, what would be my course then?

There would be, then, this difference in my action, I should *resign* my Benefice with Cure of Souls, rather than continue to minister in the public congregation of a Church which had so betrayed its own inherited position. At the bidding of either Legislature or Court of Law I should *not resign;* I should wait to be driven out by the strong hand.

And this is the counsel that, in my old age, I give my brethren. Let it be "suffering," if need be; true, patient, passive suffering. I pray to be as ready to be "deprived" now for the "Ritual" of the Blessed Sacrament, as I was twenty years ago for the Doctrine of the Blessed Sacrament.

A few points remain to be touched.

1. Authority of the Bishop to prohibit or dispense with.

I say there is no such authority at all; nor any true ground for saying that there is.

The claim of such authority belongs to a curious confusion between the position of the Bishop in a Church not established by law, and the position of a Bishop in a Church established by law. The confusion has been found convenient both by the Bishop employing it, and by the Priest justifying his submission by it. But it is a confusion all the same, and a very damaging and dangerous confusion.

In a Church not established by law, the Bishop, subject always to Canon, is the ultimate authority in matters of Ritual within his diocese: in a Church established by law, it is not only the Canon which governs the Bishop, it is Statute also. Therefore, to refer in matter of "Ritual" to the Bishop as a *governing or dispensing authority* (much as I proposed to do in 1866), is to confound two distinct conditions of things; importing into one of them the governing or dispensing power, which belongs only to the other, and which is the prime distinction between the two.

2. For the ground upon which such authority is claimed for the Bishop here in England.

This is the passage in Preface to Prayer-Book, "Concerning the Service of the Church,"—"And forasmuch," down to "the Archbishop."

Now I say that this passage has nothing whatever to do with "Ritual." The first four paragraphs refer to "order for Prayer," and for "reading of the Holy Scriptures" in the church;" the fifth paragraph to "saying and singing," according to the varying "Uses" in different parts of England; then follows the paragraph, "And forasmuch," &c. There is not one word about "Ceremonial." The next succeeding portion of the Preface is, "Of Ceremonies, why some be abolished, and some retained." Here the paragraph finds no place.

The sum of all this is, that the paragraph in question, being the one ground alleged for reference to the Bishop in matter of Ceremonial, has been very improperly forced into doing duty in justifying a reference which is not, nor ever can be, admissible in the case of a Church "established by law." The Bishop here is not bound and tied by Canon only; he is also bound and tied by

Statute law, such law not being incompatible with Canon, just as the Priest is; no more and no less. A Bishop may not lawfully be always shifting his position: one day appealing to *his* position as Diocesan in a Church established by law; another day tò *the* position of a Diocesan in a Church *not* established by law. He must make his choice between the two, and abide by it; and not, being in one position, invoke the authority which belongs only to the other.

3. Then there is the picking and choosing among points of Ritual, as things proper to be contended for, or to be surrendered: as if it were a matter of individual liking, or disliking, and not of the law of the Church. I have heard much talk and some argument, based upon this picking and choosing, in Committees of the Lower House, in the Lower House itself, and elsewhere. All such talk or argument is wholly beside the question. The question is, Is the Ceremonial lawful, and is it legal? Two things, not one and the same thing; and often found not to coincide. About compulsory obligation of "Ornaments Rubric" I say nothing. I have debarred myself from contending for this, if I were minded to contend for it, which I am not, by my own partial use of "Ritual;" I speak only of the "lawfulness" and of the "legality." I have contended throughout for both in themselves; though I did fall into the snare of "reference to the Bishop" not many years ago. Those who deny either, would deny anything and everything "Catholic," if it suited their purpose at the time. Either they are incapable of apprehending what "Catholic" means; or, apprehending it, they side with the world in the attempt, as foolish as it is wicked, to "put it down."

Nov. 23, 1867, I took part in bringing together a great meeting in St. James's Hall, Lord Nelson in the chair, to claim for Churchmen their lawful liberty, and to protest against any interference with the Book of Common Prayer.

In 1871-2, I had my difference with my own Bishop

in the matter of the "Ritual" in use in East Brent Church. When I refused to give up any part of it, the Bishop took away my Curates' licences. It appeared to me that, as the whole responsibility was my own, and not that of my Curates at all, it was I, not they, who ought to have been made responsible: accordingly, I advised my nephew, Henry Phipps Denison, to appeal to the Archbishop. He gained his appeal, and recovered his licence; but it cost £600 to do it. This is one of the pleasing features of our quasi-ecclesiastical proceedings in Courts of Law: you gain your cause; and when you have gained it, you find that you have to pay a very high price for what it is your plain right to have for nothing. When, two or three years ago, Lord Shaftesbury called attention to the Courts Ecclesiastical, he wrote to me to say that he heard I had been a great sufferer, and asked for information. I told him, in reply, that I would readily give it, provided he would read my letter in the House of Lords; which he did. The whole condition of the case is as bad as may be. I remember, after the decision in our favour costing £600, the Archbishop's Secretary putting in a claim for £46 from us, for his attendance in the matter upon the Archbishop. I said, "Not one farthing." He then allowed that he had no legal claim. It is a pity that there should be room for these things: the scandal and the hindrance in the way of getting justice is very great.

The uniform kindness of the Bishop of Bath and Wells has made it easy to put out of sight altogether all the conflict of our difference; the difference itself remaining just where it was.

I abstain from dipping my fingers into the sea of contradictory Judgments of the Judicial Committee in the matter of "Ritual." All these are upon record; and besides, as I reject *in toto* the authority of the Judicial Committee to judge at all in matters of Faith and Worship,

I do not trouble myself about their proceedings. I am very thankful to have lived long enough to see Churchmen occupying distinctly and definitely the one ground upon which the battle of Church Authority, as against the hostile Indifferentism of the Civil Power, can be fought,—the ground of absolute denial of Jurisdiction in things Spiritual. A great deal of time has been wasted in fighting about this or that point, or points, of Ritual submitted for decision to the Judicial Committee. This has been virtually, and indeed by express act, to admit the authority of the Judicial Committee to consider and decide. We have at last, I hope, got rid of all this: we see our way clearly to the manner of the fight: we will not appear, we will not plead, either by ourselves, or by counsel. If the "Ornaments Rubric" is to be destroyed or tampered with, let it be done by a National Synod. We should then have to re-consider the position of continuing to minister in a Church which had, with its own hand, severed the link of Catholic tradition, usage, practice, worship. I know well what, in such case, would be the issue of my own re-consideration.

Meantime, the Judgments of the Judicial Committee in matter of Faith or Worship, whether *for* us or *against* us, are like only so much waste paper. The Judicial cannot come into the place of the Legislative; cannot *repeal* and *re-enact* under pretext of interpreting, and contrary to express statute. As for the attempt to get rid of the "Ornaments Rubric" by the help of Advertisements, in the Ridsdale case,—this has been so shattered to pieces by many hands,—among them, by the very incisive hand of my dear friend C. S. Grueber[c],

---

[c] "Consistent or Inconsistent: Honest or Dishonest: Truthful or Untruthful: Which is the Church of England? A Last Appeal to the Archbishops and Bishops of the Church, with Ways of Peace respectfully submitted: being a Fourth Letter to the Rt. Rev. the Lord Bishop of Bath and Wells. By the Rev. C. S. Grueber, S. James, Hambridge, Diocese of Bath and Wells." (Oxford: Parker, 1878.)

and finally and conclusively by the hands of another kind friend, James Parker [d],—that it would not be necessary to say a word upon it, even if I could regard the Court making the attempt as a true authority in the matter.

For the Judicial Committee, with its snare laid to catch weak-minded and unwary people,—I mean the presence in it of Bishops of the Establishment, either as Judges or Assessors,—I have laboured long and much in Convocation [e], and out of it, to get rid at least of the snare, if we could not get rid of the Court; and so take away all ground of pretence that there was any admixture of the spiritual element in the decision of the Court. At one time, some four years ago, in conjunction with two dear friends, one now dead, the other living still, I thought the work was done; and so indeed it was, so far as the vote of the House of Commons was concerned, by a well-timed and well-aimed stroke, carried out within six-and-thirty hours. In the House of Lords other counsels prevailed; and it has ended in our having Bishops, no longer indeed as Judges, but, what is even worse, as Assessors. It is a very unhappy and damaging position, full of all manner of danger to the maintaining unimpaired the Deposit of The Faith.

As Chairman of Committee on the Address of the Church in Canada, presented to the Convocation of the Province of Canterbury, February, 1866, I had contributed what I could to the bringing together of the Lambeth Synod in 1867. I did not anticipate, certainly, the bringing together of Bishops from all parts of the world, for three days at Lambeth.

[d] "Did Queen Elizabeth take 'Other Order' in the 'Advertisements' of 1566? A Letter to Lord Selborne, in reply to his Lordship's Criticisms on the 'Introduction to the Revisions of the Book of Common Prayer,' by James Parker, Hon. M.A. Oxon." (Oxford: Parker, 1878.)

[e] See Debate on Mr. Fendall's resolution, May, 1, 1866, and the carrying of my amendment by 35 to 14.

For the proposed Synod of 1878, I cannot augur well for it under the Presidency of the present Archbishop of Canterbury. The Archbishop has always been personally most kind to me; but I know of no Church question which I am content to see principally in his hands: I can only hope and pray that my anticipations may prove to be unfounded.

May 4, 1866, the Rev. J. Bramston, now Dean of Winchester, moved for a Committee upon the Constitutions and Canons Ecclesiastical. The resolution was carried unanimously. I was a member of the Committee, and when Mr. Bramston ceased to sit as Proctor, became Chairman in his room. In 1872 Mr. Bramston returned to the House in right of his Deanery, and kindly consented, at my request, to re-occupy the chair of the Committee.

The Committee has been sitting and conferring with the Convocation of the sister Province twelve years. I have ceased to sit upon the Committee, but I have a printed notice from my kind friend this morning, May 19, 1878, of a meeting of the joint Committee of the two Provinces, Thursday, June 20, 11.30, in the Jerusalem Chamber; from which it appears that the work is still under consideration.

Very early in the work of the Committee I became persuaded that I had been too sanguine; that the work could not be brought to the desired issue. That persuasion was confirmed as the sittings proceeded. I have no belief that Canons can be made in our time,—such as the Church of England is bound to make, if it make any,—which will be ratified by consent of the Crown, that is to say, of the House of Commons. I believe that, after all the time and labour spent upon the work, it will be found that the thing cannot be done. As for any other manner of Canons,—Canons to "suit the times,"—this is a thing which may not be taken in hand lawfully.

I come now to state the principal causes which have

combined to place me in a position which, till very lately, I had not at any time contemplated: a position full of regret and pain; but out of which I see no way or prospect of escape.

I refer to the fact of my having this year withdrawn myself from taking active part in the Sessions of Convocation. I am bound upon all accounts to state explicitly what these causes are. In stating them as they present themselves to me in their conclusive character, I am not tying myself down absolutely not to return to my place under any circumstances of the position of the Church of England which may arise, and which may, I fear, not improbably arise in the future of my time, if it have a future; but I am simply saying why I have ceased to be in my place now. I think I owe this to others as to myself.

The principal causes, then, are in number four:—

1. The action of Convocation in the matter of "Ritual."
2. The action of Convocation in the matter of Revision of the Authorized Version.
3. The action of Convocation in the matter of Confession to, and Absolution by, the Priest.
4. The non-action of Convocation in respect of the desecration, at the hands of the Judicial Committee of Privy Council, of the Sacrament of the BODY and the BLOOD.

Before I state them, I must refer to the position of the House in February and May, 1870, in the matter of "National Education," when it had become clear that Government was prepared with a Bill containing provisions directly opposed to the whole policy of the House since 1852.

February 10, 1870, Canon Hopkins moved five resolutions on the subject of "National Education."

Resolution 4 accepted the principle of a "Conscience Clause." I moved, as an amendment, and carried, with consent of Canon Hopkins, the appointment of a Committee: of that Committee I was Chairman. May 3, 1870, I presented the Report. Finding myself, *for the first time since* 1852, at issue upon this matter with many with whom I had acted for more than twenty years, I stated to the House that I was unable to move the Resolutions appended to the Report, and declined to have anything further to do with the Report, except to oppose it: see "Chronicle," May 3, 1870, p. 236, and May 6, 1870, pp. 407—9. "The National Society for the Education of the Poor in the Principles of the Established Church" had gone over to the enemy; the Diocesan Board of Education for the Diocese of Bath and Wells, with the other Diocesan Boards, had done the like; the Lower House of Convocation of Canterbury followed at last; and the Church Schools of the Church of England, for which I had contended for three-and-twenty years, were finally surrendered into the hands of the Civil Power, for the purposes of the policy of Indifferentism in Religion, first formally set in motion in 1839.

This conclusion of the labour of many years could not be without its grievous pain.

It was my last day in Convocation before my illness some six weeks later. When I could return, after some months, to think upon public matters, I found the Act passed. In respect of it, I hold to every word that I said in the House, May 6. The experience of eight years has been quite enough to prove to many who were not with me then, what are the inevitable issues of the Elementary Education Act of 1870.

I return now to my four causes.

First for "Ritual."

The action of Convocation in this matter appears to me to have been not simply unsatisfactory, but unworthy of Convocation.

What has been its point of departure?

It has dealt with the revival of Ritual much more as a nuisance to be abated, as a wrong to be redressed by Courts of Law, than as a return to the Catholic use of the Church of England according to the law of this Church and Realm, after long years of neglect and disuse, to be sympathised with, welcomed, and regulated by the only considerations which can legitimately be interposed; considerations of tenderness and charity and cautious care for a people guided into, and encouraged to persevere in, the neglect and disuse by its own Bishops and Priests.

Then for the action itself.

This has been throughout, as is natural in the case of an unsound basis, illogical and confused.

Approaching the subject in the spirit I have described, as if the revival were a thing, in itself, not right but wrong, it has, from the first commencement of taking action upon it, by the stereotyped use of the term "excesses of Ritualism," admitted that the thing itself is right; that it is not the thing, but only some manner of it, which is wrong.

All the action taken upon this basis of self-contradiction has been necessarily illogical and confused.

The general impression conveyed to "the public mind" has been, that which "the public mind" in its ignorance and prejudice was well prepared to endorse, namely, that the revival of "Ritual" is a public wrong. This point once reached, any lurking scruple as to the means employed for "putting down" goes for nothing; and the whole position becomes not only illogical and confused, but inequitable and unjust; in one word, anti-Catholic. The weight of the Church Corporate is thrown into the scale, and persecution at law is not slow to begin.

It is true that fine words have been used here and there in both Houses,—words about the self-denial, moral goodness, unsparing labour among and for CHRIST'S people, high and low, rich and poor, which are eminent characteristics of the "Ritual" movement. But the fine words are always spoken with a kind of deprecating, if not contemptuous, pity for men good, but weak, deluded into contending about trifles. Are they trifles in any sense to the "Ritualist?" no man in his senses says they are or can be. Are they trifles to the anti-Ritualist? Why, then, does the "anti-Ritualist" make such frantic and unscrupulous effort to "put them down"? The self-contradiction is too evident to need another word: it would only be ludicrous, if it were not full of pain on account both of persecutor and persecuted.

This deprecating, if not contemptuous, pity is, I think, about the substance of all that has been put into the "Ritualist" scale by "friends;" that is to say, into the scale of the reviver of the long-neglected and disused Ceremonial of the Church of England.

Now for the term "excesses." Where there is "excess," there is "mean" and "defect." Nobody in Convocation, or out of it, seems to me to trouble themselves much about the defect. Priests might have gone on for ever, as so many of them are doing at this moment, and have been doing all their time, so to speak, rioting in "defect," without thought even of bringing any law, Ecclesiastical or Civil, to bear upon them.

But suppose this disclaimed,—though to be sure the disclaimer cannot be said to carry much weight with it in the face of facts,—suppose it disclaimed, and the assertion accepted in its room that all that is wanted is the "mean."

What is the "mean?" A jumble between Catholic and Protestant; between Sacramental and anti-Sacramental; between Church law and popular pleasure. Who is set up to judge about the "excess?" "The British public," with all its ten thousand forms of faith and worship. Not the Synod, but "the British public." There is something in the Old Scriptures about "pleasing the people and obeying their voice;" there is something also about the penalty of "pleasing the people and obeying their voice" in a matter of Divine Commission and Trust. Now the "Ritualist" acts, if he acts truly and faithfully, as obeying GOD rather than men wheresoever the two paths diverge definitely, and as accepting the consequences of men's anger patiently and cheerfully, yea, and thankfully, as what is sent to him of GOD.

I am bound to sum up here by saying that, so far as I have been able to see, and I have watched the whole proceeding anxiously and narrowly, Convocation has both approached and dealt with the revival of "Ritual" very much more after the fashion of "the British public," than after the fashion of a Synod of the Church.

All this had begun to weigh heavily on my mind when I became a member of the Committee on Ritual, which sat in the Chapter-house of St. Paul's in 1874—6; and I made more than one attempt, and once all but succeeded, to get the Report placed upon what appeared to me to be its only true lines :—

(*a*.) An enquiry into, and conclusion upon, the relation of "Ritual" to Doctrine,—searching, exact, complete in all its parts.

(*b*.) A like enquiry into, and conclusion upon, the "Ornaments Rubric."

If I had succeeded in carrying these things, I should have proposed two Sub-Committees, applying themselves severally to these two primary portions of the matter in hand. For the second, it would have been necessary to call in the assistance of eminent jurists.

Upon this basis, the Report would have been a "Church and State" paper of great value and authority, as governing details of the question. As the Report stands, I cannot regard it as a document, after all the time and labour spent upon it, of any substantial value.

There was one more point which I pressed persistently upon the Committee, but which I could not carry. My dear friends, Sir George Prevost and Canon Gregory, carried it afterwards in a small House, by 26 to 16, April 25, 1877, see "Chronicle," p. 87; but they had opposed it in Committee. Afterwards the question was raised again, in a house of some seventy members, and carried against my two friends by the casting-vote of the Prolocutor.

I mean the deprecation of going to Parliament for legislation, the subject-matter of such legislation being the Prayer-Book of the Church of England. I am bound to repeat here what I have said all along in Convocation, and out of it,—that I am persuaded that no greater mistake can be made, under any circumstance and condition of the time, than the bringing Bills into either House of Parliament which touch the Prayer-Book.

Carry the Prayer-Book into Parliament, and in the natural order of things it will not come out of Parliament the same Book. Will it come out a better Book? The advocates of legislation say, "Yes." Upon what ground I have tried hard to understand, but find it every way impossible. I believe that it must necessarily come out a very damaged Book. The Anglo-Catholic does not think the Prayer-Book incapable of improvement; he desiderates many things in it: but he is content to work with what he has got, to watch and wait, because he finds in it the foundations of Catholic Faith and Worship. Once carry the Book into Parliament, and a large part of these will disappear.

Seeing, therefore, that there is nothing to be gained, very much to be lost; seeing, moreover, that there is, *in limine*, an insuperable objection upon principle to any such legislation by the Imperial Legislature as now constituted; when I found that the House, the Prevost and Gregory resolution notwithstanding, was engaged in promoting such legislation, just as if no such resolution had been passed; that it had become, so to speak, the chief subject-matter of its action; that I could take no part in it but to protest against it at every step; that to concern oneself with details of the Church's life when the principles were, if not abandoned formally, yet so damaged by perpetual compromise, as to be well-nigh crumbling in the hand; that if the main line was in an unsound state, the branch lines would not yield much profit, if any,— I was driven towards the conclusion that I was better away from the House.

In the earlier part of the time during which these considerations were working upon my mind, a thing had been done by the House, May 5, 1870, which I have never been able to think of without feelings of the deepest and most painful regret, and this upon grounds private as well as public. The House had consented to, I might almost say had welcomed, the admission of a man denying the ETERNAL GODHEAD OF THE SON as a Member of the joint Committee appointed for Revision of the Authorized Version of the Holy Scriptures. I state the fact in its nakedness,—it is more than enough: I can add nothing to it, except to refer with deep thankfulness to the speech of the Bishop of Winchester in the Upper House, Feb. 14, 1871.

Two things more were coming: when they came, the added weight broke me down. I had hitherto fought with myself: I could fight no more.

The first is the non-action of the House, and even of its Committee, on the matter of the desecration of the Blessed Sacrament at the hands of the Judicial Committee of Privy Council in the case of Jenkins *v.* Cook.

February 17, 1876, I said in my place in the House :—

"I have to present a *Gravamen*, which I will read; and at the same time I desire to give notice that, during to-morrow's Session, I shall move that the standing orders be suspended, in order to the discussing this Schedule of *Gravamen*, with a view to its adoption as *Articulus Cleri*. The *Gravamen* is as follows :—

"1. Whereas, by the Judgment of the Judicial Committee of Privy Council in the case of Jenkins *v.* Cook, delivered yesterday, 16th inst., upon appeal from the Judgment of the Court of Arches, it has been declared, that to print and publish a volume entitled, 'Selections from the Old and New Testaments,' in which volume every passage setting forth, or referring to, certain Doctrines of the Catholic Faith is systematically omitted, on the specific ground alleged by the appellant in his letter of July 20, 1874, as recited in the said Judgment, that such passages are 'quite incompatible with religion or decency,' supplies, nevertheless, no sufficient ground for concluding that the person so printing and publishing rejects such Doctrines :

"2. And whereas it is thereupon pronounced in and by the said Judgment, that the person so printing and publishing may not lawfully be repelled from Holy Communion :

"3. And whereas this has been done in respect of the most solemn ordinance of the Worship, and of the most responsible function of the Bishops and Priests, of the Church of England:

"4. And whereas the Discipline of the Church has therein and thereby by direct consequence, and its Doctrine and Worship by necessary implication, been brought into contempt:

"5. And whereas nothing could be devised by man tending more powerfully to destroy belief in the Catholic position of the Church of England, and to reduce it in the eyes of men to the position of a creature and tool of the Civil Power:

"6. And whereas the said Judgment does dishonour to GOD, to HIS Word, and to HIS Church here in England:

"Now I, George Anthony Denison, M.A., Vicar of East Brent, Archdeacon of Taunton, do hereby, in my place in this Synod, enter my complaint of, and protest against, the said Judgment, given on the part of the Civil Power by a Court claiming to represent 'the Church of England as by law established;' and do appeal from such Judgment to the Judgment of the Synods of the Church of England; and do pray the Upper House to take into immediate consideration, in what manner the wrong done by the said Judgment may best be repaired.

"Witness my hand,
"GEORGE ANTHONY DENISON."

February 18, 1876, I said:—

"Finding, as I expected to find, that it is most probable that my motion for suspension of standing orders will not be carried, I think it best and most respectful to the House to ask leave to withdraw that motion, and to place my *Gravamen* in the hands of the Prolocutor to carry up as the *Gravamen* of myself. I have now only to hope that some member, more happy than myself in obtaining the concurrence of the House, may devise some means of expressing what is, I am persuaded, the general judgment and feeling of this House."

After this, I had much consultation with my kind friend, Canon Miller. It issued, May 10, 1876, in the motion of Canon Miller, seconded by Canon Gregory, for an Address to the Upper House, praying for direction to appoint Committee "to consider the law of discipline in the Church of England, in reference to the power of the Clergy to repel from Holy Communion on the ground of false doctrine and immorality; and to report to the House whether any, and if any, what, alteration in that law be desirable for the better avoiding of the profanation of this Holy Sacrament, and the scandal consequent thereon: provision being made, on the one hand, against the violation of the conscience of the Clergyman, and on the other hand, against any undue infringement upon the liberty of the Christian laity."

May 12, 1876, such Committee was appointed by direction of the Upper House, and Canon Miller was chosen Chairman.

What has been the issue? The Committee has met once; has abandoned proceeding in the matter. Whether it has reported this to the House, and has, in consequence, been discharged, I do not know.

But I say this, that if proof of the unreality of the position of Convocation were lacking, here it is supplied in a manner and to an extent from which it is impossible to escape.

The last thing I have to adduce, that which has filled up the cup, is the action of the Lower House, July 4, 1876, when the House was asked to express its "*general* concurrence in the Declaration on the subject of Confession, sent down to it from the Upper House for consideration:"

My reasons (*a*.) against the Declaration itself, (*b*.) against asking the House to assent to it without touching it, (*c*.) against the stultification of the House by proposing *general* concurrence upon a question of *particular, close*, definite Doctrine (as, indeed, upon any question of Doctrine), are to be found in the "Chronicle of Convocation," July 4, 1877, pp. 245, 6. I need not repeat them here. I moved afterwards two amendments, pp. 246, 53; the first was lost by 52 to 15, the second by 45 to 18. The resolution as above was then carried by 62 to 6.

I left the House that day, persuaded that it would be the last group of Sessions at which I should be present, if spared to see another: this persuasion has become established by all subsequent reflection. As I said above, it may be that the position of the Church of England in its relations to the Civil Power, and the effect and issue of those relations, may force me again into my place; I cannot tell; but I can hardly see what remains to make those relations worse than they are now. I think they have reached, whatever fine words may be used about them, their lowest point.

Let me try to put in very few words what that point is.

In the lack of anything to be called Corporate Unity, the Church of England has become a collection of Congregations embracing almost every manner of divergence of belief and of practice, not in point of detail only, but in point of principle. Under these actual conditions of the case, the only reasonable and equitable rule is that of the belief and practice of the Congregations. And this *is* the rule for the Protestant, or ultra-Protestant, but it *is not* the rule for the Catholic, Congregation. Here authorities Ecclesiastical and Civil interfere; in every other case, they do not interfere. But the "British public" have not learnt yet what "Catholic" means, and the British public have to be soothed and pleased at all costs.

The Protestant, or ultra-Protestant, Congregation is allowed to do exactly as it pleases; to obey or to neglect, to inculcate or to disparage, if not openly to condemn, the Church's law, just as it pleases: the Bishops look on. The Catholic Congregation is forbidden to obey the Church's law; and as this is found, the more the matter is enquired into, to be Catholic law, new law has to be made and put into its place, by some marvellous jumble of the Legislative and the Judicial.

The vote of the Lower House, July 4, 1877, had compelled me to part with the lingering hope that the Convocations of the Church of England "as by law established," would yet be found on the side of the Catholic

Revival," born in 1832; growing and increasing year by year by way of natural, and sooner or later, necessary development among all orders and conditions of men. The Church of England Working Men's Society is one of the happiest illustrations of this fact. Early in 1877 I had finally ceased to have faith in the "Establishment," and had joined the "Church League." My friends in the Lower House told me that I had thereby "broken up the party;" much as I had been told when, in 1853, I first did what I could to take away Mr. Gladstone's seat for the University of Oxford.

My reply was, that I had been at no pains to conceal for many years,—beginning in 1851 with "Why should the Bishops continue to sit in the House of Lords?" and summing up, in 1874, with "Episcopatus Bilinguis,"—my conclusions about the nature and operation of the "Establishment;" and that "the party" was, in my eyes, a very secondary thing.

I turned elsewhere for the sympathy and conjoint action which was no longer mine in the Lower House, and found it in the "Confraternity of the Blessed Sacrament," and in the "Society of the Holy Cross," of both of which I became a member in 1877. I had become some years before this a Member of "The Society for the Maintenance of The Faith."

Meantime the Bishops, in close accord with the antiCatholicism of Parliament and People, continued, and with renewed vigour after the vote of July 4, 1877, their endeavour to "put down" Confession to, and Absolution by, a Priest. This is now the guiding policy of the antiCatholic movement.

Both Bishops and People "imagine a vain thing."

The anti-Catholic assault, passing onward from "Church Rate" and "Schools," had come in contact with the Doctrine of THE REAL PRESENCE, and had suffered defeat. It had got encouragement, but nevertheless in its primary object had suffered defeat. Then it fell upon "Ritual;" and, aided by certain unscrupulous processes on the part of Episcopal legislation and Judicial authority; by the substitution of "Roman Catholic" for "Catholic;" by hoisting the flag of "no Popery," and keeping it before the eyes of the "British public," as against the manifestation of Doctrine by Ceremonial, which is the handmaid of Doctrine; by the use of the strong hand of the arm of the law of the land, as against the law of this Church and Realm, has succeeded, to some extent, in the "putting down" policy. It has repressed for a time what it cannot overcome. The Doctrine of the Blessed Sacrament, it has learnt, it cannot touch by any legal process: the Ritual of the Blessed Sacrament it can. About the manner and the means it has no hesitation; using all things freely as they come to hand, without troubling itself about what the things are.

The other day—I name no names, but I state a fact—an English gentleman, having with much difficulty overcome the reluctance of his son to join him in his "anti-Ritual" campaign, called in his butler to make up the party of the three aggrieved parishioners.

In the Diocese of Gloucester and Bristol, the Bishop has closed one of the best churches in his Diocese, and robbed the congregation of the Blessed Sacrament therein, upon the information of three "aggrieved" people, whose names and descriptions he has not ventured to make public—*Quousque tandem?*

Priests are harried and ruined, and of late, imprisoned, their people being all the time with them in what they do, because "for conscience' sake" they are constrained to revive the Ritual of the Blessed Sacrament; and, being thereupon prosecuted in the name of the three aggrieved, to refuse to listen to an authority which is not the authority of "this Church and Realm¹."

But all the temporary success of these manners of "putting down" notwithstanding, Ritual was holding on its way steadily; and even the "British public" were getting a little tired of the strife, when the book, "The Priest in Absolution," was laid hold of, and applied to rekindle the dying flame.

The Society of the Holy Cross was identified with

¹ The Ordering of Priests.

the book, as it seems to me not at all unreasonably, all the disclaimers of members of it notwithstanding: on the other hand, as it seems to me not blameably, for though I have not read the book, I am entirely satisfied by the evidence of others who have, that there is nothing in the book to blame; very much to be thankful for. The next step was to identify every "Ritualist" with the Society of the Holy Cross. This had no warrant; but then "warrant" in these things is what men do not much concern themselves about. By this process every "Ritualist" was once more held up before the eyes of the "British public" as a man to be avoided, shunned, abominated.

Hic niger est, hunc tu, Romane, caveto.

It will all fail in the end, if it seem to have some success for a time, as other unscrupulosities have failed as before the Truth.

Meantime, I have one great regret which I cannot help stating here.

It is that, in any manner or degree, Members of the Society of the Holy Cross should have yielded to the anti-Catholic pressure, and have either withdrawn from membership, or be prepared to modify the original position.

My feeling and deliberate judgment about things of this nature is, as it has always been: either do not take a thing in hand at all, as a means to holiness of life, and devotion of it to the work of CHRIST, or, whatever comes of your taking the thing in hand, abide by it. Above all things, look to it that you surrender no jot or tittle of it under anti-Catholic pressure. Better never to have taken the thing in hand at all, than to surrender it at the bidding of the "British public."

Meantime, August 10, 1873, I had preached in the Cathedral Church of St. Andrew, Wells, a Sermon entitled "Confession, Absolution, and Holy Communion," and had published some thousands of it.

In November, 1877, I published a Letter to the Bishop of Ely, my old kind friend, upon a portion of his Charge delivered that year.

One of the best judges of reasoning that I have known wrote to me upon my Letter as follows:—

"As to those two or three pages of your Letter, 15—18, I cannot tell you how unanswerable, original and important I think them. I had written something myself (on the extent of the Sacerdotal Ministry as a protection of the Blessed Sacrament, and the only Discipline practically remaining for the generality), but it is not half so telling as yours, and not so demonstrable."

The English Church Union reprinted the pages in leaflet shortly after. I reproduce the reprint here:—

"FALLACY OF 'RESTRICTED OR EXCEPTIONAL CONFESSION TO A PRIEST.' Extract of LETTER to the LORD BISHOP OF ELY from ARCHDEACON DENISON.— *Nov.*, 1877. (James Parker and Co., Oxford and London.)

"EXPOSURE OF FALLACY.

" 1. *Universal obligation to receive Holy Communion.*
" 2. *Universal duty of quieting the conscience thereto, by one or other of the two ways prescribed by the Church of England: with the great peril of neglecting the same.*

"For the vital question of the 'restricted' or 'exceptional' character of Confession to a Priest, I find that you make, not one exception only as in the Bury St. Edmund's report, but two exceptions:—

" 1. The case of a sick man having his conscience troubled with some weighty matter.
" 2. The case of a 'doubting Communicant' unable to quiet his own conscience.

I am thankful to have found this, for I would not willingly overstate.

"But, after all, is there any real difference between two exceptions and one exception? Rather, I should say, is there any room for the doctrine of 'exceptions' at all?

" Let us see.

"The Church admonishes *all* her children,—

"(*a.*) That it is necessary to Salvation to come to Holy Communion.

"(*b.*) That to come worthily it is necessary to have a quiet conscience.

"(*c.*) That there are two ways by which a quiet conscience may be had.

"1. By Confession of sins to ALMIGHTY GOD, with full purpose of amendment of life.

"2. By Confession of sins to, and Absolution by, GOD'S Priest, if any man find that he cannot quiet his own conscience by the way and means first stated.

"Now the obligation to come to Holy Communion being imperative upon *all;* the use of the means for attaining to the quiet conscience, which is essential to coming worthily, is imperative upon *all* also; and wheresoever the first is found to fail, the second is to be resorted to for the specific purpose of being enabled to come worthily.

"It is the overlooking this, which is, first and last, the use and the object of Confession to a Priest, the being enabled, that is, to come worthily to Holy Communion, that has issued in the doctrine of 'exceptions,' and of the 'occasional' use only of Confession to a Priest. And it is important to a true understanding of this matter, to note that it is specifically in her 'Order for the Administration of the LORD'S Supper or Holy Communion' that the Church has chosen to deliver her teaching touching Confession to a Priest. The place in the Prayer-Book in which the teaching is found, the first Exhortation, leads the mind at once to the *universal, not occasional, the general, not particular*, use and object of Confession to a Priest, as one of the two ordained means of attaining to the quiet conscience, which is essential to the receiving worthily what is necessary to Salvation.

"Now, even of the comparatively small number of Church-people who are Communicants, a considerable and a growing proportion are in the habit of Confessing to a Priest. Others, no doubt many, attain to a quiet conscience without Confession to a Priest. But the vast majority of Church-people are not Communicants.

"Is their conscience quiet? we must conclude, as we must hope, that it is not.

"The Church cries aloud to all these unceasingly, Come to Holy Communion. It is necessary to Salvation. What is the answer, felt, if not spoken, unless the heart be hardened; often felt and spoken? I cannot, I dare not; my conscience is not quiet; I am not at peace with GOD and man.

"What is the Church's reply? You require then further comfort or counsel. Go therefore to GOD's Priest, open your grief to him, that you may receive the benefit of absolution, together with ghostly counsel and advice to the quieting of your conscience, and avoiding all scruple and doubtfulness.

"Now, then, I should like to know what becomes of the doctrine of 'exceptions,' and of 'occasional' resort to Confession to a Priest; both which are taught so glibly by high authorities.

"How can that be an exceptional and occasional rule of the life in CHRIST, which applies generally and always to the vast majority of Church-people in respect of the Blessed Sacrament, necessary to Salvation?

"Is it not, on the contrary, abundantly plain that your second exception, the restriction to the 'doubting communicant,' cannot be maintained, any more than that to the 'sick bed [8]'?

"The Church admonishes *all* Communicants, not the 'doubting Communicant' only, as *all* non-Communicants. For even those who can quiet their own conscience before GOD need to be often admonished to take heed how they do it.

"And the sum of the whole matter is this:— It is not Confession to a Priest which is a thing 'exceptional.' The thing 'exceptional' is, as matter of fact, the having a quiet conscience at peace with GOD and man, *without* Confession to, and Absolution by, a Priest. Let those who have it bless GOD for His mercy to them, and His Church for her loving care, in all humbleness of heart. And let all remember that it is not the Church that minimises, excepts, restricts; turns general into particular, and habitual into occasional. Nay, rather, it is the Church which magnifies, recognising to the full; and applies to the Salvation of souls, in all the vast and true and Divine proportions of a mighty Mystery, Confession to and Absolution by GOD's Priest."

---

[8] "'*As well to the sick* as to the whole.'—'Ordering of Priests.'"

In 1874 I received, on Harvest Home Day, a second address from a large number of parishioners, including some 90 Communicants. The address reverts, among other things, to the fact of the increase of Communicants. The number on Easter Day that year having been 76, 46 of whom received at the Early Celebration; the number of Communicants has increased steadily. Easter Day this year we had 88 Communicants, 60 receiving at the Early Celebration.

August 16, 1873, I began Daily Celebration. From Advent, 1876, to Advent, 1877, the Celebrations were 412; the Communions 3080. Average, over 7.

At this point I close these "Notes of my Life." The chapter remaining is a Summary of the Argument and of the Position, as evidenced by the "Notes."

I have laid a heavy, and what to the great body of my countrymen will appear to be a grievous, indictment. It will be said of me, that it has been my purpose to draw as dark an outline as I could of the Position of "the Church of England as by law established."

I must bear the burden, because I may not understate the truth. No man, I hope, acknowledges more thankfully than I the move upwards of the last fifty years; but it is a move of individuals and congregations. The move of the Church Corporate, as measured by its relations to the Civil Power, relations which lie at the door of Bishops, Priests, and People, quite as much as at the door of an Indifferent Civil Power, is not upwards; nor, so far as I am able to see, is there any prospect of its taking that direction. In one particular indeed, of utmost importance, the maintaining and exercising the Trust of "Spiritual censure," the Civil Power has been more true to principle, and more careful than the Bishops, Priests, and People of the Church. I refer to the Acts 53 Geo. III. c. 127, and 2 and 3 Will. IV. c. 93 [h].

The Bishops of the "Establishment," with many of its Priests and People, talk much of "obedience to law."

[b] See Sir R. Phillimore's "Ecclesiastical Law," vol. ii. pp. 1417-1428.

I want to know what there is of base and bad that has not been done by man to man under pretext of "public law," from the day when there arose in the Judgment Hall at Jerusalem the cry of the Jews, "We have a law, and by our law He ought to die[i]."

It is difficult, in assailing a system, to avoid the imputation of assailing rather the men who administer the system, than the system itself. I have done what I could towards shewing that it is the system making the men that I assail; not the men. I have tried not to impute wrong motives personally. For the acts of men which have brought, and are bringing us every day, more and more into extremity of distress, I am only doing my duty to GOD and His Church in denouncing them throughout. And with these words I leave myself to such charitable construction of my motives and my acts as may be had.

I cannot satisfy myself with any words attempting to express my deep, abiding, and thankful sense of the hearty and unvarying kindliness manifested in many ways towards me, by opponents as by friends, throughout the thirty years of public conflict. Nor, again, of the loving help and comfort I have had at home, in the face of much necessary absence, distraction of thought, and occupation of time, at the hands of many Curates. Above all, at the hands of him who is my Curate now, my dear nephew, Henry Phipps Denison[k].

---

[i] St. John xix. 7.

[k] I have omitted to state in its place that, in 1867, a "Memorial on the Doctrine of the Eucharist," agreed to after long consultation by Clergy assembled at All Saints', Margaret-street, was forwarded by me as Chairman to the Archbishop of Canterbury. It is contained in Appendix F, pp. 128, 9, to the First Report of Commissioners on Ritual.

For the last twelve years I have had a very interesting occupation, in supplying the village of East Brent with pure drinking-water. See Appendix B.

CHAPTER XI.

SUMMARY OF THE ARGUMENT AND OF THE POSITION.

IN putting together these "Notes of my Life," I have had before me one especial purpose. The purpose has been to trace the successive steps by which, in the last half-century, 1828—78, the ultimate triumph of Indifferentism in Religion has been *statutably* accomplished, as the religious position of the English nation; to gather up, by way of induction of particulars, what has been the policy—religious policy I cannot call it, policy in respect of religion I can—of the Imperial Government.

The conclusion to which each successive particular severally and jointly tends, is,—

That whereas in Century XVI. it was "the Church established by law" which was the object proposed and attained; in Century XIX. it is "Indifferentism established by law" which has been proposed, and has been attained.

"Indifferentism" professes to be a passive thing; but in Religion—as respects, on the one hand, the thousand negations of "the Catholic Faith," and, on the other, the one affirmation of "the Catholic Faith"—it is the most active thing in the world. It is not simply in its nature favourable to the first, but encouraging and promoting at every opportunity: to the second, it is not simply in its nature unfavourable, but actively hostile. There is no fallacy, no practical lie, so great as "Indifferentism in Religion."

It is curious to note here, that it took about the same number of years in Century XVI., and the same part of the Century, to build up "the Church as by law established," which it has taken in Century XIX. to pull it down.

The position of Century XIX. is the natural and necessary sequel of the position of Century XVI. The substance of the controversy then, so far as it was doctrinal, was about the Blessed Sacrament of the BODY and the BLOOD: it is the substance of the controversy now. For reasons other than doctrinal, reasons valid and invalid, the supremacy of Rome was rejected. Social and political exigencies, combined with great and confessed abuses, and with sundry and divers novel teachings touching the Blessed Sacrament, the inventions of the time, the natural offspring of minds suddenly let loose, and discharged from obedience to any authority except their own, led the way to a novel order of Church Polity, to a basis and superstructure hitherto unknown to the Church Catholic: heresies manifold touching the Blessed Sacrament, became not only tolerated within the Church of England, but were admitted to places of influence and power side by side with Catholic Truth.

The position of the Church of England in the phase of its existence, subsisting for the last three hundred years, is not the position of a Church of the "one Faith." As it was in Century XVI., so is it in Century XIX.; but with this considerable modification, that, as *malum in pejus semper ruit*, the position, in its public development, and as promoted by the action of the Civil Power, has become an infinitely worse position. Catholic Truth, and not anti-Catholic Heresy, in respect of the Blessed Sacrament, was set forth then, as now, in the Prayer-Book and in the Articles of Religion. Heresies in the same particular were allowed not to disqualify from possession of Benefice with Cure of Souls. Heresies once admitted always gain strength. The non-exclusion of Heresies made the basis unsound; the building raised upon it unsound: and so, in our time, anti-Catholic belief in respect of the Blessed Sacrament has become the prevailing belief of the English people; and can boast of large encouragement by authorities ecclesiastical and civil. The position is more than a modified, it is an inverted position. What was tolerated three hundred years ago, is dominant now. The right to Benefice, with Cure of Souls, of those who hold and teach Catholic Truth, is called in question before "Courts of Law;" and when admitted, it has been only the fear of disruption as the consequence of non-admission which has admitted it. The admission is carefully made to include disparagement. All that can *safely* be done against Catholic Truth on the part of the Civil Power, and I must needs add, the Ecclesiastical Power, all this is carefully done.

In the great distress of the Church of England, the mercy of GOD has vouchsafed in our own time a Revival of true Religion; and the absolute difference between the Catholic Truth of the Church and the "Protestant" corruptions of it, is day by day becoming more definitely and distinctly marked, more widely and better understood.

It is a poor and shallow wisdom which does not grasp, a blindness either of ignorance or of will, which does not look in the face, the facts of the present religious condition of the English people.

The facts are,—

1. Multiplied and multiplying religious division, both within and without the Church. Not one Religion, but many religions; not one Faith, but many faiths, and no faith.

    Within (*a.*) "High Church" Ritual; non-Ritual; subdivisions of both.

    Differentia.—Apostolical Commission and Succession; Authority of Church Catholic; Doctrine of Sacraments; Distinct and inherent functions of Spiritualty.

    (*b.*) "Low Church;" subdivisions:—

    Differentia.—Indiscriminating rejection of Roman Catholic; No ultimate Church authority; Bible, and nothing but the Bible; right of private judgment; Preaching first, second Sacraments.

(*c.*) "Broad Church;" subdivisions:—
Differentia.—Rejects Apostolical Commission and Succession; does *not* "contend for The Faith;" Good moral life, with or without Doctrine; Illustration of—

"For forms of faith let wrangling bigots fight;
He can't be wrong whose life is in the right."

(*d.*) Establishmentarian *pur et simple.*
Differentia.—Acts of Parliament.

Without, (*e.*) No Church.
Differentia.—No Priest—if any, yourself; No belief in particular.

I believe "Broad Church" to represent the great majority of the English people. It has many powerful and seductive advocates, and is fast occupying the place of the Church Catholic; being very largely assisted in the occupation by the hesitating, or the negative character of teaching by Bishops and Priests.

For the "Establishmentarian" position, *pur et simple*, there is no truer illustration than what it has brought about in Wales.

A century ago, there was no Dissent in Wales; but neither under the Hanoverian policy, as against the Jacobite, could there be said to be, so to speak, much Church. The Bishoprics were filled with Englishmen; the livings with English pluralists and absentees; the Curates were such as could be got.

The natural issue of all this was, that when Whitfield came, he found a people with deep religious feeling, and craving after the food of the spiritual life, but with little food or feeding power: and so they fell into his arms straightway. It is State policy that has lost Wales to the Church.

2. This division, hostile division and irreconcileable, generally regarded, not as a thing to be deplored, as con-

trary to the Institution and Law of CHRIST, but as a thing to be welcomed, and made matter of unbounded national self-congratulation; on the ground that there is no authority in respect of the Religion of CHRIST binding upon a man, save only that which it is his will and pleasure to bind upon himself.

3. The country so divided, with, nevertheless, a "National Church," recognised as an integral part of the Constitution, bound up and intertwined with all the order and administration of the Body Politic; with "power to decree Rites and Ceremonies," and with "Authority in Controversies of Faith;" with large possessions still remaining to it, after the sacrilege and spoliation of Century XVI. under pretext of Religion,—possessions guaranteed to it by Common and by Statute Law; with many possessory rights; some already destroyed by law, others in the way of being destroyed as the popular will finds opportunity and power; with the near prospect of dis-Establishment and dis-Endowment, unless it formally abandon and surrender, as into a common stock of religious possession and possessory right, those things which still, all its internal and irreconcileable divisions notwithstanding, make it to be exclusively "the Church of England."

4. The earthly Head of this Church *de jure* the Sovereign, a Communicant of the Church, judging in temporal causes by temporal judges; in spiritual causes by spiritual judges. The earthly Head *de facto* the House of Commons, representing every form of faith that is, or is to be, and also the form of no faith at all.

5. As is the nature and wont of popular dominion, the lines of public policy becoming year by year, not only more divergent from, but more actively hostile to, the lines of the Church. The Church here in England tolerated, and barely tolerated, by the Civil Power.

6. The ancient and rightfully-inherited position of the

Church turned against it. For example, it has suited public policy to seize upon and adapt to its own uses of "Indifferentism" Church Universities and Church Schools, endowed and other. Public policy has done this without stint or scruple, and not without large encouragement in highest places.

As I write, I have lying before me the Report of the Annual Meeting of the "National Society for the Education of the Poor in the Principles of the Established Church," Wednesday, May 22, 1878.

I find in the Report speeches of the Archbishop of Canterbury, and of the Bishop of Carlisle.

The Archbishop is a kindly and able man; but his measure of the "width" of the Church of England has, for many years, appeared to me to make it no "Church" at all. It is at least beyond my poor powers of understanding how it is possible to make it apply to a "Church." I will therefore say no more about it.

The Bishop of Carlisle is also a kindly and able man. He calls the "Education" Act of 1870 "a noble, humane, and Christian measure." If he had said that Mr. Forster thought it so, I believe that to be quite true. But he speaks of the fact of the case, not of Mr. Forster's judgment about it; and the fact is not true: it is as far as possible from being true. It is a strange assertion for a Bishop to make: not more strange than many other assertions of Bishops in our time, but very strange and very ominous.

Is that a "noble" measure, which violates a Churchman's conscience by making him pay an "Education Rate?" Is that a "humane" measure, which compels under penalty the poor man to send his child to a "School Board School?" Is that a "Christian" measure, which not only makes no provision for teaching the Faith of CHRIST, but forbids it to be taught in the "School Board School," and interferes violently with the teaching of it in the so-called "Church School?"

The time which can not only admit, but applaud, such

language from a Bishop, is plainly "out of joint." If I had been at the meeting I should have said all this then and there. But as I have long ago ceased to have any favourable regard for the proceedings of a Society which has become an agent of the Committee of Council on "Education," and do not therefore go to its meetings, I say it here. A little time will shew what is the issue of the "noble, humane, Christian measure."

7. Courts of Law, unconstitutional in their character, pretending not to define the Doctrine of the Church, or to regulate its Discipline and Worship, but as matter-of-fact, defining and regulating all three in every successive case; and this without so much as a reference to a National Synod: enforcing Secular Decree by Secular Penalty.
8. A Judge of the Court Secular created for the first time three years ago by Act of Parliament, and having no particle of a Church Court about it, or in it, inhibiting, imprisoning, depriving Priests who cannot, for conscience sake, obey the Court Secular in things spiritual.
9. Non-authority of the Judicial Committee of Privy Council in matters of Faith and Worship.
10. Acts of such Judicial Committee:—
    (*a.*) In respect of the Sacrament of Holy Baptism, allowance of heresy in the person of Mr. Gorham: herein and hereby condoning the False.
    (*b.*) In respect of the Sacrament of the LORD'S Supper, where disallowance of Truth could not as yet be ventured upon, disparagement of Truth in lieu of such disallowance. The Doctrine of THE REAL PRESENCE could not safely be disallowed, it might safely be disparaged in the person of Mr. Bennett. Herein and hereby the condoning of the True.
    (*c.*) The sanctioning the Desecration of the Blessed Sacrament in the case of Jenkins *v.* Cook.
    (*d.*) A single instance of not condoning heresy in

the Heath case; No excuse for Indifferentism being ready to hand, because no fear of "consequences" at the time.

(*e.*) In respect of Worship, contradictory decisions many and special; bias against Catholic worship the same throughout.

(*f.*) In Ridsdale case, repeal and re-enactment by a Court of Law upon a non-Catholic basis of Law of this Church and Realm, upon grounds judged sufficient to build sentence upon, but so shallow and futile, that a very little historical enquiry has sufficed to scatter it to the winds.

(*g.*) In the same case, so much of allowance of Catholic Worship as *could not* be withheld, made upon a ground which had nothing to do with the real question involved; that is to say, the question of "the Sacrifice."

I have always thought the "Bennett Judgment" a most discreditable document. The "Ridsdale Judgment" is in the same category.

I submit that I have proved my case. My case is that in the last fifty years the World of England has fought openly and formally by a series of acts of the Civil Power, legislative and judicial, and has won, as against the Church of England, the battle of Indifferentism in Religion; and that it has been largely assisted in winning the battle by Churchmen of the Church "as by law established."

If it be said that, allowing this to be matter-of-fact, as indeed there is no room to dispute, it has been not matter of choice, but, matter of necessity imposed by social and political considerations, out of which has come a form of Public Polity Indifferent by its own nature, and therefore acting only upon the principle originating and governing its existence.

The rejoinder is twofold.

First, that this is a true account of the fact of the position.

Second, that it is conclusive as against the present, or any like, connection between the Church and the Civil Power. It is impossible for a connection to be sound and good and true, where the principles of the two parties connected are absolutely opposed the one to the other. In such case, one party or the other must necessarily suffer harm, loss, defeat. So far all the harm, loss, defeat, has been on the side of the Church corporate. The World of England, with Indifferentism in Religion as its war-cry, has won the battle.

So far as it can be called "a battle:" for it is unhappily true, not only that Churchmen in Parliament and in Synod, and out of Parliament and Synod, have made a miserable fight of it; as yet no fight that can be called "the good fight of faith;" but that among the chief helpers of the World, as against the Church, have been found, and are found, vast numbers of Churchmen, Archbishops, Bishops, Priests, Deacons, People.

These say they are contending for the Church. What they are contending for is "the Establishment," at the expense of "the Church."

Now there is doubtless a good deal to be said for "Establishment," where the Governing power of a country is a "Church" power. On the other hand, when this has ceased to be, there is nothing to be said for it. And even in the best case I believe that, upon the whole, the conclusion is against it, as being rather injurious than helpful to truth and earnestness of Religion. I think this is the teaching of all experience.

I often ponder upon a problem which seems to me a principal—if not the principal—problem of national life.

The highest blessing of a Christian people is Religious Obedience; that the people be "obedient to The Faith."

This in things spiritual.

Then, in things temporal, the highest blessing is Civil

Liberty, the parent of national greatness, as respects the things of this life; of true social intercourse; of active development of mental and bodily faculties; of progress in science and in art.

But the two blessings are never found together in the same people: rather must it be said, that the last always, more or less, repels and excludes the first.

Is it that man's touch mars the best things of GOD, bearing therein and thereby mournful witness to the abiding power of the Fall? Is it that Civil Liberty, in itself a precious gift, begets self-reliance; that self-reliance, if not watched and fenced round with many prayers, and with that humbleness of heart which is the proper dignity of the redeemed and regenerated nature, degenerates into unregulated and presumptuous self-confidence in the reasoning power generally, and particularly in the conclusions of scientific research, and in the productions of art as ministering more than all else to the pride of civilization; and intruding even into the province of the Divine Mysteries, things beyond the scope and grasp of reason, becomes the prolific parent of heresies and schisms? As Civil Liberty, thus abused, passes into Licence, so Religious Obedience disappears before this presumptuous self-confidence; and its place is filled, first with doubtings and questionings about Divine Revelation; then with formal scepticism; in the end with infidelity; and the people, once "obedient to The Faith," becomes a people of a hundred religions, and of no religion.

If I am asked, upon all this, whether I despair of the recovery of the Church of England, I reply that I believe it would be great and sinful thanklessness so to despair. If I am asked what I think of the hope of bringing "the Establishment of England" more and more into harmony with "the Church" of England, I reply that there is no man that has the power to go deeply into the question, who will not arrive at the conclusion that any such hope is delusive, idle, empty, profitless.

What, then, is the issue of the last fifty years? It is this; that the "Establishment" of England, representing for the time the Church of England, has been overcome by the World of England, and lies prostrate at its feet. I am not forgetting here, nor am I unthankful for, that Revival of Religion within the "Establishment," which has been manifested during the above period in individuals and in congregations. But of the corporate life of the Church of England, as represented by the "Establishment,"—that life by which it stands or falls,— I say that it has been overcome by the life of the World of England; and that it is only to shut our eyes to facts, to look to a recovery of the Church's life under any existing or probable conditions of the "Establishment:" rather must we look to a continual and accelerated "*descensus.*" The logic of facts is not to be overcome.

For the fifty years have seen the principle of Indifferentism a primary principle of the World, put publicly and formally into the place of the principle of Dogma, a primary principle of the Church; and this, not only without repudiation by the "Establishment" of England, but rather with its welcome. They have seen all the legislation of the Civil Power touching or affecting the Church, based and carried out upon the principle of Indifferentism touching Religion: they have seen the "Establishment," by the Peers Spiritual and Temporal, by the House of Commons, by the Convocations, a party to such legislation. Now we are told that "there must be heresies;" but we are not told that heresies are to be regarded as having equal claims with the "One Faith:" on the contrary, we are told that heresies are permitted, "that they which are approved may be made manifest." It is true enough that a Parliament, which is not of the "One Faith," cannot be expected to care much for the Church which is, or at least claims to be, of the "One Faith." But then, that of itself is a sufficient and conclusive argument, why Parliament should give up absolutely all attempt to legislate for the Church.

This Indifferentism, being thus a vicious and unhallowed thing,—a thing of this World only,—has, by a natural law, passed on from bad to worse. Indifferentism is not indifferent: it has become first dominant, then exacting; then persecuting, in the necessary order of its development. Having no rule but that of its own shallow presumption, self-sufficiency, and worldly convenience, it is specially intolerant of its antagonist; of the reason, that is, which finds its highest and most reasonable exercise in implicit acceptance of the Faith, Worship, and Discipline of the Church; and in the refusal to admit, in respect of them, or any one of them, the intervention of any Secular authority, or quasi-Secular authority [a].

For the Faith, and the Worship, and the Discipline of the Church are the trust of Church people. A Civil Power now saturated with Indifferentism, and representing alike all forms of religion, and no religion, interferes nevertheless legislatively [b] and judicially [c] with the Faith, Worship [d], Discipline of the Church: it interferes on the ground that the Church is an "Establishment;" that *as such*, it holds its position, its privileges, and its endowments by the national will. Now this is true enough as matter of might, though not of truth, nor right. But the argument, if it prove anything, proves too much: for by this rule, the "Establishment" ought to include all the "religions" which are found in the nation as represented in Parliament. This seems, so far as I am able to comprehend it, the view of the present Archbishop of Canterbury.

It has then come to this, that, in the eye of the Civil Power of England, the Religion of the Church is only one form of religion out of a great many; a form hap-

---

[a] Such, for example, as the authority of Bishops applied simply to the enforcing the sentence of the Court Secular, whatever that sentence may be.

[b] "Public Worship Regulation Act."

[c] "Gorham case," "Bennett case," "Ridsdale case."

[d] "Flavel Cook and Jenkins case."

pening, from certain antecedents of this people, to be "established by law;" and liable to be, at any time, disestablished and disendowed [e] by law, as may suit political, social, economical convenience: and with this little matter added, that, as the Church is so highly and largely privileged, it may reasonably, so long as it is established, be interfered with; and, more than this, may be safely robbed, after a fashion which cannot be adopted in respect of religious bodies not "established." On this rule the Civil Power acts; and the Bishops, the creatures of the Civil Power, do all they can to help; the Convocations making no real resistance.

The entire public authority of the country then,—positively, as respects its Executive, Legislative, Judicial, Episcopal character; negatively, as respects its Synodical character,—is thrown into the scale of a persecuting Indifferentism. If this were not so as respects Bishops, it could hardly be that disobedience to the express law of the Church, shewn in systematic neglect of the requirements of the Prayer-Book, should be, as it is, entirely condoned by them; they take no real notice of it, much less "institute proceedings" against it. But for "Ritualism," the exponent of the Doctrine of the Sacraments, the stern, the steadfast enemy of Indifferentism; spending all, and being spent, in the service, and for the "One Faith," of CHRIST: for this, that is, for exact and faithful observance of the requirements of the Prayer-Book, Bishops have nothing but hard words and names, every species of discouragement, proceedings at law, monition, inhibition, deprivation, ruin [f].

The other forms of persecuting Indifferentism—the form Executive, the form Legislative, the form Judicial—require no demonstration besides their own acts.

[e] Disestablishment and disendowment are two things; but two things *not separable*.

[f] I instance here in the late "proceedings" of the Bishop of Gloucester and Bristol against the Rev. A. H. Ward, St. Raphael's, Bristol. Anything worse, both in respect of the matter and the manner of the Bishop's action, it would be impossible to find.

The Creed of Indifferentism—for it has a Creed—is that Creeds are indifferent things. If it stopped here, it would only be a vain, and silly, and self-stultifying thing: but, as we have seen, it does not stop here. The Indifferentist is not only content with, he is proud of, his Creed; he claims for it the praise of an enlarged and enlightened Christianity, a Christianity whose office it is to "put down" dogmatism: in other words, rejecting Christianity, he is, upon his own estimate of himself, a Christian of the Christians; he is the Apostle of "the Church of the future;" about which nothing is known certainly, save that it has nothing in common with the Church of the past, nor of the present. He is the persecuting Apostle of the Church of the future.

Indifferentism has now culminated in England. It is the child of the dislocation, and mixed novel combination and complication, religious, social, political, of Century XVI.[g]: it runs side by side with the Infidelity, the Deism, and the Atheism, of which the Englishmen, Herbert and Hobbes, were, next to Socinus, the first fathers in modern times. Indifferentism is always converging towards Infidelity; and, sooner or later, merges into it: all along, the distinction between the two—if, indeed, there be a distinction in kind—is subtle and evanescent.

It is to Indifferentism that Bishops, Priests, People of the Church of England are being every day more and more tempted; and into which they have been already largely drawn in many chief particulars, by the close connection of the Church with the Civil Power, commonly called "the Establishment."

The Bishops of the "Establishment" are the creatures of the Civil Power. The Civil Power is indifferent, as for or against any form of religion, save only as against Catholic Religion; because it is, in the Providence of GOD, the opposing force to Indifferentism. The Bishops follow the lead of the Civil Power.

[g] See my "Episcopatus Bilinguis." (Parker, Oxford and London, 1874.)

For coercive authority, and, in great measure, for discretionary also, the Bishops have none except under Statute, as prescribed and limited by Statute: but then whatever the Court Secular may interpret Statute to mean, that the Bishops accept and act upon, as being "law of this Church and Realm."

The day of "Establishment" is gone. It would be impossible now to create "Establishment" in any country. That of it which exists is fast drawing to its close; and it is difficult to conceive of any future condition of the world in which it will be found again. All indications seem to point to a state of things when the Catholic will be designated, not as a member of the Church of this or that country, or of the Church of East or West, but as a member of the Church Catholic gathered out of all nations throughout the world.

Here, then, is the issue of the conflict of the last fifty years. The seeds of it, sown in Cent. XVI., were forced on not a little in 1688; but it is the fifty years between 1828 and 1878, which have witnessed their rapid growth, and their maturity.

If I am asked, "Why, seeing these things are so, do you not, as many of your friends and coadjutors have done, betake yourself elsewhere?" my answer is as easy as it is simple: "I am in the place to which GOD has called me: it is mine by inheritance, and by the law of this Church and Realm." I have never been able to understand, I cannot even now understand, in all the extremity of the present distress, in all the destruction of the power of confidence in the Archbishops and Bishops, in all my loss of faith in the Convocations, the temptation to abandon the Church of England. We have here in England—blessed be GOD!—we have here in England what the merely human creations of Century XVI. elsewhere have not: we have the old Church in its essentials; the Orders, and, by consequence, the Sacraments.

With this, then,—holding fast all the Trust of Faith,

Worship, Discipline, committed to me in my Ordination, and sworn to by me as before GOD; keeping it; delivering it as I have received it; surrendering no particle of it at the bidding of the Court Secular, or of the Bishop enforcing its sentence, as superseding and governing his Diocesan authority, an authority in its turn prescribed and limited by Statute law,—with this, then, it is my privilege, as it is my duty, to be content; and to wait for GOD.

And so, under all the trials of the position, past, present, and to come, I die where I have lived; I die, to use once more the words of Bishop Ken:—

"As for my religion," says Bishop Ken in his will, "I die in the Holy Catholic and Apostolical Faith, pro-"fessed by the whole Church before the disunion of East "and West. More particularly, I die in the Communion "of the Church of England, as it stands distinguished "from all Papal and Puritan innovation, and as it ad-"heres to the Doctrine of the Cross."

There is a thought of very absorbing and almost overwhelming power, connected closely and inseparably with the claim to hold exclusively the One Truth of GOD, as committed to His Church, and as set forth in these words of Bishop Ken.

I have more than once adopted them for my own. Now what is the thought inseparable from such adoption? It is this:—

That the man who claims to live and die by this rule, must take good heed that his life and conversation correspond to the claim. He affirms of himself the highest position which it is possible for man to hold on this side the grave,—The position of humble but absolute acceptance in all its parts by his own free-will, prevented and assisted by Grace, of the Will of GOD, as revealed and committed to the Church of GOD. He means, if he mean anything, that this is GOD'S gift to him personally. If his life and conversation be not in accordance with, and in due proportion to, the gift received, where will he be in the Judgment, relatively to the man who has not received the gift at all, or with the man who has only received it in part? GOD is the GOD of mercy: Blessed be His Name! but He is also the GOD of justice. To whom much has been given, of him will much be required. It is, I repeat, an almost overwhelming thought to those who claim to have received the gift of GOD in all its fulness. O GOD, help me, who claim the gift for my own, to strive and pray to make the return as best I may, by Grace preventing, furthering!

For Secession to Rome, I have a few words to say. I have at no time been tempted to it myself, any more than I am tempted to it now: that is to say, in no manner or degree. I have known very many, not a few intimately, who have seceded. For some time, a good many years ago, I kept a list of names, and had some thirty or forty names upon it: it became so painful to me, that I ceased to keep it. I make two remarks only in connection with it.

1. That at least two-thirds of the seceders were men who had begun life as "Low Churchmen." I do not feel sure that I am not under-estimating the proportion; I am certain I do not over-estimate it.
2. That Secession to Rome, with return, is a thing to me wholly incomprehensible. There is only one ground upon which a man can come to the conclusion that he must needs desert the Communion in which he was baptized, and that is, that such Communion is not a "Church" at all; or if not this, then, what comes to the same thing, that it is in wilful schism.

Suppose a man to have seceded to Rome from England upon this ground, and, still affirming the ground, to be nevertheless so disappointed by what he finds in Rome, that he comes back again, alleging the disappointment as the ground of return. He went upon a principle; the only principle that could justify or excuse his going. He retains the principle, but he returns in defiance of it. If he went upon the principle, he has, by returning, denied and stultified himself; and has given just cause for suspecting that he did not go upon principle at all, but only upon weariness of spirit, and illegitimate craving for "rest."

At the end of my book I have some words to say upon a principal, widely-spread, and increasing distress of our time. I mean the use that is being made of what are called "Scripture difficulties." Before and by this use the faith of high and low, rich and poor, is perishing daily.

The Death of the Cross has overcome death; the first and the second death. The Resurrection of the Crucified has overcome Sin, by which death came into the World. It remains for man to "lay hold on Eternal Life[h]."

Here comes in the mystery of grace and free-will. It is of the way of dealing with this and other mysteries of GOD, as being "Scripture difficulties," i.e. things which have to be subjected to the free use of the reasoning faculty; and which, being found to be without explanation by the reasoning faculty, become a ground for rejecting Scripture wholly; or partially at first, and wholly afterwards; it is upon this distress that I have some concluding words to say.

The fight for "Eternal Life" is a fight such as there is none other: none so fierce; none so enduring through all time. We cannot fight the fight at all without preventing and assisting Grace. We have, each one of us, need of our brother's help, encouragement, teaching, example; that we may "fight the good fight of faith," and "lay hold on Eternal Life."

Wherein lies the "hope of Eternal Life[i]?" It lies in simple, childlike, unquestioning faith in CHRIST[j], and in the keeping of His Commandments by the power of Love: faith in CHRIST as revealed to us in the Holy Scriptures

---

[h] 1 Tim. vi. 19. [i] Titus i. 2.
[j] Cf. St. Luke x. 21, the one place in which it is recorded of our LORD that He "rejoiced." Cf. St. Matt. xi. 25.

of the New and the Old Testament, committed to the Church by THE SPIRIT to seal and to deliver unto men.

Is there then anything more cruel, more unlike brotherly love, than not to give such help as best we may, that the foundation may be good [k]?

There is one thing more cruel,—not only unlike a brother, but very like murdering a brother, if indeed it be not murder itself,—and that is, to disturb and shake first our own, and then, by way of natural consequence, our brother's faith in the Holy Scriptures, as committed to, and interpreted by, the Church. To take away therein and thereby the "foundation," having no "foundation" to put into its place.

But, all this notwithstanding, it is a thing common among men of our time to be employing other chief gifts of GOD,— learning, scholarship, science, power of thought and expression,—to the undermining and general defacing and mutilation of Holy Scripture.

The cry of these men,—who are throwing all the weight they can into the scale of the discredit of Holy Scripture; into the scale of the chief temptation of man, "the pride of life;" that which is called distinctively the temptation of the Devil,—the cry of these men is "the difficulties of Holy Scripture."

Now when people talk about "difficulties of Scripture," meaning difficulties intellectual, moral, religious, talk very common in our time, and giving utterance to thoughts even more commonly present than expressed,—they forget *in limine* that Scripture, being the record of the operation of the Infinite, must needs contain *à priori* many such "difficulties;" inasmuch as the reasoning faculty of the finite cannot, in the nature of things, be a measure of the operation of the Infinite. And when to "finite" is added, "imperfect," "sinful," "mortal," the case, as submitted to the true exercise of the reasoning faculty, is conclusive as against so much as the use of the term "Scripture difficulties," as being properly subject-matter of such exercise.

[k] See 1 Tim. vi. 19.

If, all this notwithstanding, the mind allows itself employment about "difficulties of Scripture," then in natural order and issue the undue occasional use of the reasoning faculty becomes habitual abuse of it; ground first of complaint; then of shaken faith; then of scepticism, passive and active; lastly, of pronounced unbelief.

Now it is of small power to place before a mind in such condition, or in the way to it, that to question Scripture at all is to deny the only authority upon which Scripture is Scripture,—That is, the authority of the Church Catholic under the guidance of THE HOLY SPIRIT. That, therefore, to call in question the Divine character of any portion of Scripture, is to call in question the authority of the Church, by which alone, in the Providence of GOD, such Divine character has been stamped upon it, and, once for all, sealed. The mind relying upon itself only, rejects all other authority, especially when comprising what it regards as only a human element. To a mind in such condition, the authority passing through the Church is, so to speak, discredited by the very fact of its passing through the Church. And yet,—so absorbing is the self-contradictory process going on in the mind when once gone astray from the simplicity of faith,—it is demanding authority, in the act of rejecting the only authority which can be had. Now, if the demand in such case found a hearing, and the authority for believing Scripture to be Scripture came in the shape of a miracle, it does not follow at all that even evidence of miracle would not be rejected also. "Though He had done so many miracles before them, yet they believed not on Him[1]." And, moreover, we have His own express warning, that men who reject the proof supplied to them in the ordinary Providence of GOD, will not be persuaded by manifestation of His extraordinary Providence: "If they hear not Moses and the Prophets, neither will they be persuaded, though one rose from the dead[m]."

However, all this said, the mind I am supposing has to be approached by another way. It has to be brought

---

[1] St. John xii. 37. [m] St. Luke xvi. 31.

face to face with the real "difficulty," if it be allowable to use the term in the case. A difficulty of which it is impossible to so much as conceive that it can be taken out of the way of any mind, believing or disbelieving, on this side the grave. It is possible, perhaps, metaphysically,—I trust I speak with all reverence,—to conceive of what are commonly meant by "Scripture difficulties," difficulties about the Creation, the time and manner of it; the existence of the Evil Spirit; Grace and Free Will; the Temptation; the Fall; the coming in and the enduring power of Sin; the Incarnation; the Temptation of CHRIST; the Atonement; the Death; the Resurrection; the coming of THE HOLY GHOST; Apostolical Commission and Succession; Prophecy; Miracles; History; Divine commands; Inspiration, plenary and other; Eternal Punishment. It is possible, perhaps, to conceive that these might be removed from the path of the belief of the finite being, if GOD saw fit in His Infinite Wisdom, Power, Mercy. But, if they were all so taken away,—and the supposition is an extreme supposition, and put only *argumenti causâ*,—the primary difficulty out of which all these come, and into which all have ultimately to be resolved, would remain just where it was, unapproachable by the finite, without so much as a possibility of conceiving metaphysically that it could be removed. I mean the difficulty of the Being of THE ETERNAL GOD, without Beginning and without End.

I say, then, that when men entertain what are commonly included under the term "Scripture difficulties," and entertaining them, proceed from entertaining to doubt; from doubt to scepticism; from scepticism to unbelief, because of them; they do not, or will not, see that the true account of the miserable process, from first to last, is that what they are really and in substance doubting about, and finally end in disbelieving, is the Being of THE ETERNAL GOD, without Beginning and without End. That all their doubts and questionings are but secondary instances and manifestations of this primary doubt, and primary disbelief. That the only way out of "Scripture difficulties," is not inventions or explanations, or so-called solutions by the finite of what is part of the Infinite, things good for nothing at the best, or rather, worse than nothing; but that the way is to receive them as they are sent, knowing whence it is that they come, as coming from the Infinite source of all things; the source from which all things come, and to which all things return.

Believe, with childlike belief in THE ETERNAL GOD, and there is no darkness that can fall upon man in the life of this world, through which the light does not shine; no difficulty of Scripture which can disturb or shake. Doubt about THE ETERNAL GOD, and every page of Scripture is filled with rocks, upon which repentance and faith and love suffer shipwreck. One man says he cannot be a believer because of the Doctrine of Eternal Punishment; another because of the Doctrine of Plenary Inspiration. Would it not be truer and more like a reasonable being to say, that in the first case, the source of their unbelief is the existence of Sin; in the second, the determination to make human learning and knowledge of authority rather than the Word of GOD? Would it not be even more deeply and universally true to say that unbelief in every shape, and under its most seductive disguises, comes as from its primary source out of the resolve, that the Eternal and Infinite GOD is not what He has revealed Himself to be, and has committed to the Church to declare, but what the reason of the finite prescribes, limits, concedes, regulates; and demands that it be received in the place of the Revelation of the Infinite, *because*, if not so received, men "will not believe[n]."

I repeat, then, that if all the difficulties commonly intended under the term "Scripture difficulties" were removed; difficulties of prophecy, miracles, commands of

---

[n] See p. xlix. of Preface to "Eternal Hope." Five Sermons preached in Westminster Abbey, November and December, 1877, by the Rev. Frederic W. Farrar, D.D., F.R.S., Canon of Westminster, Chaplain in Ordinary to the Queen, late Master of Marlborough College, Hulsean Lecturer, and Fellow of Trinity College, Cambridge.

GOD, difficulties of history, science, criticism, and the like; that if all these were taken out of the way by a stroke, the difficulties out of which all the others come, the difficulty of the Being and Operation of GOD, the difficulty of the existence of sin, would remain exactly where they were before. So that what it comes to is this,—that the removal of the secondary "difficulties" would have done nothing for the soul. It would only have brought it face to face with the primary "difficulty;" and the only alternatives remaining would be, unconditional surrender into GOD'S hands, or denial of the Being of GOD. Then, I rejoin,

If a man believe in GOD, he believes in the GOD of Infinite Goodness, Knowledge, Power, Love, Justice, Mercy.

But, it is said, there are things in Scripture, not a few, which are not consistent with the Goodness, Love, Justice, Knowledge, Mercy—

And *therefore* we disbelieve Scripture.

Who is it that says the things intended are inconsistent? The finite speaking of the Infinite. Man applying a human measure to things Divine: abolishing faith and waiting upon GOD, and putting reason and the haste of an imperfect nature into the place of faith and patience. Now "he that believeth shall not make haste[o];" and, "if we hope for that we see not, then do we with patience wait for it[p]."

But, it is retorted, this is to ask a reasonable being not to be guided by his reason. Has GOD given reason for unreasonable uses? Is it not the highest use of reason to draw the line where the province of the finite ends, and not to intrude into "the secret things" of GOD?

If, all this notwithstanding, men will so intrude, there is no possible ultimate issue of the attempt persevered in, and abided by, other than disbelief, not only in the exercise of the attributes of GOD, but in GOD Himself.

And this is what the "Scripture difficulties" men have to be brought face to face with.

[o] Isa. xxviii. 16.   [p] Rom. viii. 25.

In sum, the suggestion of "Scripture difficulties" is nothing but a snare of the Tempter, enticing into denial of GOD. To so much as entertain them, is to make reason unreasonable; to pervert its use; and to stultify its power. Man, if he would be saved, has to accept the Salvation as it is sent. When he cannot understand, to humble himself as in the Presence of the Almighty; to watch, to pray, to wait, till the darkness of this World pass away, and the light of Heaven come.

APPENDIX A[a].

(P. 14.)

Epistola XLII.

"Christianis professoribus interdicit lectione Græcorum auctorum [b]."

Παιδείαν ὀρθὴν εἶναί νομίζομεν, οὐ τὴν ἐν τοῖς ῥήμασιν, οὐδὲ τῇ γλώττῃ πολυτελῆ εὐρυθμίαν. ἀλλὰ διάθεσιν ὑγιῆ νοῦν ἐχούσης διανοίας, καὶ ἀληθεῖς δόξας ὑπέρ τε ἀγαθῶν καὶ κακῶν καλῶν τε καὶ αἰσχρῶν. Ὅστις οὖν ἕτερα μὲν φρονεῖ, διδάσκει δὲ ἕτερα τοὺς πλησιάζοντας, αὐτὸς ἀπολελεῖφθαι δοκεῖ τοσούτῳ παιδείας, ὅσῳ καὶ τοῦ χρηστὸς ἀνήρ εἶναι. Καὶ εἰ μὲν ἐπὶ σμικροῖς εἴη τὸ διάφορον τῆς γνώμης πρὸς τὴν γλῶτταν, κακὸς μὲν εἰς τόδε, ὅμως τῷ τοσῷ γίνεται· εἰ δὲ ἐν τοῖς μεγίστοις ἄλλο μὲν φρονοίη τις, ἐπ᾽ ἐναντίον δὲ ὧν φρονεῖ, διδάσκει, πῶς οὐ τοῦτο ἐκεῖνο καπήλων ἐστίν, οὔ τι χρηστῶν, ἀλλὰ παμπονήρων βίος ἀνθρώπων; οἳ μάλιστα παιδεύουσιν, ὅσα μάλιστα φαῦλα νομίζουσιν, ἐξαπατῶντες καὶ δελεάζοντες τοῖς ἐπαίνοις, εἰς οὓς πετατιθέναι τὰ σφέτερα ἐθέλουσιν, οἶμαι, κακά. Πάντας μὲν οὖν χρῆν τοὺς καὶ ὁτιοῦν διδάσκειν ἐπαγγελλομένους, εἶναι τὸν τρόπον ἐπιεικεῖς, καὶ μὴ μαχόμενα τοῖς δημοσίᾳ μεταχαρακτηρίζοντας, τά. ἐν τῇ ψυχῇ φέρειν δοξάσματα· πολὺ δὲ πλέον ἁπάντων οἶμαι δεῖν εἶναι τοιούτους, ὅσοι ἐπὶ λόγοις τοῖς νέοις συγγίγνονται, τῶν παλαιῶν ἐξηγηταὶ γενόμενοι συγγραμμάτων, εἴτε ῥήτορες, εἴτε γραμματικοί, καὶ ἔτι πλέον οἱ σοφισταί. βούλονται γὰρ πρὸς τοῖς ἄλλοις

---

[a] I am indebted to my dear friend, Herbert A. Grueber, British Museum, for some considerable trouble in searching for the original of Appendix A, and also for the Latin and English translations of it appended. The same kind hand has largely assisted me with *précis* of debates in Parliament, and with dates and facts.

[b] The Latin title does not describe clearly the scope and purpose of the Epistle; this is to ridicule, and to stigmatise as dishonest, the Christian professor employing heathen authors in his teaching, who believed in gods whom he rejects as false.

οὐ λέξεων μόνον, ἠθῶν δὲ εἶναι διδάσκαλοι, καὶ τὸ κατὰ σφᾶς εἶναί φασι τὴν πολιτικὴν φιλοσοφίαν. Εἰ μὲν οὖν ἀληθὲς ἢ μή, τοῦτο ἀφείσθω νῦν· ἐπαινῶν δὲ αὐτοὺς οὕτως ἐπαγγελμάτων καλῶν ὀρεγομένους, ἐπαινέσαιμ᾽ ἂν ἔτι πλέον, εἰ μὴ ψεύδοιντο, μηδ᾽ ἐξελέγχοιεν αὐτούς, ἕτερα μὲν φρονοῦντες, διδάσκοντες δὲ τοὺς πλησιάζοντας ἕτερα. Τί οὖν; Ὁμήρῳ μέντοι, καὶ Ἡσιόδῳ, καὶ Δημοσθένει μέντοι, καὶ Ἡροδότῳ, καὶ Θουκυδίδῃ, καὶ Ἰσοκράτει, καὶ Λυσίᾳ θεοὶ πάσης ἡγοῦνται παιδείας. Οὐχ οἱ μὲν Ἑρμοῦ σφᾶς ἱεροὺς, οἱ δὲ. Μουσῶν ἐνόμιζον; Ἄτοπον μὲν οἶμαι, τοὺς ἐξηγουμένους τὰ τούτων ἀτιμάζειν τοὺς ὑπ᾽ αὐτῶν τιμηθέντας θεούς. Οὐ μὴν ἐπειδὴ τοῦτο ἄτοπον οἶμαι φημὶ δεῖν αὐτοὺς μεταθεμένους τοῖς νέοις· συνδίδωμι δὲ αἵρεσιν, μὴ διδάσκειν ἃ μὴ νομίζουσι σπουδαῖα, βουλομένους δέ, διδάσκειν ἔργῳ πρῶτον, καὶ πείθειν τοὺς παθητὰς, ὡς οὔτε Ὅμηρος, οὔτε Ἡσίοδος. οὔτε τούτων τις, οὓς ἐξηγοῦνται καὶ κατεγνωκότες εἰσὶν ἀσέβειαν ἄνοιάν τε, καὶ πλάνην εἰς τοὺς θεούς, τοιοῦτός ἐστιν. Ἐπεὶ δ᾽ ἐκεῖνοι ἐξ ὧν γεγράφασι παρατρέφονται μισθαρνοῦντες, εἶναι ὁμολογοῦσιν αἰσχροκερδέστατοι, καὶ δραχμῶν ὀλίγων ἕνεκα πάντα ὑπομένειν. Ἕως μὲν οὖν τούτου πολλὰ ἦν τὰ αἴτια τοῦ μὴ φοιτᾶν εἰς τὰ ἱερὰ καὶ ὁ πανταχόθεν ἐπικρεμάμενος φόβος ἐδίδου συγγνώμην ἀποκρύπτεσθαι τὰς ἀληθεστάτας ὑπὲρ τῶν Θεῶν δόξας. ἐπειδὴ δὲ ἡμῖν οἱ Θεοὶ τὴν ἐλευθερίαν ἔδοσαν, ἄτοπον εἶναί μοι φαίνεται διδάσκειν ἐκεῖνα τοὺς ἀνθρώπους, ὅσα μὴ νομίζουσιν εὖ ἔχειν. Ἀλλ᾽ εἰ μὲν οἴονται σοφὰ ὧν εἰσιν ἐξηγηταί, καὶ ὧν ὥσπερ προφῆται κάθηνται, ζηλούτωσαν αὐτῶν πρῶτον τὴν εἰς τοὺς Θεοὺς εὐσέβειαν· εἰ δὴ εἰς τοὺς τιμιωτάτους ὑπολαμβάνουσι πεπλανῆσθαι, βαδιζόντων εἰς τὰς τῶν Γαλιλαίων ἐκκλησίας, ἐξηγησόμενοι Ματθαῖον καὶ Λουκᾶν· οἷς πεισθέντες, ἱερείων ὑμεῖς ἀπέχεσθαι νομοθετεῖτε. Βούλομαι ὑμῶν ἐγὼ καὶ τὰς ἀκοὰς, ὡς ἂν ὑμεῖς εἴποιτε, καὶ τὴν πλῶτταν ἐξαναγεννηθῆναι τούτων, ὧν ἔμοιγε εἴη μετέχειν ἀεί, καὶ ὅστις ἐμοὶ φίλα νοεῖ τε καὶ πράττει. Τοῖς μὲν καθηγεμόσι καὶ διδασκάλοις οὑτωσὶ κοινὸς κεῖται νόμος. Ὁ βουλόμενος γὰρ τῶν νέων φοιτᾶν, οὐκ ἀποκέκλεισται. Οὐδὲ γὰρ οὐδὲ εὔλογον ἀγνοοῦντας ἔτι τοὺς παῖδας ἐφ᾽ ὅ, τι τρέπωνται, τῆς βελτίστης ἀποκλείειν ὁδοῦ, φόβῳ δὲ καὶ ἄκοντας ἄξειν ἐπὶ τὰ πάτρια.

APPENDIX A. 401

Καίτοι δίκαιον ἦν, ὥσπερ τοὺς φρενιτίζοντας, οὕτω καὶ τούτους ἄκοντας ἰᾶσθαι· πλὴν ἀλλὰ συγγνώμην ὑπάρχειν ἅπασι τῆς τοιαύτης νόσου καὶ γάρ, οἶμαι, διδάσκειν, ἀλλ' οὐχὶ κολάζειν χρὴ τοὺς ἀνοήτους.

Epistola XLII.

Doctrinam rectam esse arbitramur, non verborum linguæve magnificum et exquisitum sonum : sed mentis bene constituæ sanam affectionem, et veras certasque de bonis et malis, honestis et turpibus, sententias. Quare quisquis aliud sentit, aliud suos discipulos docet, is tantum videtur a scientia, quantum a probitate abesse. Ac si de parva re sit linguæ animique dissensio, in hoc ipso etiam est improbus, tametsi modum non excedat sceleris magnitudo: sin vero in maximis rebus aliud sentit, contraque ac sentit, docet, nonne hæc cauponum, non dico bonorum, sed nequissimorum, vita est ? Quippe cum id maxime doceant, quod maxime malum existimant, fallentes atque inescantes eos laudibus, quibuscum sua, ut arbitror, mala commutare volunt. Quamobrem omnes, qui quidvis docere profitentur, bonis moribus esse debent, neque opiniones novas et a sensu populari abhorrentes afferre: sed imprimis tales esse debent, qui adolescentes in veterum scriptis instituunt, sive sint Rhetores, sive Grammatici, et præcipue Sophistæ, qui non solum verborum, sed etiam morum magistros se esse volunt, et ad se philosophiam de administrandis rebus publicis pertinere contendunt. Hoc verum sit, necne, in præsentia omitto, laudo eos, quod doctrinam tam præstantem expetant ; plus certe laudaturus, si non mentirentur, neque de ipsi refellerent, dum aliud sentiunt, aliud discipulis tradunt. Quid ? Homerus, Hesiodus, Demosthenes, Herodotus, Thucydides, Isocrates, Lysias, Deos habent doctrinæ suæ duces et auctores. Nonne eorum alii Mercurio, alii Musis sacros se esse arbitrabantur ? Quare absurdum est, qui horum libros exponunt, Deos vituperare, quos illi coluerunt. Neque tamen, quia id absurdum puto, idcirco eos discipulorum causa sententiam mutare jubeo, verum do optionem, ut ne doceant quæ non bona esse sentent; sin docere malunt, doceant reipsa primum et persuadeant discipulis, neque Homerum, neque Hesiodum, neque quemquam earum, quos interpretati sunt, quosque impietatis, amantiæ, et erroris erga Deos condemnarunt, talem esse. Nam alioqui cum ex illorum scriptis alantur mercedemque capiant, avarissimos plane et sordidissimos se esse fatentur, paucarumque drachmarum gratia quælibet sustinere. Atque hactenus quidem multa erant, quæ eos templorum, aditu prohiberent: et timor undique impendens excusabat, quo minus verissimæ de Diis sententiæ explicarentur. Nunc autem cum Deorum munere atque concessu libertate potiamur, absurdum mihi videtur et homines docere, quæ non bona esse arbitrentur. Quod si in iis quæ docent, et quorum quasi interpretes sedent, sapientiam esse ullam arbitrantur, studeant primum illorum in Deos pietatem imitari. Sin in Deos sanctissimos putant ab illis auctoribus peccatum esse, eant in Galilæorum Ecclesias, ibique Matthæum et Lucam interpretentur: quibus vos obtemperantes a victimis abstinere jubetis. Cupio ego et aures, et linguam vestram (sicut vos loqueremini) renasci in iis rebus, quarum utinam et ego sim semper particeps, et omnes qui me diligunt. Doctoribus quidem et præceptoribus communis hæc lex statuatur. Adolescentes enim qui ire volunt, minime prohibentur; iniquum siquidem fuerit, pueros adhuc ignaros quo se vertant, ab optima via rejicere, ac metu coactos ad patria instituta deducere. Quamvis justum esset istos tanquam impotentes et insanos, etiam invitos ac repugnantes, sanare: attamen liceat omnibus per nos isto morbo detineri. Docere enim amentes, non punire, oportet.

English Translation.

We are of opinion that the fruit of true education is found, not in the choice and order of words, of fine and elegant language, but in the sound disposition of a healthy mind, and true judgment touching what is good or evil, honourable or disgraceful. Whosoever, therefore, thinks one thing and teaches another to his followers, he seems to be a man as far away from truth of teaching, as from moral goodness. And if, indeed, it be a small matter in which there is this difference between the mind and the tongue, even here he is wrong; but if in a matter of the greatest concern a man thinks one thing, and teaches the contrary of what he thinks, in what degree does his life differ from that of traders, base and depraved men, who affirm what things they know to be mostly false, cheating and deceiving with praises those to whom, as I think wickedly, they wish to dispose of their goods. Therefore, it behoves that all those who profess to teach should be of good moral character; and, believing strongly in their own opinions, should not entertain such as are opposed to those of the people; and especially of such character, I think, all those should be who instruct the youth, being themselves the exponents of the ancient writers, whether orators or grammarians, or, still more, Sophists, for these latter ones wish to be esteemed teachers to others, not only of words, but of ethics; and they say that political philosophy belongs to them alone, i.e. is their peculiar province. Whether, therefore, this be true or not, I shall not at present consider; but, whilst praising those who offer such good promises, I should commend them still more, if they did not deceive or falsify themselves by thinking one thing, and teaching another to their followers. What then! Were not Homer, Hesiod, Demosthenes, Herodotus, Thucydides, Isocrates, and Lysias, esteemed the leaders of all erudition? Did not some of them consider themselves sacred to Mercury, others to the Muses? I think, therefore, that it is absurd that those who explain the works of these men, should despise the gods whom they honoured. I do not say that they should change their opinions to instruct the youth, for that would be absurd; but I give them the choice, either not to teach what they themselves consider false, or, wishing to teach, that they should first teach and persuade their disciples that neither Homer, nor Hesiod, nor any of them whose works they expound, and whom they accuse of impiety, madness, and error concerning the gods, are such as they represent them to be. For if these men live by what they have written, and receive pay, they seem to me to be most basely greedy, and to venture anything for the sake of a few drachms. Hitherto, indeed, many causes have prevented their frequenting the temples; and the danger which everywhere impended, gave them an excuse for concealing that belief in the gods which is the truest. But since the gods have granted us liberty, it seems to me to be unreasonable that men should teach those things which they judge to be bad in kind. And if they think that there is any wisdom in the writings of those whom they expound, and of whom they sit as interpreters, they should first zealously emulate their piety towards the gods. But if they think they have erred in the conception of the most holy gods, let them go into the churches of the Galilæans, and expound Matthew and Luke, by whom you are persuaded to abstain from sacrifices. I wish that your ears and your tongues, to use your own phraseology, were regenerated in those things of which may I myself, and whosoever cares for me, always be partakers. Let this, then, be the common law of masters and teachers. But if any youth wishes to be taught as I have described, he shall not be prevented doing so. For it would be as unreasonable to exclude children, as yet ignorant which way they should turn, from the right path, as to lead them by fear and by force to the institutions of their fathers. It would, indeed, be only strict justice that minds in such condition should be cured against their will, as though they were minds of madmen; yet it may be permitted that those who are suffering under so great disease, should be dealt gently with: for I think it best to instruct, not to punish the ignorant.

> "Juliani Imperatoris, quæ feruntur Epistolæ, &c., Ludovicus Henricus Heyler." (Moguntiæ, 1828, Ep. xlii. p. 78.)

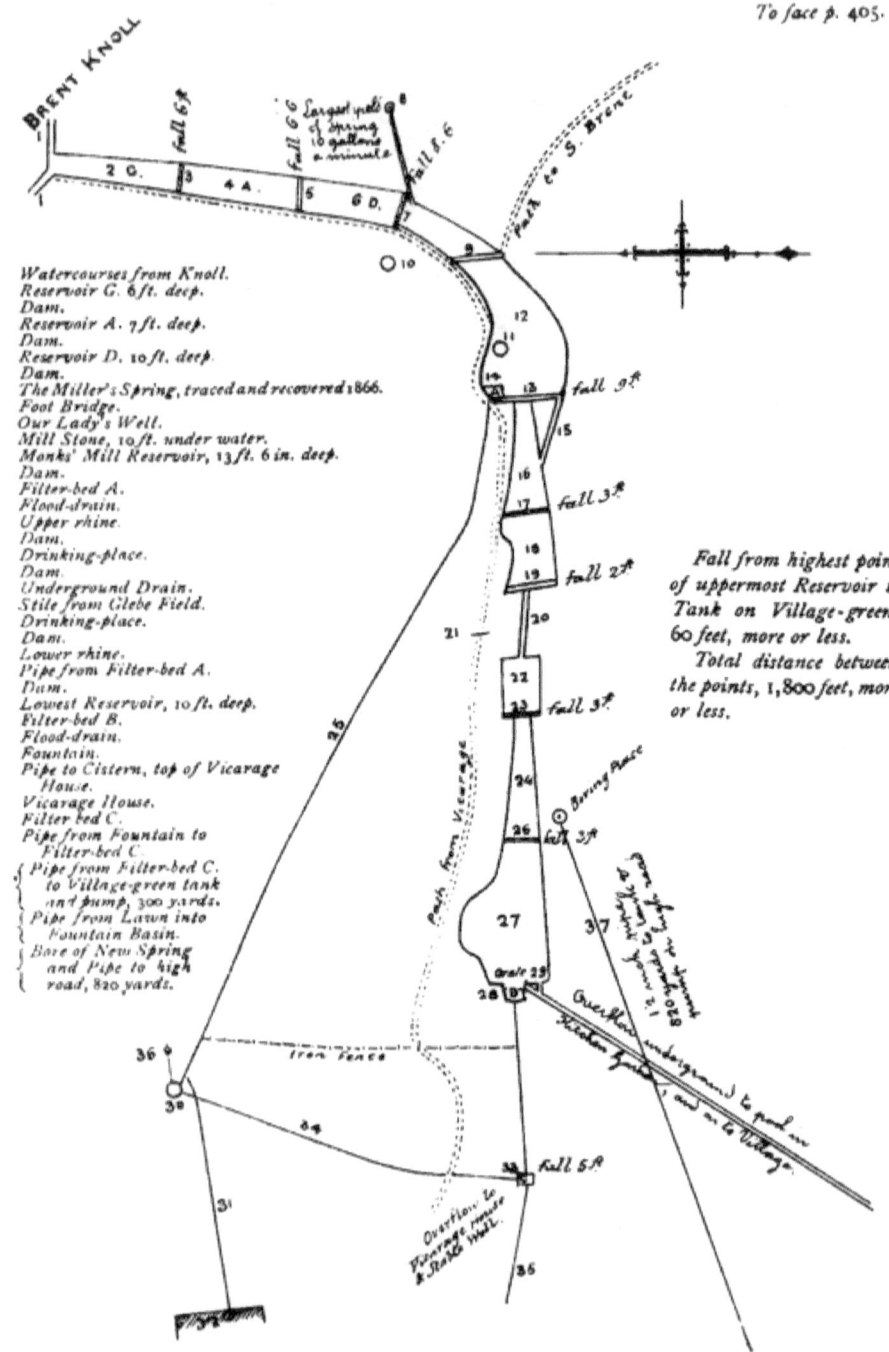

APPENDIX B.

SUPPLY AND STORAGE OF WATER AT EAST BRENT.

By ARCHDEACON DENISON.

Read by James Thompson, M.D., at the Leamington Congress of the Sanitary Institute of Great Britain, October, 1877.

THE natural advantages for supply and storage of pure drinking-water at East Brent are very great; but the supply would be nothing without the storage. Last year, during a four months' drought, I was enabled to give such water not only to my parishioners, but to many others at some distance; and, when the drought was over, my reservoirs were three parts full. I have since that time much enlarged them, and am adding further to them at this time. When I came to East Brent in 1845, I found hardly any pure water except in two shallow wells, the "Lady Well," or "Well of the Virgin," to whom the church is dedicated, and the "Dripping Well," both near the foot of the Knoll at some considerable distance from the village, and of limited power of supply, though never wholly failing. Drinking-water was taken generally from the ditches forming the drainage, into which the sewage of the place all found its way. Three times in thirty years, 1845 to 1875, the place suffered from epidemic—each time in conjunction with severe drought. The obvious explanation being that, in time of drought, the proportion of sewage to the whole amount of water in the ditches was so large as effectually to poison the water.

The village lies on the east side of Brent Knoll, an isolated hill, about four miles round at its base; from 400 to 500 feet above the level of, and two-and-a-half miles distant from, the Bristol Channel. I am told by geologists that it has three strata: (1.) Top, "Superior oolite;" (2.) Middle, "Upper and middle lias;" (3.) Low ground, "Lower lias."

The flat, out of which the hill rises, is bounded to the north and east by Mendip, to the south by Poldon-hill, and runs up to

Glastonbury and Wells. The boundary nearest to the Knoll is part of Mendip, about four miles away.

The Knoll is full of springs; a natural reservoir. It also, in rainy time, collects and discharges great abundance of surface-water down its several water-courses. There are no houses on the hill, and the surface-water is as free as may be from impurity.

On the east side of the Knoll the main water-supply is by three water-courses. The middle course, that yielding the largest supply, comes down opposite the Vicarage-house, and is that out of which the reservoirs have been constructed. See sketch annexed.

In a long drought the water in the water-course ceases, and the only supply is by a spring traced and recovered by me in 1866. It appeared from the depth I had to go before coming to the water, that the spring had been choked for a great number of years.

The spring never fails; but in long drought its yield falls to a gallon a minute: ten gallons a minute is the largest yield that I have noted. It is excellent water, with a good deal of iron in it.

It was the recovery of this spring that put me upon providing for storage of water. I believe, from many indications upon which I came in excavating, that there was a pump over it long ago for the use of the mill-house standing just above the mill-dam, the foundations of which, as of the wall carrying the water-wheel, I found, in 1866; large hewn stones and fragments of mullions. Last year, in widening Reservoir No. 4, I found a mill-stone 4 ft. 6 in. in diameter and 8 in. thick. The material, Draycot stone from Mendip, ten miles away across the flat. It lies where I found it, and is now 10 ft. below the surface of the water. I have records of the mill in the Glastonbury Papers at Longleat, kindly supplied to me by the Rev. Canon Jackson, of Leigh Delamere, up to 1187; and I cannot doubt that it was there long before that date.

I had then before me a water-course, some 1,000 ft. in length, in places of some depth: in its widest part, 45 ft. wide; in its narrowest, 12 ft. The upper end of it about 50 ft. above the level of the front-door of the Vicarage-house.

The reservoirs were thus half-made to my hand; and permission having been kindly given me by the late Rev. Dr. Symons, in respect of all that part of it which lies outside the glebe, that is, of at least two-thirds of it, all that was required was to clear away the brambles and brushwood from waste ground of no value, to excavate, deepen, and shape, and to build a succession of dam-walls, giving out the water from each, when in a dry time there is little or no overflow, either by tap or by syphon.

The construction of these reservoirs has enabled me (1.) to throw the water to the roof of the Vicarage-house; (2.) to have a fountain in the flower-garden; (3.) to supply a tank with a ball-cock and pump in the village, 300 yards from the Vicarage. All the water so supplied passing through two filtering-beds.

I hope to be able, before I have done, to carry the supply to another tank and pump at the further end of the village.

May, 1878. I am enabled, by the kind assistance of my brother Alfred, to carry the supply 820 yards to another tank and pump on the high road at the further end of the village. I am at this time securing a fresh supply of water.

APPENDIX C.

REPORT OF "DILAPIDATIONS" COMMITTEE[a], DIOCESE OF BATH AND WELLS, NOV., 1876.

Your Committee report as follows :—

That the necessity for further legislation in the matter of Ecclesiastical Dilapidations is generally conceded: see Report of Select Committee of House of Commons, 1 June, 1876, p. vi.

That the question arises "*in limine*" (*a*.) whether such legislation should be by way of amendment of existing system, or (*b.*) by way of creation of new system. Report, H. of C., pp. v., vi.

That (*a.*) has the vantage ground of possession and prescription; but that the argument against it, and in favour of (*b.*) is very strong. Report, H. of C., p. vi.

For there are radical defects of existing system which no amendment of it could remove, both in respect of its operation, and of the character of its administration.

For its operation, the liability to pay "Dilapidations" falls at the precise time, and upon the precise persons, when and upon whom it least ought to fall; and to provide, by way of compulsory insurance of life, for meeting the liability, is full of difficulties.

On the other hand, if no such provision be made, one of two things happens in a great many cases; either the "Dilapidations" money is lost in whole or in part, or the liability to pay it is fastened, as by present law, on the incoming Incumbent, who is left to recover it as he can from the late Incumbent, or his representatives. This appears to be a manifest injustice done

[a] MEMBERS OF COMMITTEE.

Archdeacon of TAUNTON, *Chairman*.   Rev. Prebendary BULLER, R.D.
Archdeacon of BATH.   Rev. Prebendary SANFORD, R.D.
Archdeacon of WELLS.   Rev. Prebendary CLARK, R.D.
Rev. Preb. GOLDNEY, R.D., *Secretary*.   Rev. W. W. ROWLEY, R.D.
Rev. C. CAREY, R.D.

to the incoming Incumbent, as the other is a constantly recurring source of injury to the trust property of the Church; and where this last is not so, the pressure and hardship incurred in satisfying " Dilapidations " charges is in many cases extreme.

For the administration of the system,—

There appears to be no sufficient account to be given why such administration should be, as at present, in the hands of the Clergy. A Bishop or Archdeacon, or Priest other than Bishop or Archdeacon, is not by his calling the fittest person to conduct such administration. The subject-matter of such administration, the condition, repair, and maintenance of buildings, &c., has nothing properly ecclesiastical about it. That in earlier times the Clergy should have been the administrators is easy to understand; but, as matter of fact, the Clerical element has long been superseded in this part of its function by the lay professional element; and to make a show of retaining the old system of Clerical administration, by tacking on the Bishop or Archdeacon to the Surveyor, is a delusion, and worth less than nothing. It is also, so far as Bishops are concerned, an undue and serious encroachment upon their time and attention. Here and there a Bishop, or Archdeacon, or Priest other than Bishop or Archdeacon, may be able to judge soundly about the necessity of a survey, but in no case can he be the fit person to carry out such survey. It is no proper part of his calling or office so much as to judge in the matter; and, if it were, the power of so judging is rare, and cannot be depended upon as the foundation of a system, or even as an ingredient of a system.

Whether, then, we look to the existing system itself, or to the administration of it, the defects appear to be inherent and incurable. It can serve no good purpose to be either continually losing " Dilapidations " money, or to be securing its payment by imposition of unjust liability. Nor, again, to be throwing an ecclesiastical covering over a matter which is, in its nature and substance, not ecclesiastical, but civil. It makes no difference as to the essentials of repair and tenantable condition, whether a building be an ecclesiastical or a civil building. The thing to be done in both cases alike is the same; the knowledge and the power to deal with it soundly and effectually the same; the hands to execute the same. Doubtless the comfort and the just economy of Clergy have to be carefully considered and provided for in this matter so far as is possible. But the point here contended for is, that this is better in other hands than in theirs; and that, it being impossible to relieve them from the charges incident to a life-tenancy of trust-property, the legislature has to provide that the liability be enforced in a manner at once the least onerous and the most effectual.

In sum, the history of the system itself, and of its administration, both before and since 1871, is not favourable to retaining it; nor, again, to attempting to cure its faults by way of further "amendments."

It is therefore submitted by your Committee—

1. That the present system of ascertaining, recovering, and applying "Dilapidations" money be done away.

2. That a Board of three persons be constituted, the nomination being in the Crown, to sit in London, with Trustees, Treasurer, and Secretary; such Board to have the entire management and control of[b] all repairs and maintenance of Ecclesiastical buildings, &c.; and of all additions to, or removal of such buildings; to receive and apply all monies charged upon Incumbents in respect of such repair and maintenance; to invest from time to time for the uses of the Board all surplus money so received, after providing for current expenses of management and repair: or that the same powers be given to a lay Committee of Queen Anne's Bounty Board.

3. That the Board appoint a Surveyor-in-chief, to be resident in London, and such number of local Surveyors in each Diocese as it may judge to be sufficient.

4. That the remuneration of the Surveyor-in-chief, as of the paid Member or Members of the Board and of the Secretary, be by salary; the remuneration of the local Surveyors according to the number of cases of survey: the amount in each case as

---

[b] The words in Draft were "repair and maintenance, &c." In Committee "all repairs" was substituted for "repair." Upon this the question arises, whether repairs, such as, e.g. replacing a slate, or putting in a pane of glass, or fresh papering, or inside painting, or whitewashing, be meant to be included under "all repairs."—*Chairman of Committee.*

the Board may provide; but that no part of such amount be provided for by fees of Clergy.

5. That all such fees in respect of "Dilapidations" cease and determine; and that the only payment in this respect, and in respect of all office charges (except appeals when decided against the appellant), to be made by Incumbents under the new system, be a yearly payment, to be assessed upon each benefice at the vacancy next ensuing [e], or before such vacancy if the Incumbent so arrange with the Board. The amount of such payment to be subject to revision at each succeeding vacancy; and to be made easily recoverable by the Board when one month overdue.

6. That if a new Board be constituted, the "Dilapidations" money now in the hands of the Bounty Board, with all liabilities attaching thereto, be transferred to such new Board.

7. That existing Incumbents be empowered to make such arrangements with the Board, for the transfer to the Board of their prospective liability, and for coming under the operation of the new system, as may appear to the Board to be reasonable and equitable. And that, in default of such arrangement, the present law, with such amendments of it as are necessary, remain in force as respects existing Incumbents: provided only that, in every such case, the amount of "Dilapidations" assessed be recoverable by the Board from the late Incumbent or his representatives: and that all appeal in every such case be to the Surveyor-in-chief.

The amendments of present Act intended here are principally these:—

1. A Definition of "Dilapidations." What the term means: what it does not mean. The necessity for this has been created, not so much by as under the Act. Before the Act was passed, though there were here and there some differences of opinion, the necessity for such definition could have not been said to exist, as it exists now.

For, under the Act, the term "Dilapidation" has been confounded with the term "Restoration," the terms not being co-extensive. Every "Dilapidation" is matter of "Restoration;" but every "Restoration" is not matter

---

[e] The Chairman of Committee proposes to insert here words as they stood in Draft of Report, but which were omitted in Committee upon difference of opinion, viz. "according to value of benefice, and extent and condition of its buildings."

of "Dilapidation." Doubtless all "Restoration" of Ecclesiastical buildings is an excellent thing: but if to be had, under all circumstances, at the cost of the outgoing Incumbent, then "Restoration" and "Dilapidation" become co-extensive terms.

This result has, very reasonably, greatly alarmed the Clergy; and is one principal cause of the prevailing dissatisfaction with the Act of 1871, and with its administration.

2. The spreading over a larger number of years than at present the repayment with interest of money borrowed for building or re-building.
3. The free choice of Surveyors by the Clergy in each case.

It does not appear that a more general election by Clergy of Surveyors for Dioceses, or parts of Diocese, would meet the grievance. What is wanted under any such Act as the present is free choice by the Clergy in each case.

4. The regulation and amount of fees. At present these do not appear to bear a just proportion to amount of "Dilapidations." Where "Dilapidations" are small the trouble is comparatively small. See p. v. of Report, H. of C.
5. A real liberty of appeal in place of the present unreal liberty. Appeal should always be to a Surveyor-in-chief, resident in London; and the cost of it should be moderate, and be divided equally between outgoing and incoming Incumbent; or, what is most reasonable, should follow the decision of the Appeal Judge.
6. The repeal of the unjust provision created by the Act which makes the incoming Incumbent ultimately responsible for amount of "Dilapidations."

There may be other things in the Act which require amendment in order to making it a fair and reasonable law for existing interests, pending the coming into full operation of the new system; but these appear to be the primary things. A good law your Committee believe it cannot be made; and that, if the alternative be the retaining of it as it is, or the simple repeal of it and return to the old state of "Dilapidations" law, the latter is to be preferred. But your Committee believe that the real remedy is to be found, not in the amendment of the present system but, in the creation of a new system of the nature of that sketched in this Report.

8. That the only ordinary Survey and repair be upon each successive vacancy: or, if judged more expedient, at the expiration of every five years. The first such period of five years to commence from the completing of the repairs undertaken by the Board upon such vacancy. Any Incumbent desiring to be relieved from such quinquennial Survey to pay at some higher rate of yearly charge.

9. That if an Incumbent see cause to propose extraordinary survey during his Incumbency, he may arrange with the Board for the purpose: and that he do nothing to alter the buildings, &c., of the benefice without the knowledge and the sanction of the Board.

10. That the charge for fire Insurance be covered by the yearly payment.

The advantages of the system here proposed, when in full operation, and *pari passu* with its coming into gradual operation, would be these :—

1. That Bishops, Archdeacons, and Rural Deans would be relieved from an administration which is no proper part of their calling and office. Bishops and Clergy generally from payment of " Dilapidations," and the Church from the loss of them. The Board receiving everything by yearly charge upon each benefice, and paying everything out of the monies so received.

2. That appeals would all be to one central authority; and would be confined to cases in which, after representation and suggestion made by those whose interests are affected to the local Surveyor, there remained difference of judgment as to what ought or ought not to be done.

3. That the security *against* useless or illegitimate outlay, and *for* necessary and legitimate outlay, would be ample; it being the interest of the Board to see to both.

4. That there would be no necessity for any attempt to define " Dilapidations." What ought, or ought not, to be done in each case being in the ultimate discretion, and if done, at the cost, of the Board.

5. That the administration would be uniform, and in competent hands, and the whole arrangement very simple.

It does not appear to your Committee that the inconvenience to poor Incumbents of a yearly payment in lieu of "Dilapidations" can reasonably be set against the ultimate inconvenience, and unseasonable pressure, with other mischiefs, of the present system.

It would appear to be just that the system should include under its provisions Lay Rectors as well as Clerical, in respect of Chancels and other Ecclesiastical buildings.

The general issue of adoption of scheme is as follows :—

1. Yearly rent [d] in place of "Dilapidations," and of all repairs, building and rebuilding.
2. Ordinary Survey only upon vacancy, or every five years.
3. Extraordinary Survey only at instance of Incumbent during Incumbency.
4. The Church the Landlord as now.
5. The property mixed freehold and trust as now.
6. The Legislature provides an agent, to be paid out of the yearly charge upon Incumbents, and responsible to the Church and to the Legislature for the due execution of the agency.
7. Check upon over-building. This cannot be said to exist now, whether upon Bishops' Palaces, Deans' and Canons' Houses, or Glebe Houses.

Signed, by order of the Committee,
GEORGE ANTHONY DENISON,
Chairman.

HIGHBRIDGE,
November 14, 1876.

---

[d] Rent is nothing new to Incumbents, though a permanent rent is. The Chairman gives here his own instance of rent, &c., paid during thirty years of Incumbency.

Two Incumbencies.	Broadwinsor, Dorset.		East Brent, Somerset.	
	Gross value.	Sum borrowed.	Highest rent paid to Queen Anne's Bounty Board.	Lowest do.
Broadwinsor, seven years	£775	£2,000	£146	£70
East Brent, twenty-three years	1,000	1,500	110	52

Over and above this rent, the sum expended during seven years of Incumbency at Broadwinsor, where the Vicarage House with its surroundings had to be created, cannot be put at less than £1000; and during thirty-one years of Incumbency at East Brent the sum expended upon necessary repairs and upon substantial improvements at less than £800. "Dilapidations" are in prospect.

APPENDIX C.

Resolutions affirming principles of Report, to be moved at Wells, Dec. 7, by Chairman of Committee.

1. That a yearly payment from each Benefice for repair and maintenance of the buildings belonging to such Benefice is to be preferred to "Dilapidations" at close of Incumbency.
2. That the administration and application of the Fund accruing by such yearly payments are better in other hands than those of Bishops and Clergy.
3. That central administration of such Fund—if, upon full and careful enquiry by competent persons ascertained to be practicable, and not burdensome to Clergy—is to be preferred to local: subject always to right of representation and suggestion by Patron, or Incumbent, or both, to Surveyor acting under Central Board; with right of appeal from such Surveyor to Surveyor-in-chief.

APPENDIX D.

(P. 59.)

"In 1663 Convocation gave four subsidies to the Crown, and this was the last time the clergy imposed a tax upon themselves, the agreement already referred to being effected soon afterwards. Speaker Onslow makes the following note to a passage in Burnet, containing the history of this transaction. 'It was first settled by a verbal agreement between Archbishop Sheldon and the Lord Chancellor Clarendon, and tacitly given in to by the clergy in general, as a great ease to them in taxations. The first public act of any kind relating to it, was an Act of Parliament in 1665, by which the clergy were, in common with the laity, charged with the tax given in that Act, and were discharged from payment of the subsidies they had granted before in Convocation; but in this Act of Parliament in 1665, there is an express saving of the right of the clergy to tax themselves in Convocation, if they think fit; but that has never been done since, nor attempted as I know of, and the clergy have been constantly from that time charged, with the laity, in all public aids to the Crown, by the House of Commons. In consequence of this (but from what period I cannot say), without the intervention of any particular law for it, except what I shall mention presently, the clergy (who are not lords of Parliament) have assumed, and without any objection enjoyed, the privilege of voting in the election of members of the House of Commons, in virtue of their ecclesiastical freeholds.

"'This having constantly been practised from the time it first began, there are two Acts of Parliament which suppose it now a right. These Acts are, the 10th of Anne, c. 23, and 18th of Geo. II., c. 18; and here it is best the whole of this matter should remain, without further question or consequence of any kind. As it now stands, both the Church and the State have a benefit from it. Gibson, Bishop of London, said to me, that this was the greatest alteration in the constitution ever made without an express law.'

"The effect of this abandonment of the power of taxing the

clergy has operated, in the peculiar religious circumstances of this country, unfavourably to the meeting of Convocation. Collier, the Church historian, foresaw this effect. 'Being,' he observes, 'in no condition to give subsidies and presents to the Crown, 'tis well if their Convocation meetings are not sometimes discontinued, if they do not sink in their insignificancy, lie by for want of a royal licence, and grow less regarded when their grievances are offered.'

"It may well be questioned whether this discontinuance has not worked mischief to the State as well as the Church. Probably, if Convocation had been allowed to sit to make the reforms, both in its own constitution, and generally in the administration of spiritual matters, which time had rendered necessary, the apathy and erastianism which at one time ate into the very life of our Church, the spiritual neglect of our large cities at home in England, and of our colonies abroad, and the fruit of these things—the schism created by the followers of Wesley—would not have occurred; and the State would have escaped the evil of those religious divisions, which have largely influenced, hampered, and perplexed the legislation of her parliaments, and the policy of her statesmen."—*Phillimore, Eccles. Law*, vol. ii. pp. 1932, 3.

www.ingramcontent.com/pod-product-compliance
Lightning Source LLC
Chambersburg PA
CBHW020546300426
44111CB00008B/816